Concep

Jepson Studies in Leadership

Series Editors: George R. Goethals, Terry L. Price, and J. Thomas Wren

Managing Editor: Tammy Tripp

Jepson Studies in Leadership is dedicated to the interdisciplinary pursuit of important questions related to leadership. In its approach, the series reflects the broad-based commitment to the liberal arts of the University of Richmond's Jepson School of Leadership Studies. The series thus aims to publish the best work on leadership not only from management and organizational studies but also from such fields as economics, English, history, philosophy, political science, psychology, and religion. In addition to monographs and edited collections on leadership, included in the series are volumes from the Jepson Colloquium, which bring together influential scholars from multiple disciplines to think collectively about distinctive leadership themes in politics, science, civil society, and corporate life. The books in the series should be of interest to humanists and social scientists, as well as to organizational theorists and instructors teaching in business, leadership, and professional programs.

Books Appearing in This Series:

Conceptions of Leadership

Enduring Ideas and Emerging Insights

Edited by
George R. Goethals, Scott T. Allison,
Roderick M. Kramer, and David M. Messick

palgrave
macmillan

First published in 2014 by
PALGRAVE MACMILLAN®
in the United States—a division of St. Martin's Press LLC,
175 Fifth Avenue, New York, NY 10010.

Where this book is distributed in the UK, Europe and the rest of the world,
this is by Palgrave Macmillan, a division of Macmillan Publishers Limited,
registered in England, company number 785998, of Houndmills,
Basingstoke, Hampshire RG21 6XS.

Palgrave Macmillan is the global academic imprint of the above companies
and has companies and representatives throughout the world.

Palgrave® and Macmillan® are registered trademarks in the United States,
the United Kingdom, Europe and other countries.

ISBN: 978–1–137–47201–4 (Hardback)
ISBN: 978–1–137–47202–1 (Paperback)

Library of Congress Cataloging-in-Publication Data

Conceptions of leadership : enduring ideas and emerging insights /
edited by George R. Goethals, Scott T. Allison, Roderick M. Kramer, and
David M. Messick.
pages cm.—(Jepson studies in leadership)
Includes bibliographical references and index.
ISBN 978–1–137–47201–4 (hardcover : alk. paper)—
ISBN 978–1–137–47202–1 (pbk. : alk. paper)
1. Leadership—Social aspects. 2. Leadership—Psychological aspects.
I. Goethals, George R.

HM1261.C643 2014
303.3′4—dc23   2014021671

A catalogue record of the book is available from the British Library.

Design by Newgen Knowledge Works (P) Ltd., Chennai, India.

First edition: December 2014

To our friend and colleague Edwin P. Hollander,
in gratitude for his leadership legacy.

CONTENTS

TABLES

ACKNOWLEDGMENTS

Foremost, we wish to thank the contributors to this volume. All of you have been exceedingly cheerful about strict deadlines, unusually thoughtful in your chapters, and wonderfully cooperative in all stages of putting this book together. Your helpfulness is gratefully acknowledged.

We are indebted to Terry L. Price and J. Thomas Wren, co-series editors for Jepson Studies in Leadership. Your support and encouragement at crucial junctures is very much appreciated.

We want to thank the dean of the Jepson School of Leadership Studies, Sandra J. Peart. We are grateful for your support for the series as a whole and for this particular volume.

We are deeply indebted to Tammy Tripp, managing editor of Jepson Studies in Leadership, for her gracious and timely nudging and her careful competence, to Michele Bedsaul for her heroic work in applying the finishing touches, and to Lisa Rivero for her excellent and timely handling of the index.

Brian Foster and Casie Vogel at Palgrave Macmillan have been helpful and encouraging at every step in the process of crafting this book. We thank you. In addition, we are grateful to Bradley Showalter for effectively guiding us through the production phases.

To all, we appreciate all that you have contributed to our project.

PART I

Conceptions of Leadership

CHAPTER ONE

Introduction and Commentary

DAVID M. MESSICK

In the spring of 1999, two of this book's editors, Kramer and I, met for lunch at the Sheraton Hotel in Chicago. Kramer was on the faculty of the Graduate School of Business at Stanford University and I was on the faculty of the Kellogg School at Northwestern University. One of the topics that we talked about during lunch was the shift in emphasis in both business schools away from cooperation, trust, communication, coordination, and the like, to the related but distinct topic of leadership. Kramer and I were social psychologists and knew that the topic of leadership had been an important theme in some of the earliest research on group processes. However, as social psychology experienced an infatuation with the "cognitive" revolution in psychology, the topic of leadership shrank into obscurity. By the turn of the millennium, though, there were some new ways of thinking about leadership that had not been introduced to the business school environment. Why not, we thought, have a conference and invite some of social psychology's most creative innovators to a conference to discuss these new approaches to leadership and then publish a book based on the talks? The conference was held in August of 2000 at the Kellogg School of Management, and the book based on this conference, *The Psychology of Leadership,* was published in 2005. Two of the creative innovators who were invited to the conference and who wrote chapters for the book are the other two editors of the current book, Allison and Goethals.

Now, a decade, more or less, later, and there has been a virtual tsunami of books and articles about leadership. When the issue of updating the earlier book was first raised, Kramer and I wondered what the point of a revision would be. We then became aware of the creative work by Allison and Goethals and realized that there was indeed a body of research that had not been described in their earlier book. So Kramer and I discussed the idea of a revision with Allison and Goethals, and we all agreed that such a project was worth exploring. After much discussion and the exchange of scads of ideas, the current book was agreed upon by all of us, who, we should note, are all associated with the University of California, Santa Barbara, where I was a faculty member, Allison and Kramer were graduate students, and Goethals was a visiting scholar.

The familiarity of us four editors with each other is a blessing but also a shortcoming. We are all male, white, North American university professors. These facts surely limit our views of what constitutes good leadership and who qualifies to be thought of as a leader. Famous people from around the world, people like Nelson Mandela, Mahatma Gandhi, Martin Luther King, Mother Teresa, are all well known and admired. But there are many others who would be unrecognized by most Americans. Take, for instance, Lee Kuan Yew (familiarly known in Asia as LKY). LKY was the first prime minister of Singapore and one of the most famous and admired political leaders in Asia. When one of us (DM) taught in Hong Kong to a broad mix of Asian executives, LKY was one of the most popular figures executives wrote about to illustrate excellence in leadership. Consider also Molly Melching, about whom a book has appeared (Molloy, 2013). She is a volunteer in a not-for-profit organization in Senegal who spends time in rural villages where the practice of female genital cutting is a well-established cultural tradition. She has begun the process of gradually eliminating this barbaric practice from hundreds of villages in Senegal but remains relatively obscure in the United States. Finally, think of Simon Bolivar. His name is recognized by a fraction of US scholars, but he is famous throughout Latin America for having led the South American people in a rebellion against Spanish domination. Indeed he has one nation named after him (Bolivia) and is widely known as *el Libertador* throughout Central and South America. He is to Latin America what George Washington is to the United States.

Inescapably then, we editors are constrained by our backgrounds in our selection of "core" issues about leadership, and we are constrained in ways that will often be invisible to us. For instance, we are all social psychologists and have read much of the same literature on leadership. But that literature is different from that which a political scientist or a journalist or a military historian will have read. Their books on core concepts would be different from ours—not better, necessarily, nor worse, just different. The way we define leadership is likely to differ from the way people whose backgrounds and experiences are different from ours define leadership. This fact is true about professional experiences and it is equally true about political and social differences. Most citizens of the United States, for instance, would not consider Fidel Castro to be a hero and a leader, but most Cubans would. Most North Koreans think their leaders have almost godlike qualities and most Americans think these leaders are monomaniacal lunatics. What is implied by these differences is that leadership, like beauty, may be in the eye of the beholder. If history is written by winners, one will either be viewed as a hero or a terrorist depending on who wins.

But winning or losing may depend partly on unpredictable geological events like storms, earthquakes, or droughts, or equally unpredictable social events, and who is a hero and who is a villain acquires a random element. Flip a coin. Heads you have a leader and hero; tails you have a scoundrel. This fact, along with the subjective nature of leadership judgments mentioned above, may be inevitable and immutable. But they can also be problematic for one trying to create a logic of leadership that is "objective," in the sense that judgments of leadership do not depend on one's own position, and systematic, in that these judgments do not depend on random events. Eliminating the impact of chance is probably a more difficult challenge than eliminating the impact of one's position. A major reason why this is so lies in what has been called the "outcome bias" (Baron & Hershey, 1988). The outcome bias refers to the fact that in judging the quality of an act, the result of the act—the outcome—is used as a cue. If the outcome is a good one, the act or the decision is seen as good; if the outcome is poor, the act or decision is judged to have been poor. This relationship characterizes judgments even when it is clear that the outcome depends not only on the decision but also on a random event over which the decision maker has no control. So imagine two people at a roulette table deciding to place a large bet on a single number. The first is lucky and wins her bet but the second is unlucky and loses hers. People will judge the first person to be a better decision maker than the second, despite the fact that they made identical decisions. The outcome bias violates the principle that the quality of a decision must be assessed on the basis of the information that was available to the decision maker at the time the decision was made, not on the basis of a subsequent outcome. The outcome will influence a judgment of how lucky the decision makers were, but not the quality of the decision per se.

The rule is this as it applies to leadership. Only those individuals who have made a significant difference in the world, in one way or another, are considered leaders. But to make a significant difference one must be lucky as well as skilled. We cannot count the number of business executives who tried but failed to build lasting organizations, failed often because of poor economic conditions, competition from unexpected places, the sudden introduction of new and better products, political advantages given to competitors, and so on. Leadership books are written about those who survived and thrived, even if they did essentially everything the failures did except experience bad luck. Just as we as a species are the result of a long process of evolution for which we can take no credit, successful people are the result of an evolutionary process which has eliminated many others with similar qualities. The survivors were lucky. The failures were not. A difference between biological evolution and the selective pressures for success in one's lifetime is that the survivors of the latter often attribute their success to their qualities rather than to luck. One result of this process is the flood of "leadership by autobiography" books on the market.

A principle that accompanies the outcome bias is what Fischoff and Beyth (1975) call "creeping determinism." When an event that is a priori uncertain happens, we tend to think that it was inevitable. Thus explaining the past, where everything is mostly known, is very different from predicting the future. People tend to be very good at the former, and very poor at the latter. When we think about tomorrow, the world is "iffy." When we think about yesterday, what happened must have been destined to happen. The paradox is that the future is highly uncertain whereas the past is deterministic. What this means for studies of leadership is that winners appear to have been destined to win, not just lucky. Their successes must reflect qualities that are stable, permanent, and exceptional. We can illustrate this principle with a recent sports example. In the 2013 NBA championship, in game 6 between the San Antonio Spurs and the Miami Heat, with essentially no time left and San Antonio ahead by three points, Heat guard Ray Allen shot a three-point shot from the corner. This shot had at best a 40 percent chance of going in. If it did not, the Spurs win the title. If it did go in, the game is tied and goes into overtime. At this point, the outcome is totally dependent on chance. The shot does go in and the Heat goes on in overtime to defeat the Spurs, and the Heat also wins game 7 to win the series and become the NBA Champions for the second straight year. The press writes about the Heat as a team of destiny. But what seems clear is that the Spurs and the Heat are two excellent teams either of which could have won the series and the championship. It was pure luck that the Heat won on Allen's three-point shot but it was not pure luck that the Heat was within striking distance so that the three pointer could do the trick. In other words, both skill and luck were necessary for victory.

Here is another example that is more pertinent to the content of this book. In the early years of the last century, two parties set out to be the first to reach the South Pole. A British party was led by Robert Falcon Scott, a Captain in the Royal Navy and an experienced explorer. A Norwegian party was led by Roald Amundsen, an explorer with extensive experience in polar conditions. Each of these teams set out in the summer of 1910 (Amundsen left Oslo on June 7 in the *Fram* and Scott sailed out of London on the *Terra Nova* on June 10). While they had different routes to sail to Antarctica, both teams arrived on the Antarctic continent in the antipodean spring (Northern autumn). After enduring the winter of 1911, both expeditions left for the pole in the spring, Amundsen on October 20 and Scott and his team on November 1. The round-trip journey was to be approximately 1,500 miles—on foot! In a competition of this sort, there are at least two goals. The first is to be the first team to the goal and thereby win eternal fame in the annals of exploration. This goal can only be achieved by one of the groups. This race will have one winner and one loser. The second goal is to return safely with all the team members. This goal is not zero-sum and both teams can win in this game against a viciously cold nature.

Amundsen won both contests. He reached the Pole on December 14, 1911, and he and all of his men returned safely to the coast and then to Norway. Scott not only arrived at the Pole after Amundsen, on January 16, 1912, but he and all of his men died of starvation and hypothermia on the long, arduous trek back. So Scott lost both times. He was beaten to the pole by Amundsen and his team, and he was beaten by the brutal weather in Antarctica. The most comprehensive account of this rivalry is probably that of Huntford (1999) who attributes Scott's failures to a series of blunders and irresponsible decisions. Scott was, according to Huntford, a vaingloriously inept figure who was more concerned about his image, reputation, and place in the panoply of British exploration than about overcoming the obstacles that he and his men faced. His tragic death and that of the four men with him was, according to Huntford, directly attributable to Scott's mistakes, oversights, judgmental flaws, and planning errors. But Susan Solomon (2001), in her wonderfully titled book, *The Coldest March*, takes a different spin on this historical disaster. Her book title refers to one of the coldest months of March in Antarctic history, and to the march of Scott and his men in their effort to reach a depot where food and fuel were available. (They died about ten miles from this depot.) Solomon's thesis is that Scott and his men were brave, well-organized, and prepared, and, but for the unusually bitter weather they encountered that required them to sit immobile in a tent for nearly a week, they would have prevailed. Had they not been so unlucky, she argues, Scott and his men would have returned home and been considered heroes. While they were not the first to pole, they had man-hauled their own provisions, whereas Amundsen's team had depended on dog teams to haul theirs, thus exhibiting the superiority of British grit and endurance.

Leadership generally implies getting results. Great leaders produce great things. But great results do not imply great leadership. Great leadership requires achievement of a social nature. Great leadership results in the outstanding performance of a social unit, be it an athletic team, an army, a political unit, or a business enterprise. We can illustrate this point with a sports example.

A leader of a sports team should take his or her team to the highest level—a championship or something close to it. If we examine the last 40 years of college basketball teams that won the NCAA tournament to claim to be the best team in the United States, we find that in only 5 years of these 40 did that championship team include the player selected by the Associated Press as the National Player of the Year. So the best player was usually not on the best team. Outstanding individual performance is not tantamount to outstanding leadership. The fastest person, the best shot, the strongest, the brightest, the most generous or the least generous, these people are not necessarily excellent leaders. They may be extraordinary, but they are not necessarily extraordinary leaders.

Leadership requires something more, something different. Many of the chapters in this book explore what these qualities might be. There are several points to be stressed here. The first is that leadership in different contexts may require very different talents. What are the qualities required to be a top-notch general? Are they the same that are needed to lead a platoon into dangerous combat? Are they the same as those needed to be a successful college basketball coach? And are these qualities the same as those needed to be the captain of the college basketball team? We can ask about the extent to which different domains require different types of leaders. Is what we need in politics the same as what we look for in sports? For that matter, does successful leadership in football, for instance, draw on the same skills as successful leadership in baseball or soccer or basketball? Is what we need in politics the same as business or sports or warfare or exploration or science or religion. Extending this question a bit, we may ask if leadership in the United States requires different skills from leadership in China, Kenya, Chile, or France. Even more specifically are the ingredients of successful leadership in politics in China similar to those needed to excel in sports in Chile? Discussions of leadership are often more concrete and meaningful when they pertain to a rather narrow and concrete domain like American politics or German soccer than when they are abstract and general. A related issue is whether leadership processes vary at different levels of the same organization. Staying with the example of German soccer, does the head of the Bundesliga, the governing body for professional German football or soccer, face different challenges from the coach of Bayern Munich, for instance, who may be an ex-player but who plays zero minutes on the field, or from the captain of the team who is on the field and in the midst of the competition. The leadership requirements for these three different levels of organization within "German soccer" are very different.

Another issue to be highlighted here is a distinction made between two types of leadership in small groups. More than half a century ago, a distinction was made between "task specialists" and "socio-emotional specialists" (Bales, 1950). Task specialists are leaders who have particular skills at solving the problems faced by the group or organization. They are the ones who seem to "know what to do" to solve a problem or to avoid a disaster. The skills needed to be task leaders will vary as widely as the spectrum of problems that could beset the enterprise. These leaders are externally oriented in that they are focused on the challenges coming form without that endanger the group or organization.

Socio-emotional specialists, on the other hand are focused on maintaining smooth and harmonious relationships within the group or organization. Their focus is on what is happening within the unit, not on the threats from outside. Creating an internal environment that supports all the members of the group is the goal of the socio-emotional leader. Sometimes, both types of leadership are exhibited by the same person. An illustration of such a combination is given by Dean Smith (2005), the legendary retired basketball coach of the University of North Carolina. Smith's book, *The Carolina Way,* is one of the most useful books about the psychology of leadership that has been written by one whose job was not psychology. We quote Smith to illustrate one detail of task leadership, and one detail of socio-emotional leadership. First, task leadership.

> If the opponent had the ball in a tie game with the shot clock off, we weren't about to back off defensively and let it hold the ball without a problem. Instead we pressured it, tried to trap out of our double teams, tried to make it uncomfortable and force a turnover. We weren't content with letting the opponent dictate the action. That followed our philosophy of being the aggressor, not the reactor. However, at ten seconds remaining, we would back off with our defense, pay special attention to the opponent's best shooter, and hope for overtime. (p. 203)

This description of a strategy for dealing with the unhappy situation that the opponent has the advantage of having the ball as time is expiring and having the chance to either win or draw is a clear example of managing an unpleasant, unlikely but important detail of the task—how best to avoid losing the game.

Now this next passage is about Smith the socio-emotional specialist, focusing on the maintenance of team coherence and reinforcing the concept that every person associated with the team is of importance and is crucial for the team's success. In basketball, attention focuses on the shooter and the player who scores the most points. Smith asks how did the shooter get the ball to make the shot in the first place. He says he discussed this idea with legendary UCLA coach John Wooden. Wooden said that he wanted the recipient of a pass that led to a basket to thank the passer or to wink at him. Smith writes,

> This was a good idea, but I wanted a stronger, more visible signal of thanks. I preferred a gesture that the fans could see. The media too. So we asked the player who scored to point to the man who gave him the pass and resulted in the basket, to show appreciation for an unselfish act that helps the team.
>
> It was a rule in the early years as head coach: Thank the passer by pointing to him. We insisted on it in practice and games. It became contagious. Soon my assistants and I were pointing to the passer; next the substitutes on the bench picked up on it; then the fans at our home games were standing in their seats pointing to the passer. The public address announcer at our home games began saying, "Assist to Karl, basket by Jones." It went just as I hoped: a show of appreciation for the passer: applause for his unselfishness; recognition of his good play. As the seasons went by I seldom had to mention it to our players. The North Carolina tradition was set in stone. Players picked up on it automatically. If they failed to do so, I didn't hesitate to remind them. (p. 165)

Dean Smith was a basketball coach whose leadership incorporated principles of both task leadership and socio-emotional leadership. His book is a priceless analysis of leadership in college sports.

Mentioning Dean Smith to illustrate excellence in leadership leads naturally to a question that lies at the very heart of the study of leadership. Is leadership always good? It seems to be so since many schools now teach "leadership" as if they are teaching virtue or goodness. Is there such a thing as bad leadership? Some scholars think that there is (Kellerman, 2004) and that bad leadership needs to be understood as well as "good" leadership. Some scholars argue that leadership always involves a shared goal between the leader and the followers (Wills, 1994), but the goal may not always be shared by others. Most Americans do not view Adolph Hitler as a great leader, but German citizens in the 1930s and early 1940s certainly did. Who is right? Or does it make sense even to pose that question? There seem to be two positions on this issue. The first is that leadership should be judged only by the process of influencing others. Take the definition offered by Gardner (1990), for instance.

> Leadership is the process of persuasion or example by which an individual (or leadership team) induces a group to pursue objectives held by the leader or shared by the leader and his or her followers. (p. 1)

Gardner says nothing about the quality of the goals. They may be laudable or they may be larcenous. This definition does not discriminate. It focuses on the process of leadership not on its objectives. By this standard, we may judge Hitler to have been as good a leader as Churchill or Eisenhower (except for the fact that he lost the war and they won). Hitler rallied the German people and many others to his cause and by Gardner's definition he illustrated leadership. (Notice that Gardner does not say anything about achievement.) However there are those who argue that Gardner's view of leadership is incomplete, that leadership involves inducing others to pursue admirable, moral, ethical objectives. You cannot praise the leadership skills of the men who organized the attack on the World Trade Center on September 11, 2001, according to this alternative view. One form of bad leadership has to do with guiding people or leading people to do bad things. Realizing that people may differ about what is and is not moral or ethical, we may generally call leadership that guides others to commit or support immoral or unethical "unethical bad leadership."

Some leaders may simply be incompetent and that is a different category of bad leadership, "incompetent bad leadership." As we noted earlier, leaders often have task requirements that need executing and leaders are expected to know how to accomplish these tasks. But sometimes they do not. They may think that they have the skill to perform well when in fact they do not. In other circumstances the tasks may simply be too difficult for the leader to manage. In this domain we encounter the issue of achievement again; incompetent leaders cannot achieve the goals that are expected of him or her. Incompetence, unfortunately, is rife. We see almost daily examples of executives who failed to achieve corporate goals, of military officers who simply cannot meet their objectives, of political leaders who fail to fulfill the electoral promises they make.

A particularly virulent type of bad leadership occurs when a person is both unethical and incompetent. It is sometimes claimed that two wrongs make a right, but in this case two wrongs make for a uniquely sinister and dangerous combination. The type of bad leadership that we have in mind here is the type that conceals the true objective of the leader and also conceals that inability of the leader to achieve the false objective. A superb illustration of this type of leader is the notorious Bernie Madoff, the investment guru who promised investors impossible returns on their investments while concealing his Ponzi scheme from them, his followers, and concealing his inability to create the kinds of returns he promised. He was incompetent as an investor—indeed he did no investing at all—and his goal was the immoral one of stealing from people who trusted him.

So leadership is not always "good" leadership just as accounting is not always "good" accounting and brain surgery is not always "good" brain surgery. But the goal of those who want to learn about leadership and those of us who teach about leadership is to focus on "good" leadership and the qualities and skills that create and maintain it. In this book we hope to highlight some of the core concepts that promote good leadership (and also good followership). So we turn now to the chapters in the book.

Conceptions of Leadership

We have called this book "Conceptions of Leadership" to highlight the fact that there are many concepts of leadership. We have not called the book, "*The* Conceptions" because we do not claim to be exhaustive about the ideas presented here. Go to Amazon.com and type in "Leadership Books." (I just did this.) You will find that there are over 100,000 entries. I can promise the reader that there are not 100,000 ideas about leadership that are worth examining. There are probably fewer than 50. What we are offering is a subset of these conceptions, a subset that we think contains some of the most important ones. Some of these conceptions are enduring, they have been around for a long time (e.g., Idiosyncratic credit), and some are relatively new or emergent (e.g., Heroic leadership). We have roughly organized these conceptions into two broad and somewhat overlapping categories, "Conceptions of Leadership" and "Processes of Leadership." The first section deals with the beliefs about, the qualities of, and the obligations of leaders. The second part of the book focuses more on the "how" of leading and some of the attendant consequences thereof. In our second chapter, Lipman-Blumen traces some historical views about leadership. She notes how the concept has evolved from Grecian times to modern times. What is especially interesting about her chapter is the mapping of the changes in views about leadership to the changing requirements of leaders. For instance, Greek philosopher kings were not elected and they did not have to appeal to a large and diverse electorate. The American view of leadership changed to reflect the growth of American corporations and the needs of managers to understand much more than simply speech-making. Her chapter documents the point made earlier that tasks of leaders change as we move era to era, from nation to nation, and from domain to domain. Leaders of today's multinational corporations must be global to an extent never imagined by Machiavelli, for instance. Next, Bazerman highlights the obligation of modern leaders, especially of corporations, to stay aware of what is happening in the organizations they lead. Leaders must *notice* what is going on in order to stop undesirable or unethical actions done by subordinates. This surveillance becomes challenging in today's multinational corporations. How does one create a surveillance process that can alert a leader to potential problems while not violating rights to privacy? If it is the ethical duty of the CEO to shape the conduct of his or her organization, how can that be accomplished? In the last quarter of a century we have seen the failure of major corporations whose demise is directly attributable to either corrupt (immoral) or incompetent leadership.

The following two chapters both focus on individual differences in leadership qualities, but in very different ways. Simonton examines the methods that scholars use to study people, sometimes quite deceased, who have been important leaders, particularly political leaders. Suppose one wishes to study men who have been president of the United States, he asks. All but four of these men are dead. He then reviews methods that can be employed to attempt to assess the qualities of these people and illustrates one of the methods by having experts rate the characteristics of each of the past presidents. Hoyt's contribution examines the differences between men and women in leadership roles and highlights the difficulties women have in attaining such roles as a result of stereotypes about women in general, or women in masculine roles in particular. She also addresses the double burden saddling some women of being female and African American at the same time. She argues that women may be handicapped by stereotype threat, the well-established decrement in performance by members of stereotyped subgroups if they are faced with a task threatens to validate the stereotype. For instance a woman's performance on a "masculine" task, such as arithmetic computation or giving orders, may be diminished by the concern that she is expected to do less well than a comparable man.

In the first of the final two chapters in this section, Caruso, Fleming, and Spector explore recent research on the important quality of emotional intelligence in leadership. They review research indicating that standard intelligence tests fail to measure some of the essential qualities of effective leadership, qualities such as decisiveness and self-confidence. Emotional intelligence purports to measure competencies involved in reasoning with and about emotions, competencies that are essential in leading others. Much of the chapter explores methods of assessing emotional intelligence.

In the final chapter in this section, Goethals and Allison explore the quality of "charisma," a special aura that emanates from some persons that gives them a nearly spiritual feeling. The authors illustrate this quality by discussing the "three kings" in the late twentieth-century America, Dr. Martin Luther King, Elvis Presley, and Muhammad Ali, and transporting their inferences about the qualities of these men to Abraham Lincoln. This chapter is rich in speculations about the evolutionary and psychological origins of our human vulnerability to charismatic leadership and its quasi-theological appeal.

The second section of the book deals roughly with things that leaders do to enhance their effectiveness. This is not to say that they intentionally manipulate followers, although they may, but to adduce activities that leaders perform that help enhance the adherence of followers. In the first of these chapters, Kramer and Elsbach feature the central role of the crucial but elusive concept of trust. Without trust, either in the benevolence or competence (or both) of the leader, followers have little incentive to be loyal. Creating trust therefore is an essential task for a leader. The creation and maintenance of trust is accomplished to some degree by the types of stories or narratives that circulate, formally or informally, about the leaders. And it is this aspect of leading that McAdams explores in his chapter. We all create narrative life stories, McAdams argues, but those of leaders have some special qualities. He illustrates his position by reference to Barack Obama and George W. Bush, two recent presidents of the United States. Despite their stark political differences, he argues, there are notable similarities in their life stories; they are both stories of redemption. Allison and Goethals, in the next chapter, stress the central role of narratives in leadership. They introduce the concept of the heroic leadership dynamic to refer to the processes by means of which stories of heroes and leaders inspire and inform people. People are informed about appropriate modes of action and about deeper truths about human existence. They are inspired to reach for goals that may seem unreachable, like immortality. Stories of heroic accomplishment seem to be present in all human societies and may be considered to satisfy a fundamental need in human growth.

The final three chapters deal with the process of influence, broadly speaking, a topic of central concern to social psychologists. Forsyth presents a thorough review of research on the processes through which people influence each other. One of the important points he makes in this chapter is that various influence strategies have differing depths of impact, which is to say some modes of influence yield mere compliance while others produce true internalization. In other words, not all followership is the same. Some is deep and some is shallow. Hollander's chapter echoes this theme while spotlighting the role of followers in allowing leaders latitude in action, a phenomenon he labels, "idiosyncrasy credit." Hollander emphasizes the dual nature of influence in leader-follower relationships; leaders certainly influence followers but followers also have an impact on their leaders in terms of the expectations that the leaders must meet to maintain the position of leadership. Influence is a two-way street, Hollander reminds us, not one-way as some authors tend to imply.

The final chapter in the book examines the use and misuse of power—one form of influence—by leaders and asks the question, "Why do leaders sometimes behave in ways that are predictably counter to their own interests?" Kramer explores the processes that might support and promote such self-defeating behavior and provides insights into traps that leaders might fall into in their efforts to be successful. His chapter might be thought of as a psychological analysis of the types of actions that the brilliant historian Tuchman (1984) chronicled. Kramer asks how such disasters could have happened and shows that it is actually not that difficult.

This book does not pretend to say everything important that there is to say about leadership. But what it does say about leadership is important and useful in understanding and promoting good leadership.

References

Bales, R. F. (1950). *Interaction process analysis*. Cambridge, MA: Addison-Wesley.

Baron, J., & Hershey, J. C. (1988). Outcome bias in decision evaluation. *Journal of Personality and Social Psychology, 54*(4), 568–579.

Fischoff, B., & Beyth, R. (1975). "I knew it would happen." Remembered probabilities of once-future things. *Organizational Behavior and Human Performance, 13*, 1–16.

Gardner, J. W. (1990). *On leadership*. New York: Free Press.

Huntford, R. (1999). *The last place on earth*. New York: Modern Library.

Kellerman, B. (2004). *Bad leadership*. Boston: Harvard Business School Press.

Messick, D. M., & Kramer, R. M. (Eds) (2005). *The psychology of leadership*. Mahwah, NJ: Lawrence Earlbaum.

Molloy, A. (2013). *However long the night*. New York: HarperOne.

Smith, D. E. (2005). *The Carolina way*. New York: Penguin.

Solomon, S. (2001). *The coldest march*. New Haven, CT: Yale University Press.

Tuchman, B. W. (1984). *The march of folly*. New York: Random House.

Wills, G. (1994). *Certain trumpets*. New York: Touchstone.

CHAPTER TWO

The Essentials of Leadership: A Historical Perspective

JEAN LIPMAN-BLUMEN

From earliest times, and presumably without pondering its plight, the animal kingdom—from apes to zebras—has sorted itself into leaders and followers. In the process, hierarchy ensued. Brains and brawn counted. The young and eager routinely mounted competitive challenges, which robust, more mature leaders handily crushed. Eventually, however, age, wisdom, and infirmity would give way to youth and vigor. Over time, the cycle, with some variation, simply repeats itself.

The history of human leadership offers a surprisingly similar, but considerably more complex, picture. Human leaders existed in the most primitive nomadic groups seeking sustenance, shelter, and safety from enemies and natural hazards. Leaders, as we understand that concept today, were the ones who acted first. The rest of the group simply followed them to the watering hole, the protective cave, the hunt, or the battle.

Leaders continue to appear in all kinds of groups, from families, to small work groups, to large, complex organizations and societal institutions. Perhaps, because we find ourselves and those who most exquisitely represent us endlessly fascinating, the study of human leaders and leadership relationships has held us in its thrall, at least since the invention of the written word.

Human leadership has been examined through many distinct lenses: philosophy, psychology, sociology, physiology, anthropology, medicine, art, literature, and several other disciplines, to boot. Unfortunately, however, until recent decades, different disciplinary lenses have been used independently, preventing the integration of these multiple views of leadership. Rost (1991/1993) noted the relatively late (circa 1980s) evolution of "leadership studies" as a welcome elaboration of previous single-disciplinary scholarship.

To capture what I believe to be an emerging paradigmatic shift in leadership studies would stretch this chapter into multiple volumes. Here, to the reader's relief, we shall have to settle for much less. Rather, given the current state of the field, I shall examine briefly and very selectively the more neglected historical arc of leadership contemplation and research, from its earliest days to late twentieth century. Although scholars around the world have added important perspectives, because of space considerations, we shall limit our attention primarily to US scholars writing before 2000. More recent developments and more global inclusion must be left to others.

Venturing to summarize a field that has developed over centuries provides considerable frustration. Topics seem to capture researchers' imaginations for a period of time, then disappear, only to resurface decades later with a new twist. More than half a century ago, Bennis (1959) complained, "Probably more has been written and less is known about leadership than about any other topic in the behavioral sciences." Almost two decades later, James MacGregor Burns (1978) echoed the same sentiments.

This leaves one with a sense of disarray, incompletion, and recapitulation, particularly when trying to do justice, in limited space, to this rambling venture. Perhaps, we should consider this chapter essentially an effort to whet the reader's appetite for the following chapters, as well as for the several outstanding leadership compendia that cover more recent decades.

I shall attempt to deal with this unwieldy task—probably vainly—by charting the trajectory of concerns with leaders, leading, and leadership as the interest in these various facets has ebbed and flowed. Our lens will focus on leaders primarily as positive forces in various contexts. Toxic leadership, worthy of its own chapter, falls beyond our current purview, as does the burgeoning corpus of female leadership and more recent work on followership.

Way Back When...

Among humans, the earliest recorded contemplation of leadership is commonly attributed to Lao-Tzu (an honorific title translated as "old master"). The presumed founder of Taoism, Lao-Tzu (604 BC– 531 BC), succinctly depicted leadership as a subtle art, in which the followers were virtually unaware that their accomplishment had been guided by the leader. His most oft-quoted wisdom on leadership demonstrates Lao-Tzu's (1998) nuanced understanding of good versus bad leadership.

A leader is best when people barely know he exists, when his work is done, his aim fulfilled, they will say: We did it ourselves.

The Greek Philosophers' "Take" on Leadership

In the intervening centuries, virtually every topic still bedeviling contemporary leadership scholars today was seriously considered in the very earliest philosophical writings on the subject. Socrates, Plato, and Aristotle essentially identified—mind you, without benefit of Factor Analysis—the core roster of leadership conundrums that continues to intrigue contemporary analysts.

Socrates's (469 BC–399 BC) leadership wisdom is known primarily through the work of his student, Plato (427 BC–347 BC). Later, Plato's prized student, Aristotle (384 BC–322 BC), addressed leadership issues, as well, particularly the ethics required of leaders. Ciulla, 1998, more recently has pinpointed the endurance of ethics as "the heart of leadership" (p. 4).

Plato

Following Socrates, Plato (1992) contemplates the philosopher-king in the context of the ideal political state (*polis*), an individual whose main purpose (*telos*) is to enable the citizens to become "good" *(demiurge)*. The ultimate goal was achieving "happiness."

Initially, in *The Republic*, Plato (1992) insists that philosopher-kings must rule because they, alone, understand the abstract, ideal "form" of the "good." They also demonstrate the ability to rule in accordance with that knowledge. In the *Dialogues*, Plato suggests that philosopher-kings, drawing on scientific principles, actually can learn the "art of ruling."

The most important of several virtues with which philosopher-kings must be endowed is "prudence," a gift possessed by few. Plato notes that those philosophers with the wisdom, proclivity to truth-seeking, and integrity necessary for good leadership rarely wish to pursue such political roles. (Truth-seeking and integrity, as we shall see, are never far from the minds and empirical findings of leadership scholars down through the ages.) Consequently, most leaders fall short of the philosopher-king ideal. Plato also warns against the rhetoric and persuasion of would-be leaders, as opposed to the wisdom and reason of true philosopher-kings.

Because philosopher-kings, graced with moral strength and political wisdom, seldom feel inclined to rule, law, embodied in a state constitution, must be developed. Only in this way can the masses be protected against imperfect leaders, whose numbers rarely wane. Even in those singular instances when philosopher-kings do assume the mantle of leadership, *their* actions, too, must conform to the law.

Plato's writings prefigure numerous leadership issues with which subsequent scholars continue to wrestle: the roles of charisma, truth, and integrity; the management of meaning through symbolic action; the raising of followers to a higher state of being; and the dilemma posed by the reluctant leader. These were then and, alas, still are today the core issues surrounding leadership. Perhaps, this offers greater testimony to the enduring, enigmatic qualities of leadership than to the inadequacy of subsequent scholarship.

Aristotle

While the leadership wisdom of Aristotle can hardly be reduced to a few sentences, the nub of his argument revolves around the leader's virtue (excellence of character or integrity, reflected in habits and action) and how this virtue may be encouraged, practiced, and honed. Leaders' virtue rests upon their moral trustworthiness.

Aristotle suggests that the virtue of leaders always involves voluntary actions. Three well-springs nourish virtue: the object of the action, the leader's noble intention, and the circumstances surrounding the action. Goodness must characterize all three elements.

In addition, the leader and follower must voluntarily share a common noble purpose. The result: "ethics lies at the very heart of leadership," buttressed by technical competence (Ciulla, 1998, p. xv). The relationship between leader and follower involves a moral, reciprocal bond, "based on trust, obligation, commitment, emotion, and a shared vision of the good" (Ciulla, 1998, p. xv). "Leaders and followers rely upon and influence one another" (Ciulla, 1998, p. xv). (This concept of a reciprocal leader-follower relationship, however, would lie dormant for centuries.)

Aristotle also paid serious attention to the leader's capacity to communicate, particularly to persuade, based on the leader's trustworthiness. Leaders' credibility, according to Aristotle, rested upon their practical wisdom (*phronesis*), virtue (*arête*), and good will (*eunoia*). These were indispensable qualities for a leader communicating in that ancient democracy, where all citizens had both the right and the obligation to engage in civic discourse about their government.

Niccolò Machiavelli (1469–1527)

In his best-known treatise, *The Prince (Il Principe)*, Machiavelli (1992) offers pragmatic advice about effective leadership behavior. *The Prince,* written in sixteenth-century Florence, is remembered largely for its advocacy of unethical behavior when and if the leader deems it absolutely necessary.

Perhaps, *The Prince* is most renowned for its even-then shocking recommendation to value inculcating fear over love in one's followers. In considering these alternatives, Machiavelli recognized the rarity of evoking both. To resolve this dilemma, he suggested,

> *One would like to be both the one and the other; but because it is difficult to combine them, it is far safer to be feared than loved if you cannot be both.*

Machiavelli acknowledges that, ideally, the Prince should act virtuously. If the circumstances demand, however, Machiavelli rather pragmatically recommends abandoning those virtues in favor of less stellar qualities—from brutal force to deceit—for the sake of surviving to lead another day. He hard-headedly advises:

> *Yet the way men live is so far removed from the way they ought to live that anyone who abandons what is for what should be pursues his downfall rather than his preservation; for a man who strives after goodness in all his acts is sure to come to ruin, since there are so many men who are not good.*

Machiavelli argues that, because there are so many good qualities to be developed, it is quite impossible for the Prince to embody them all. Rather, the Prince should aim at creating the *appearance* of these exemplary qualities, while retaining the flexibility to abandon them as necessity demands. In fact, Machiavelli suggests, circumstances may arise in which one must deliberately opt for evil, although, if possible, one should try to avoid such dire situations.

William Shakespeare (1564–1616)

William Shakespeare's second tetralogy of history plays, *Richard II*, *Henry IV*, and *Henry V*, reveals Machiavelli's pragmatic influence, paradoxically intertwined with the Tudor political-religious philosophy supporting the inviolable "Divine Right of Kings." Primogeniture, the firstborn's right to inherit the crown, was similarly sacrosanct. The duty of the ruled was simply to accept unequivocally all decisions of the ruler, despite any personal misgivings.

As Machiavelli would have it, rulers must be politically savvy, intelligent, strong, captivating, knowledgeable in the art of war, even dissembling, when necessary. Machiavelli counseled the Prince to avoid the cardinal blunder of appropriating subjects' property or women, advice Richard II casually ignored, to his great detriment. Thus, for Shakespeare, both anointed status and political acumen must be married in the King, who answers only to God.

In his second tetralogy, The Bard presents three types of rulers who meet these requirements quite differently. Richard II is legitimately entitled to his throne, as well as his subjects' absolute obedience, despite his abject lack of political intelligence and moral rectitude. Henry IV embodies the latter, but lacks the former: he displays great political genius, but has ascended to the throne by overthrowing Richard, rather than by "Divine Right."

For Shakespeare, Henry V embodies both requisites for leadership. A legitimate "firstborn" royal, Henry V also exemplified immense political intelligence. Henry V developed this ability during his "wayward youth" as Prince Hal, consorting with Falstaff, a braggart-cum-prevaricator, and his like. Once enthroned, however, Henry V deftly transforms his engaging, wily ways into royal grandeur. He demonstrates a knack for the art of war (so essential to Machiavelli), still enchants his subjects, and—in a gesture worthy of Machiavelli—he dramatically renounces Falstaff.

Moving Forward...

The Great Man: The "Born or Made" Controversy

The question of what makes a good leader would not be settled, even by Shakespearean genius. In fact, the issue of "born to rule" would take on new meaning in the years ahead. The "born vs. made" debate erupted with the question posed by Thomas Carlyle, the Scottish philosopher: "Is leadership innate or learned?"

Carlyle developed the "great man theory" of leadership in his collected lectures (1841) (see T. Carlyle, Thomas with James Fraser, 1840/1993). Since the publication of Carlyle's work, argument about the "born vs. made" leader has waxed and waned, but never entirely withered away. Traits such as intelligence, self-confidence, and introversion/extroversion (read "charisma"), integrity, and determination seem to reappear across the years. More recently, however, newer "cousin constructs," such as social intelligence, emotional intelligence, and self-monitoring have joined the list of usual suspects (Zaccaro, Kemp, & Bader, 2004). Witness Avolio's 2005 volume (Avolio, 2005) dedicated to that same question, which continues to percolate. And, if the evolutionary leadership theorists have their way, it most likely will just keep going (Van Vugt, 2012).

The Weberian Influence

By the twentieth century, Max Weber (1978), the renowned German social theorist, had reintroduced the concept of charisma in his influential treatise on the "Types of Legitimate Domination." There, Weber (p. 241) insisted that

> *The term "charisma" will be applied to a certain quality of an individual personality by virtue of which he is considered extraordinary and treated as endowed with supernatural, superhuman, or at least specifically exceptional powers or qualities. These are such as are not accessible to the ordinary person, but are regarded as of divine origin or as exemplary, and on the basis of them the individual concerned is treated as a "leader."*

According to Weber, charismatic leaders are "born of distress," that is, most likely to appear in times of crisis. Many, it seems, are simply waiting impatiently in the wings for the most propitious conditions to offer an opening. Perhaps, more tellingly, Weber warned we are "compelled to regard them with awe." What, then, is a mere mortal follower to do?

Weber contrasted charismatic authority with two other distinct bases of authority: traditional and legal-rational (often called "bureaucratic"). In more recent egalitarian eras, *traditional*, particularly monarchical leadership, gradually has lost considerable favor in both Western political life, as well as the leadership literature. Moreover, since Weber's time, *bureaucratic* leadership, which the German sociologist considered superior to the charismatic variety, has revealed its own oxymoronic character. Continuous global revelations of the inefficiency, as well as corruption, of bureaucratic authority must certainly be roiling Weber's grave.

Still, charisma has maintained its allure, both in academia and the popular imagination. It retains its appeal despite leadership scholar James

MacGregor Burns's (1978) conclusion that the term's "ambiguity" and "overlapping meanings" have left it so "overburdened as to collapse under close analysis." Consequently, Burns recommended that "charisma" be retired from "analytical duty." As with most good advice, Burns's recommendation has been largely ignored.

In fact, the romantic appeal of "charisma" (from the Greek, χάρισμα *khárisma,* frequently translated "gift of grace") has continued to surface in the leadership literature—both positively and negatively—ever since. To wit, Amazon.com's 6,399 volumes on charismatic leadership offer strong testimony to the topic's continuing attraction.

Transactional and Transforming Leadership: James MacGregor Burns

By distinguishing between "transactional" and "transforming" leadership, James MacGregor Burns, in his landmark work, *Leadership* (1978, p. 4), drew upon, but sought to move beyond, the fixation with charisma. He saw the relations of "most leaders and followers" as

> *transactional—leaders approach followers with an eye to exchanging one thing for another: jobs for votes, or subsidies for campaign contributions. Such transactions comprise the bulk of the relationships among leaders and followers, especially in groups, legislatures, and parties.*

By contrast, Burns described a "more complex," "more potent" form of leadership that he labeled "transforming" leadership. According to Burns,

> *The transforming leader recognizes and exploits an existing need or demand of a potential follower. But, beyond that, the transforming leader looks for potential motives in followers, seeks to satisfy higher needs, and engages the full person of the follower. The result of transforming leadership is a relationship of mutual stimulation and elevation that converts followers into leaders and may convert leaders into moral agents.* (p. 4)

Despite Burns's rejection of the term "charisma," his description of "transforming" leaders retained echoes of the Weberian concept. This persisted, despite Burns's distinct effort to differentiate between charismatic and transforming leaders by explicitly articulating the concept of "heroic leaders" to address leadership based on personal magnetism, etc.

Burns's concept of transforming leaders ignited decades of scholarly work dedicated to the nuances of leaders who go beyond mere transactional exchanges with their followers to accomplish an honorable task dedicated to improving the world. Burns's "transforming" leaders raised both their followers and themselves by guiding and inspiring them to engage in noble enterprises. Echoes of earlier Platonic musings.

From Leadership to Management

While leaders and leadership have teased the imagination of philosophers and other scholars since the time of Socrates, Plato, and Aristotle, the concern with management was to come much later. This interest in management only emerged around the turn of the twentieth century, in the shadow of industrialization and large-scale, clumsy, even chaotic organizations.

Early "Executive" Scholars in the Industrial Era

Well into the twentieth century, the reverberations of the Industrial Revolution, initiated in the 1760s in Great Britain, were still affecting America. Consequently, during that time, much of the focus in the leadership field took its cue from industrial organizations, with their rigid hierarchies of executives, managers, clerks, and "workers." How should we manage these sprawling, disorganized leviathans? In 1916, H. Fayol famously identified *planning, organizing, staffing,* and *controlling* as the basic responsibilities of management.

In the 1930s, Chester I. Barnard (1938/1964) identified "executive capacity" as "the most general strategic factor in human cooperation" (p. 282). For Barnard, the quality of leadership "derives from the breadth of the morality upon which it rests" (p. 282). Barnard saw leadership as

> that indispensable social essence that gives common meaning to common purpose, ... infuses the subjective aspect of countless decisions with consistency in a changing environment, ... inspires the personal conviction that produces the vital cohesiveness without which cooperation is impossible.
>
> Executive responsibility, then, is that capacity of leaders by which, reflecting attitudes, ideals, hopes, derived largely from without themselves, they are compelled to bind the wills of men to the accomplishment of purposes beyond their immediate ends, beyond their times. (p. 283)

Organizational Leaders vs. Managers

Inevitably, leadership in organizations came under serious and increasing scrutiny, energizing a discourse that continues even today. Within the organizational setting, scholars and practitioners examined the differences between leaders and managers, raising questions about the alignment of organizations and their members' needs and goals.

Stogdill and Bass

Ralph Stogdill (1948), an early leadership scholar prominent in the Ohio State Leadership Studies, focused on leaders in organizational settings.

Stogdill trained his lens on a wide range of organizational leaders, from senators to presidents of labor unions, corporations, and universities. Beginning with his initial survey of the leadership literature, Stogdill helped turn leadership researchers' attention to the field of management, which, even now, compels their interest.

Stogdill developed various measures of leadership behavior, including the RAD Scale, which measured organizational responsibility (R), authority (A), and delegation (D). Stogdill subsequently worked with numerous colleagues to focus on managerial/administrative settings and develop other leadership measures (see, e.g., Stogdill & Coons, 1957; Stogdill & Shartler, 1948). Alone and later with Bernard Bass (Bass & Stogdill, 1990), Stogdill produced several encyclopedic volumes on leadership and "managerial applications."

Bernard Bass extended the work of James MacGregor Burns on transactional and transforming leadership. (Allegedly, Bass changed Burns's original term, "transforming," to "transformational.") Bass integrated the small groups research of social and organizational theorists with the work of historians and political scientists, who had produced important biographies of well-known leaders.

In addition, Bass developed the *Multifactor Leadership Questionnaire* (MLQ), an instrument for measuring transformational leadership as he reconceptualized it. According to Bass's formulation, transformational leadership comprised four factors: Idealized Influence (charismatic leadership), Inspirational Motivation (team spirit); Intellectual Stimulation (encouragement of creativity), and Individual Consideration (concern with follower' needs, desires, and development). Bass collaborated with and inspired other leadership scholars to consider not only the antecedents, but also the nuances, of transformational leadership (Bass & Riggio, 2006).

Readers who wish to follow Bass's later work on transformational leadership should consult his seminal 1999 paper (Bass, 1999), in which he also indicated that women had a greater tendency than men to engage in transformational leadership, an insight that has been debated both before and since (see Robinson & Lipman-Blumen, 2003). Eagly and her colleagues subsequently conducted impressive meta-analyses of this large and informative body of work indicating the widespread consistency of this finding (Eagly, Johannesen-Schmidt, & van Engen, 2003).

Leadership and Small Groups

Circling back to the 1950s and 1960s, the impact of the leader's behavior on small groups became the major focus of research at the University of Michigan, where D. Cartwright and A. Zander (1960), D. Katz and R. L. Kahn (1951), and, subsequently, R. Likert (1961, 1967) conducted their work. That research program concentrated on two major leadership behaviors: employee orientation and production orientation.

Emanating from the Human Relations School, these researchers suggested that leaders with strong employee orientations paid particular attention to employees as human beings with unique feelings, interests, and needs. The production orientation, by contrast, revolved around the leader's attention to workers primarily as those who were directly responsible for performing work and accomplishing organizational goals (i.e., who could "crank out" the work). At the outset, the Michigan researchers saw these two orientations—employees and production—as polar opposites. That is, a leader who was keenly interested in employees would have little concern for production issues and vice versa. Eventually, however, Kahn (1956) distinguished these two orientations as separate phenomena. Thus, a leader could care strongly and simultaneously about employee satisfaction *and* production.

Blake and Mouton's Managerial (Leadership) Grid

Following in the tradition of managerial behavior, R. R. Blake and J. S. Mouton introduced the Managerial Grid (1964) (later renamed the "Leadership Grid"). Much like the Ohio State approach and the University of Michigan researchers' two-factor model, Blake and Mouton highlighted two familiar orientations: concern for people and concern for production. Combining these two concerns, the Leadership Grid resulted in five leadership styles:

- *The Authority-Compliance* style focused on goal accomplishment, with little concern for individual employees or interpersonal relationships, only for getting the job done.
- *The Country-Club Management* style, by contrast, attended primarily to interpersonal relationships and workers' personal needs, with scant concern for goal achievement.
- The *Impoverished Management* style described the passive, apathetic leader, with minimal interest in either goal achievement or interpersonal relationships.
- The *Middle-of-the-Road Management* style stood mid-way on both goal achievement and interpersonal relationships, emphasizing a stress-free environment and, if necessary, acceptance of mid-level productivity.
- The *Team Management* style embodied concern for both goal achievement, based on common purpose and interpersonal relationships, as well as team participation, characterized by excitement, trust, respect, openness, and determination.

In addition, Blake et al. introduced two additional elements: *Paternalism/Maternalism* and *Opportunism*. Leaders who favored *Paternalism/Maternalism* took a parental stance toward employees, articulating goals, setting the rules, and promoting positive interpersonal relationships. Like strict parents, these leaders also expected unequivocal obedience and achievement. (There's no free lunch, after all.)

The *Opportunistic* leaders presented quite a different kettle of fish. They cared primarily about their own personal advancement, with little regard for the group's members or goals. Unlike other leaders on the Managerial Grid who usually relied upon one favorite style (with a back-up choice when necessary), the Opportunistic leader did not favor any particular Grid style. In fact, Opportunistic leaders demonstrated great agility in combining or moving from one style to another, as the situation demanded, but always with their own fortunes front and center (Blake & Mouton, 1985).

Dignifying the Manager: Peter Drucker

Peter Drucker, widely considered the "Father of Modern Management," had little interest in leadership until the very last years of his life. Instead, Drucker essentially devoted his career to creating the "discipline of management" as a liberal art and dignifying the role of manager. As late as 1994, Drucker wrote to a colleague that he "didn't believe in leadership." He later announced that position publicly, in his role as "discussant" of a conference paper by leadership scholar Martin Chemers. Chemers humorously replied, "Good, that leaves the field completely to me."

In Drucker's (1973) original *magnum opus*, he was at great pains to downplay individual leadership, instead describing managers as constituting the "leadership group." There were no "leaders" *per se*. Drucker argued (p. 368):

> The managers of institutions are *collectively* the leadership groups of the society of organizations. But *individually* a manager is *just another fellow employee* (emphasis added)...It is therefore inappropriate to speak of managers as leaders. They are "members of the leadership group."

Drucker conferred on managers all the dignity of the traditional professions (p. 368):

> Essentially being a member of a leadership group is what traditionally has been meant by the term "professional." Membership in such a group confers status, position, prominence, and authority.

Eventually, Drucker recognized that the distinction between managers and leaders could not be so summarily dismissed. In fact, in his later writings, Drucker acknowledged leaders' distinguishing characteristics: their need to do what they can do well, their capacity to determine a significant purpose, their ability to frame and act consistently upon the organization's mission, and their talent for avoiding distractions.

In fact, Drucker (1973) ultimately defined leadership very similarly to James MacGregor Burns's description of "transforming" leaders. According to Drucker,

> Leadership is lifting a person's vision to higher sights, the raising of a person's performance to a higher standard, the building of a personality beyond its normal limitations. (p. 289)

Once again, we detect Platonic and Burnsian echoes of these key insights.

Unlike many others in the field, Drucker had little use for "leadership qualities" or "leadership personality," much less the highly touted concept of "charisma," which he insisted easily became "the undoing of leaders." In fact, he saw leadership as "mundane, unromantic, and boring. Its essence *is performance*" (p. 289).

For Drucker, leaders identified and exemplified a "few basic standards" (p. 290). They set those standards, molded their behavior to reflect them, and demanded that others do the same.

The "second requirement" for leadership, according to Drucker, was the leader's recognition that leadership was a "responsibility, rather than...rank and privilege" (p. 290). When things go awry (and Drucker was quick to suggest that "they always do"), leaders don't pass the buck. They admit "the buck stops here," à la the sign on President Harry S. Truman's desk.

Good leaders, according to Drucker, surround themselves with the strongest people, encouraging them to greater heights and taking vicarious pleasure in their accomplishments. Effective leaders enabled others to carry on where they left off, rather than setting up their successors for failure to demonstrate their own indispensability. And, finally, Drucker (1973) described the critical importance of leaders' integrity ("...the one absolute requirement of managers and leaders" pp. 290–291) by which they earned the trust—not necessarily the affection—of their supporters.

Resuscitating the Leader

During the decades when Drucker focused his intellectual passion on managers, Warren G. Bennis and his various coauthors contributed a treasure trove of writing on leaders and secondarily on managers (Bennis, 1959). Bennis and Nanus's (1985) most oft-quoted dictum revolved around the distinction between leaders and managers (a quotation ironically often attributed to Drucker):

> Managers are people who do things right, and leaders are people who do the right thing.

Bennis and Nanus argued that leadership involved vision and influence, whereas management focused on perfecting routines and performing activities.

Later, Bennis (1989/2003) would add that leaders "master the context, (while managers) surrender to it." He drew other distinctions, as well. He saw leaders as innovators, "originals," oriented toward people, rather than to systems or structure. Bennis believed leaders inspired trust, developed long-range perspectives, asked "what" and "why" (not "how" and "when"). Leaders kept their "eye on the horizon" (vs. the bottom-line orientation of managers), always challenging the status quo.

In a similar vein, John P. Kotter (1990) also differentiated sharply between leaders and managers, but insisted that organizations could not prosper without both. For Kotter, leaders were the strategic visionaries, who "got the big picture," aligning individuals by "communicating goals," "seeking commitment," and "building coalitions." In addition, leaders "motivate" and "inspire" their employees by "energizing and empowering" them, as well as by addressing their "unmet needs."

Managers, in Kotter's view, kept the organization stable by "planning and budgeting," "organizing and staffing," as well as "controlling" and solving problems. Managers created agendas, tied to timetables and carefully allocated resources. They designed and protected the structure, buttressing it by "rules and procedures" and assigning individuals to appropriate jobs. When problems arise, it is the manager's place to develop "creative solutions" and "take corrective action."

Kouzes and Posner (1987, 2002) identified five practices that mid-level and senior managers used to achieve outstanding results: "modeling the way," "inspiring a shared vision," "challenging the process," "enabling others to act," and "encouraging the heart." Based on these practices, Kouzes and Posner developed a widely-used 360° assessment of leadership competencies, *the Leadership Practices Inventory (LPI)*.

The Manager vs. Leader Question Redux

In an oft-quoted *Harvard Business Review* article, Abraham Zaleznick (1992) posed the question, "Managers and Leaders: Are They Different?" Predictably, Zaleznick's paper ignited a fresh round of debate. Zaleznick's answer: a resounding "Yes," with leaders winning out by virtue of their vision, risk taking, yearning for change, capacity to excite others, creativity, ethical behavior, and empathy. That essentially left managers far behind in the heavy dust of rationality, control, negotiation, tolerance for "mundane work," preservation of the "existing order," and a focus on process. And the "leader vs. manager" beat goes on.

A New Angle

Leavitt's Corporate Pathfinders

Harold J. Leavitt (1986), a "pioneer in the academic field of organizational behavior," took a somewhat different approach. He differentiated among three types of managers: *pathfinders, problem solvers*, and *implement-ers*. For Leavitt, *pathfinders* were creative visionaries, who relied upon wisdom, imagination, and an instinct to achieve their goals. *Problem finders*, by contrast, used their quantitative and other analytical skills to detect and control organizational problems. *Implementers*, Leavitt's third managerial category, counted on their political skills, including emotional and social intelligence (before these terms were coined), to reduce stress, build consensus, and establish teams. Together, these three groups of managers could achieve major organizational goals.

Leadership across Cultures: The GLOBE Research Program

Anthropologist and international management scholar Geert Hofstede's (1980) study of cross-cultural dimensions, in 50 countries, gathered data from more than 100,000 participants. The prodigious Hofstede research effort focused on five work-related dimensions that differentiated cultures. Hofstede's work, however, did not attempt to link these values specifically to leadership.

To address this gap, in 1991, organizational behavior and international management scholar Robert J. House and his colleagues (House, Javidan, Hanges, & Dorfman, 2002) tracked the influence of culture and leadership effectiveness in 62 countries. These researchers were interested in "organizational leadership, not leadership in general."

For their understanding of leadership, House et al. drew upon several theoretical frameworks. They described their conceptual model as

> an integration of implicit leadership theory (Lord & Maher, 1991), value/belief theory of culture (Hofstede, 1980), implicit motivation theory (McClelland, 1985), and structural contingency theory of organizational form and effectiveness (Donaldson, 1993; Hickson, Hinings, McMillan, & Schwitter, 1974).

Implicit leadership theory, according to Lord and Maher (1991), argues that people generally hold implicit beliefs and expectations about how leaders, both effective and ineffective, behave. They apply these implicit understandings to individuals they observe in leadership roles. In this view (pp. 171–233), leadership is defined by the *perceptions* of the observer, *not* by the actual behaviors of the person being defined as the leader.

The overarching goal for House and his principal collaborators was to develop an empirically based theory to describe, understand, and predict the impact of cultural variables on leadership and organizational processes and the effectiveness of these processes (House, R., Hanges, P., Ruiz-Quintanilla, S., Dorfman, P., Javidan, M., & Dickson, M., 1999).

More specifically, House and his collaborators set out to "extend (Hofstede's) study to test hypotheses relevant to relationships among societal-level variables, organizational practices, and leader attributes and behavior." In addition to Hofstede's five cultural differentiation dimensions, they developed four additional categories.

House, Hanges, Javidan, Dorfman, and Gupta (2004) published numerous findings regarding the influence of cultural factors on leadership and organizational processes, as well as many other organizational issues. Commonly referred to as the "GLOBE" studies (Global Leadership and Organizational Behavior Effectiveness), this work reports the findings from approximately 17,000 middle managers in 825+ local organizations in 61 countries, all in the financial, telecommunication, or food processing industries.

House et al. identified ten country clusters that demonstrated "within group" consistency, but were clearly distinguishable from one other. The findings, too complex in their entirety to record here, identified the dimensions on which each country cluster scored high or low, as well as those dimensions on which each group was distinctive.

The GLOBE project isolated 22 "valued" leadership characteristics essentially universally endorsed (with minor exceptions, like the Middle East). For most of the countries, extremely effective leaders were perceived as displaying high integrity, charismatic/values-based leadership behavior, and interpersonal skills (Dorfman, Hanges, & Brodbeck, 2004). (Are we beginning to see a pattern here?) Ineffective leaders, on the other hand, were perceived as authoritarian, self-protective, and lacking in interpersonal skills. These characteristics of organizational leaders, however, were studied without considering the situation or context in which they were acting, as earlier studies had done (Fiedler, 1964, 1967; Fiedler & Chemers, 1974; Fiedler & Garcia 1987).

Contingency Theory of Leadership: Fiedler and Associates

Social psychologist Fred E. Fiedler (1964), with various colleagues, developed a contingency theory of leadership, which directly addresses the match between leaders' capacities and the situations in which they must act. Here, too, the task orientation and relationship/people orientation come into play. Similar to other studies, *task orientation* or *motivation* focused primarily on accomplishing the task, while *relationship orientation/motivation* was driven by a desire to establish positive interpersonal relationships.

For Fiedler et al., leadership effectiveness was contingent upon the situation, which, in turn, presented three key dimensions: *leader-member relations, task structure,* and *position power. Leader-member relations* spoke to the ambience of the group, the degree to which members of the group felt loyal to, believed in, and were drawn to the leader. In groups exhibiting a high degree of these characteristics, *leader-member relations* were evaluated as positive. When these characteristics were in short supply, researchers rated *leader-member relations* as negative.

Clearly specified tasks, with explicitly described requirements, were defined as "highly-structured." High structure allowed the leader more control over group members whose assignment was to accomplish those tasks. For effective leadership, a task must be highly structured, with only a limited number of possible solutions and implementation strategies. Poorly defined, unclear tasks ("low" structure) made it difficult for the leader to maintain control and, thus, interfered with the leader's effectiveness.

The third dimension of the situation, position power, referred to the degree to which the leader legitimately could reward or discipline group members by hiring, promoting, demoting, dismissing, or increasing or slashing pay. The legitimacy of leaders' authority flowed directly from their organizational position.

Situations that were likely to produce effective leadership displayed positive *leader-member relations*, highly structured tasks, and leaders with *high position power*. The findings, however, held some interesting surprises. Leaders who were very task-oriented were judged effective both in situations that were going well, as well as their opposites, that is, situations that were going quite poorly. By contrast, leaders who cared more about relationships than tasks were most effective in situations which were neither completely within, nor completely beyond, their control. The reasons for these rather unexpected patterns were relatively unfathomable, belonging to a range of unexplained phenomena that Fiedler described as "black box problems" (Fiedler, 1993).

Contingency theory recognized that leaders may be effective in some, but not other, situations. Success was, therefore, *contingent* upon the match between the leader's style and the demands of the context. It also allowed greater predictability about the likelihood of the leader's success in a given situation.

Fiedler's methodology involved developing a widely used instrument for measuring leaders' style: The *Least-Preferred Coworker Scale* (LPC). Although the complexity of administering the LPC presents certain difficulties, the test-retest reliability of the scale has enhanced its use by many researchers (Fiedler & Garcia, 1987).

Path-Goal Leadership Theory: Robert House and Colleagues

The path-goal leadership theory, developed by Robert House (1971), with both G. Dessler (House & Dessler, 1974) and R. Mitchell (House & Mitchell, 1974), was more concerned with employees' performance, satisfaction, and motivation, than with leadership behavior, *per se*. Drawing on expectancy theory, House and his associates based their research on the assumption that employees' expectation that they could, in fact, do well under certain circumstances would help them to perform better. Thus, the general idea of the path–goal leadership theory revolves around the leader's efforts to determine what the employee needed to accomplish a particular task—whatever might be necessary to strengthen that individual's performance. Helping the employee by defining the goal, clarifying the path to the goal, removing obstacles, and providing personal support constituted the leader's basic responsibilities.

The path–goal theory is essentially a contingency theory, since the leader's choice of his/her own behavior was deemed contingent both upon the leader's assessment of the employee's needs and the nature of the task. The leader had several behavioral choices: directive, supportive, participative, or achievement-oriented. Moreover, the leader was not limited to any one behavior with a particular employee and could change behaviors, depending upon the needs of the situation. And, of course, the leader's behavioral choice varied from one employee to the next

Locus of control, that is, whether the individual felt s/he should control what happened, provided another factor that the path–goal researchers took into account. Employees who scored high on internal locus of control responded optimally to leaders who used participative behavior, inviting the employees into the entire decision-making and implementation process.

The path–goal researchers focused on specific aspects of the task: the primary work group for the task, the organization's formal authority system, and the design of the task. When the task is vague and unstructured, in an organization without a strong authority system and effective group norms, leadership intervention is usually necessary. Then, the leader must take into account the demands of the task, as well as the characteristics of the employee, in determining exactly which leadership behavior(s) to utilize.

Two decades after House originally introduced the path–goal research, he revised the theory by expanding the types of leadership behaviors to a full complement of eight. (The basic contingency model remained essentially the same.) The four new leadership behaviors were work facilitation, group-oriented decision process, work-group representation/networking, and "value-based" leadership behavior.

New Leadership for a New Century

In 1991, Joseph C. Rost declared most of the previous scholarship on leadership as outdated, reflecting a bygone industrial age, replete with organizational managers and subordinates. He identified the need to reconceptualize leadership for a postindustrial era. Roth proposed his own conceptualization: "Leadership is an *influence relationship* among leaders and followers who intend real changes that reflect their mutual purposes" (p. 102).

For Rost, acknowledging James MacGregor Burns's influence, leadership entails four "essential elements":

- Influence, that is "using persuasion to have an impact...in a 'non-coercive' and 'multidirectional' relationship between leaders and followers" (p. 102).
- "Mutual purposes" (not goals) that "become common purposes" (p. 106).
- A relationship between leaders and active followers that is "inherently unequal because the influence patterns are unequal" (p. 106).
- "Multiple, transforming changes" intended by the leaders and followers (p. 106).

For Rost, leaders and active followers "do leadership" together (p. 106).

Leadership for a New, Connective Era

In the early 1990s, J. Lipman-Blumen (1992) agreed existing leadership models were inadequate, but for somewhat different reasons. She contended that the nascent historical moment—the Connective Era—was creating new sociopolitical conditions in which everyone and everything were rapidly becoming interconnected and interdependent.

These rapidly changing conditions created two major and burgeoning challenges—diversity and interdependence—that pulled in opposite directions, often sparking conflict. Diversity called for *in*dependence and self-expression, while *inter*dependence required collaboration and teamwork. With technology tightening interdependence among diverse, often antagonistic, groups, only new and dramatically different leadership strategies would suffice.

Consequently, Lipman-Blumen (1995) argued for a new model of leadership, which she labeled "Connective Leadership." The Internet offered an apt metaphor for this new, entangling Connective Era. Connective leaders use a broader repertoire of strategies that can integrate—not exacerbate—these proliferating tensions. This new global context demands leaders who can enable parties, with distinctive, often inimical, agendas and world views, to work and live together harmoniously and productively.

Using a "politics of commonalities," (rather than a "politics of differences"), connective leaders create short-term (vs. long-term "NATO-like") coalitions to work on mutual problems. Relying upon integration, rather than compromise, connective leaders help disagreeing parties to identify areas of mutual, if admittedly limited, interest and agreement. Starting there, connective leaders bring the vision, skills, authenticity (consistent dedication to the group's cause), accountability (transparency), adaptability, accessibility, and know-how to enlarge conflicting parties' areas of mutual concern.

Connective leaders identify and work with their supporters on noble enterprises, thereby transforming the world, while simultaneously helping their supporters deal with their own existential anxiety. These connective leaders adeptly use symbolic, counterintuitive gestures to draw supporters to their goals. And here, too, we see that integrity, with all that it entails, serves as a cornerstone of connective leadership. Integrity, it seems just won't go away—fortunately.

Lipman-Blumen and Leavitt's Achieving Styles: An Underlying Behavioral Model

Beyond articulating the conceptual model of Connective Leadership, Lipman-Blumen linked that model to years of earlier (1973) behavioral research in which she and Harold J. Leavitt, at Stanford Graduate School of Business, had developed a nine-factor Model of Achieving Styles. They defined "Achieving Styles" as the learned, characteristic behaviors or behavioral strategies that individuals repeatedly call upon to accomplish their tasks and achieve their goals (Leavitt & Lipman-Blumen, 1980). The ideal Connective Leader, Lipman-Blumen later understood, would need to have easy access to all nine behavioral strategies.

To apply just the right combination of Achieving Styles, connective leaders needed to apprehend the "situational cues" in each particular context. So, both emotional and social intelligence come seriously into play in the effective, nimble adjustments that connective leaders must make as they move from one situation to the next.

The Achieving Styles Model comprises three major sets of behavioral strategies for achieving one's goals and/or completing one's tasks: the *Direct, Instrumental,* and *Relational Set.* Each of the three Achieving Styles Sets includes three distinctive Achieving Styles, resulting in a nine-factor model:

The three Direct styles include: *Intrinsic, Competitive,* and *Power.* The *Direct* styles emphasize deriving *intrinsic* satisfaction from mastering a challenging task, outdoing others through *competitive* action, and using *power* to take charge and reduce chaos by coordinating everyone and everything. These are the styles most closely linked to diversity and its various expressions of one's unique individualism.

The three *Instrumental* Achieving Styles include: *Personal, Social,* and *Entrusting.* The *Instrumental Achieving Styles* enable individuals *to* call upon themselves and others openly, unabashedly, and ethically to accomplish mutual goals. The personal, social, and political savvy embedded in these styles helps to diminish interpersonal friction among people and groups with opposing agendas. The *Personal Instrumental* style uses the total array of one's *personal* strengths—including intelligence, wit, charisma, physical appearance, humor, counterintuitive gestures, as well as negotiating and mediating skills—to attract supporters. The *Social Instrumental* style involves creating and working through social networks and alliances with those individuals and groups with clearly relevant experience, skills, and contacts to accomplish common tasks. The *Entrusting Instrumental* style allows leaders to impart their vision to other trusted individuals whom they empower and entrust with a shared goal *without* concern about their relevant experience, skills, or contacts. This is "leadership by expectation."

The third and last Achieving Styles Set, the *Relational Set,* also includes three styles: *Collaborative, Contributory,* and *Vicarious.* This set attracts individuals who prefer respectively to work with others on group tasks, to contribute behind the scenes to other people's success, or simply to take pleasure and a sense of personal achievement from the success of others with whom they identify.

Since Achieving Styles are learned behavioral preferences, Leavitt and Lipman-Blumen believed that they could be modified by awareness and training. To this end, beginning in 1973, they developed the *L-BL Achieving Styles Inventory (ASI 13-R)* to assess the behavioral strategies individuals use to accomplish their goals (1983). Subsequently, they developed an organizational version, the *L-BL Organizational Achieving Styles Inventory (OASI),* to measure the Achieving Styles organizations value and reward (i.e., the organizational culture), thereby creating an individual/organization assessment duo addressing identical behavioral dimensions. Subsequently, a *360° Achieving Styles Inventory (ASI 360°)* and a *Situational Evaluation Assessment (ASSET),* which matches individuals' personal Achieving Styles profiles to the demands of specific roles or tasks were developed. More recently, Lipman-Blumen has designed aspirational versions of the individual, organizational, and 360° assessments.

Invisible Leadership: Hickman and Sorenson

At this end of the historical arc, and as this chapter comes to a close, it seems quite fitting that we hear echoes of Lao Tsu in Gill Robinson Hickman and Georgia Sorenson's (2014) work on "invisible leadership." The concept of "invisible leadership" brings us full circle, at least for the moment. Invisible leadership points to the "compelling common purpose (that) inspires exceptional leadership." The leader slips into the shadows, behind the common purpose. Thus, charisma, with its compelling attraction (as Weber warned us) is now attached to the common purpose, rather than the leader. There, too, however, we need to be on guard, lest a common purpose, aglow with charisma, leads us down a primrose path.

Coda

At the outset, we indicated our intent to reach back to the earliest musings on leadership and then selectively move toward the dawn of the twenty-first century, focusing primarily on American leadership literature. We also stated that certain more recent twentieth-century leadership topics—from gender, to toxicity, to followership—regrettably fall beyond the bounds of this chapter.

As we passed the century mark, many of the leadership scholars whose work we've included have continued to contribute to the field, while new scholars have added their voices. Fortunately, the new century has already brought an exciting wave of leadership scholarship, both from the United States and around the world. Even more recently, the academic movement toward transdisciplinary scholarship has begun to shed new light on leadership.

In fact, the field of leadership studies appears poised at an inflection point. Multiple signals suggest that scholars in many fields, from neuroscience to mathematical modeling, are beginning to realize the value, as well as the difficulty, of integrating the knowledge drawn from different conceptual frameworks and methodologies. Perhaps, Van Seters and Field's (1990) early prediction of an integrated theory of leadership will soon come to fruition. Given the vast array of research from numerous disciplines, a transdisciplinary understanding of leadership, with its conjoined twin, followership, is clearly gestating. Without a doubt, the venture of perusing the twenty-first-century leadership oeuvre beckons enticingly.

References

Avolio, B. J. (1994). The "natural": Some antecedents to transformational leadership. *International Journal of Public Administration, 17*, 1559–1581.

Avolio, B. J. (2005). *Leadership development in balance: MADE/Born*. New York: Psychology Press.

Barnard, C. I. (1938/1964). *The functions of the executive* (6th ed., p. 282). Cambridge, MA: Harvard University Press.

Bass, B. M. (1985). *Leadership and performance beyond expectations*. New York: Free Press.

Bass, B. M. (1999). Two decades of research and development in transformational leadership. *European Journal of Work and Organizational Psychology, 8*, 9–32.

Bass, B. M. & Riggio, R. E. (2006). *Transformational leadership* (2nd ed.). Mahwah, NJ: Lawrence Erlbaum.

Bass, B. M., & Stogdill, R (1990). *Bass & Stogdill's handbook of leadership: Theory, research, & managerial applications* (3rd ed.). New York: Free Press.

Bennis, W. (1959). Leadership theory and administrative behavior. *Administrative Science Quarterly, 4*, 259–301.

Bennis, W. G. (1989/2003). *On becoming a leader* (p. 40). Cambridge, MA: Perseus Books.

Bennis, W. G., & Nanus, B. (1985). *Leaders: The strategies for taking charge* (p. 221). New York: Harper & Row.

Blake, R. R., & Mouton, J. S. (1964/1985). *The managerial grid*. Houston, TX: Gulf.

Burns, J. M. (1978). *Leadership* (pp. 4–102). New York: Harper & Row.

Carlyle, T., & Fraser, J. (1840/1993). *On heroes, hero-worship, and the heroic in history*. Berkeley, CA: University of California Press.

Cartwright, D., & Zander, A. (1960). *Group dynamics research and theory*. Evanston, IL: Row, Peterson.

Ciulla, J. B. (1998). Leadership ethics: Mapping the territory. In J. Ciulla (Ed.), *Ethics, the heart of leadership* (pp. xv–xix, 3–26). Westport, CT: Praeger.

Donaldson, L. (1993). *Anti-management theories of organization: A critique of paradigm proliferation*. Cambridge: Cambridge University.

Dorfman, P. W., Hanges, P. J., & Brodbeck, F. C. (2004). Leadership and cultural variation: The identification of culturally endorsed leadership profiles. In R. House, P. Hanges, M. Javidan, P. Dorfman, & V. Gupta (Eds.), *Culture, leadership, and organizations: The GLOBE study of 62 societies* (pp. 669–722). Thousand Oaks, CA: Sage.

Drucker, P. F. (1973) *Management: Tasks, responsibilities, practices.* New York: Harper & Row.

Eagly, A. H., Johannesen-Schmidt, M. C., & van Engen, M. J. (2003). Transformational, transactional, and laissez-faire leadership styles: A meta-analysis comparing women and men. *Psychological Bulletin, 129,* 569–591.

Fayol, H. (1916). *General and industrial management.* London: Pitman.

Fiedler, F. E. (1964). A contingency model of leadership effectiveness. In L. Berkowitz (Ed.), *Advances in experimental social psychology* (Vol. 1, pp. 149–190). New York: Academic Press.

Fiedler, F. E. (1967). *A theory of leadership effectiveness.* New York: McGraw-Hill.

Fiedler, F. E. (1993). The leadership situation and the black box in contingency theories. In M. M. Chemers & R. Ayman. (Eds.), *Leadership theory and research: Perspectives and directions* (pp. 1–28). San Diego, CA: Academic Press.

Fiedler, F. E. & Chemers, M. M. (1974). *Leadership and effective management.* Glenview, IL: Scott, Foresman.

Fiedler, F. E., & Garcia, J. E. (1987). *New approaches to leadership: Cognitive resources and organizational performance.* New York: Wiley.

Hickman, G. R., & Sorenson, G. J. (2014). *The power of invisible leadership: How a compelling common purpose inspires exceptional leadership.* Thousand Oaks, CA: Sage.

Hickson, D. J., Hinings, C. R., McMillan, J., & Schwitter, J. P. (1974). The culture-free context of organization structure: A tri-national comparison. *Sociology 8,* 59–80.

Hofstede, G. (1980). *Culture's consequences: International differences in work-related values.* Beverly Hills: Sage.

House, R. J. (1971). A path-goal theory of leader effectiveness. *Administrative Science Quarterly, 16,* 321–328.

House, R. J., & Dessler, G. (1974). The path-goal theory of leadership: Some *post hoc* and *a priori* tests. In J. Hunt & I. Larson (Eds.), *Contingency approaches in leadership* (pp. 29–55). Carbondale, IL: Southern Illinois University Press.

House, R. J., & Mitchell, R. R. (1974). Path-goal theory of leadership. *Journal of Contemporary Business, 3,* 81–97.

House, R. J., Javidan, M., Hanges, P., & Dorfman, P. (2002). Understanding cultures and implicit leadership theories across the globe: An introduction to project GLOBE. *Journal of World Business, 37,* 3–10.

House, R., Hanges, P., Javidan, M., Dorfman, P., & Gupta, V. (Eds.) (2004), *Culture, leadership, and organizations: The GLOBE study of 62 societies.* Thousand Oaks, CA: Sage.

House, R., Hanges, P., Ruiz-Quintanilla, S., Dorfman, P., Javidan, M., & Dickson, M. (1999). Cultural influences on leadership and organizations. In William H. Mobley (Ed.), *Advances in Global Leadership* (Vol. I, pp. 171–233). Greenwich, CT: JAI Press, Inc.

Kahn, R. I. (1956). The prediction of productivity. *Journal of Social Issues, 12*(2), 41–49.

Katz, D., & Kahn, R. L. (1951). Human organization and worker motivation. In L. R. Tripp (Ed.), *Industrial productivity* (pp. 146–171). Madison, WI: Industrial Relations Research Association.

Kotter, J. P. (1990). *A force for change: How leadership differs from management.* New York: Free Press.

Kouzes, J. M., & Posner, B. Z. (1987/2002). *The leadership challenge: How to get extraordinary things done in organizations.* San Francisco: Jossey-Bass.

Leavitt, H. J. (1986). *Corporate pathfinders.* New York: Dow-Jones-Irwin and Penguin Books.

Leavitt, H. J., & Lipman-Blumen, J. (1980). A case for the relational manager. *Organizational Dynamics, 9,* 27–44.

Likert, R. (1961). *New patterns of management.* New York: McGraw-Hill.

Likert, R. (1967). *The human organization: Its management and value.* New York: McGraw-Hill.

Lipman-Blumen, J. (1992). Connective leadership: Female leadership styles in the 21st century workplace. *Sociological Perspectives, 35,* 183–203.

Lipman-Blumen, J. (1996). *The connective edge: Leading in an interdependent world.* San Francisco, CA: Jossey-Bass. (Paperback edition, *Connective Leadership: Managing in a Changing World.* New York: Oxford University Press.)

Lipman-Blumen, J., Handley-Isaksen, A., & Leavitt, H. J. (1983). Achieving styles in men and women: A model, an instrument, and some findings. In J. T. Spence (Ed.), *Achievement and achievement motives: Psychological and sociological approaches* (pp. 147–204). San Francisco: W. H. Freeman and Company.

Lord, R., & Maher, K. J. (1991). *Leadership and information processing: Linking perceptions and performance.* Boston: Unwin-Everyman.

Machiavelli, N. (1992). *The prince.* New York: Dover Publications.

Plato. (1992) *The republic* (2nd ed.). Cambridge, MA: Hackett.

Robinson, J. L., & Lipman-Blumen, J. (2003). Leadership behavior of male and female managers, 1984–2002. *Journal of Education for Business, 79,* 28–33.

Rost, J. C. (1991/1993). *Leadership for the twenty-first century.* Westport, CN: Praeger.

Stogdill, R. M. (1948). Personal factors associated with leadership: A survey of the literature. *Journal of Psychology, 25,* 35–71.

Stogdill, R. M. (1974). *Handbook of leadership* (1st ed.). New York: Free Press.

Stogdill, R. M., & Coons, A. E. (1957). *Leader behavior: Its description and measurement.* Columbus: Ohio State University, Bureau of Business Research.

Stogdill, R. M., & Shartle, C. L. (1948). Methods for determining patterns of leadership behavior in relation to organization structure and objectives. *Journal of Applied Psychology, 32,* 286–291.

Tzu, L. (1998). *Tao de ching.* New York: Shambhala Press.

Tzu, L. (2004). *Ancient quotes Lau-Tzu quotations.* N.D. Web. September 10, 2014. http://www.quotes.stevenredhead.com/ancient/Lau-Tzu.html.

Van Seters, D. A., & Field, R. H. G. (1990). The evolution of leadership theory. *Journal of Organizational Change Management, 3,* 29–45.

Van Vugt, M. (2012). The nature in leadership: Evolutionary, biological, and social neuroscience perspectives. Ch. 5. In David V. Day & John Antonakis (Eds.), *The Nature of Leadership* (2nd ed., pp. 141–175). Thousand Oaks, CA: Sage.

Weber, M. (1978). *Economy and society: An outline of interpretive sociology.* In G. Roth & C. Wittich (Eds.) (p. 241). Berkeley, CA: University of California Press.

Zaccaro, S. J., Kemp, C., & Bader, P. (2004). Leader traits and attributes. In J. Antonakis, A. T. Cianciolo, & R. J. Sternberg (Eds.), *The nature of leadership* (pp. 101–124). Thousand Oaks, CA: Sage.

Zaleznik, A. (1992). Managers and leaders: Are they different? *Harvard Business Review,* 70(2), 126–135.

CHAPTER THREE

Ethical Leadership and Noticing

MAX H. BAZERMAN

Four times in recent years (2006, 2008, 2009, and 2011), *Time* magazine named JPMorgan Chase CEO Jamie Dimon as one of the world's 100 most influential people. *Institutional Investor* included Dimon on its Best CEOs list every year from 2008 through 2011. In 2009, *Newsweek* declared Jamie Dimon to be "America's Most Important Banker" and particularly the US government's banker of choice (*Newsweek* staff, 2009). By 2011, though, the glowing praise for Dimon had begun to dim, and one story in particular explains why.

In the aftermath of the financial crisis, which JPMorgan had weathered better than most large US banks, Dimon faced demands from shareholders to improve the bank's profitability. To allow for more flexible trading strategies, Ina Drew, the bank's chief investment officer, dropped JPMorgan's requirement to sell investments when losses exceeded $20 million. A strong supporter of Drew, Dimon paid less and less attention to her operations as large profits flowed in. In fact, Dimon encouraged Drew to further boost profits through greater risk taking. Speaking to a large audience of JPMorgan Chase executives in February of 2011, Dimon emphasized that it was the job of the bank's leadership to be bold, saying "Ina is bold" (Dominus, 2012). Dimon, like all CEOs, was a very busy leader, focused on profits; he saw Drew's returns and failed to notice weaknesses in the bank's review systems.

On April 4, 2012, Dimon read an article in the *Wall Street Journal* about a JPMorgan Chase trader in London, Bruno Iksil. According to the article, Iksil was making huge bets with the bank's money, bets that turned out to be in the wrong direction, and huge losses were accruing. The size of his bets and his risk taking had earned Iksil the nickname "the London whale." Four days later, Drew assured Dimon and the operating committee of JPMorgan Chase that Iksil's large trades would turn out fine, and she argued that the *Wall Street Journal* story was "blown out of proportion"

(Langley, 2012). Based on Drew's assessment, Dimon stated publicly that the trades were a "complete tempest in a teapot" (Dominus, 2012).

Unfortunately for Iksil, Drew, Dimon, and JPMorgan Chase more broadly, the losses associated with Iksil's trades grew. Finally, on April 30, Dimon demanded that Drew show him the details of the trading positions that resulted from Ilsil's action. Only after looking at the data did Dimon realize that a huge problem existed. Two weeks later, he admitted, "The last thing I told the market—that it was a tempest in a teapot—was dead wrong," the *Journal* reports. Dimon came to blame himself "for failing to detect the group's exposure" (Langley, 2012). He acknowledged the magnitude of the losses in a conference call on May 10, and he requested and received Drew's resignation in the days that followed. By late 2013, the total estimated cost of the trading losses from this episode were $6.2 billion.

Drew and Dimon failed to notice important information. The London and New York offices of JPMorgan Chase did not get along. The London unit that included Iksil consisted of "quants," analysts who relied on highly sophisticated (or perhaps just complicated) quantitative analyses when making trades. Iksil's assignment was to create complex investments using derivatives based on the direction the market was likely to move. Many speculate that Drew did not fully understand the quants' methods, and Dimon certainly was not monitoring Drew's supervision of London. Drew did question Iksil's superiors in the London office about his positions, but received ambiguous, incomplete answers. Iksil's group dodged Drew's questions, Drew failed to sufficiently demand clearer answers, and she never fully understood the magnitude of the risks being taken by the London-based investment unit.

After the damage was done, Dimon told the US Senate Banking Committee that "It morphed into something I can't justify" (Kopecki, Mattingly, & Benson, 2012). He also told his wife that he had "missed something bad." The *Wall Street Journal* later reported that Dimon said: "The big lesson I learned: Don't get complacent despite a successful track record" (Langley, 2012). Iksil's boss and one of his subordinates were indicted, and JPMorgan agreed to pay $920 million in fines. Senior management was also accused of hiding its losses from its own board's audit committee (Kopecki, 2013).

Unfortunately, the London whale story was just one of a number of major scandals to hit JPMorgan Chase in very recent history. The bank is also being investigated based on its acquisition of Bear Stearns in 2008, specifically regarding the rights the bank gained to sell electricity from power plants in Michigan and California. The complicated story has many pieces that have Enron-like aspects to it, but ample evidence suggests that JPMorgan Chase was involved in illegally manipulating energy markets. The Federal Energy Regulatory Commission (FERC) investigators have argued that JPMorgan Chase executives made "scores of false and misleading statements and material omissions" in an attempt to cover up the scandal (Silver-Greenberg & Protess, 2013).

In addition, during the more than two decades that JPMorgan Chase served as Bernard Madoff's primary bank, it claims that it never noticed anything suspicious worth reporting to regulators. The US Office of the Comptroller of the Currency argues that JPMorgan Chase failed to conduct adequate due diligence into Madoff's investments. This was true despite the fact that ample evidence suggests that even an average level of financial expertise should have allowed JPMorgan Chase to notice that Madoff's consistent above-market returns were not feasible.

JPMorgan Chase was also among the many large financial institutions implicated in the LIBOR manipulation scandal. LIBOR, the London interbank offered rate, is a key metric that sets interest rates for trillions of dollars in financial instruments. In a nutshell, JPMorgan Chase is accused of colluding with other banks and providing false information to a daily survey by the British Bankers' Association. This survey asks lenders how much it would cost to borrow money from each other.

After studying these scandals in more detail than I can document in this brief chapter, and reading about Jamie Dimon's experience, I conclude that:

(1) Jamie Dimon is a very intelligent leader, has a moral compass similar to that of many admired leaders, and has good intentions of being an ethical citizen of society.
(2) Jamie Dimon failed to notice unethical behavior and unacceptable risks being taken in his organization even when plenty of evidence was available.
(3) Jamie Dimon led an organization that had institutionalized a set of structures and practices that created an environment where unethical behavior was likely to occur.

The story of Jamie Dimon and JPMorgan Chase is broadly consistent with a growing literature that documents that even reasonably good people have the capacity to act unethically—often without their own awareness (Chugh, Bazerman, & Banaji, 2005; Chugh & Kern, 2009; Bazerman & Tenbrunsel, 2011; Messick & Bazerman, 1996).

The Dimon episodes highlight the core of this chapter; Leaders not only have the responsibility to act ethically, but they also have responsibilities (1) to notice when others around them are engaging in unacceptable behavior and (2) to create and maintain systems that do not reward or encourage unethical actions. Jamie Dimon has failed on these two leadership tasks. This chapter overviews the contemporary literature on bounded ethicality, or the psychology behind good people doing bad things. (For more extensive overviews of bounded ethicality, see Banaji & Greenwald, 2013, and Bazerman & Tenbrunsel, 2011.) I then discuss the core leadership challenges of (1) noticing the unethical actions of others and (2) creating organizational systems that encourage ethical behavior. In the process, I define noticing and the creating of organizational systems as the unique ethical challenges of leaders that go beyond the challenges facing other professionals.

Bounded Ethicality

Bounded ethicality refers to the systematic ways in which people act unethically without their own awareness (Banaji & Bhaskar, 2000; Chugh et al., 2005; Kern & Chugh, 2009). The core argument is that people engage in behaviors that they would avoid and condemn upon further reflection or awareness. Bounded ethicality has a number of specific manifestations.

Implicit associations. Perhaps the most well-developed research stream studies implicit attitudes/associations, or how people act in racist, ageist, and sexist ways without being aware that they are doing so (Banaji & Greenwald, 2013; Chugh et al., 2005). Implicit attitudes also cause people to favor members of their in-group, without awareness of the impact this will have on out-groups. To take one example, mortgage loan discrimination against minorities is much more likely to result from lenders' unconscious favoritism toward in-groups than from explicit hostility toward out-groups (Messick, 1994). But, bounded ethicality also manifests itself beyond discrimination.

Overly discounting the future. We overly discount the future, increasing the burden of government debt and destroying the ecosystem, often without awareness that we are acting in ways that may harm future generations (Wade-Benzoni, 1999). At an individual level, when we do not save enough for retirement, the burden becomes our own. But, when others incur the costs, discounting the future moves from an issue of rationality to an issue of ethicality. And often, we impose such burdens on future generations without intentional defection.

Overclaiming credit. We often claim more credit than we deserve. Ross and Sicoly (1979) first observed overclaiming in a study of married couples. They asked participants the percentage of household activities, such as washing the dishes, they each personally performed. When the two percentages were added, the per-couple average far exceeded 100 percent. Since this original demonstration by Ross and Sicoly, overclaiming of credit for work performed has been demonstrated in a variety of contexts, including academics claiming credit for coauthored publications (Caruso, Epley, & Bazerman, 2006).

Moral disengagement. One set of challenges for behavioral ethicists is how to integrate the observations that many people lie and cheat on a daily basis (just a little), yet hold very positive general images of ourselves as good and moral people. Shu, Gino, and Bazerman (2011) attempt to reconcile this inconsistency through Bandura's (1990) concept of moral disengagement. In short form, when people engage in actions that are at odds with their moral standards, they tend to modify their beliefs about their bad actions through moral disengagement in order to alleviate cognitive dissonance. Moral disengagement redefines the unethical conduct in a way that is personally acceptable by redefining the questionable behavior as morally permissible (Bandura, 1990).

Understanding bounded ethicality is important, since it leads to a very different set of strategies for how to create more ethical organizations and societies than the dominant strategies of today. If unethical behavior is intentional, as many presume, then we only need to worry about those who will intentionally commit unethical acts. But, if unethical behavior occurs unintentionally, as growing research suggests, this creates a broader set of concerns. It also highlights the fact that ethics training should be focused not just on turning bad apples into good ones, but on identifying the bad tendencies of good apples as well.

The lens of bounded ethicality can also identify when we need to be most worried about unethical behavior. For example, Kern and Chugh (2009) find that our ethics are swayed by the framing of information. That is, we are more likely to cheat to avoid losses than to obtain gains, even when the difference between whether we are thinking about losses versus gains is based on the framing of the same objective information. This highlights the need for greater awareness of the possibility of such behavior in difficult economic times.

The Leadership Challenge of Noticing

Many different definitions of leadership exist, and I make no claim to be able to identify the correct one. For our purposes, it is sufficient to note the most obvious task of leadership: leading other people to perform at their best. Some of those people might not always do the right thing, and when they don't, it is the job of the leader to notice. Regarding this aspect of ethical behavior, Jamie Dimon appears to have failed his organization and society at large.

The story of Bernard Madoff highlights the leadership challenge of noticing. Madoff's Ponzi scheme created enormous losses for many people—up to $65 billion, depending on what accounting you prefer. As we now know, Madoff sold most of his investments via feeder funds. That is, other funds sold investments to their retail (typically rich) customers, and invested all or most of these funds with Madoff. These feeder funds were well rewarded, typically earning a small percentage of the funds invested plus 20 percent of any investment profits earned (common in the hedge fund world). As Madoff racked up an amazing record of success, the feeder funds performed quite well in parallel.

As you know, Madoff turned out to be a crook. But his intentional illegal and unethical actions are not our focus here. Rather, we focus on the leadership failures of many of those who surrounded Madoff—people who, unlike him, were not consciously aware that their actions could and likely would harm others. Financial experts have concluded that Madoff's consistent returns, which outperformed the market with very little fluctuation, were statistically impossible. This simple analysis can be easily explained to undergraduate students (which I have done on multiple occasions). Nonetheless, many of the leaders of the feeder funds failed to notice that Madoff's performance reached an impossible level of return and stability. Lots of evidence reveals that many feeder funds had hints that something was wrong but lacked the incentives needed to see the readily available information. Consider René-Theirry Magon de la Villehuchet, a wealthy French aristocrat who invested his own fortune and his clients' funds with Madoff as the founder and CEO of investment firm Access International Advisors (AIA). De la Villehuchet ignored numerous warnings that Madoff's returns were not possible; he ignored the data that he did not want to see. AIA lost $1.5 billion in the Madoff scandal, including de la Villehuchet's personal fortune. Two weeks after Madoff's arrest, de la Villehuchet killed himself in his office in New York.

Leaders at many feeder funds, leaders of the SEC, leaders at Madoff's primary bank (JPMorgan Chase), his accountant, and many of his employees also didn't notice. Research is beginning to clarify the magnitude by which people fail to notice, the conditions in which leaders most commonly fail to notice, and the prompts they can use to highlight the need to pay attention. This section overviews research on three well-studied types of noticing failures: (1) when ethics erode on a slippery slope, (2) when we haven't seen the bad outcome yet, and (3) when others do their dirty work through intermediaries.

Slippery slope. Imagine that an accounting firm is auditing a client. For several years in a row, the client's books look just fine. The auditing firm approves the books and has a good relationship with its client. Then, one year, the client commits some clear transgressions in its financial statements, breaking the law in multiple ways.

Now consider an alternative story. The first year, the auditing firm notices that the corporation stretched, but did not break, the law. The auditing firm approves the books. The next year, the firm was even more unethical, committing a minor violation of federal accounting standards. Again the auditing firm signs off on the financials. By the third year, the violations have increased in magnitude but are not technically illegal. Once again, the auditing firm approves the numbers. And in the fourth year, the auditing firm has committed the same illegal behavior described in the prior paragraph.

Is the auditing firm more likely to notice, speak up, and act on the accounting improprieties in the first or the second paragraph? My work with Francesca Gino (Gino & Bazerman, 2009) suggests that the auditor would be more likely to notice and speak up in the first story. In the second version, the fact that the client's behavior eroded slowly over time makes it less likely that the auditor would notice the same severe ethical transgression.

In our experimental work, we conducted a series of laboratory studies showing that study participants are more likely to accept others' unethical behavior when ethical degradation occurs slowly rather than in one abrupt shift. Our "auditors" are given a task to notice if the client is cheating.

Our consistent result is that our auditors are less likely to notice and act on the actions of others when their behavior erodes gradually, over time, rather than in one abrupt shift. Gino and I (2009) refer to this as the *slippery slope effect*. Much of this effect occurs due to bounded awareness, our work suggests; that is, our auditors fail to notice the ethical erosion when it occurs gradually rather than in one fell swoop.

Ethical outcome bias. Baron and Hershey (1988) conducted early, fascinating work showing that we evaluate people based on the outcomes they produce much more than on the quality of their decisions. Thus, we are more positive about an employee who makes a lousy decision that turns out well than about an employee who makes a good decision that turns out poorly, even when we have ample access to information on the quality of the decision. Similarly, Cushman, Dreber, Wang, and Costa (2009) show that we are far more likely to condemn the same unethical behavior when it leads to a negative outcome than when it leads to a positive outcome.

In a typical study in the Cushman et al. (2009) paradigm, study participants (choosers) choose between the following two options:

Option A: You roll a six-sided die. If it comes up 1–4, you get $10, and the other party gets $0. If it comes up a 5, you get $5, and the other party gets $5. If it comes up a 6, you get $0, and the other party gets $10.

Option B: You roll a six-sided die. If it comes up a 1, you get $10, and the other party gets $0. If it comes up 2–5, you get $5, and the other party gets $5. If it comes up a 6, you get $0, and the other party gets $10.

It is easy to notice that Option A is the greedier choice, as it offers the chooser a higher probability (four out of six) to claim $10 for herself. In contrast, Option B is the "fair" choice; as it offers four opportunities for the $10 to be split evenly, and asymmetric options are symmetric in terms of who benefits.

In the original version of this design, after choosing, the decision maker rolls the die, the money is distributed, and the recipient (the other player) is given the opportunity to punish her partner without incurring any cost. The consistent result in this paradigm is that the recipient pays far more attention to the equality of the result of the rolled die than to the chooser's choice of die. This result holds even when a third party decides whether and how strongly to punish the chooser.

People too harshly blame others for making ethical decisions that have unfortunate outcomes and fail to blame others for unethical decisions that do not cause a clearly observable harm. Most people now question the ethics behind George W. Bush's decision to invade Iraq in 2003, particularly the administration's misrepresentation of the "facts" that prompted the war. Yet in the early months, when the war was going well from an American military perspective, few Americans offered criticism. Only after the war dragged on and the mistakes mounted did large numbers of

Americans begin to notice Bush's prewar unethical behavior. And, unfortunately, leaders have a general tendency to not pay attention until after the bad outcome occurs.

Indirectness of ethical infractions. In the early 1990s, Rhône-Poulenc sold a five-milliliter vial of the drug H.P. Acthar Gel to patients for about $50. The drug disappeared from the market for a while. When it reappeared in 2013, that same five-milliliter vial sold for $28,000 (this is not a typo) (Pollack, 2012). Before I share the details, it seems appropriate for me to mention that I have worked as a consultant for many pharmaceutical organizations and believe it is appropriate for drug companies to earn healthy profits when they create new solutions to our health challenges. That said, I find $28,000 per five-milliliter vial to be an amazing and problematic number.

H.P. Acthar Gel became an Aventis product when Aventis acquired Rhône-Poulenc. Both Rhône-Poulenc and Aventis had a limited ability to institute dramatic price increases for this small-market product due to the public attention that large pharmaceutical firms receive from the media. After selling only about $500,000 per year of Acthar in 2000, in 2001, Aventis sold the intellectual property rights to the drug to Questcor, a much smaller pharmaceutical company, for $100,000 plus profit sharing. The interesting aspect of this transaction was that Questcor did not have much of a brand image to protect and was less concerned about publicity than Aventis. This is the typical pattern when smaller pharmaceuticals buy small-market drugs from larger pharmaceuticals. Questcor quickly changed the price of Acthar from $50 to $700 per five-milliliter vial and continued to periodically raise the price until it reached $28,000 in 2013.

Most media accounts of this story blame Questcor and let Aventis off the hook, despite Aventis's role in the price increase. Aventis sold the drug to a company that could be predicted to dramatically increase its price and then share the profits with Aventis. Clearly, Aventis got Questcor to do its dirty work. But this story is hardly new. In 2006, the *New York Times* described what happened to a cancer drug called Mustargen that was being produced by Merck (Berenson, 2006). Mustargen was a small-market drug, with loyal cancer patients as its customers. Merck had incentives to raise prices, but negative publicity would be a problem. Merck's solution was to sell the rights to Ovation Pharmaceuticals, a much smaller company that specializes in buying slow-selling medicines from big pharmaceutical companies. Ovation quickly raised the price of Mustargen by 1,000 percent, despite facing no R&D or manufacturing expenses (Merck continued to manufacturer the drug on a contract basis). Because of its relative obscurity, Ovation was relatively unconcerned about its brand taking a hit, and Merck avoided the negative publicity of directly raising the price of the drug tenfold.

The Merck story motivated several of my colleagues and I to design a set of studies (Paharia, Kassam, Greene, & Bazerman, 2009) aimed at examining the dysfunctional tendency of people to ignore price gouging if the gouging occurs through an intermediary. We showed that people typically ignore unethical action if the unethical actor has an intermediary do its dirty work. We asked study participants to consider a situation where:

> A major pharmaceutical company, X, had a cancer drug that was minimally profitable. The fixed costs were high and the market was limited. But, the patients who used the drug really needed it. The pharmaceutical was making the drug for $2.50/pill (all costs included), and was only selling it for $3/pill.

We asked one group of participants to assess the ethicality of the following action:

A: The major pharmaceutical firm raised the price of the drug from $3/pill to $9/pill.

We asked a second group to assess the ethicality of a different course of action:

B: The major pharmaceutical X sold the rights to a smaller pharmaceutical. In order to recoup costs, company Y increased the price of the drug to $15/pill.

As predicted, participants judged Action A more harshly than those who read Action B, despite the smaller negative impact of Action A on patients. This work, as well as the work of Coffman (2011; Paharia, Coffman, & Bazerman, 2012), finds that our minds fail to notice when people do their dirty work through others. More broadly, research shows that we often fail to notice when others behave poorly. This is a leadership challenge, and one that behavioral ethicists have the power to address.

Finally, Kramer (2006) does an amazing job of showing how US presidents (e.g., Eisenhower, Nixon, and G. H. W. Bush) hired chiefs of staff to do their dirty work, so that they themselves could keep their hands (and images) clean and look "presidential." Kramer calls this tactic intimidation by proxy. The leader can remain the good guy, knowing their subordinates will do the dirty work that the media and public might find problematic.

The Leadership Challenge of Creating a High-Integrity Organization

The dark side of goal setting. Ethical leadership requires leaders not only to notice the unethical actions of others, but also to notice how the organizational structures they create can lead to predictably unethical behavior. Consider the classic story from the early 1990s, where Sears imposed a visible sales quota on employees performing auto repairs: each staff member was expected to bring in work worth at least $147/hour. This goal was quite consistent with the recommendations of the literature on goal setting, which promoted moderately difficult goals as an effective tool for improving employee motivation and performance (Locke & Latham, 2006). Across hundreds of studies, dozens of tasks, and thousands of participants on multiple continents, the clear conclusion was that specific, challenging goals boost performance results in comparison to having no goals, vague goals, or easy goals (Locke & Latham, 1990). "So long as a person is committed to the goal, has the requisite ability to attain it, and does not have conflicting goals, there is a positive, linear relationship between goal difficulty and task performance," Locke and Latham (2006) wrote.

The advocates of goal setting have provided ample evidence that they are correct about this conclusion. The problem, however, is that goals have a dark side. Namely, the same specific, challenging goals that improve performance also inspire an overly narrow focus that causes us to neglect performance criteria that are not part of our goal set. As a result, such goals reduce intrinsic motivation, damage interpersonal relationships, and—most important, for the purposes of this chapter—increase the likelihood of unethical behavior, as employees will bend or break rules and laws in order to achieve their goal (Ordóñez, Schweitzer, Galinsky, & Bazerman, 2009). The goal that Sears gave its mechanics notoriously led them to overcharge for their work and perform unnecessary repairs across the company, a trend that became a national scandal (Barsky, 2007; Disheau, 1992). Sears's "goal setting process for service advisers created an environment where mistakes did occur," Sears chairman and CEO Edward Brennan eventually admitted (Santoro & Paine, 1993). As Brennan learned too late, goals can motivate employees to deceive customers.

Similarly, during the years that Enron was consistently written up as one of the most admired firms in the world, the company's specific, challenging goals were pinpointed as a key to its success. From 1996 to 2000, Enron's revenues and assets grew at an astounding rate. Enron employees learned to meet their goals, but they did so by engaging in a variety of unethical and illegal behavior.

Conflicts of interest. Not only do leaders ignore how their goals can contribute to unethical behavior, but they also ignore other aspects of how their structure and reward systems guide employees toward unethical behavior. One of the most commonly ignored organizational conditions that creates unethical behavior is the existence of conflicts of interest. Lawyers who bill by the hour take more time to resolve cases than lawyers who are paid a commission of the settlement. Surgeons view surgery to be necessary more often than other doctors do, and real estate agents usually think that it's the right time to sell your home. People form these judgments without noticing that their advice is biased and potentially wrong (Moore, Cain, Loewenstein, & Bazerman, 2005).

Conflicts of interest occur across industries and at a larger societal level, and leaders too often fail to see how allowing such conflicts of interest to exist will predictably lead to unethical behavior. The institution of using outside auditors to validate the books of corporations was created so that outside parties could trust the information that the firm provides. Yet, for decades, our auditing institutions have created powerful conflicts of interest by asking auditors to provide unbiased evaluations of their clients' books even as they curry their clients' favor and seek to expand their business with them. Audit failure is typically viewed as a result of corruption, but intentional fraud is only the most extreme manifestation of a far more pervasive and pernicious problem in auditing: unconscious bias. Extensive psychological evidence shows that when people are motivated to reach a particular conclusion they are incapable of objectivity or, as the auditing industry calls it, independence.

Don Moore, Lloyd Tanlu, and I (2010) show that accountants are more likely to endorse a company's ambiguous accounting when the company is their client. In our experiments, just the suggestion of a hypothetical relationship with a "client" distorts our participants' judgment. It becomes clear that in the real world, auditors who want to be rehired by their clients, who want to sell other services to the same clients, and who may want to work for the client firm at a future date, cannot disregard their own self-interest, even when they try hard to do so. With these incentives in place, even the most honest auditors will continue to view the world in a biased way, and failures of auditor independence will continue.

It is tempting to attribute the scandals of the new millennium to a few bad eggs. But across the scandals at Enron, Waste Management, Sunbeam, Cendant, Rite-Aid, and Phar-Mor, and the subsequent fiascoes at WorldCom, Adelphia, Global Crossing, Halliburton, Tyco, Xerox, and Bernard Madoff's office, the auditors failed us. To attribute all of these auditing scandals to deliberate corruption by the on-site auditors would be to suggest that the accounting profession is rife with crooks. The actual evidence points to the likelihood that most auditors are good people who are not acting independently because of the conflict of interest inherent in the institutions that we have created.

The most serious ethical failure occurring within these firms is committed by the leaders of the auditing firms, who continue to manipulate our political institutions to prevent society from making the changes needed to create true auditor independence. Our national leaders (across many countries) have also failed us by not taking legislative action to create auditor independence. When we allow our institutions to enable conflicts of interest that will predictably lead to unethical action and the failure to notice it, the leaders who created those institutions are to blame. High-integrity leaders would work to prohibit audit firms from providing other services to clients, impose term limits on audit relationships to prevent auditor/client "partnerships," and bar auditors from working for their former clients. Leaders would create an environment where auditors serve not as "partners" or "advisors" to their clients, but in more impartial, distant roles, similar to that of tax collectors.

The bounded ethicality aspect of understanding conflicts of interest is critical. If conflicts of interest play out in people intentionally acting for financial gain rather than meeting their professional responsibility, then integrity could protect us. But, if the problem is that good people are affected by conflicts of interest without their own awareness, integrity is not a solution, and the institution must be changed.

Without reflection, our leaders can repeat the same mistakes across industries. Just as auditing firms exist to vouch for the financial condition of firms they audit, credit-rating agencies exist to independently assess the creditworthiness of issuers of debt obligations so that stakeholders can be informed about the risks of investment securities. When a financial firm wants to sell securities to the public, the securities must be rated by Moody's, Standard & Poor's, or Fitch Group.

As the housing bubble developed in 2007 and 2008, debt issuers sold subprime and other high-risk home loans as mortgage-backed securities. It is now clear that credit-rating agencies were far too lenient and failed in their task of assessing these securities. The agencies gave the securities their highest rating despite having all the data they needed to know that the securities were highly risky (Bazerman, 2014).

Just as firms pay auditors for unbiased assessments of their books, credit-rating agencies are paid by the companies whose securities they rate. The credit-rating agencies were not rewarded based on the accuracy of their assessments. Rather, the agency with the most lax standards had the best chance of winning business from new clients, creating a race to the bottom. In another parallel to auditing, credit-rating agencies were selling consulting services to the firms whose securities they were rating.

In most cases, those who are caught up in a conflict of interest honestly believe they are immune from its negative effects. This bounded ethicality aspect of conflicts of interest is what makes them a leadership challenge. Leaders must step forward and change broken systems, rather than relying on the unreasonable hope that people will be immune from the downsides of conflicts of interest. Ethical leadership must go far beyond promoting honesty and integrity. If leaders benefit from the actions of their subordinates, they must also be responsible when they create an environment where unethical action is predictable. One of the clearest results from the last century of psychological research is that the environment matters far more than most of us realize. It is the job of leaders to understand this and to create environments that more predictably lead to ethical action.

Closing Comments

Starting with the collapse of Enron, society has called on us to create more ethical employees. This is consistent with the tendency to look for the "bad apples" who present the most obvious ethical challenges. I am confident that most leaders want to weed out the bad apples, and I doubt that I have much new to tell them on this front.

Rather, my goal has been to highlight what research tells us about how leaders can get the majority of their employees to notice the unethical actions of others and create organizations that will be less susceptible to unethical behavior. Far too often, leaders are judged, and judge themselves, by assessing the ethicality of their own actions. But, leaders are responsible for their organizations, and their responsibility does not end with their own ethicality.

References

Banaji, M. R., & Bhaskar, R. (2000). Implicit stereotypes and memory: The bounded rationality of social beliefs. In D. L. Schacter & E. Scarry (Eds.), *Memory, brain, and belief* (pp. 139–175). Cambridge: Harvard University Press.

Banaji, M. R., & Greenwald, A. G. (2014). *Blind spot: Hidden biases of good people.* New York: Delacorte Press.

Bandura, A. (1999). Moral disengagement in the preparation of inhumanities. *Personal and Social Psychology Review, 3,* 193–209.

Baron, J., & Hershey, J. C. (1988). Outcome bias in decision evaluation. *Journal of Personality and Social Psychology, 54,* 569–579.

Barsky, A. (2007). Understanding the ethical cost of organizational goal-setting: A review and theory development. *Journal of Business Ethics, 81*(1), 63–81.

Bazerman, M. (2014). *The power of noticing: What the best leaders see.* New York: Simon & Schuster, 2014.

Bazerman, M. H., & Tenbrunsel, A. E. (2011). *Blind spots: Why we fail to do what's right and what to do about it.* Princeton, NJ: Princeton University Press.

Berenson, A. (2006, March 12). A cancer drug's big price rise is cause for concern. The *New York Times,* http://www.nytimes.com/2006/03/12/business/12price.html?pagewanted=print&_r=0.

Caruso, E. M., Epley, N., & Bazerman, M. H. (2006). The costs and benefits of undoing egocentric responsibility assessments in groups. *Journal of Personality and Social Psychology, 91*(5), 857–871.

Chugh, D., Bazerman, M. H., & Banaji, M. R. (2005). Bounded ethicality as a psychological barrier to recognizing conflicts of interest. In D. Moore, G. Loewenstein, D. Cain, & M. H. Bazerman (Eds.), *Conflicts of interest: Challenges and solutions in business, law, medicine, and public policy* (pp. 74–95). New York: Cambridge University Press.

Coffman, L. (2011). Intermediation reduces punishment (and reward). *American Economic Journal, 3*(4), 77–106.

Cushman, F. A., Dreber, A., Wang, Y., & Costa, J. (2009). Accidental outcomes guide punishment in a "trembling hand" game. *PLoS ONE 4*(8),e6699. doi:10.1371/journal.pone.0006699.

Disheau, D. (1992, June 23). Sears admits mistakes at auto shops; Overhauling its sales system. The Associated Press Newswire.

Dominus, S. (2012, October 3). The woman who took the fall for JPMorgan, *the New York Times,* http://www.nytimes.com/2012/10/07/magazine/ina-drew-jamie-dimon-jpmorgan-chase .html?pagewanted=all.

Gino, F., & Bazerman, M. (2009). When misconduct goes unnoticed: The acceptability of gradual erosion in others' unethical behavior. *Journal of Experimental Social Psychology, 4*(4), 708–719.

Kern, M., & Chugh, D. (2009). Bounded ethicality: The perils of loss framing. *Psychological Science, 20*(3), 378–84.

Kopecki, D. (2013, September 20). JPMorgan pays $920 million to settle London Whale probes. *Bloomberg News,* http://www.bloomberg.com/news/2013-09-19/jpmorgan-chase-agrees-to -pay-920-million-for-london-whale-loss.html.

Kopecki, D., Mattingly, P., & Benson, C. (2012, June 13). Dimon fires back at complex system in U.S. Senate grilling, *Bloomberg BusinessWeek,* http://www.bloomberg.com/news/2012-06-13 /dimon-faces-senators-over-jpmorgan-s-hedge-fund-style-trading.html.

Kramer, R. M. (2006). The great intimidators. *Harvard Business Review, 84,* 88–96.

Langley, M. (2012, May 18). Inside J.P.Morgan's blunder. *The Wall Street Journal,* http://online.wsj .com/news/articles/SB10001424052702303448404577410341236847980.

Locke, E. A., & Latham, G. P. (1990). *A theory of goal setting and task performance* (p. 544). Englewood Cliffs, NJ: Prentice Hall College Division.

Locke, E. A., & Latham, G. P. (2006). New directions in goal-setting theory. *Current Directions in Psychological Science, 15*(5), 265–268.

Messick, D. M. (1994, March 1). Mortgage-bias complexities. *Chicago Tribune.*

Messick, D. M., & Bazerman, M. H. Ethics for the 21st century: A decision making approach. *MIT Sloan Management Review, 37*(2), 9–22.

Moore, D. A., Tanlu., L, & Bazerman, M. H. (2010). Conflict of interest and the intrusion of bias. *Judgment and Decision Making, 5*(1), 37–53.

Moore, D., Cain, D., Loewenstein, G., & Bazerman, M. H. (2005). *Conflicts of interest: Problems and solutions from law, medicine, and organizational settings.* New York: Cambridge University Press.

Newsweek staff (2009, September 10). Jamie Dimon: America's most important banker. *Newsweek,* http://www.newsweek.com/jamie-dimon-americas-most-important-banker-79437.

Ordóñez, L. D., Schweitzer, M. E., Galinsky, A. D., & Bazerman, M. H. (2009). Goals gone wild: The systematic side effects of over-prescribing goal setting. *Academy of Management Perspectives, 23*(1), 6–16.

Paharia, N., Coffman, L., & Bazerman, M. H. (2012). Intermediation and diffusion of responsibility in negotiation: A case of bounded ethicality. In G. Bolton & R. Croson (Eds.), *The Oxford handbook of economic conflict resolution* (pp. 37–46), New York: Oxford University Press.

Paharia, N., Kassam, K., Greene, J., & Bazerman, M. (2009). Dirty work, clean hands: The moral psychology of indirect agency. *Organizational Behavior and Human Decision Processes, 109*(2), 134–141.

Pollack, A. (2012, December 29). Questcor finds profits, at $28,000 a vial. The *New York Times,* http://www.nytimes.com/2012/12/30/business/questcor-finds-profit-for-acthar-drug-at -28000-a-vial.html?pagewanted=all&_r=0.

Ross, M., & Sicoly, F. (1979). Egocentric biases in availability and attribution. *Journal of Personality & Social Psychology, 37*(3), 322–336.

Santoro, M., & Paine, L. (1993). Sears auto centers. Harvard Business School Case 9–394–010.

Shu, L. L., Gino, F., & Bazerman, M. H. (2012). Ethical discrepancy: Changing our attitudes to resolve moral dissonance. In D. De Cremer & A. E. Tenbrunsel (Eds.), *Behavioral business ethics: Shaping an emerging field* (pp. 236–280). New York: Routledge.

Silver-Greenberg, J., & Protess, B. (2013, May 2). JPMorgan caught in swirl of regulatory woes. The *New York Times,* http://dealbook.nytimes.com/2013/05/02/jpmorgan-caught-in-swirl-of -regulatory-woes/.

Wade-Benzoni, K. A. (1999). Thinking about the future: An intergenerational perspective on the conflict and compatibility between economic and environmental interests. *American Behavioral Scientist, 42*(8), 1393–1405.

CHAPTER FOUR

The Personal Characteristics of Political Leaders: Quantitative Multiple-Case Assessments

DEAN KEITH SIMONTON

A fundamental principle of political psychology is that psychology matters in the understanding of politics. Because both psychology and politics represent complex phenomena, with many manifestations, this tenet can adopt many different specific forms. Nonetheless, for the purposes of this chapter, two points stand out. First, an important subdiscipline of psychology deals with the personal characteristics of people. This subdiscipline is most commonly referred to as *differential* psychology, that is, the study of individual differences (Chamorro-Premuzic, Stumm, & Furnham, 2011). Second, a critical feature of politics is its leaders—the phenomenon of *political leadership*. Especially important are heads of state, whether presidents, prime ministers, monarchs, or dictators (Ludwig, 2002). These persons are reputed to have an exceptional influence, for good or ill, on their political system, whether democracy, autocracy, or oligarchy. Because political leaders remain persons, despite their exalted status in society, they too can vary in their personal characteristics. Furthermore, this variation can have consequences for their leadership, such as their ideology, decision making, or performance (Simonton, 1995). Hence, a central research topic must necessarily include the differential psychology of political leadership—the study of the personal characteristics of political leaders.

Now a defining feature of this topic must be emphasized: Differential psychologists are inherently engaged in quantitative multiple-case assessments. In the first place, individual differences do not even exist without having multiple individuals. For example, it is impossible to say whether someone is very bright or very dull without having other individuals with whom to compare. More specifically, the intelligence of a political leader must be judged in comparison to either other political leaders or their followers (Simonton, 2009a). Moreover, this comparison must entail some amount of quantification. For instance, as a first approximation, an ordinal scale might be used to indicate the relative intelligence of a set of N political leaders, from the first to the Nth. Better yet, the assessments might be executed on a numerical scale, such as assigning an IQ score to each political leader (e.g., Cox, 1926). In most studies, these multiple-case quantitative assessments must also be carried out for leadership criteria, such as evaluations of performance, eminence, or greatness (e.g., Deluga, 1997, 1998; Simonton, 1981; Spangler & House, 1991). By combining these quantified variables, it then becomes possible to examine how the personal characteristics relate to political leadership.

In theory, quantitative multiple-case assessments can be executed using the standard instruments in differential psychology. Political leaders might be given IQ tests, personality inventories, and various measures of interests and values. The resulting scores can then be correlated with leadership measures. In practice, this direct approach rarely happens (cf. Costantini & Craik, 1980). One reason is that most political leaders would not be inclined to expose themselves to direct psychometric scrutiny. After all, the results might undermine their credibility as candidates for high office. Yet another reason is even more obvious: The political leaders of interest might already be deceased. To illustrate, suppose a researcher wanted to determine whether certain personality traits predict the final performance ratings of former US presidents. Only a small number of past chief executives remain alive at any one time—currently just the two Bushes, Carter, and Clinton. An $N = 4$ is way too small to conduct any useful statistical analyses.

The alternative is to use at-a-distance techniques that can be applied to any historical figure, alive or not (Craik, 1988; Song & Simonton, 2007). More succinctly, psychometric assessment can be replaced by historiometric assessment. The latter adapts psychometric measures for application to historical materials, such as speeches, correspondence, archival records, and biographies (Suedfeld, Guttieri, & Tetlock, 2003; Winter, 2002). In the case of US presidents, for instance, historiometric research is applicable to all who have occupied that position, from George Washington to Barack Obama. Such an application then generates a truly multiple-case sample, with N in the dozens rather than just a few fingers on one hand. Now it becomes feasible to introduce complex statistical analyses. Because of this asset, this chapter will stress historiometric assessments.

It should be also apparent that the historiometric approach differs categorically from other ways of studying the personal characteristics of historic political leaders (Simonton, 2003). Historiometry most strongly differs from political psychobiography, which is almost invariably single-case and qualitative (Tetlock, Crosby, & Crosby, 1981). It also differs from qualitative comparative studies that examine multiple cases without quantifying any variables, whether personality or performance (e.g., Barber, 2008). Accordingly, the method to be discussed in this chapter can provide a unique perspective on the phenomenon.

Below I discuss the history of this method, review some of central findings, go over some new approaches, provide a specific illustration, and treat some broader applications beyond political leadership.

History

The very first attempt to quantify the personal characteristics of numerous political leaders can be found in the book *Mental and Moral Heredity in Royalty* by Frederick Woods (1906). The sample consisted of hundreds of hereditary monarchs and their immediate relatives (i.e., the royal family). Using biographical materials, each was accessed along a 10-point scale on "intellect" and "virtues." A few years later, Woods (1909, 1911) coined an official name for the method, namely historiometry, and indicated that the method's history dates back to Francis Galton's (1869) *Hereditary Genius*. His final publication using this technique was the 1913 *The Influence of Monarchs* in which he assessed hundreds of heads of state in several European nations on their personal leadership, and then correlated those scores with a general measure of the welfare of the nation that these monarchs led (both on a 3-point scale). The leadership ratings were also based on biographical materials.

Just a few investigators followed up Woods's biography-based assessments of hereditary monarchs (see Simonton, 2001a, for review). Thirty years later, Edward L. Thorndike (1936) conducted a replication of Woods (1906) in order to obtain a better estimate of the correlation between intellect and morality in rulers (cf. Sorokin, 1926). Much later still, the author of this chapter combined the data in both Woods (1906) and Woods (1913) with new data to examine how individual differences in intellect and morality are related to both leadership and historical eminence in a sample of 342 hereditary monarchs (Simonton, 1983, 1984b). Like Thorndike (1936), these later two studies also provided a validation of biography-based assessments of personal characteristics.

Many historiometric studies using this particular at-a-distance approach use samples that are more heterogeneous. Not only will different kinds of leaders be included, but also the leaders will be combined with various kinds of creators. For example, Cox's (1926) classic study of intelligence and personality included politicians, revolutionaries, commanders, and religious leaders as well as scientists, philosophers, writers, artists, and composers (see also Miles & Wolfe, 1936; Simonton & Song, 2009). About a quarter century later, Thorndike (1950) assessed 91 historic leaders and creators on 48 characteristics using a 13-point scale (also see Knapp, 1962). Some of these characteristics were shown to predict the relative eminence attained (Simonton, 1991b). Interestingly, although Thorndike (1950) claimed to assess 48 "traits of personality," three of those traits actually concerned biographical circumstances, namely, parental wealth, paternal indulgence, and maternal indulgence. This practice has become rather common, more objective aspects of the family environment and educational experiences serving as assumed proxy variables for personal characteristics that supposedly resulted from these developmental conditions.

Thus far, quantitative multiple-case studies were piecemeal rather than being an integral part of extended and coherent research programs. That deficiency was to change in the 1970s and 1980s. Because these developments took place during my career, they cannot possibly be considered "history." Therefore, these advances become the subject of the next section.

Review

In this section, I provide an overview of the key developments in research applying at-a-distance quantitative multiple-case assessments to political leaders. These developments can be assigned to three broad categories: samples, assessments, and analyses.

Samples

Whereas the first historiometric studies concentrated on hereditary monarchs, and later studies expanded the samples to include creators as well as leaders of various kinds, in the early 1970s research largely turned to presidents of the United States (Donley & Winter, 1970; Wendt & Light, 1976; Winter, 1973). These studies represented the onset of extensive research on the role of motivation in presidential leadership, with special emphasis on the power motive (Winter, 1987). A major impetus behind this increased attention to US chief executives was probably the availability of "greatness ratings" generated by surveys of historians and other experts (Kynerd, 1971). These surveys began shortly after World War II but picked up steam going into the 1970s and 1980s (e.g., Maranell, 1970; Murray & Blessing, 1983). Moreover, these global performance evaluations revealed a very strong and stable consensus on the relative merits of those political leaders who served in the nation's highest office (Simonton, 1985b, 1991a). In addition, because most of the early researchers were Americans, they enjoyed ready access to more objective measures of leader performance, such as recorded in US histories, biographies, encyclopedias, and government archives. For example, several studies have exploited the archival records of the chief executive's use of the power to veto congressional legislation (Copeland, 1983; Lee, 1975; Ringelstein, 1985; Rohde & Simon, 1985).

Nonetheless, eventually investigators began to turn to political leaders in other nations as well as to political leaders who were not the actual heads of state (Hermann, 1980b). Examples include Canadian prime ministers (Ballard & Suedfeld, 1988), members of the UK Parliament (Tetlock, 1984), the US Senate (Tetlock, 1981a; Tetlock, Hannum, &

Micheletti, 1984), and the Politburo of the old Soviet Union (Hermann, 1980a; Tetlock & Boettger, 1989), presidential advisors and cabinet members (Etheredge, 1978), US vice presidents (Wendt & Muncy, 1979), presidential candidates (Gottschalk, Uliana, & Gilbert, 1988; Miller & Stiles, 1986; Zullow & Seligman, 1990) as well as various political leaders in southern Africa (Winter, 1980) and the Middle East (Suedfeld, Wallace, & Thachuk, 1993). These changes in the samples of political leaders studied were accompanied by expansions in the personal characteristics that could be assessed on those political leaders.

Assessments

Biography-based assessments have both advantages and disadvantages. On the one hand, biographies are exceptionally rich in information that can be quantified into useful assessments. On the other hand, biographies are very often written after the leader has left office, and even long after they have passed away, meaning that they could be contaminated by hindsight bias. As a result, historiometric studies should not rely on this method alone. By using multiple assessment methods, researchers can ensure that their evaluations are not contingent on the idiosyncrasies of any single measurement technique. Fortunately, in the early 1970s two new methods emerged.

The first involves surveys in which experts are directly asked to evaluate political leaders on one or more personal characteristics. For example, Maranell (1970) had American historians assess US presidents on performance criteria but also on two individual traits, namely, flexibility and idealism (see also Ridings & McIver, 1997). Occasionally, experts will generate valuable evaluations that might seem unlikely. For instance, the First Ladies of the US presidents have been assessed on a very impressive array of personal characteristics that can also contribute to the success of the chief executive (Simonton, 1996). Finally, I must mention recent work using experts on the US presidents to assess them on standard personality variables (Rubenzer & Faschingbauer, 2004; Rubenzer, Faschingbauer, & Ones, 2000; Watts et al., 2013). This endeavor is important because it connects political leaders with the general population. Just as average persons on the street can vary on extraversion or neuroticism, so can the leaders sitting in the Oval Office.

The second new at-a-distance assessment technique involved the content analysis of written documents or transcribed oral communications (Smith, 1992). This method first emerged when coding schemes were devised to assess speeches on motivational content, especially the power, achievement, and power motives (Donley & Winter, 1970; Winter, 1973). About a decade later, content analysis could tap into more cognitive variables, most notably conceptual and integrative complexity (Suedfeld & Rank, 1976; Suedfeld, Tetlock, & Ramirez, 1977). The range of personal characteristics that can be assessed in this manner has become quite impressive (Smith, 1992). Furthermore, considerable progress has been made in devising coding schemes sufficiently objective and precise to lend themselves to computerized content analysis (e.g., Hart, 1984). A particularly current example is recent research on political leadership using Profiler Plus text analysis software (see http://socialscience.net/partners/research.aspx).

Most researchers now routinely calculate reliability coefficients for their assessments of personal characteristics. These reliabilities tend to be comparable to those seen in direct psychometric instruments (viz. in the .80s and even .90s). For example, a biography-based rating of presidential charisma featured a coefficient alpha reliability of .90 (Simonton, 1988). Indeed, the training of raters in content analyses will often stipulate that those raters first meet a specified reliability standard before their scorings can even be used (e.g., Suedfeld, Tetlock, & Streufert, 1992). Naturally, the reliabilities for computerized content analyses are technically perfect given that such assessments can always be exactly replicated. The only real question in these applications is the validity of the coding scheme and representativeness of the document sample to which the analysis is applied.

Although the three main techniques—biography-based, expert-survey, and content-analytical—differ in major ways, research shows that they can triangulate on the same measurements. For instance, a biography-based measure of presidential charisma correlates with a computerized content analysis of speeches (Emrich, Brower, Feldman, & Garland, 2001). Similarly, a content analytical measure of power motivation correlates positively with a biography-based indicator of forcefulness and negatively with indicators of moderation and pacifism (Simonton, 1986c). Alternative methods thus seem to be tapping into the same underlying constructs (see also House, Spangler, & Woycke, 1991).

Analyses

The earliest quantitative multiple-case assessments often went no further than calculating bivariate associations between personal characteristics and leader political performance (e.g., Holmes & Elder, 1989; Wendt & Light, 1976; Winter, 1987). However, simple bivariate relations can lead to misleading conclusions (Simonton, 2013). For example, even if power motivation correlates positively with assessed leader performance, a correlation cannot tell us whether that relation represents a direct effect, an indirect effect (mediated by another variable), or a spurious relationship (where both are caused by an underlying third variable). To circumvent this problem, it is most often necessary to introduce a multiple regression analysis (e.g., Curry & Morris, 2010; Spangler & House, 1991). If the effect is indirect, and the mediating variable is included in the equation, then the effect will be reduced to zero. Similarly, if the relationship is spurious, and the underlying third variable is included, then the relationship will become zero. For instance, by this means power motivation has been shown not to have a direct effect on presidential greatness (Simonton, 2008). Any effect is most likely indirect, through its impact on the direct predictors, such as war and assassination.

Multiple regression analysis can also test for complex causal relations, including nonadditive and nonlinear effects. Nonadditive effects are alternatively termed interaction or moderated effects. For example, in the case of US presidents, the impact of flexibility on his use of the veto power, and his success in the implementation of that power, is contingent on the political context in which he entered office, namely, the size of his electoral mandate and the degree to which his party controls both houses of Congress (Simonton, 1987). This constitutes an instance of an Individual X Situational interaction effect. Nonlinear effects can assume many forms, but the most common are curvilinear quadratic functions that describe single-peaked or single-trough functions. For instance, the eminence of a European absolute monarch is a U-shaped function of his or her morality, the most famous kings, queens, and sultans being either supremely virtuous or insidiously evil (Simonton, 1984b). In an almost parallel fashion, the greatness ratings of the US presidents are a roughly U-shaped function of their personal dogmatism (i.e., idealistic inflexibility; Simonton, 1981). In contrast, an absolute monarch's influence on the welfare of his or her nation is roughly described by in inverted-U function of age, indicating an optimal or peak age for positive political impact (Simonton, 1984a).

Other more advanced correlational methods include factor analysis and structural equation models (e.g., House, Spangler, & Woycke, 1991; Wendt & Muncy, 1979). None of these sophisticated techniques is applicable unless the researcher has first acquired quantitative assessments of personal character for multiple cases of political leadership.

New Approaches

The quantitative multiple-case assessments described above are all applied to what have been called "significant samples" (Simonton, 1999). The political figures under scrutiny are eminent individuals who have importance beyond some hypothetical population to which most statistics are designed to generalize (e.g., *Homo sapiens*, or at least college undergraduates). Indeed, these studies very often deal with the *entire* population rather than a mere *sample* from that population. For example, investigators who study *all* past presidents of the United States have perforce exhausted the population of available cases. To be sure, one might ask whether any findings can be generalized to current and future presidents. Yet that is not a question that statistics are designed to address. The "sampling error" is zero. If an empirical finding that holds from George Washington to George W. Bush fails to apply to Barack Obama, that failure cannot be simply attributed to a statistical fluctuation. President Obama was not randomly drawn from the same population of elected presidents. Therefore, each time a new former president is added to the list, earlier studies really should be replicated on the larger sample to see if the empirical results still apply. These replications are becoming increasingly common in the case of the US presidents (e.g., Simonton, 2001b, 2002). The replications will often include new assessments as well (Balz, 2010; Cohen, 2003; Curry & Morris, 2010; Simon & Uscinski, 2012; Simonton, 2006; Watts et al., 2013).

A second new development is the application of quantitative methods to single cases (e.g., Simonton, 1998). If a sufficient comparative baseline has been established in prior multiple-case studies, then these single-case inquiries become comparable to using a standardized psychometric instrument to assess a single individual. These applications can then provide a "profile" of a given political leader that proves useful in analyzing his or her leadership performance (Feldman & Valenty, 2001). An excellent illustration is the use of content analytical motive scores to explain some peculiarities in the political career of Richard M. Nixon (Winter & Carlson, 1988). This objective and quantitative approach avoids some of the pitfalls in applying more subjective and qualitative perspectives (Simonton, 1999). It is also of interest to compare the results of these alternative approaches to the profiling of a single political leader (Post, 2003).

Both of the foregoing developments take full advantage of a special feature of significant samples, namely, "unit replicability" (Simonton, 1999). That is, researchers can study the exact same cases. Hence, if two investigators obtain different results for the same sample of political leaders, the basis for the replication failure is much easily pinpointed (Simonton, 2014). If the assessments of personal character differ, then they can be directly compared. If the assessments agree, but the statistical analyses vary, then the analyses can be redone to see if the same results obtain. This asset of significant samples is augmented when researchers actually publish the scores on the assessment variables (e.g., Simonton, 1986c, 1988; Winter, 1987). This advantage will be seen in the next section.

Illustration

As already mentioned, among all political leaders, the US presidents have become the favorite target of quantitative multiple-case assessments of personal characteristics. Although the presidents have long been part of more inclusive samples of eminent creators and leaders (e.g., Cox, 1926; Thorndike, 1950), investigators began concentrating on the US chief executives in the 1970s (Donley & Winter, 1970; Wendt & Light, 1976). I was attracted to this particular group of political leaders in the late 1970s, and for the next three decades published numerous historiometric studies on presidential leadership (e.g., Simonton, 1981, 1985, 1988, 1991c, 2006). Because some of the earlier pioneers continued their efforts, and new investigators later joined the expanding cottage industry, a rather rich literature emerged (for recent reviews, see Simonton, 2008, 2013). Here I can only provide enough highlights to illustrate this approach (see also Goethals, 2005, for a broader perspective).

Put simply, most quantitative multiple-case assessments of presidential leadership can be divided into two parts. The first part consists of the performance criteria by which those leaders are to be judged. These criteria can include subjective and global evaluations, such presidential greatness ratings, as well as objective and specific measures, such as success in the use of the legislative veto power. The second part concerns the personal characteristics that are hypothesized to predict the performance criteria. These may entail any combination of biography-based indicators, expert surveys, and content analytical measures. Moreover, biographical sources are often used to define measures of family background and educational attainments, such as socioeconomic class, birth order, college graduation, professional experience.

Because most research in the 1970s was small scale, concentrating on just a handful of variables and often a subset of presidents, Simonton (1981) initiated an exhaustive investigation designed to identify the various possibilities. The main sample consisted of the 38 presidents from Washington to Carter. A subset of 33 of these had been rated by 571 American historians on 7 characteristics, namely, general prestige, strength of action, presidential activeness, idealism versus practicality, flexibility, administration accomplishments, and respondent's amount of information (Maranell, 1970). A factor analysis consolidated these measures into just two dimensions, namely, a greatness factor and a dogmatism (idealistic inflexibility) factor (see also Wendt & Light, 1976). Using available historical data, a large inventory of variables were defined that assessed both the president's biographical characteristics and the critical events taking place during his presidency, as well as his transition into office and his transition out of office. About three-quarters of the variance in a president's assessed greatness was predicted using only five variables: the administration's duration, number of war years, unsuccessful assassination attempts, administration scandals, and his publication record prior to entering office. In contrast, family background, personal characteristics, education, occupation, and political experiences provided relatively few predictors of presidential performance (see also Balz, 2010). The one exception was that succession to office via the vice-presidency had a rather broad negative impact on performance in the areas of legislation and appointments (see also Simonton, 1985).

The above study was only preliminary. Especially problematic was its reliance on a 1970 survey that soon became obsolete with the appearance of three new surveys in the early 1980s, especially the extensive survey of 846 experts published by Murray and Blessing (1983). Not only was this latter measure vastly superior to any so far published, but it enabled the addition of more recent presidents. The first investigation to take advantage of these new leadership evaluations was published only a couple of years later (Simonton, 1986b). This inquiry first established the substantial consensus exhibited by more than a dozen different performance evaluations. It next used the three most recent evaluations to determine the main predictors of presidential greatness. After testing hundreds of possible predictors, just five predictors replicated across the alternative measures: number of years in office, the number of years served as wartime commander-in-chief, administration scandal, assassination, and having been a national war hero prior to entering office. The main predictors were also found in the 1981 investigation. Significantly, Simonton also tested to determine whether these predictors were transhistorically invariant and could not reject the null hypothesis that the same variables operated just as much in the nineteenth century as they did in the twentieth.

Conspicuously absent from the preceding studies was any attempt to assess personality traits and other individual differences, such as intelligence. Any personal characteristics were biographical in nature. This absence is all the more noticeable given that earliest studies tended to stress personality. That oversight was soon rectified. First, Simonton (1986c) published a quick follow-up in which he had a team of independent raters evaluate the presidents on the 300 descriptors in the Gough Adjective Check List (using anonymous personality sketches drawn from biographical sources; cf. Simonton, 1986a). Two years later Simonton (1988) used a similar method to extract scores on each president's leadership style, such as the charismatic and deliberative styles (see also Simonton, 2009b; cf. Hermann, 2005). Independently of this work, Winter (1987) revived and extended the practice of extracting motivational measures by content analyzing presidential inaugural addresses (see also Winter, 2003).

Over the next 20 years, many more researchers joined in the discussion, with special focus on the personal characteristics that predict the presidential greatness ratings (cf. Kenney & Rice, 1988; Nice, 1984). Although this line of research was not without controversy (McCann, 1992; Simonton, 1991c, 1992), the introduction of new variables and additional cases in the late 1990s and early 2000s helped settle the principal issues with respect to the prediction of greatness (Simonton, 2008, 2013; but see Curry & Morris, 2010). In particular, a six-variable equation finally emerged that accounts for about 80 percent of the variance in presidential greatness. The first five predictors simply replicate what was discovered earlier: total years in office, war years, successful assassination, administration scandals, and prior status as war hero (Simonton, 1986b). However, the sixth predictor was Intellectual Brilliance, a factor analytic measure that was originally generated by applying the Gough ACL to anonymous personality sketches (Simonton, 1986c). Presidents scoring high on this personal characteristic tend to score high on the following ACL adjectives Interests wide, Artistic, Inventive, Curious, Intelligent, Sophisticated, Complicated, Insightful, Wise, and Idealistic but score low on Dull and Commonplace (coefficient alpha = .90). Although these scores were initially estimated for presidents from Washington to Reagan, they were later updated to include G. H. W. Bush, Clinton, and George W. Bush. Jefferson had the highest score, Harding the lowest. Two additional aspects of Intellectual Brilliance deserve mention.

First, although presidential Intellectual Brilliance correlates positively with both estimated IQ and estimated Openness to Experience (one of the Big Five Personality Factors), it provides a superior predictor of presidential greatness than either of these two closely related variables (Simonton, 2006; cf. Rubenzer & Faschingbauer, 2004; Simonton, 2002). In a sense, that predictive superiority comes from the fact that it incorporates both of these more specialized variables, one more cognitive and the other more dispositional.

Second, Intellectual Brilliance correlates with other interesting personal characteristics of the US presidents. In particular, presidents scoring high on this factor rate higher in two leadership styles: the creative and the charismatic (Simonton, 1988). Creative leaders tend to be innovators, initiating new legislation, and charismatic leaders tend to be highly dynamic and influential with respect to the public at large. It is also worth mentioning that such presidents tend to be more prolific book authors before entering office (Simonton, 1986c). This tendency thus explains explaining the predictor found earlier (Simonton, 1981). Extensive authorship was merely serving as a proxy variable for Intellectual Brilliance.

Applications

As pointed out earlier, quantitative multiple-case assessments have already been applied to rather heterogeneous samples of eminent personalities (e.g., Bass, Avolio, & Goodheim, 1987; Thorndike, 1950). Besides purely political leaders, these samples will include military and religious leaders as well as creative geniuses in the arts and sciences. This heterogeneity actually has certain assets relative to samples that concentrate on just political leaders. Most importantly, high achievers in other domains of leadership and even creativity can provide useful baselines for comparing political leaders. If it is not always easy to compare politicians with the average person, at least they can be compared to other individuals of comparable achievement or eminence. For example, political leaders exhibit general intelligence higher than military leaders but lower than philosophers and writers (Cox, 1926; Simonton & Song, 2009). Political leaders are somewhat less likely to display psychopathology than holds for creative geniuses, especially in the arts (Ludwig, 1995; Post, 1994; cf. Davidson, Conner, & Swartz, 2006). These contrasts in personal characteristics may account for why young talents gravitate to one domain of achievement rather than another.

Although the examples just given involved biography-based assessments, other assessment techniques can be applied as well, particularly content analysis. A case in point is the extensive research assessing integrative complexity (Suedfeld, 2010). In simple terms, integrative complexity is the cognitive state in which a person can view an issue or problem from multiple perspectives and then integrate those perspectives into a coherent position. The coding system for assessing this state can be applied to a wide range of documents, such as personal correspondence, public speeches, and interview transcripts. Accordingly, integrative complexity has been assessed in political leaders, such as presidents, monarchs, and revolutionaries, as well as supreme court justices, military generals, terrorists, scientists, writers, and composers (e.g., Porter & Suedfeld, 1981; Suedfeld & Bluck, 1993; Suedfeld, Corteen, & McCormick, 1986; Suedfeld & Leighton, 2002; Suedfeld & Rank, 1976; Tetlock, 1981b; Tetlock, Bernzweig, & Gallant, 1985; Thoemmes & Conway, 2007).

At the same time, certain areas do not lend themselves as well to such treatment. Each assessment method makes an essential assumption about the availability of certain types of data. Biography-based assessments require adequate biographies, expert-based assessments presume able and willing experts, and content analytical assessments demand appropriate personal documents. Particularly for historical figures in the remote past, one or more of these data types may not exist to a degree necessary to support multiple-case quantifications of personal characteristics. To give an extreme but obvious example, anyone who wanted to study the personalities of the victorious athletes in the ancient Greek Olympic competitions will get nowhere, all of Pindar's surviving *Odes* to the victors notwithstanding.

Nonetheless, I believe that the methods described in this chapter remain underutilized. Particularly with the advent of the Internet and online databases, the available data are becoming more extensive and detailed. Furthermore, the content analytical procedures applied to personal documents can eventually be extended to other sources of information, such as biographical entries. The personal characteristics of many luminaries remain to be revealed—including political leaders in the present and future.

Nevertheless, one caveat must be imposed on these future applications: the perpetually prominent impact of situational factors in political leadership. All of the past research implementing multiple-case assessments has found that the political context accounts for more variance in leader performance than any personal characteristic or set of personal characteristics. This holds as much for absolute monarchs as for US presidents (Simonton, 2001a, 2013). Furthermore, even when some personal characteristic plays a major role, its effect is moderated by situational factors (e.g., House, Spangler, & Woycke, 1991; McCann, 1995; Simonton, 1987; Winter, 1987). Seldom if ever can we speak of the "great leader" without adding the stipulation that he or she was "at the right place at the right time."

References

Ballard, E. J., & Suedfeld, P. (1988). Performance ratings of Canadian prime ministers: Individual and situational factors. *Political Psychology*, *9*, 291–302.

Balz, J. (2010). Ready to lead on day one: Predicting presidential greatness from political experience. *PS: Political Science and Politics, 43*, 487–492.

Barber, J. D. (2008). *The presidential character: Predicting performance in the White House* (4th ed.). Englewood Cliffs, NJ: Prentice-Hall.

Bass, B. M., Avolio, B. J., & Goodheim, L. (1987). Biography and the assessment of transformational leadership world-class level. *Journal of Management, 13*, 7–19.

Chamorro-Premuzic, T., Stumm, S., & Furnham, A. (Eds.) (2011). *The Wiley-Blackwell handbook of individual differences.* New York: Wiley-Blackwell.

Cohen, J. E. (2003). The polls: Presidential greatness as seen in the mass public: An extension and application of the Simonton model. *Presidential Studies Quarterly, 33*, 913–924.

Copeland, G. W. (1983). When Congress and the president collide: Why presidents veto legislation. *Journal of Politics, 45*, 696–710.

Costantini, E., & Craik, K. H. (1980). Personality and politicians: California party leaders, 1960–1976. *Journal of Personality and Social Psychology, 38*, 641–661.

Cox, C. (1926). *The early mental traits of three hundred geniuses.* Stanford, CA: Stanford University Press.

Craik, K. H. (1988). Assessing the personalities of historical figures. In W. M. Runyan (Ed.), *Psychology and historical interpretation* (pp. 196–218). New York: Oxford University Press.

Curry, J. L., & Morris, I. L. (2010). Explaining presidential greatness: The roles of peace and prosperity? *Presidential Studies Quarterly, 40*, 515–530.

Davidson, J. R. T., Conner, K. M., & Swartz, M. (2006). Mental illness in U.S. presidents between 1776 and 1974: A review of biographical sources. *Journal of Nervous and Mental Disease, 194*, 47–51.

Deluga, R. J. (1997). Relationship among American presidential charismatic leadership, narcissism, and related performance. *Leadership Quarterly, 8*, 51–65.

Deluga, R. J. (1998). American presidential proactivity, charismatic leadership, and rated performance. *Leadership Quarterly, 9*, 265–291.

Donley, R. E., & Winter, D. G. (1970). Measuring the motives of public officials at a distance: An exploratory study of American presidents. *Behavioral Science, 15*, 227–236.

Emrich, C. G., Brower, H. H., Feldman, J. M., & Garland, H. (2001). Images in words: Presidential rhetoric, charisma, and greatness. *Administrative Science Quarterly, 46*, 527–557.

Etheredge, L. S. (1978). Personality effects on American foreign policy, 1898–1968: A test of interpersonal generalization theory. *American Political Science Review, 78*, 434–451.

Feldman, O., & Valenty, L. O. (Eds.). (2001). *Profiling political leaders: Cross-cultural studies of personality and behavior.* Westport, CT: Praeger.

Galton, F. (1869). *Hereditary genius: An inquiry into its laws and consequences.* London: Macmillan.

Goethals, G. R. (2005). Presidential leadership. *Annual Review of Psychology, 56*, 545–570.

Gottschalk, L. A., Uliana, R., & Gilbert, R. (1988). Presidential candidates and cognitive impairment measured from behavior in campaign debates. *Public Administration Review, 48*, 613–619.

Hart, R. P. (1984). *Verbal style and the presidency: A computer-based approach.* New York: Academic Press.

Hermann, M. G. (1980a). Assessing the personalities of Soviet Politburo members. *Personality and Social Psychology Bulletin, 6*, 332–352.

Hermann, M. G. (1980b). Explaining foreign policy using personal characteristics of political leaders. *International Studies Quarterly, 24*, 7–46.

Hermann, M. G. (2005). Assessing leadership style: A trait analysis. In J. D. Post (Ed.), *The psychological assessment of political leaders* (pp. 178–212). Ann Arbor: University of Michigan Press.

Holmes, J. E., & Elder, R. E. (1989). Our best and worst presidents: Some possible reasons for perceived performance. *Presidential Studies Quarterly, 19*, 529–557.

House, R. J., Spangler, W. D., & Woycke, J. (1991). Personality and charisma in the U.S. presidency: A psychological theory of leader effectiveness. *Administrative Science Quarterly, 36*, 364–396.

Kenney, P. J., & Rice, T. W. (1988). The contextual determinants of presidential greatness. *Presidential Studies Quarterly, 18*, 161–169.

Knapp, R. H. (1962). A factor analysis of Thorndike's ratings of eminent men. *Journal of Social Psychology, 56*, 67–71.

Kynerd, T. (1971). An analysis of presidential greatness and "President rating." *Southern Quarterly, 9*, 309–329.

Lee, J. R. (1975). Presidential vetoes from Washington to Nixon. *Journal of Politics, 37*, 522–546.

Ludwig, A. M. (1995). *The price of greatness: Resolving the creativity and madness controversy.* New York: Guilford Press.

Ludwig, A. M. (2002). *King of the mountain: The nature of political leadership.* Lexington, KY: University Press of Kentucky.

Maranell, G. M. (1970). The evaluation of presidents: An extension of the Schlesinger polls. *Journal of American History, 57*, 104–113.

McCann, S. J. H. (1992). Alternative formulas to predict the greatness of U.S. presidents: Personological, situational, and zeitgeist factors. *Journal of Personality and Social Psychology, 62*, 469–479.

McCann, S. J. H. (1995). Presidential candidate age and Schlesinger's cycles of American history (1789–1992): When younger is better. *Political Psychology, 16*, 749–755.

Miles, C. C., & Wolfe, L. S. (1936). Childhood physical and mental health records of historical geniuses. *Psychological Monographs, 47*, 390–400.

Miller, N. L., & Stiles, W. B. (1986). Verbal familiarity in American presidential nomination acceptance speeches and inaugural addresses. *Social Psychology Quarterly, 49*, 72–81.

Murray, R. K., & Blessing, T. H. (1983). The presidential performance study: A progress report. *Journal of American History, 70*, 535–555.

Nice, D. C. (1984). The influence of war and party system aging on the ranking of presidents. *Western Political Quarterly, 37*, 443–455.

Porter, C. A., & Suedfeld, P. (1981). Integrative complexity in the correspondence of literary figures: Effects of personal and societal stress. *Journal of Personality and Social Psychology, 40*, 321–330.

Post, F. (1994). Creativity and psychopathology: A study of 291 world-famous men. *British Journal of Psychiatry, 165*, 22–34.

Post, J. M. (Ed.). (2003). *The psychological assessment of political leaders: With profiles of Saddam Hussein and Bill Clinton.* Ann Arbor, MI: University of Michigan Press.

Ridings, W. J., Jr., & McIver, S. B. (1997). *Rating the presidents: A ranking of U.S. leaders, from the great and honorable to the dishonest and incompetent.* Secaucus, NJ: Citadel Press.

Ringelstein, A. C. (1985). Presidential vetoes: Motivations and classification. *Congress & the Presidency, 12*, 43–55.

Rohde, D. W., & Simon, D. M. (1985). Presidential vetoes and congressional response: A study of institutional conflict. *American Journal of Political Science, 29*, 397–427.

Rubenzer, S. J., & Faschingbauer, T. R. (2004). *Personality, character, & leadership in the White House: Psychologists assess the presidents.* Washington, DC: Brassey's.

Rubenzer, S. J., Faschingbauer, T. R., & Ones, D. S. (2000). Assessing the U.S. presidents using the revised NEO Personality Inventory. *Assessment, 7*, 403–420.

Simon, A., & Uscinski, J. (2012). Prior experience predicts presidential performance. *Presidential Studies Quarterly, 42*, 514–548.

Simonton, D. K. (1981). Presidential greatness and performance: Can we predict leadership in the White House? *Journal of Personality, 49*, 306–323.

Simonton, D. K. (1983). Intergenerational transfer of individual differences in hereditary monarchs: Genes, role-modeling, cohort, or sociocultural effects? *Journal of Personality and Social Psychology, 44*, 354–364.

Simonton, D. K. (1984a). Leader age and national condition: A longitudinal analysis of 25 European monarchs. *Social Behavior and Personality, 12*, 111–114.

Simonton, D. K. (1984b). Leaders as eponyms: Individual and situational determinants of monarchal eminence. *Journal of Personality, 52*, 1–21.

Simonton, D. K. (1985). The vice-presidential succession effect: Individual or situational basis? *Political Behavior, 7*, 79–99.

Simonton, D. K. (1986a). Dispositional attributions of (presidential) leadership: An experimental simulation of historiometric results. *Journal of Experimental Social Psychology, 22*, 389–418.

Simonton, D. K. (1986b). Presidential greatness: The historical consensus and its psychological significance. *Political Psychology, 7*, 259–283.

Simonton, D. K. (1986c). Presidential personality: Biographical use of the Gough Adjective Check List. *Journal of Personality and Social Psychology, 51*, 149–160.

Simonton, D. K. (1987). Presidential inflexibility and veto behavior: Two individual-situational interactions. *Journal of Personality, 55*, 1–18.

Simonton, D. K. (1988). Presidential style: Personality, biography, and performance. *Journal of Personality and Social Psychology, 55*, 928–936.

Simonton, D. K. (1991a). Latent-variable models of posthumous reputation: A quest for Galton's G. *Journal of Personality and Social Psychology, 60*, 607–619.

Simonton, D. K. (1991b). Personality correlates of exceptional personal influence: A note on Thorndike's (1950) creators and leaders. *Creativity Research Journal, 4*, 67–78.

Simonton, D. K. (1991c). Predicting presidential greatness: An alternative to the Kenney and Rice Contextual Index. *Presidential Studies Quarterly, 21*, 301–305.

Simonton, D. K. (1992). Presidential greatness and personality: A response to McCann (1992). *Journal of Personality and Social Psychology, 63*, 676–679.

Simonton, D. K. (1995). Personality and intellectual predictors of leadership. In D. H. Saklofske & M. Zeidner (Eds.), *International handbook of personality and intelligence* (pp. 739–757). New York: Plenum.

Simonton, D. K. (1996). Presidents' wives and First Ladies: On achieving eminence within a traditional gender role. *Sex Roles, 35*, 309–336.

Simonton, D. K. (1998). Mad King George: The impact of personal and political stress on mental and physical health. *Journal of Personality, 66*, 443–466.

Simonton, D. K. (1999). Significant samples: The psychological study of eminent individuals. *Psychological Methods, 4*, 425–451.

Simonton, D. K. (2001a). Kings, queens, and sultans: Empirical studies of political leadership in European hereditary monarchies. In O. Feldman & L. O. Valenty (Eds.), *Profiling political leaders: Cross-cultural studies of personality and behavior* (pp. 97–110). Westport, CT: Praeger.

Simonton, D. K. (2001b). Predicting presidential greatness: Equation replication on recent survey results. *Journal of Social Psychology, 141*, 293–307.

Simonton, D. K. (2002). Intelligence and presidential greatness: Equation replication using updated IQ estimates. *Advances in Psychology Research, 13*, 143–153.

Simonton, D. K. (2003). Qualitative and quantitative analyses of historical data. *Annual Review of Psychology, 54*, 617–640.

Simonton, D. K. (2006). Presidential IQ, Openness, Intellectual Brilliance, and leadership: Estimates and correlations for 42 US chief executives. *Political Psychology, 27*, 511–639.

Simonton, D. K. (2008). Presidential greatness and its socio-psychological significance: Individual or situation? Performance or attribution? In C. Hoyt, G. R. Goethals, & D. Forsyth (Eds.), *Leadership at the crossroads: Vol. 1, Psychology and leadership* (pp. 132–148). Westport, CT: Praeger.

Simonton, D. K. (2009a). The "other IQ": Historiometric assessments of intelligence and related constructs. *Review of General Psychology, 13*, 315–326.

Simonton, D. K. (2009b). Presidential leadership styles: How do they map onto charismatic, ideological, and pragmatic leadership? In F. J. Yammarino & F. Dansereau (Eds.), *Research in Multi-Level Issues: Vol. 8. Multi-level issues in organizational behavior and leadership* (pp. 123–133). Bingley, UK: Emerald.

Simonton, D. K. (2013). Presidential leadership. In M. G. Rumsey (Ed.), *Oxford handbook of leadership* (pp. 327–342). New York: Oxford University Press.

Simonton, D. K. (2014). Significant samples—not significance tests! The often overlooked solution to the replication problem. *Psychology of Aesthetics, Creativity, and the Arts, 8*, 11–12.

Simonton, D. K., & Song, A. V. (2009). Eminence, IQ, physical and mental health, and achievement domain: Cox's 282 geniuses revisited. *Psychological Science, 20*, 429–434.

Smith, C. P. (Ed.). (1992). *Motivation and personality: Handbook of thematic content analysis.* Cambridge, England: Cambridge University Press.

Song, A. V., & Simonton, D. K. (2007). Studying personality at a distance: Quantitative methods. In R. W. Robins, R. C. Fraley, & R. F. Krueger (Eds.), *Handbook of research methods in personality psychology* (pp. 308–321). New York: Guilford Press.

Sorokin, P. A. (1926). Monarchs and rulers: A comparative statistical study. II. *Social Forces, 4*, 523–533.

Spangler, W. D., & House, R. J. (1991). Presidential effectiveness and the leadership motive profile. *Journal of Personality and Social Psychology, 60*, 439–455.

Suedfeld, P. (2010). The cognitive processing of politics and politicians: Archival studies of conceptual and integrative complexity. *Journal of Personality, 78,* 1669–1702.

Suedfeld, P., & Bluck, S. (1993). Changes in integrative complexity accompanying significant life events: Historical evidence. *Journal of Personality and Social Psychology, 64,* 124–130.

Suedfeld, P., & Leighton, D. C. (2002). Early communications in the war against terrorism: An integrative complexity analysis. *Political Psychology, 23,* 585–599.

Suedfeld, P., & Rank, A. D. (1976). Revolutionary leaders: Long-term success as a function of changes in conceptual complexity. *Journal of Personality and Social Psychology, 34,* 169–178.

Suedfeld, P., Corteen, R. S., & McCormick, C. (1986). The role of integrative complexity in military leadership: Robert E. Lee and his opponents. *Journal of Applied Social Psychology, 16,* 498–507.

Suedfeld, P., Guttieri, K., & Tetlock, P. E. (2003). Assessing integrative complexity at a distance: Archival analyses of thinking and decision making. In J. M. Post (Ed.), *The psychological assessment of political leaders: With profiles of Saddam Hussein and Bill Clinton* (pp. 246–270). Ann Arbor, MI: University of Michigan Press.

Suedfeld, P., Tetlock, P. E., & Ramirez, C. (1977). War, peace, and integrative complexity. *Journal of Conflict Resolution, 21,* 427–442.

Suedfeld, P., Tetlock, P. E., & Streufert, S. (1992). Conceptual/integrative complexity. In C. P. Smith (Ed.), *Motivation and personality: Handbook of thematic content analysis* (pp. 393–400). Cambridge, England: Cambridge University Press.

Suedfeld, P., Wallace, M. D., & Thachuk, K. L. (1993). Changes in integrative complexity among Middle East leaders during the Persian Gulf crisis. *Journal of Social Issues, 49,* 183–199.

Tetlock, P. E. (1981a). Personality and isolationism: Content analysis of senatorial speeches. *Journal of Personality and Social Psychology, 41,* 737–743.

Tetlock, P. E. (1981b). Pre-to postelection shifts in presidential rhetoric: Impression management or cognitive adjustment. *Journal of Personality and Social Psychology, 41,* 207–212.

Tetlock, P. E. (1984). Cognitive style and political belief systems in the British House of Commons. *Journal of Personality and Social Psychology, 46,* 365–375.

Tetlock, P. E., & Boettger, R. (1989). Cognitive and rhetorical styles of traditionalist and reformist Soviet politicians: A content analysis study. *Political Psychology, 10,* 209–232.

Tetlock, P. E., Bernzweig, J., & Gallant, J. L. (1985). Supreme Court decision making: Cognitive style as a predictor of ideological consistency of voting. *Journal of Personality and Social Psychology, 48,* 1227–1239.

Tetlock, P. E., Crosby, F., & Crosby, T. L. (1981). Political psychobiography. *Micropolitics, 1,* 191–213.

Tetlock, P. E., Hannum, K. A., & Micheletti, P. M. (1984). Stability and change in the complexity of senatorial debate: Testing the cognitive versus rhetorical style hypothesis. *Journal of Personality and Social Psychology, 46,* 979–990.

Thoemmes, F. J., & Conway, L. G., III (2007). Integrative complexity of 41 U.S. presidents. *Political Psychology, 28,* 193–226.

Thorndike, E. L. (1936). The relation between intellect and morality in rulers. *American Journal of Sociology, 42,* 321–334.

Thorndike, E. L. (1950). Traits of personality and their intercorrelations as shown in biographies. *Journal of Educational Psychology, 41,* 193–216.

Watts, A. L., Lilienfeld, S. O., Smith, S. F., Miller, J. D., Campbell, W. K., Waldman, I. D., ...Faschingbauer, T. J. (2013, October 8). The double-edged sword of grandiose narcissism: Implications for successful and unsuccessful leadership among U.S. presidents. *Psychological Science,* online first doi:10.1177/0956797613491970

Wendt, H. W., & Light, P. C. (1976). Measuring "greatness" in American presidents: Model case for international research on political leadership? *European Journal of Social Psychology, 6,* 105–109.

Wendt, H. W., & Muncy, C. A. (1979). Studies of political character: Factor patterns of 24 U.S. vice-presidents. *Journal of Psychology, 102,* 125–131.

Winter, D. G. (1973). *The power motive.* New York: Free Press.

Winter, D. G. (1980). An exploratory study of the motives of southern African political leaders measured at a distance. *Political Psychology, 2,* 75–85.

Winter, D. G. (1987). Leader appeal, leader performance, and the motive profiles of leaders and followers: A study of American presidents and elections. *Journal of Personality and Social Psychology*, *52*, 196–202.

Winter, D. G. (2002). Motivation and political leadership. In L. Valenty & O. Feldman (Eds.), *Political leadership for the new century: Personality and behavior among American leaders* (pp. 25–47). Westport, CT: Praeger.

Winter, D. G. (2003). Measuring the motives of political actors at a distance. In J. M. Post (Ed.), *The psychological assessment of political leaders: With profiles of Saddam Hussein and Bill Clinton* (pp. 153–177). Ann Arbor, MI: University of Michigan Press.

Winter, D. G., & Carlson, D. G. (1988). Using motive scores in the psychobiographical study of an individual: The case of Richard Nixon. *Journal of Personality, 56*, 75–103.

Woods, F. A. (1906). *Mental and moral heredity in royalty*. New York: Holt.

Woods, F. A. (1909, November 19). A new name for a new science. *Science, 30*, 703–704.

Woods, F. A. (1911, April 14). Historiometry as an exact science. *Science, 33*, 568–574.

Woods, F. A. (1913). *The influence of monarchs*. New York: Macmillan.

Zullow, H. M., & Seligman, M. E. P. (1990). Pessimistic rumination predicts defeat of presidential candidates, 1900 to 1984. *Psychological Inquiry, 1*, 52–61.

CHAPTER FIVE

Social Identities and Leadership: The Case of Gender

CRYSTAL L. HOYT

Social identities matter in the leadership process. Renowned American politician Shirley Chisholm observed this first hand. She notes, *"I was the first American citizen to be elected to Congress in spite of the double drawbacks of being female and having skin darkened by melanin. When you put it that way, it sounds like a foolish reason for fame. In a just and free society it would be foolish. That I am a national figure because I was the first person in 192 years to be at once a congressman, black and a woman proves, I think, that our society is not yet either just or free."* Members of society's nondominant social groups, such as women and minorities, experience greater difficulty in reaching elite leadership positions than dominant group members (Eagly & Carli, 2007). Taking a quick glimpse across the top influence wielding bodies in the United States we can see a disproportionate prevalence of white males in top leadership positions. For example, although white males account for only 34 percent of the electorate (US Census, 2012), 67 percent of the seats are occupied by white men in the 2013 US congress. However, women, who account for 52 percent of the electorate (US Census, 2012), hold only 18.3 percent of the congressional seats and women of color hold a mere 4.5 percent (Center for American Women and Politics, 2013). The numbers are not much different in the top echelons of the business world. For example, leadership on the boards of the Fortune 500 companies is dominated by white men; white men hold 95.5 percent of board chair positions with minority men (3.9%), white women (2.0%), and minority women (.6%) significantly underrepresented in these positions (Alliance for Board Diversity, 2011).

Why does this matter? Representation of women, minorities, and other nontraditional leaders in public office and leadership positions is a matter of justice and equity. As Susan B. Anthony said, *"There never will be complete equality until women themselves help to make laws and elect lawmakers."*

Not only does increasing parity in representation show movement toward fulfilling democratic principles of equal opportunity to participate in the public sphere, but members from these marginalized groups can bring to office important perspectives and priorities that may be underrepresented. For example, increases in the empowerment of women as political leaders are associated with increases in policy making that represents the concerns of families, women, and ethnic and racial minorities (Markham, 2012; UNICEF, 2006). The greater empowerment of women in the political realm predicts increases in standards of living, education, infrastructure, and health (Beaman, Duflo, Pande, & Topalova, 2006; Markham, 2012). Furthermore, research suggests that when women hold political office there is an increased responsiveness to the needs of constituents, greater cooperation across party and ethnic groups, and when they are involved with peace negotiations and post-conflict governance and reconstruction there is a greater chance of lasting success (Cammisa & Reingold, 2004; Chinkin, 2003; Markham, 2012; Rosenthal, 2001). Similarly, women have been shown to bring unique perspectives and priorities to the business world that are associated with a greater focus on corporate sustainability including environmental issues (e.g., investing in renewable energy), social issues (e.g., improving access to health care), and governance issues (e.g., demonstrating high levels of transparency; McElhaney & Mobasseri, 2012).

Many factors contribute to the underrepresentation of marginalized individuals in leadership and limit their access to power. Theoretical perspectives are vast, ranging from those focusing on economic disadvantage and resultant limited access to educational, social, and cultural opportunities, to those focusing on how members of the dominant group work to maintain their privileged status, to focusing on how members of marginalized groups justify the system and the status quo (Haines & Jost, 2000; Jost, Banaji, & Nosek, 2004; Sidanius & Pratto, 1999). Focusing specifically on women, researchers have identified important factors contributing to women's lesser access to power including their greater family responsibilities as well as organizational cultures and structures that are more amenable to men's lives than women's (Eagly, 2012). The perspective that I will take in this chapter is that social identities matter in large part because they shape expectations (Major, 2012). These expectancies influence the way we as observers respond toward others as well as the way we as actors think about ourselves and behave (Deaux, 2012). Finally, in this chapter I will focus primarily on gender with a particular emphasis on the social category of women. Furthermore, most of the research that I draw upon has been undertaken in Western contexts. Given that these social identity findings stem largely from the culturally defined roles of women in society, the Western perspective I take in this chapter may not generalize well to cultures in which the roles of women differ.

Gender and Leadership: An Overview

Leadership researchers largely ignored social identities as a focus of research until the 1970s when they turned their attention to one social identity in particular: gender (Chemers, 1997; Hoyt, 2013a). There is now a robust scholarly interest into questions surrounding gender and leadership, with much focus on the topics that occupied the earliest scholars: examining style and effectiveness differences between women and men. The governing questions have changed dramatically over the past decades; first, researchers asked "can women lead?" and now many are asking "are women superior leaders than men?" In short, decades of research reveals that there appears to be small sex-related differences in leadership style and effectiveness (see Eagly, Gartzia, & Carli, 2014 for a comprehensive review). For example, women are slightly more likely to use democratic or participatory as opposed to autocratic leadership styles (Eagly & Johnson, 1990; van Engen & Willemsen, 2004). Women are also more likely than men to engage in transformational leadership behaviors and these behaviors are associated with contemporary notions of effective leadership (Eagly, Johannesen-Schmidt, & van Engen, 2003). Importantly, the leadership context can play an influential role in effectiveness. Women experience slight effectiveness disadvantages in masculine settings, whereas settings that are less masculine and male-dominated offer women some advantages.

Both pundits and researchers are now starting to focus on other ways in which female and male leaders may differ. For example, national journalists recently heralded the 20 female US Senators as the driving force behind the end to the government shutdown in 2013. According to the *New York Times*, "*In a Senate still dominated by men, women on both sides of the partisan divide proved to be the driving forces that shaped a negotiated settlement.*" *TIME* magazine further argued that "*women are the only adults left in Washington*" and that the 20 women are "*setting new standards for civility and bipartisanship.*" Focusing on exploring differences in values and attitudes, researchers have found that women are more likely than men to endorse social values that promote the welfare of others (Eagly et al., 2014; Schwartz & Rubel, 2005). Research focused on ethical decision making has shown that women are less likely to support unethical decisions than are men (Borkowski & Ugras, 1998; Franke, Crowne, & Spake, 1997). These differences in values and ethics can help explain important gender-linked differences in leadership outcomes. For example, female politicians are more likely to promote policies related to women, children, and families, are more focused on the public good, and are less involved in political corruption (Beaman, Chattopadhyay, Duflo, Pande, & Topalova, 2009; Dollar, Fisman, & Gatti, 2001; Eagly et al., 2014; Paxton, Kunovich, & Hughes, 2007; Swamy, Knack, Lee, & Azfar, 2001). Organizations with greater numbers of women at the top are associated with greater philanthropy, fewer employee lay-offs, and fewer unethical business practices (Boulouta, 2013; Eagly et al., 2014; Williams, 2003). Recently, there has been considerable focus on the financial performance of companies with more or less gender diversity in their upper echelons. Although early research found that greater levels of female leadership promoted financial success, closer scrutiny of the data reveals that increasing numbers of women at the top do not necessarily promote firm success (see Eagly et al., 2014). However, research does point to a number of important society-levels effects of having more women in leadership positions including a reduced gender wage gap, greater national wealth, and greater levels of societal gender equality (Cohen & Huffman, 2007; Eagly et al., 2014; World Bank, 2012).

Scholars have also long been interested in the difficulties that women face in attaining positions of influence and leadership. As Madeleine Albright astutely noted, "*The world is wasting a precious resource today. Tens of thousands of talented women stand ready to use their professional expertise in public life; at the same time, they are dramatically underrepresented in positions of leadership around the world.*" The *glass ceiling* is a term originally coined by two *Wall Street Journal* reporters in 1986 (Hymowitz & Schellhardt, 1986) to refer to the invisible barrier preventing women from ascending into top corporate leadership positions. Women even face this barrier in female-dominated occupations, professions where men ride a *glass escalator* up to the top positions (Maume, 1999). Although the glass ceiling metaphor served a useful purpose in placing this topic in the national spotlight, it has limitations and has recently been replaced with the image of a leadership labyrinth (Eagly & Carli, 2007). The glass ceiling implies that women do not face barriers at lower-level positions and that they face one large, indiscernible, and impassable barrier higher up. This new metaphor conveys the image of a journey riddled with challenges throughout that can be, and has been, successfully navigated. Women encounter many obstacles on this journey, including those stemming from an often disabling division of domestic labor. In this chapter, however, I will focus primarily on those barriers that stem from gender stereotypes and that shape expectations thereby influencing our beliefs and behaviors.

Social Identities: Shaping Expectations of Perceivers

Leadership Is in the Eye of the Beholder

I think the important thing about my appointment is not that I will decide cases as a woman, but that I am a woman who will get to decide cases.
— Sandra Day O'Connor

Social identities influence who we see as "fitting" the preconceived notion of a leader. To the extent that leadership begins with "the process of being perceived by others as a leader" (Lord & Maher, 1991, p. 11), nontraditional leaders are at a distinct disadvantage. Ample research indicates that people evaluate their leaders and potential leaders in reference to their intuitive notion of an ideal leader (Forsyth & Nye, 2008; Kenney, Schwartz-Kenney, & Blascovich, 1996; Lord & Maher, 1991). These lay conceptions of what it means to be a leader are called implicit leadership theories and they commonly revolve around task-oriented and people-oriented traits and behaviors, such as being determined and influential as well as being caring and open to others' ideas (Forsyth & Nye, 2008). These implicit leadership theories often reflect characteristics associated with traditional leaders and can result in biased perceptions and evaluations of people who do not fit the image of a leader, such as women (Hoyt & Chemers, 2008). For example, during Supreme Court Justice Sonia Sotomayor's confirmation hearing there was considerable apprehension about how her experiences and background, as a Latina woman, might bias her ability to be impartial. Building off the inherent assumption in these concerns that white men are uniquely impartial and immune to having life experiences shape their own views and biases, Stephen Colbert cleverly observed:

> In America, white is neutral ... The personal backgrounds [of Supreme Court justices] had nothing to do with the all neutral [white] court's decision that it was legal to send Japanese Americans to internment camps in 1942. Imagine how the life experiences of an Asian judge would have sullied that neutrality.

People's implicit leadership theories often reflect the masculinity standard that is associated with leadership. Ample research demonstrates that these intuitive notions of leaders are culturally masculine (Eagly & Carli, 2007; Koenig, Eagly, Mitchell, & Ristikari, 2011). Historically, positions of power and influence in society have traditionally been occupied by men whereas women have held lower status positions and have been more likely to work in the home. This division of labor has brought about gender roles, or consensually shared beliefs about what women and men usually do and what they should do (Eagly, 1987). According to role congruity theory, bias against female leaders emerges from the conflicting expectations between the female gender role and the leader role (Eagly, 2004; Eagly & Karau, 2002; Heilman, 2001). Significant research demonstrates that people have less favorable attitudes toward female than male leaders and women experience a greater difficulty than men in attaining top leadership roles and to being viewed as effective in these roles (Eagly & Karau, 2002).

Gender stereotypes both describe beliefs about the attributes of women and men and prescribe how women and men ought to be (Burgess & Borgida, 1999; Glick & Fiske, 1999). These stereotypes are activated easily and can result in biased perceptions and evaluations of others (Fiske, 1998; Kunda & Spencer, 2003). A vivid illustration of gender-based prejudice can be seen in the selection processes for members of symphony orchestras. In the 1970s and 1980s, male-dominated symphony orchestras made one simple change that resulted in a radical change in the proportion of women in symphony orchestras: applicants were asked to audition while hidden behind a screen (Goldin & Rouse, 2000). Although the content of gender stereotypes is vast, the particular stereotypes that influence the perception and evaluation of individuals in leadership are those maintaining that "women take care" and "men take charge" (Dodge, Gilroy & Fenzel, 1995; Heilman, 2001; Hoyt, 2010). Women are associated with communal characteristics that highlight a concern for others, whereas men are viewed as possessing agentic characteristics that emphasize confidence, self-reliance, and dominance (Deaux & Kite, 1993; Eagly, Wood, & Diekman, 2000; Williams & Best, 1990). Thus, descriptive gender stereotypes make it such that men are more likely than women to be seen as possessing traits that "fit" with the leadership role because the qualities used to describe men are similar to those used to describe effective leaders (Koenig et al., 2011).

The stereotype-based discrimination that women face in the leadership domain often comes in subtle forms and can be difficult to detect. In one clever experimental approach to illuminating this bias, termed the *Goldberg paradigm* (Goldberg, 1968), identical information, such as resumes or vignettes, are given to participants for evaluation with only one change across conditions: the name attached is either male or female. In a meta-analytic review of studies using this paradigm for leadership selection, researchers found a strong bias toward selecting men for masculine positions, including leadership positions, and gender-neutral positions and a preference for selecting women for feminine jobs, such as nurse (Davison & Burke, 2000).

Female leaders often find themselves in a double bind: highly communal women are criticized for being deficient leaders and highly agentic women experience backlash for not being female enough (Eagly et al., 2014; Heilman, 2001; Heilman & Okimoto, 2007; Heilman, Wallen, Fuchs, & Tamkins, 2004). That is, successful female leaders can engender hostility in terms of not being liked and being personally derogated (Heilman et al., 2004; Rudman & Glick, 1999, 2001). Relative to men, women are more likely to be penalized for expressing anger, talking more than others, and negotiating for their salary (Bowles, Babcock, & Lai, 2007; Brescoll, 2011; Brescoll & Uhlmann, 2008). This hostility women encounter for being successful at leadership stems from the perceived violation of the communal gender role. As Shirley Chisholm once noted, "*One distressing thing is the way men react to women who assert their equality: their ultimate weapon is to call them unfeminine. They think she is anti-male; they even whisper that she's probably a lesbian.*" This backlash experienced by effective female leaders who are perceived to be disregarding the prescription of femininity is exemplified in the 1989 Supreme Court case *Price Waterhouse v. Ann Hopkins* (Fiske, Bersoff, Borgida, Deaux, & Heilman, 1991). Hopkins was told by Price Waterhouse that she would not make partner because she was too masculine and that she should "*walk more femininely, talk more femininely, dress more femininely, wear make-up, have her hair styled, and wear jewelry."* Thanks in part to the empirical and theoretical literature on gender stereotyping, the court ruled that Price Waterhouse was discriminating against Hopkins based on gender stereotypes.

Gender–Based Preferences in Leadership Are Changing

Although women have more difficulty than men in attaining positions of authority from the boardroom to the senate floor, there has been an enormous shift toward accepting women as leaders over the last half century (Eagly & Carli, 2007; Hoyt, 2010). For example, when Gallup asked Americans in 1995 whether they would prefer to work for a man or woman 46 percent indicated preference for a male boss, only 19 percent preferred a female boss, and 33 percent indicated no preference. However, when asked the same question in 2011, the most popular response was no preference (44%), followed by preference for a male boss (32%), and then preference for a female boss (22%). Thus, even though there is still a preference for male over female bosses, this preference has decreased over the years and preference for a female boss and no preference have increased. Research has shown that there has been a cultural change such that leadership is increasingly being thought of as an androgynous endeavor requiring both agency as well as communal relational skills (Koenig et al., 2010).

Not only have biases against female leaders decreased considerably over the years but there is great variability in how people respond to women in leadership positions. There is ample evidence demonstrating that people's expectations about the roles of men and women in society and their attitudes toward women in positions of authority can be important predictors of gender-biased leader evaluations. Research has shown that more traditional attitudes toward women in positions of authority predict bias against women in positions of power (Rudman & Kilianski, 2000; Simon & Hoyt, 2008). Although the majority of the research focuses on anti-women bias, recent research has highlighted the bias in favor of women that can emerge when people hold progressive attitudes toward women in authority (Hoyt & Burnette, 2013). Similarly, Hoyt (2012) demonstrated that whereas individuals who support the gender role status quo, conservatives, discriminate against women in employment decisions, individuals who actively reject the status quo, liberals, show favor toward female candidates. Finally, recent research has shown that the extent to which people rely on their gender attitudes when making leader evaluations depends on the extent to which they believe human attributes are malleable. Consistent with past research showing that those who believe attributes are fixed, as opposed to malleable, pay greater attention to stereotype-consistent information and rely more on social group and trait-related information when perceiving others, those who believe attributes are fixed are more likely to rely on their gender role attitudes when evaluating female and male leaders (Hoyt & Burnette, 2013).

The findings that progressive, as opposed to traditional, gender role attitudes predict bias *in favor of* female leaders contributes to a relatively new and growing literature demonstrating a shift in gender-based preferences in leadership. For example, across both experimental and archival studies, researchers have shown that women are preferred over men to lead organizations during times of organizational failure (Ryan & Haslam, 2007). Thus, women are more likely than men to be appointed to *glass cliffs*: precarious situations associated with greater risk and criticism (Haslam & Ryan, 2008; Ryan, Haslam, Hersby, Kulich, & Atkins, 2008). Women who are put in these risky positions are often highly criticized and used as scapegoats when the struggling organizations fail. Examples of women who have found themselves on glass cliffs include Carly Fiorina when she took over as CEO at Hewlett-Packard and Katie Couric when she took over as evening news anchor at CBS. In related research, Brown, Diekman, and Schneider (2011) have shown that under conditions of threat people prefer a change in leadership and they favor female leaders. These findings are consistent with a role congruity perspective in that the preference for female leaders ensues from the congruency between qualities deemed necessary in that leader role (change) and gender-stereotypic characteristics associating females, more so than males, with change.

Intersecting Identities

There are other important social identities besides gender that influence who we see as "fitting" the preconceived notion of a leader. In addition to imposing a masculinity standard, our lay theories about the traits and qualities of leaders also impose a white standard. That is, being white has been shown to be a central component of the leader prototype in America (Rosette, Leonardelli, & Phillips, 2008). In reality we all have many various identities that interrelate and are not independent. Our experiences and perceptions of others are overwhelmingly shaped by the simultaneous influences of these various identities. The importance of intersecting identities can be traced back to Sojourner Truth's (African–American abolitionist and women's rights activist) famous 1851 speech *Ain't I a Woman?* In this speech Truth interrogates the intersections of race and sex, implying that all too often the category woman refers to white women.

> *That man over there says that women need to be helped into carriages, and lifted over ditches, and to have the best place everywhere. Nobody ever helps me into carriages, or over mud-puddles, or gives me any best place! And ain't I a woman?*
>
> —Sojourner Truth

Much social science research, however, examines people's various social identities in isolation. An intersectionality perspective considers and accounts for the intersection of multiple categories of social group membership (Cole, 2009). Researchers are starting to take the importance of intersecting identities seriously and in doing so we discover important new findings that may counter and expand our established wisdom.

Recent research has shown that the backlash that female leaders can experience when they demonstrate agency is moderated by race (Livingston, Rosette, & Washington, 2012). This research shows that black female leaders do not experience the same backlash for expressing dominance that white women experience. The authors argue that black women can be rendered "invisible" as they are neither a prototypical black person (who is male) nor a prototypical female (who is white). Thus, they may be buffered from some of the hostilities encountered by members of these non-dominant social groups. In this research they also found that black men are penalized for expressing dominance, unlike white men. These findings regarding black men are consistent with research showing that black male leaders, unlike white males, benefit from having a nonthreatening baby-faced appearance (Livingston & Pearce, 2009). These findings are complemented by recent research examining the role of gender and race in leader selection. In their research, Galinsky, Hall, and Cuddy (2013) showed that when asked to assign leader candidates to either a masculine leadership role (requiring the candidate to be competitive and contentious) or a feminine position (requiring collaboration and relationship building), participants were more likely to assign black women and white men to the masculine position than they were to assign white women or black men.

Although research shows that black women do not seem to experience the same negative repercussions for exhibiting agency as white women and black men do, black women do appear to experience double jeopardy, or a heightened disadvantage due to their dual-subordinate identities, under conditions of organizational failure (Rosette & Livingston, 2012). Under conditions of organizational success black women are evaluated similarly positive as white women and black men, all of whom are evaluated somewhat less positively than white men. Things change, however, when people evaluate leaders of failing organizations. In short, white men receive somewhat of a pass, black men and white women are evaluated more negatively than white men, and black women are evaluated the most negatively. One thing that is abundantly clear from this nascent literature examining both race and gender in leadership: to gain a better understanding of the role of social identities in leadership, it is imperative for social scientists to incorporate intersectionality into their theoretical and methodological approaches.

Social Identities: Shaping Our Own Behaviors and Beliefs

The expectancies associated with social categories not only influence how we perceive and act toward others, but they also shape the way we think about ourselves and the way we behave. Later in her life Eleanor Roosevelt acknowledged both the gendered expectations she faced as well as her inability to quietly abide these boundaries when she wrote, "*I could not, at any age, really be contented to take my place in a warm corner by the fireside and simply look on.*" Regardless of whether the culturally dominant stereotypes are endorsed or not, members of marginalized social groups are keenly aware of the pervasive stereotypes surrounding their social group and are aware that others may treat them accordingly. How people respond to these stereotypes are varied but one thing is clear: successful leaders are able to successfully navigate these biases.

Social identity threat occurs when one's social identity is at risk of being devalued in a specific context (Steele, Spencer, & Aronson, 2002). Experiencing threat in the face of negative stereotypes, termed *stereotype threat*, is a pervasive form of social identity threat. Stereotype-based expectations of inferiority can place a large psychological burden on individuals (Steele, 1997; Steele & Aronson, 1995; Steele et al., 2002). Researchers have shown that leaders who experience stereotype threat may perform less well, be less likely to take on leadership roles, and experience lower levels of well-being when they think they are being evaluated through the lens of negative stereotypes (Bergeron, Block, & Echtenkamp, 2006; Davies, Spencer, & Steele, 2005; Hoyt & Blascovich, 2007, 2010). For women in leadership positions, stereotype threat can come in many forms including a blatant threat, such as explicit exposure to stereotypes, or a more subtle threat, such as having solo status as the lone woman leading a group of men. For example, exposure to gender stereotypic commercials has been shown to undermine women's leadership aspirations (Davies et al., 2005), when gender stereotypes are activated implicitly women perform less well than men on a masculine sex role-typed managerial task (Bergeron et al., 2006) and on a negotiation task (Kray, Thompson, & Galinsky, 2001), and explicit stereotype activation adversely impacts leadership performance, self-perceptions, and the well-being of women who do not have high levels of leadership self-efficacy (Hoyt & Blascovich, 2007). Stereotype threat, however, does not always result in detrimental responses. For example, there are situational factors, such as telling women there are no gender differences in the leadership task (Davies et al., 2005) or presenting them with a feminine sex role-typed leadership task (Bergeron et al., 2006), that can nullify the detrimental impact of stereotype threat.

At times, however, people are able to react to negative stereotype-based expectations with constructive responses. US Supreme Court justice Sonia Sotomayor acknowledges that one of her biggest challenges is dealing with others' expectations of her. She has faced a number of negative stereotypic expectations including those associated with being an "affirmative action admittee," an "emotional Latina," or a "poor Latina from New York." Sotomayor, the third-ever female and first Latina justice on the highest court in the United States, has admitted to having fun proving her doubters wrong. In an early research demonstration of stereotype reactance, Kray and colleagues showed that when blatantly presented with the gender and bargaining stereotype women react against it by increasing their negotiation performance and out-negotiating men, but they can only do so if they possess sufficient power to do so (Kray et al., 2001; Kray, Reb, Galinsky, & Thompson, 2004). Women who are highly confident of their leadership ability respond positively (by performing better on leadership tasks, identifying more with leadership, and reporting greater levels of well-being) when put in a position to confirm the gender-leadership stereotype, demonstrating an *I'll Show You* response (Hoyt & Blascovich, 2007, 2010). Although women have been shown to demonstrate reactance to certain solitary identity threats in the domain of leadership, when they experience identity threat from multiple sources they are likely to demonstrate deleterious vulnerability responses (Hoyt, Johnson, Murphy, & Skinnell, 2010). In sum, whether women meet threats to their identity with vulnerability or reactance responses depends on various factors including the leader's self-efficacy, the explicitness of the stereotype, the group sex-composition, and the power that the leader holds.

In addition to individual and situational factors, interpersonal relations can help buffer marginalized individuals from potential threats to their identities. Humans are, in large part, socially constructed beings—molded through powerful interpersonal processes (Carver & Scheier, 1998; Cooley, 1902; Rusbult, Finkel, & Kumashiro, 2009). Indeed, research highlights the important role of others in individuals' pursuit and attainment of goals (Finkel & Fitzsimons, 2011). Chief among these affiliations are friends, family members, mentors, and role models. Former Secretary of State Condoleezza Rice credits her family in large part for helping her navigate the race and gender-based biases she encountered. Rice grew up in Birmingham, Alabama, during racial segregation and was fully aware of racial hostility. Rice's success as a leader depended in part on her responses to the deeply ingrained racism in her childhood: "*My parents had me absolutely convinced that, well, you may not be able to have a hamburger at Woolworth's, but you can be President of the United States.*"

Increasingly, researchers are examining the impact of exposure to positive role models on individuals who are underrepresented in leadership in part due to negative stereotypic expectations. Recent research has shown that the implementation of gender quotas for women that increased their representation on Indian village councils resulted in greater numbers of women subsequently vying for office, greater career and educational aspirations for local girls, and decreases in the educational gender gap (Beaman, Duflo, Pande, & Topalova, 2012). These role models can be effective, in part, because they demonstrate that success is indeed attainable and they can increase a sense of social belonging and inoculate people's sense of self against identity threats (Dasgupta, 2011; Marx, Ko, & Friedman, 2009; Marx & Roman, 2002; McGlone, Aronson, & Kobrynowicz, 2006). As Sonia Sotomayor acknowledges, "*. . . a role model in the flesh provides more* *than inspiration; his or her very existence is confirmation of possibilities one may have every reason to doubt, saying, 'Yes, someone like me can do this.'"*

Research on the impact of role models, however, has been equivocal. Upward social comparisons with successful role models have the potential to be inspiring and offer hope particularly when people focus on similarities with the role model (Collins, 1996, 2000; Suls, Martin, & Wheeler, 2002; Wood, 1989). However, exposure to superior others can also result in self-deflating contrast effects by demonstrating how relatively deficient one is compared to the superior other (Lockwood & Kunda, 1999; Suls et al., 2002). Exposure to highly successful business leaders has been shown to negatively influence women's self-rating of competence (Parks-Stamm, Heilman, & Hearns, 2008). Similarly, Rudman and Phelan (2010) found that exposure to counterstereotypical role models (e.g., a female surgeon or a female business executive) decreased women's leadership self-concept and lowered their interest in traditionally masculine occupations. One factor that can influence whether leader role models will be injurious or inspiring to women is the extent to which individuals are able to identify with them and deem their success as attainable. Hoyt and Simon (2011) found that exposure to elite female leaders had self-deflating effects on female participants' leadership aspirations and self-perceptions following a leadership task, whereas similar exposure to less elite role models, whom the women could identify with more, did not have this negative impact.

Other research has shown, however, that elite female leader role models can have inspiring effects on women. Latu, Schmid Mast, Lammers, and Bombari (2013) have recently shown that subtle, implicit exposure to a picture of elite female role models was effective in positively influencing women's behavior and self-appraisals during stressful leadership tasks. Other researchers have examined factors associated with women that influence how they respond to explicit and intentional exposure to role models. Recent research has shown that, compared to those with lower efficacy, women with high levels of leadership efficacy were more inspired by the elite role models and subsequently showed heightened levels of leadership aspiration, leader self-identification, and performance (Hoyt, 2013b). Finally, recent research has shown that the more people endorse the idea that leadership abilities are malleable and can be cultivated, as opposed to believing they are fixed, the more positive they respond to leader role models (Hoyt, Burnette, & Innella, 2012).

Hillary Clinton: America's Exhibit A

Hillary Rodham Clinton's tenure as former US Secretary of State, US Democratic presidential candidate, US Senator from New York, and First Lady vividly demonstrates many of the ways in which social identities can shape expectations and experiences of leaders. Social identities matter in part because members from marginalized groups may bring to office important and distinct perspectives, values, and priorities. Coming of age during a time of great social change offered Clinton opportunities women before her did not have and instilled in her a commitment to social justice. In 1998 Clinton gave a speech in Seneca Falls at the 150th anniversary of the campaign for women's suffrage led by Susan B. Anthony and Elizabeth Cady Stanton, remarking:

> The future, like the past and present, will not and cannot be perfect. Our daughters and granddaughters will face new challenges, which we today cannot even imagine. But each of us can help prepare for that future by doing what we can to speak out for justice and equality, for women's rights and human rights, to be on the right side of history, no matter the risk or cost.

Clinton has worked tirelessly both in her early years as First Lady and her more recent days as an elected official to improve the status and dignity of women and children in the United States and around the world. During her term as First Lady, Clinton began to actively shape domestic policy related to women, children, and families. For example, Clinton was instrumental in passing the State Children's Health Insurance Plan, creating the Office on Violence Against Women at the Department of Justice, and creating and passing the Adoption and Safe Families Act. Her focus on empowering women reaches well beyond the United States. In 1995 Clinton made headlines at the Beijing women's conference proclaiming "*Let it be that human rights are women's rights, and women's rights are human rights, once and for all.*" As Secretary of State, Clinton was able to enact these values on an international stage and she did just this by crafting an American foreign policy that, in her own words, "*put women on the agenda and made it a center-piece*" of all that the United States did globally (Baker, 2013).

Throughout her various leadership experiences Clinton has faced many obstacles that stem from both the descriptive and prescriptive nature of gender stereotypes. Clinton confronted gender role-based limitations early on; for example, as a young girl her interest in space exploration was met with a letter from NASA telling her they were not accepting girls into the program. Morphing over the years, various forms of gender-based restrictions have followed Clinton throughout her life. During her days as First Lady, Clinton confronted head on the ambivalence stemming from the incongruity between the female gender role and the leadership role. As she remarked in her autobiography *Living History* (2003):

> People could perceive me only as one thing or the other—either a hardworking professional woman or a conscientious and caring hostess . . . It was becoming clear to me that people who wanted me to fit into a certain box, traditionalist or femi-nist, would never be entirely satisfied with . . . my many different, and sometimes paradoxical, roles . . . We were living in an era in which some people still felt deeply ambivalent about women in positions of public leadership and power. In this era of changing gender roles, I was America's Exhibit A. (pp. 140–141)

America's exhibit A found herself walking on a precarious tightrope when running for the US democratic presidential nomination. The contradictory expectations associated with being both a proper woman and an effective leader complicated many things from deciding what to wear to navigating the proper emotional expression. Like many female leaders, Clinton's appearance was scrutinized by the media and general public. Here too female leaders find themselves trying to balance proper femininity with adequate masculinity. For example, Margaret Thatcher, arguably, "struck this balance, in part, by always dressing stylishly, carrying a handbag, and wearing her signature pearls. She consciously adopted a very feminine appearance to complement her very masculine political behavior" (Carroll, 2009, p. 6). Clinton understood this balancing act; however, although she tried to soften her appearance, she was often seen as looking very masculine. Indeed, her signature pantsuit took on a life all its own. At one point Clinton herself jokingly referring to her presidential campaign staff as "The Sisterhood of the Traveling Pantsuits."

Navigating these contradictory expectations becomes particularly important and tricky for female leaders when it comes to emotional expression. When Clinton's eyes welled up talking at a campaign rally a number of pundits opined that those tears were proof she is not fit to be president. Never mind that a male republican party hopeful, Mitt Romney, teared up twice on the campaign trail with little notice. In response, Clinton astutely observed that male politicians get emotional at times as well: "*We have gone through years of male political figures who have done everything from cry to scream who have been our presidents.*" Clinton, however, was not too worried about being seen as too weak for the office of US President. Indeed, these apprehensions that Clinton would not be "man" enough to be commander-in-chief were overshadowed with concerns that she wasn't "woman" enough. As she noted, "*They know that I can make decisions. But I also want them to know I'm a real person.*"

The prescriptive nature of gender stereotypes can result in women being disliked and vilified if they are seen as engaging in dominant behaviors and violating the prescription for feminine niceness. Clinton has been no stranger to this gender-based backlash; in fact, on this front she is certainly America's exhibit A. Clinton has been demonized as a woman, wife, and mother, having been labeled a "radical feminist," "militant feminist lawyer," and, most notably, "bitch." The backlash phenomenon was on clear display in the media coverage of the 2008 US presidential primaries. As Katie Couric noted after Clinton bowed out of contention, "*One of the great lessons of that campaign is the continued and accepted role of sexism in American life, particularly the media ... if Senator Obama had to confront the racist equivalent of an 'Iron My Shirt' poster at campaign rallies or a Hillary nutcracker sold at airports ... the outrage would not be a footnote, it would be front page news*" (Couric & Co., 2008). Of course, Clinton is far from the first or only woman taking a leading role in public life to experience this backlash. In a private meeting with Clinton in 1995, then prime minister of Pakistan Benazir Bhutto told Clinton, "*Women who take on tough issues and stake out new territory are often on the receiving end of ignorance*" (Clinton, 2003, p. 272).

Clinton is well aware that success does not happen in isolation but rather, it takes a village (1996). Although there is intuitive appeal to locate the cause of great leadership success in the individual leaders themselves, as social beings our success is inextricably intertwined with others. Clinton gained inspiration from many others all along her journey. As an undergraduate student at Wellesley College she looked to upper-level students for mentorship and in later years she turned to Eleanor Roosevelt for inspiration and guidance. Clinton has learned firsthand how role models can contribute to successful leadership experiences and the development of a healthy sense of self-confidence. Clinton's confidence in her leadership abilities undoubtedly contributed to her unwavering resilience and helped her navigate her journey through the leadership labyrinth. Now Clinton serves as a role model for many women and girls worldwide. She has been identified by Americans as the most admired woman alive for an historic 17 times (Newport, 2012). Indeed, the current First Lady of the United States, Michelle Obama, identifies Clinton as a personal role model. Clinton has served as a model First Lady, Senator, and Secretary of State. The big question left to ponder: will Hillary Rodham Clinton serve as the first role model Americans call Madam President?

In conclusion, social group memberships matter in the leadership process. Social identities can both influence the way we respond toward others as well as the way we think about ourselves. These various and subtle processes can work contrary to a just and free society by contributing to biased leader evaluations and the underrepresentation of marginalized individuals in positions of power and influence. Importantly, a greater understanding of these challenges can help give us the tools necessary to encourage and enable women and other underrepresented individuals to participate fully in the political, civil, social, economic, and cultural lives of our societies. By bringing distinctive perspectives and priorities, the increased representation of marginalized individuals in leadership positions can contribute to the development and prosperity of our communities and nations. As Clinton recently noted (2013), "*When women participate in peacemaking and peacekeeping, we are all safer and more secure. And when women participate in politics, the effects ripple across the entire society.*"

References

Alliance for Board Diversity (2011). Missing pieces: Women and minorities on Fortune 500 boards. Retrieved from http://theabd.org/ABD_datasheet.pdf

Beaman, L., Duflo, E., Pande, R., & Topalova, P. (2007). *Women politicians, gender bias, and policymaking in rural India*. Background Paper for UNICEF's *The State of the World's Children Report*. Retrieved from http://www.unicef.org/sowc07/docs/beaman_duflo_pande_topalova.pdf

Beaman, L., Duflo, E., Pande, R., & Topalova, P. (2012). Female leadership raises aspirations and educational attainment for girls: A policy experiment in India. *Science, 335* (6068), 582–586. doi:10.1126/science.1212382

Beaman, L., Chattopadhyay, R., Duflo, E., Pande., R, & Topalova, P. (2009). Powerful women: Does exposure reduce bias? *The Quarterly Journal of Economics, 124,* 1497–1540. doi:10.1162/qjec.2009.124.4.1497

Bergeron, D. M., Block, C. J., & Echtenkamp, B. A. (2006). Disabling the able: Stereotype threat and women's work performance. *Human Performance, 19*(2), 133–158. doi:10.1177/0011000010382459

Borkowski, S. C., & Ugras, Y. J. (1998). Business students and ethics: A meta-analysis. *Journal of Business Ethics, 17,* 1117–1127. doi:10.1023/A:1005748725174

Boulouta, I. (2013). Hidden connections: The link between board gender diversity and corporate social performance. *Journal of Business Ethics, 113,* 185–197. doi:10.1007/s10551–012–1293–7.

Bowles, H. R., Babcock, L., & Lai, L. (2007). Social incentives for gender differences in the propensity to initiate negotiations: Sometimes it does hurt to ask. *Organizational Behavior and Human Decision Processes, 103,* 84–103. doi:10.1016/j.obhdp.2006.09.001

Brescoll, V. L. (2011). Who takes the floor and why? Gender, power, and volubility in organizations. *Administrative Science Quarterly, 56,* 622–641. doi:10.1177/0001839212439994

Brescoll, V. L., & Uhlmann, E. L. (2008). Can an angry woman get ahead? Status conferral, gender, and expression of emotion in the workplace. *Psychological Science, 19,* 268–275. doi:10.1111/j.1467–9280.2008.02079.x

Brown, E. R., Diekman, A. B., & Schneider, M. C. (2011). A change will do us good: Threats diminish typical preferences for male leaders. *Personality and Social Psychology Bulletin, 37,* 930–941. doi:10.1177/0146167211403322

Burgess, D., & Borgida, E. (1999). Who women are, who women should be: Descriptive and prescriptive gender stereotyping in sex discrimination. *Psychology, Public Policy, & Law, 5,* 665–692. doi:10.1037/1076–8971.5.3.665

Cammisa, A. & Reingold, B. (2004) Women in state legislators and state legislative research: Beyond sameness and difference. *State Politics and Policy Quarterly, 4,* 181–210. doi:10.1177/153244000400400204

Carroll, S. J. (2009). Reflections on gender and Hillary Clinton's presidential campaign: The good, the bad, and the misogynic. *Politics & Gender, 5,* 1–20. doi:10.1017/S1743923X09000014

Carver, C. S., & Scheier, M. F. (1998). *On the self-regulation of behavior.* New York: Cambridge University Press.

Center for American Women and Politics (2013). Women of color in elective office 2013. Retrieved from http://www.cawp.rutgers.edu/fast_facts/levels_of_office/documents/color.pdf

Chemers, M. M. (1997). *An integrative theory of leadership.* Mahwah, NJ: Lawrence Erlbaum.

Chinkin, C. (2003). *Peace agreements as a means for promoting gender equality and ensuring the participation of women.* Retrieved from United Nations: Division for the Advancement of Women website http://www.un.org/womenwatch/daw/egm/peace2003/reports/BPChinkin.PDF

Clinton, H. R. (2003). *Living history.* New York: Simon & Schuster.

Clinton, H. R. (1996). *It takes a village: And other lessons children teach us.* New York: Simon & Schuster.

Baker, P. (2013, April 2). Clinton speaks up for women's issues. The *New York Times.* Retrieved from http://thecaucus.blogs.nytimes.com/2013/04/02/clinton-speaks-up-for-womens-issues/

Cohen, P. N., & Huffman, M. L. (2007). Working for the woman? Female managers and the gender wage gap. *American Sociological Review, 72,* 681–704. doi:10.1177/000312240707200502

Cole, E. R. (2009). Intersectionality and research in psychology. *American Psychologist, 64,* 170–180. doi:10.1037/a0014564

Collins, R. L. (1996). For better or worse: The impact of upward social comparison on self-evaluations. *Psychological Bulletin, 119,* 51–69. doi:10.1037/0033–2909.119.1.51

Collins, R. L. (2000). Among the better ones: Upward assimilation in social comparison. In J. Suls & L. Wheeler (Eds.), *Handbook of social comparison: Theory and research* (pp. 159–172). New York: Kluwer Academic/Plenum.

Cooley, C. H. (1902). *Human nature and the social order* (Rev. ed.). New York: Scribner's.

Davies, P. G., Spencer, S. J., & Steele, C. M. (2005). Clearing the air: Identity safety moderates the effects of stereotype threat on women's leadership aspirations. *Journal of Personality and Social Psychology, 88,* 276–287. doi:10.1037/0022–3514.88.2.276

Couric & Co. (2008). *Katie Couric's notebook: Sexism and politics.* Retrieved from http://www.cbsnews.com/blogs/2008/06/11/couricandco/entry4174429.shtml

Dasgupta, N. (2011). Ingroup experts and peers as social vaccines who inoculate the self-concept: The stereotype-inoculation model. *Psychological Inquiry, 22,* 231–246. doi:10.1080/1047840X.2011.607313

Davison, H. K., & Burke, M. J. (2000). Sex discrimination in simulated employment contexts: A meta-analytic investigation. *Journal of Vocational Behavior, 56,* 225–248. doi:10.1006/jvbe.1999.1711

Deaux, K. (2012). Categories we live by. In S. Wiley, G. Philogène, & T. A. Revenson (Eds.), *Social categories in everyday experience* (pp. 205–217). Washington, DC: American Psychological Association.

Deaux, K., & Kite, M. (1993). Gender stereotypes. In F. L. Denmark & M. Paludi (Eds.), *Psychology of women: A handbook of theory and issues* (pp. 107–139). Westport, CT: Greenwood.

Dodge, K. A., Gilroy, F. D., & Fenzel, L. M. (1995). Requisite management characteristics revisited: Two decades later. *Journal of Social Behavior and Personality, 10,* 253–264.

Dollar, D., Fisman, R., & Gatti, R. (2001). Are women really the "fairer" sex? Corruption and women in government. *Journal of Economic Behavior and Organization, 26,* 423–429. doi:10.1016/S0167–2681(01)00169-X

Eagly, A. (2012). Women as leaders: Progress through the labyrinth. In S. Wiley, G. Philogène, and T. A. Revenson (Eds.), Social categories in everyday experience. Decade of behavior (pp. 63–82). Washington, DC, US: American Psychological Association.

Eagly, A. H. (1987). *Sex differences in social behavior: A social-role interpretation.* Hillsdale, NJ: Erlbaum.

Eagly, A. H. (2004). Prejudice: Toward a more inclusive understanding. In A. Eagly, R. M. Baron, & V. L. Hamilton (Eds.), *The social psychology of group identity and social conflict: Theory, application, and practice* (pp. 45–64). Washington, DC: APA Books.

Eagly, A. H., & Carli, L. L. (2007). *Through the labyrinth: The truth about how women become leaders.* Boston, MA: Harvard Business School Press.

Eagly, A. H., Gartzia, L., Carli, L. (2014). Female advantage revisited. In S. Kumra, R. Simpson, & R. J. Burke (Eds.), *The Oxford Handbook of Gender in Organizations.* Oxford: Oxford University Press.

Eagly, A. H., & Johnson, B. T. (1990). Gender and leadership style: A meta-analysis. *Psychological Bulletin, 108,* 233–256. doi:10.1037/0033–2909.108.2.233

Eagly, A. H., Johannesen-Schmidt, M. C., & van Engen, M. (2003). Transformational, transactional, and laissez-faire leadership styles: A meta-analysis comparing women and men. *Psychological Bulletin, 129,* 569–591. doi:10.1037/0033–2909.129.4.569

Eagly, A. H., & Karau, S. J. (2002). Role congruity theory of prejudice toward female leaders. *Psychological Review, 109,* 573–598. doi:10.1037/0033–295X.109.3.573

Eagly, A. H., Wood, W., & Diekman, A. (2000). Social role theory of sex differences and similarities: A current appraisal. In T. Eckes & H. M. Trautner (Eds.), *The developmental social psychology of gender* (pp. 123–174). Mahwah, NJ: Erlbaum.

Finkel, E. J., & Fitzsimons, G. M. (2011). The effects of social relationships on self-regulation. In K. D. Vohs & R. F. Baumeister (Eds.), *Handbook of self-regulation: Research, theory, and applications* (2nd ed., pp. 390–406). New York: Guilford Press.

Fiske, S. (1998). Stereotyping, prejudice, and discrimination. In D. T. Gilbert, S. T. Fiske, & G. Lindzey (Eds.), *The handbook of social psychology* (4th ed., Vol. 2, pp. 982–1026). Boston: McGraw-Hill.

Fiske, S., Bersoff, D. N., Borgida, E., Deaux, K., & Heilman, M. E. (1991). Social science research on trial: Use of sex stereotyping research in *Price Waterhouse v. Hopkins. American Psychologist, 46*(10), 1049–1060. doi:10.1037/0003–066X.46.10.1049

Forsyth, D. R., & Nye, J. L. (2008). Seeing and being a leader: The perceptual, cognitive, and interpersonal roots of conferred influence. In C. L. Hoyt, G. R. Goethals, & D. R. Forsyth (Eds.), *Leadership at the crossroads: Leadership and Psychology* (Vol. 1, pp. 116–131). Westport, CN: Praeger.

Franke, G. R., Crown, D. F., & Spake, D. F. (1997). Gender differences in ethical perceptions of business practices: A social role theory perspective. *Journal of Applied Psychology, 82,* 920–934. doi:10.1037//0021–9010.82.6.920

Galinsky, A. D., Hall, E. V., & Cuddy, A., J. (2013). Gendered races: Implications for interracial marriage, leadership selection, and athletic participation. *Psychological Science, 24,* 498–506. doi:10.1177/0956797612457783

Glick, P., & Fiske, S. T. (1999). Sexism and other "isms": Independence, status, and the ambivalent content of stereotypes. In W. B. Swann, Jr. & J. H. Langlois (Eds.), *Sexism and stereotypes in modern society: The gender science of Janet Taylor Spence* (pp. 193–221). Washington, DC: American Psychological Association.

Goldin, C., & Rouse, C. (2000). Orchestrating impartiality: The impact of "blind" auditions on female musicians. *American Economic Review, 90*(4), 715–741. doi:10.1257/aer.90.4.715

Goldberg, P. A. (1968). Are women prejudiced against women? *Transaction, 5,* 28–30.

Haines, E. L., & Jost, J. T. (2000). Placating the powerless: Effects of legitimate and illegitimate explanation on affect, memory, and stereotyping. *Social Justice Research, 13,* 219–236. doi:10.1023/A:1026481205719

Haslam, S. A., & Ryan, M. K. (2008). The road to the glass cliff: Differences in the perceived suitability of men and women for leadership positions in succeeding and failing organizations. *Leadership Quarterly, 19,* 530–546. doi:10.1016/j.leaqua.2008.07.011

Heilman, M. (2001). Description and prescription: How gender stereotypes prevent women's ascent up the organizational ladder. *The Journal of Social Issues, 57*(4), 657–74. doi:10.1111/0022–4537.00234

Heilman, M. E. & Okimoto, T. G. (2007). Why are women penalized for success at male tasks?: The implied communality deficit. *Journal of Applied Psychology, 92,* 81–92. doi:10.1037/0021–9010.92.1.81

Heilman, M. E., Wallen, A. S., Fuchs, D., & Tamkins, M. M. (2004). Penalities for success: Reactions to women who succeed at male gender-typed tasks. *Journal of Applied Psychology, 89,* 416–427. doi:10.1037/0021–9010.89.3.416

Hoyt, C. L. (2010). Women, men, and leadership: Exploring the gender gap at the top. *Social and Personality Psychology Compass, 4,* 484–498. doi:10.1111/j.1751–9004.2010.00274.x

Hoyt, C. L. (2012). Gender bias in employment contexts: A closer examination of the role incongruity principle. *Journal of Experimental Social Psychology, 48,* 86–96. doi:10.1016/j.jesp.2011.08.004

Hoyt, C. L. (2013a). Women and leadership. In P. Northouse's *Leadership: Theory and practice, 6th edition* (pp. 349–382). Thousand Oaks, CA: Sage.

Hoyt, C. L. (2013b). Inspirational or self-deflating: The role of self-efficacy in elite role model effectiveness. *Social Psychological and Personality Science, 4,* 290–298. doi:10.1177/1948550612455066

Hoyt, C. L., & Blascovich, J. (2007). Leadership efficacy and women leaders' responses to stereotype activation. *Group Processes and Intergroup Relations, 10,* 595–616. doi:10.1177/1368430207084718

Hoyt, C., & Blascovich, J. (2010). The role of self-efficacy and stereotype activation on cardiovascular, behavioral and self-report responses in the leadership domain. *Leadership Quarterly, 21,* 89–103. doi:10.1016/j.leaqua.2009.10.007

Hoyt, C. L., & Burnette, J. (2013). Gender bias in leader evaluations: Merging implicit theories and role congruity perspectives. *Personality and Social Psychology Bulletin, 39,* 1306–1319. doi:10.1177/0146167213493643

Hoyt, C. L., Burnette, J., & Innella, A. (2012). I can do that: The impact of implicit theories on leadership role model effectiveness. *Personality and Social Psychology Bulletin, 38,* 257–268. doi:10.1177/0146167211427922

Hoyt, C., & Chemers, M. M. (2008). Social stigma and leadership: A long climb up a slippery ladder. In C. L. Hoyt, G. R. Goethals, & D. R. Forsyth (Eds.), *Leadership at the crossroads: Leadership and psychology* (Vol. 1, pp. 165–180). Westport, CT: Praeger.

Hoyt, C., Johnson, S., Murphy, S., & Skinnell, K. (2010). The impact of blatant stereotype activation and group sex-composition on female leaders. *Leadership Quarterly, 21,* 716–732. doi:10.1016/j.leaqua.2010.07.003

Hoyt, C. & Simon, S. (2011). Female leader role models: Injurious or inspiring? *Psychology of Women Quarterly, 35,* 143–157. doi:10.1177/0361684310385216

Hymowitz, C., & Schellhardt, T. D. (1986, March 24). The glass ceiling: Why women can't seem to break the invisible barrier that blocks them from the top jobs. *The Wall Street Journal*, pp. D1, D4–D5.

Jost, J. T., Banaji, M. R., & Nosek, B. A. (2004). A decade of system justification theory: Accumulated evidence of conscious and unconscious bolstering of the status quo. *International Society of Political Psychology*, *25*, 881–919. doi:10.1111/j.1467–9221.2004.00402.x

Kenney, R. A., Schwartz-Kenney, B. M., & Blascovich, J. (1996). Implicit leadership theories: Defining leaders described as worthy of influence. *Personality and Social Psychology Bulletin*, *22*, 1128–1143. doi:10.1177/01461672962211004.

Koenig, A. M., Eagly, A. H., Mitchell, A. A., & Ristikari, T. (2011). Are leader stereotypes masculine? A meta-analysis of three research paradigms. *Psychological Bulletin*, *137*(4), 616–642. doi:10.1037/a0023557

Kray, L. J., Thompson, L., & Galinsky, A. (2001). Battle of the sexes: Gender stereotype confirmation and reactance in negotiations. *Journal of Personality & Social Psychology*, *80*, 942–958. doi:10.1037/0022–3514.80.6.942

Kray, L., Reb, J., Galinsky, A., & Thompson, L. (2004). Stereotype reactance at the bargaining table: The effect of stereotype activation and power on claiming and creating value. *Personality and Social Psychology Bulletin*, *30*, 399–411. doi:10.1177/0146167203261884

Kunda, Z., & Spencer, S. J. (2003). When do stereotypes come to mind and when do they color judgment? A goal-based theory of stereotype activation and application. *Psychological Bulletin*, *129*, 522–544. doi:10.1037/0033–2909.129.4.522

Latu, I. M., Schmid Mast, M., Lammers, J., & Bombari, D. (2013) Successful female leaders empower women's behavior in leadership tasks, *Journal of Experimental Social Psychology*, *49*, 444–448. doi:10.1016/j.jesp.2013.01.003

Livingston, R. W., Rosette, A. S., & Washington, E. F. (2012). Can an agentic black woman get ahead? The impact of race and interpersonal dominance on perceptions of female leaders. *Psychological Science*, *23*, 354–358. doi:10.1177/0956797611428079

Livingston, R. W., & Pearce, N. A. (2009). The teddy bear effect: Does babyfaceness benefit Black CEOs? *Psychological Science*, *20*. 1229–1236. doi:10.1111/j.1467–9280.2009.02431.x

Lockwood, P., & Kunda, Z. (1999). Salient best selves can undermine inspiration by outstanding role models. *Journal of Personality and Social Psychology*, *76*, 214–228. doi:10.1037/0022–3514.76.2.214

Lord, R. G., & Maher, K. J. (1991). *Leadership and information processing: Linking perceptions and performance*. Cambridge, MA: Unwin Hyman.

Major, B. (2012). Self, social identity, and stigma: Through Kay Deaux's lens. In S. Wiley, G. Philogène, and T. A. Revenson (Eds.), *Social categories in everyday experience. Decade of behavior* (pp. 11–30). Washington, DC, US: American Psychological Association.

Markham, S. A. (2012) Strengthening women's roles in parliaments. *Oxford Journal of Parliamentary Affairs*, 1–11. doi:10.1093/pa/gss024

Marx, D. M., Ko, S. J., & Friedman, R. A. (2009). The "Obama Effect": How a salient role model reduces race-based performance differences. *Journal of Experimental Social Psychology*, *45*, 953–956. doi:10.1016/j.jesp.2009.03.012

Marx, D. M., & Roman, J. S. (2002). Female role models: Protecting women's math test performance. *Personality and Social Psychology Bulletin*, *28*, 1183–1193. doi:10.1177/01461672022812004

Maume, D. J. Jr. (1999). Glass ceilings and glass escalators. *Work & Occupations*, *26*, 483. doi:10.1177/0730888499026004005

McElhaney, K. A., & Modasseri, S. (2012). *Women create a sustainable future*. Center for Responsible Business. Haas School of Business, University of California, Berkeley. Retrieved from http://responsiblebusiness.haas.berkeley.edu/Women_Create_Sustainable_Value_FINAL_10_2012.pdf

McGlone, M. S., Aronson, J., & Kobrynowicz, D. (2006). Stereotype threat and the gender gap in political knowledge. *Psychology of Women Quarterly*, *30*, 392–398. doi:10.1111/j.1471–6402.2006.00314.x

Newport, F. (2012, December 31). Hillary Clinton, Barack Obama most admired in 2012. Retrieved from http://www.gallup.com/poll/159587/hillary-clinton-barack-obama-admired-2012.aspx

Parks-Stamm, E. J., Heilman, M. E., & Hearns, K. A. (2008) Motivated to penalize: Women's strategic rejection of successful women. *Personality and Social Psychology Bulletin, 34*, 237–247. doi:10.1177/0146167207310027

Paxton, P., Kunovich, S., & Hughes, M. M. (2007). Gender in politics. *Annual Review of Sociology, 33*, 263–284. doi:10.1146/annurev.soc.33.040406.131651

Rosenthal, C. S. (2001). Gender styles in legislative committees. *Women & Politics, 21*, 21–46. doi:10.1300/J014v21n02_02

Rosette, A. S., Leonardelli, G. J., & Phillips, K. W. (2008). The white standard: Racial bias in leader categorization. *Journal of Applied Psychology, 93*, 758–777. doi:10.1037/0021–9010.93.4.758

Rosette, A. S., & Livingston, R. W. (2012) Failure is not an option for black women: Effects of organizational performance on leaders with single versus dual-subordinate identities. *Journal of Experimental Social Psychology, 48*, 1162–1167. doi:10.1016/j.jesp.2012.05.002

Rudman, L. A., & Kilianski, S. E. (2000). Implicit and explicit attitudes toward female authority. *Personality and Social Psychology Bulletin, 26*, 1315–1328. doi:10.1177/0146167200263001

Rudman, L. A., & Phelan, J. E. (2010). The effect of priming gender roles on women's implicit gender beliefs and career aspirations. *Social Psychology, 41*, 192–202. doi:10.1027/1864–9335/a000027

Rusbult, C. E., Finkel, E. J., & Kumashiro, M. (2009). The Michelangelo phenomenon. *Current Directions in Psychological Science, 18*, 305–309. doi:10.1111/j.1467–8721.2009.01657.x

Ryan, M. K., & Haslam, S. A. (2007). The Glass Cliff: Exploring the dynamics surrounding the appointment of women precarious leadership positions. *Academy of Management Review, 32*, 549–572. doi:10.5465/AMR.2007.24351856

Ryan, M. K., Haslam, S. A., Hersby, M. D., Kulich, C., & Atkins, C. (2008). Opting out or pushed off the edge? The glass cliff and the precariousness of women's leadership positions. *Social and Personality Psychology Compass, 2*, 266–279. doi:10.1111/j.1751–9004.2007.00007.x

Rudman, L. A., & Glick, P. (2001). Prescriptive gender stereotypes and backlash toward agentic women. *Journal of Social Issues, 57*, 743–762. doi:10.1111/0022–4537.00239

Schwartz, S. H., & Rubel, T. (2005). Sex differences in value priorities: Cross-cultural and multimethod studies. *Journal of Personality and Social Psychology, 89*, 1010–1028. doi:10.1037/0022–3514.89.6.1010

Sidanius, J., & Pratto, F. (1999). *Social dominance: An intergroup theory of social hierarchy and oppression.* New York: Cambridge University Press.

Simon, S., & Hoyt, C. (2008). Understanding the gender gap in support for a woman for president. *Analyses of Social Issues and Public Policy (ASAP), 8*, 157–181. doi:10.1111/j.1530–2415.2008.00167.x

Steele, C. M. (1997). A threat in the air: How stereotypes shape intellectual identity and performance. *American Psychologist, 52*, 613–629. doi:10.1037/0003–066X.52.6.613

Steele, C. M., & Aronson, J. (1995). Stereotype threat and the intellectual test performance of African Americans. *Journal of Personality and Social Psychology, 69*, 797–811. doi:10.1037/0022–3514.69.5.797

Steele, C. M., Spencer, S. J., & Aronson, J. (2002). Contending with group image: The psychology of stereotype and social identity threat. In M. Zanna (Ed.), Advances in experimental social psychology (Vol. 34, pp. 379–440). New York: Academic Press.

Suls, J., Martin, R., & Wheeler, L. (2002). Social comparison: Why, with whom and with what effect? *Current Directions in Psychological Science, 11*, 159–163. doi:10.1111/1467–8721.00191

Swamy, A., Knack, S., Lee, Y., & Azfar, O. (2001). Gender and corruption. *Journal of Development Economics, 64*, 25–55. doi:10.1016/S0304–3878(00)00123–1

van Engen, M. L., & Willemsen, T. M. (2004). Sex and leadership styles: A meta-analysis of research published in the 1990s. *Psychological Reports, 94*, 3–18. doi:10.2466/PR0.94.1.3–18

Williams, R. J. (2003). Women on corporate boards of directors and their influence on corporate philanthropy. *Journal of Business Ethics, 42*, 1–10. doi:10.1023/A:1021626024014

Williams, J. (2000). Unbending gender: Why family and work conflict and what to do about it. New York: Oxford University Press.

Williams, J. E, & Best, D. L. (1990). *Sex and psyche: Gender and self viewed cross-culturally.* Thousand Oaks, CA: Sage Publications, Inc.

Wood, J. V. (1989). Theory and research concerning social comparisons of personal attributes. *Psychological Bulletin, 106*, 231–248. doi:10.1037/0033–2909.106.2.231

UNICEF (2006). *Women and children: The double dividend of gender equality.* New York: UNICEF. Retrieved from http://news.bbc.co.uk/1/shared/bsp/hi/pdfs/11_12_06SOWC2007.pdf.

US Census Bureau. (2012). *Voting and registration in the election of November 2012.* Retrieved from: http://www.census.gov/hhes/www/socdemo/voting/publications/p20/2012/tables.html

World Bank. (2012). *Gender equality and development: World development report, 2012.* Washington, DC: International Bank for Reconstruction and Development, World Bank. Retrieved from http://issuu.com/world.bank.publications/docs/9780821388105

CHAPTER SIX

Emotional Intelligence and Leadership

DAVID R. CARUSO, KERRIE FLEMING, AND
ETHAN D. SPECTOR

Emotional Intelligence and Leadership

Emotional intelligence (EI) is a critical component of effective leadership. At least, that is the new, common wisdom. But the term EI is used in many different ways, and after 25 years of scientific study of emotional intelligence it is important to ask the questions "what is emotional intelligence (EI)?" and "what is its role in leadership?" The answers to these questions are "it means many different things" and "it depends." The many meanings of EI are explored in this chapter as are the relationship of these meanings to leadership within organizations. We suggest ways in which EI should be defined and applied to leadership and discuss the promise as well as the limitations of EI in this critical domain.

There are Several Emotional Intelligences

EI means different things to different people. For the general public, it is often referred to as "EQ" which stands for emotional quotient. EQ is often viewed as the opposite of analytical ability or IQ. People can have high IQs but many of them have low EQs, at least according to various journalists and executives. This makes intuitive sense as we all know analytically brilliant people who fail as leaders or flame out on a grand scale. We've also heard claims that IQ doesn't matter for success in the workplace. There are a few problems with this view. One is that intelligences tend to cluster together, that is, in general, if you are high on one form of intelligence it is likely that you are high on others. Another problem is that EQ has come to represent a broad array of skills and personality traits, ranging from optimism to leadership to emotion recognition.

And a third problem with this view is that IQ is actually one of the more important predictors of workplace performance. What's going on here? How can so many disparate views be held about the same concept? The answer is simple: Emotional intelligence is defined in radically different ways by different people. In this chapter we will tell you about these different views of EI, how they are applied to leadership and then focus our attention on one approach, the ability model of EI, and its application to the study and practice of leadership. Finally, we discuss an approach to structured problem solving based on recent research on emotional intelligence and leadership.

Although the term had been used before, the origins of modern research on the topic of emotional intelligence can be traced to an article in 1990 by Peter Salovey and John D. Mayer. They defined EI as "a set of skills hypothesized to contribute to the accurate appraisal and expression of emotion in oneself and in others" (p. 1). EI had something in common with other "hot" intelligences proposed by intelligence researchers such as Gardner who devised the multiple intelligence theory and Sternberg who came up with the idea of a practical intelligence theory. Gardner, in 1983 theorized the existence of multiple intelligences, as opposed to the more conventional theory of intelligence which was that intelligence was a single entity consisting of one, general factor statistically speaking. Among the intelligences in Gardner's theory were an interpersonal and an intrapersonal intelligence. These intelligences dealt with the ability to read others and to read one-self (respectively). Sternberg examined abilities such as understanding tacit, or implicit, knowledge vital for career success, and the ability to solve problems in daily life. Such tacit knowledge is often not written down; it consists of the unwritten rules about how things really get done.

Salovey and Mayer published additional papers on EI, but they generated little interest or attention until 1995. It was the publication of a trade book in 1995 that put the concept of EI on the map. The book, *Emotional Intelligence: Why It Can Matter More Than IQ*, was written by a psychologist and journalist, Daniel Goleman. It became a best-selling book and the popular press around the world picked up on the title and the idea that success is not a function of how smart you are. This trade book made bold claims and expanded the concept of EI to include almost any trait, characteristic or ability that was not traditional analytical intelligence or IQ. EI was equated with character, optimism, and impulse control. Others picked up on Goleman's ideas to include almost any skill or personality trait other than traditional intelligence. The term "EQ" was used by the popular press, including a cover story in *Time* magazine. This EQ phenomenon was due, in part, to a matter of timing. Published soon after *The Bell Curve* (Herrnstein & Murray, 1994), a weighty volume by two respected researchers whose take-away message was that IQ is fixed, IQ predicts life success and IQ varies across races. Goleman's cogent arguments for the importance of other skill sets served as an antidote to the message of *The*

Bell Curve, with an especially forceful statement that "At best, IQ contributes about 20% to the factors that determine life success which leaves 80% to other factors" (Goleman, 1995, p. 34). The broad-based approach to EI is very appealing, especially in the workplace, because of its claims that EI, or EQ, can predict a large percentage of success. In psychology, however, the notion that any psychological construct, can predict 80 percent of the variance in any outcome is nearly unheard of. The claims that (1) IQ only predicts 20 percent of success and that (2) EQ (noncognitive skills and competencies) is "twice as important as IQ" can only be supported through a review of the literature and followed by some statistical sleight of hand. We next take up four central issues: disparate approaches to EI and EQ, the claimed importance of these approaches, how the statistical sleight of hand was accomplished and the importance of EI (in its various incarnations) to leadership.

Emotional Intelligence as "EQ" or a Set of Personality Traits

It is hard to deny that traits such as assertiveness, optimism, reality testing, and impulse control are unimportant descriptors of differences between people and as predictors of their well-being and behaviors. Compare that list to another set of traits: assertiveness, positive emotions, impulsiveness, and openness to feelings. The first is drawn from an "EQ" assessment consisting of 15 sub-scales and the second are some of the 30 facet scales from a standard measure of personality (NEO). One of the first attempts to capitalize on the popularity of the EQ movement was to re-label a host of traditional personality traits as a new construct: emotional quotient, or EQ.

An assessment was developed based on an unpublished dissertation on well-being which included test items drawn from mental health professionals and from various models of mental health and well-being (e.g., Jahoda, 1958). The assessment, which we call the "trait" approach to EI, measures traditional traits such as those listed above (for a full list of sub-scales see Table 6.1). These are important aspects of our personality, and

Table 6.1 Factors and Scales from the Emotion Quotient Inventory 2.0

	Factors				
	Self-perception	*Self-expression*	*Interpersonal*	*Decision making*	*Stress management*
Scales	Self-regard	Emotional expression	Interpersonal relationships	Problem solving	Flexibility
	Self-actualization	Assertiveness	Empathy	Reality testing	Stress tolerance
	Emotional self-awareness	Independence	Social responsibility	Impulse control	Optimism

they tend to be good predictors of well-being. However, such approaches are extremely similar to measures of traditional personality traits that have been around for decades.

A possible test item on a trait-based, self-report measure would ask you how much various statements describe you, such as "I am good at reading people's emotions" or "I can tell how a person is feeling by looking at them." At the same time, executives and researchers studying leaders should note that these traits often are excellent predictors of certain leadership outcomes. The issue for researchers to consider is one of incremental validity (i.e., what do such measures add to our understanding of leadership above and beyond traditional personality measures) and the issue for leaders, coaches, and others in the workplace is whether they are already looking at such factors, although under a different set of labels.

Emotional Intelligence as Traditional Leadership Competencies

Another approach to the definition and measurement of EI is that of leadership competency models (Goleman, 1998). Leadership competencies consist of a broad range of knowledge, skills, abilities, and personal characteristics. Consider two lists of leadership competencies: Decisiveness, compassion and sensitivity, taking initiative, self-awareness, problems with interpersonal relationships, difficulty changing or adapting; versus self-confidence, adaptability, positive outlook, influence, and inspirational leadership. The first list is from a standard leadership 360 (Benchmarks) while the second is from an EI competency measure called the Emotional and Social Competency Inventory (ESCI). 360-degree feedback assessment asks a leader to rate her own behaviors and these ratings are compared to those provided by one's peers, supervisees, and boss. Discrepancies between various perceptions are examined and addressed to assist in the development of a leader's behaviors.

The Self-Assessment Questionnaire (1991) formed the basis of a re-purposed assessment ESCI and is based on extensive research on workplace competencies. Thus, a standard competency model became a measure of emotional or emotional and social intelligence. These competencies are grouped into four clusters drawn from a book on EI in the workplace (Goleman, 1998), and the clusters and competencies are listed in Table 6.2.

Competencies are measured using items such as: Shows awareness of own feelings, seeks to improve own self by setting measurable and challenging goals, views the future with hope. The four clusters themselves are derived from a model which refers to awareness and emotion management in oneself and in others. A compact model, it also appeals to the everyday experience of people in leadership roles.

Table 6.2 Scales from the Emotional and Social Competency Inventory 2.0

	Clusters			
	Self-awareness	Self-management	Social awareness	Relationship management
Competencies	Emotional self-awareness	Achievement orientation	Empathy	Conflict management
	Accurate self-assessment	Adaptability	Organizational awareness	Developing others
	Self-confidence	Emotional self-control	Service orientation	Influence
		Positive outlook		Inspirational leadership
		Transparency		Teamwork & collaboration
		Initiative		Change catalyst
		Optimism		

Source: http://www.eiconsortium.org/measures/eci_360.html.

Emotional Intelligence as "EI": The Ability Model of Emotional Intelligence

Finally, emotional intelligence can be viewed as an intelligence and consisting of a set of cognitive abilities where one reasons with emotions and where you reason about emotions. Intelligence can be viewed as the ability to learn, and an emotional intelligence focuses this learning ability on emotional content. It could be argued that competencies arise from both underlying abilities, or from a combination of underlying ability with deliberate, corrective feedback and practice.

Mayer and Salovey revised their definition of EI in a 1997 chapter where they proposed that EI consisted of a set of four related abilities which developed over age: perceiving emotions in oneself, others and the environment around us; utilizing our emotional states to help us think in different ways; understanding the causes of emotions, and how emotions progressed over time; and the ability to regulate emotions in oneself and others in order to achieve positive outcomes. Mayer and Salovey made a few attempts at operationally defining these abilities and developed ability-based assessments. The latest assessment is the Mayer, Salovey, Caruso Emotional Intelligence Test (MSCEIT) which measures four abilities, each assessed with two sets of items or tasks, and these are described in Table 6.3.

These abilities are measured in ways that can seem unusual to test takers, especially leaders. For example, the ability to use emotions to facilitate thinking is measured with a set of items such as "How effective are the following in seeking errors in a spreadsheet?" which is followed by 4 or 5 emotion terms, each rated on a 5-point effectiveness scale.

Along with issues regarding factor structure and reliability, the MSCEIT's use in leadership settings can be problematic unless accompanied by

Table 6.3   The Mayer, Salovey, Caruso Emotional Intelligence Test (MSCEIT)

Ability	Task	Question types
Perceive emotions	Faces	Identify subtle emotions in faces
	Pictures	Identify emotions in complex landscapes and designs
Use emotions to facilitate thought	Facilitation	Knowledge of how moods impact thinking
	Sensations	Relate various feeling sensations to emotions
Understand emotions	Changes	Multiple choice questions about how emotions change over time
	Blends	Multiple choice emotion vocabulary definitions
Manage emotions	Emotion Management	Indicate effectiveness of various solutions to regulating emotions in oneself
	Emotional Relations	Indicate effectiveness of various solutions to regulating emotions in other people

explicit instructions regarding the unusual nature of the assessment. For example, executives may wonder how matching physical sensations to basic emotions plays a role in their day-to-day leadership decisions. In reality, this is a measure of emotional empathy or the ability to establish connections between people, to "feel their pain," and perhaps, to inspire groups.

However, the MSCEIT appears to measure something new and different. Scores on the MSCEIT are moderately, and positively, related to measures of IQ, supporting the contention that it is a form of intelligence.

Conceptual Approaches Linked to Measurement Approach

These three approaches to EI or EQ have all been operationalized with psychological assessments. Each approach to defining EI or EQ is also associated with a method of measurement. While there is a 360 version of the self-report measure, a self-report version of the main 360 competency measure, and a self-report scale based on the ability model, it is instructive to consider how models of EI/EQ are so closely aligned with a measurement approach. Therefore, the ability approach to EI uses an ability-based measure with correct answers. The competency approach to EI uses the traditional 360 approach. The trait-based model uses a self-report scale of personality traits.

We'll return to this issue of models and measurement in a moment. Let's now look at that claim that IQ is unimportant in workplace success.

Does EQ Really Predict 80 percent of Success?

The appeal of EQ is that it claims to be the key, or only, missing ingredient, in a success formula. That 20 percent of "success" due to IQ is based on various meta-analyses (reviews and compilations of multiple research studies) which indicate that analytical ability, or IQ, is indeed an excellent predictor of workplace success (e.g., Schmidt & Hunter, 1998). In psychological research, this means that IQ and workplace performance correlates in the .40–.50 range. That's a major effect. However, it also means that IQ predicts about 20 percent of the variance in workplace performance and that there is a full 80 percent of the variance due to other factors.

In spite of the strong correlation between IQ and performance, the media, and some researchers and consultants, sometimes claim that IQ is a poor predictor in school and at work. They have a point: measures of analytical ability such as high-stakes admissions testing (e.g., the Graduate Management Admissions Test, the Scholastic Aptitude Test) predict a student's first-year grades but often, little else of interest. And studies of analytical ability and job performance within a career often come up empty. Such findings allow a naïve consultant to claim that IQ doesn't matter in professional careers. It's a true statement in a way, but vastly misleading. Here's why: companies hiring professionals screen their employees on proxies of IQ. Many firms require a college degree before they consider an applicant. Many firms recruit graduates of the world's top universities. These universities use high-stakes admissions tests, which correlate highly with standard IQ measures, to admit its students. Students must then perform well enough at university to graduate. Thus, the best organizations are filled with very smart, high-IQ people. Saying that IQ is of little importance in the workplace, especially the professional workplace, is technically true because of the problem called restriction of range: if everyone is smart, if every professional is above a threshold of intellectual ability, then the correlation between intelligence and performance will be muted. There just isn't enough variation in IQ to make a difference. The real test of IQ's predictive power would be if companies, as well as universities, hired and selected people randomly. But that doesn't happen.

We can demonstrate the same statistical trick, and illustrate the absurdity of the claim that IQ is not an important factor in workplace performance, by examining data from another field: professional sports, specifically, basketball. We analyzed team statistics from the National Basketball Association's (NBA) 2012 season to examine whether height is a predictor of success in basketball. On the face of it, most people will likely conclude that height is a critical factor in professional basketball: all you have to do is tune into a single NBA game to reach that conclusion. But we decided to look at the data. We obtained data on players from two 2012 NBA teams, the New York Knicks and the Boston Celtics, to control for general team success. The Knicks finished second from the top in their division, while the Celtics finished second from the bottom. The

Table 6.4   Correlations of height with measures of success in professional basketball

Measure of basketball success	r
Points (per game)	−0.56
Points (per minute)	−0.56
Rebounds (per game)	0.36
Rebounds (per minute)	0.62
Defensive rebounds (per game)	0.31
Steals (per game)	−0.60
Steals (per minute of playing time)	−0.38
Field goal %	0.28
3-Point %	−0.68

data we collected were: player height, points per game, minutes played per game, defensive rebounds per game, offensive rebounds per game, steals per game, shooting percentage, and a few others. To control for minutes played, we changed the per game statistics to per minute by multiplying them by (1/minutes per game). As you can see in Table 6.4, we found that while rebounds per minute and field goal percentage (2 pointers) were positively correlated with height, all other statistics we recorded (steals, points per minute, and 3-point percentages) were negatively correlated with height. We also looked at early-season stats for a single team, the 2013–2014 powerhouse Miami Heat, and found that individual player height correlated −0.03 with average points per game.

How can this be? If valid, these data suggest that even a hypothetical management psychologist, at a towering 5' 7" (170 cm) tall, and a devoted New York Knicks fan as a child, should be able to demonstrate competitive play in the NBA. Or, maybe not. These correlations demonstrate that when a variable has a restriction in how much it varies that correlation can be low. In other words, height does not matter all that much in professional basketball because all of the players are tall in comparison to the general population. The shortest player on this Knicks team was 6' 1" (Raymond Felton) and the tallest was Tyson Chandler (7' 1"). However, according to the Centers for Disease Control, the average height for males in the United States is 69.3 inches, or about 5' 9" (www.cdc.gov/nchs/fastats/bodymeas.htm). Just as basketball players are tall, successful professionals are smart, possessing strong technical skills, and industry-specific knowledge. Organizations hire smart, skilled professionals, and in most organizations, they hire college graduates who have high IQs. Just like most basketball players are really tall, most professionals are really smart.

Given this state of affairs, if we select and retain the smartest, most skilled employees, whether taller than average NBA super-stars or smarter than average leaders and managers, we can further enhance their effectiveness by then selecting on other characteristics and training other skills. Some of these skills may be those defined as emotional intelligence. But what does this intelligence look like in practice and how does it relate to leadership?

EI, Leaders, and Their Organizations

In order to ultimately comprehend how EI can be utilized by leaders, it is important to evaluate its influence on contemporary organizations and their people. An international conference on the impact of EI on organizational settings held in the United Kingdom in 2013 attracted an array of academics and practitioners from across the globe. A presentation on a study of EI in the leadership of the Australian mega-project environments demonstrated that "people skills" (loosely defined as EI) were a key factor in maintaining stakeholder relationships during the long complex processes of such projects (Pisarski & Brook, 2013). Thor (2013) presented findings on a proposed relationship between leadership EI and work engagement in a US sample using an *assessing emotions* scale and suggests that those with high emotional intelligence, especially the ability to manage their emotions, are likely to have the mental strength to stay positive even when facing tough situations. He also found that an ability to develop positive emotions and their control offers an explanation as to why those who can manage their emotions are more engaged in their work. Cambridge researcher Calvo along with his Australian colleagues spoke of the importance of "affective computing" (described as human-computer interaction where technology tries to detect and respond to its user emotion and other stimuli) where emotions can be detected by classifying signals into labels or points in a dimensional space (Calvo & D'Mello, 2010). They suggest that the signals most commonly used include video of facial expressions, voice, words, and physiology and from each of these signals a number of features can be extracted. For example, smiling or frowning detected from video features offers an indication of the emotional state of the individual. Such awareness is very significant for virtual leaders who lead remotely and for whom video conferencing is a norm for communication and building relationships with their virtual teams. German researcher Apelojg and his colleagues from Magdeburg University continue this human computer interaction research and are developing a smartphone application which measures emotions in specific learning and working contexts. Students are prompted to record both the situational setting and how they felt at that exact moment over a period of days. This is a useful tool for leaders to gauge the mood of their teams and potentially offers a platform for discussion if a team member has lost focus due a personal matter which may be interrupting their ability to work effectively. Such activity can help promote self-awareness for both the employee and the leader and also offers a simple but effective method of finding links between emotions and productivity which can be applied outside the classroom setting across organizational contexts.

Other published research, examining the role of EI in organizations suggests that emotions, if properly managed, can drive trust, loyalty, and commitment, leading to productivity gains, innovations, accomplishments of individuals, teams and organizations (Gardner & Stough, 2002;

Mandell & Pherwani, 2003; McGarvey, 1997). Research also suggests that the management of certain emotions and behaviors are key determinants when matching organization values with those of employees (Gardner & Stough, 2002; Mandell & Pherwani, 2003; McGarvey, 1997). Yildirim (2004) discusses the importance of emotional intelligence as a competency in firms and suggests that human resource departments should develop and maintain EI in their present employees as well as hiring people who are emotionally intelligent. McGarvey suggests that EI is what employees and bosses need to build successful organizations. Gardner and Stough demonstrate that ability to identify and apply knowledge of their own and other's emotions when solving problems evokes a climate of organizational learning. Halsell, Shumate, and Blum (2007) suggest that EI should be incorporated into orientation and training programs, as its inclusion in training departments allows employees to cooperate better, increase motivation, increase productivity, and increase profits. This and continuing research suggests that EI can address a host of organizational ailments and the curiosity of the concept of EI, now in its third decade, is unabated. On the surface, this continuing curiosity either suggests inconclusive findings or wild claims which will not translate into real world practice. However, the concept of emotional intelligence does offer a useful means for us to begin to pay attention to the importance of and complexity of human capital in organizations. So, what about the leaders of such complex environments? Do they "need" EI and if so, how do they use it?

Why EI Might be Important for Effective Leadership

Previously, IQ and experience were at the forefront of determining leadership quality but evidence would now suggest that these are necessary but not sufficient skills for leaders coping with current organizational demands. This new leadership has evolved due to the explosion of knowledge workers who will simply not accept authoritarian instruction but value proper debate and indeed sensitivity to their needs and feelings, both as employees and human beings. Such sensitivity must be managed carefully as leader reactions and emotional displays often provide cues for followers on how to react in similar situations. This is similar to Jung's view of transference, where children mimic the feelings and reactions of their parents in similar situations (Jung, 1969). However, inappropriate displays of leader emotions (such as weeping uncontrollably or throwing a stapler at someone in fury!) may simply turn off followers and suggest that such a leader is incapable of leading them successfully. This can impact their perception of the leaders' credibility and coping skills in stressful situations (Lewis, 2000). For example, a leader consumed by sadness may be perceived as lacking in self-confidence, while anger is often associated with strong leadership but also can mean a lack of control, which Goleman (1998), linked with leader ineffectiveness. However, this is not always the case, as the founder of Apple Inc., Steve Jobs's disdain for his team's innovative ideas made them strive to work even harder to gain his approval. This was not an unconscious leadership trait but one which was described by his employees as a very powerful emotion management strategy by Jobs (Issacson, 2011). The pressure for modern leaders to understand and control their own emotions and those of others, reflects a move from individualistic notions of leadership to inclusive relational perspectives and offers new suggestions into the effective practice and performance of leadership (Avolio, Walumbwa, & Weber, 2009; Bolden & Gosling, 2006). There is however, no right or wrong way to lead and in order to be effective, authenticity and honesty may be what is most important. This is often contrary to what bestselling books on leadership suggest, where certain leadership styles are proffered, but take no account of the heterogeneous nature of people. If you are an engineer who has been given a team of 100 people to lead, your inherent characteristics and abilities may prohibit you from oozing the charisma the latest leadership book suggests will charm your people into submission. Therefore, it is best to remain true to who you are but flex your communication style in the moment as needed. This true self is what creates trust between leaders and their people. That is why self-awareness is such a key ingredient to successful leadership. So, we now know what a contemporary leader "should" look like, let's examine the scientific evidence to investigate if EI can increase leader success. In order to paint an accurate picture of what is aspirational and what is realistic, we will separate the personality or trait and ability-based emotional intelligence research. If you are subsequently still impressed and want to develop some self-awareness and evolve your emotional intelligence, we suggest a blueprint to help with this development.

Personality and EQ competency-based research (nonabilities) provides a raft of studies linking EI and transformational leadership and claims that EI is crucial in assisting leaders to make good decisions about new products, markets, managing followers. Examples include Cooper et al. (1997) who suggest that a leader who pays attention to emotions saves time, expands opportunities, and focuses energy for better results. George (2000) suggests that leaders need emotional intelligence to manage employee emotional states and reduce leader's unconscious behavior transference to their followers. Johnson and Indvik (1999) suggest that managers who develop their emotional intelligence will have a workforce willing to engage with passion and employees will have managers who are open and receptive to their needs. Sirkwoo, Myeong-Gu, and Shapiro (2008), in a sample of 192 fulltime managers undertaking an MBA, found that the effects of EQ on transformational leadership vary according to the leader's emotional experience. They found that in periods of high emotional intensity, there is a tendency for the cognitive resources of leaders to become drained and subsequently cause them to lack focus on their followers. Law, Wong, and Song (2004) using a self-report measure called Wong and Law

EI (WLEIS) scale found a significant relationship between EQ and job performance. In other studies of organizational effects of EQ, Goleman (1998) reported on research involving 121 companies worldwide which revealed that EI competencies rank more than twice as crucial for excellence as technical abilities. Again, however, keep in mind the restriction of range issue discussed earlier when interpreting such results. Other trait research also demonstrates positive links to groups and team performance: Stubbs Koman, and Wolff (2007) collected data from 422 respondents representing 81 teams in a military organization and found that emotionally intelligent managers and leaders foster and support emotional competence leading to the creation of emotionally competent group norms. Jordan et al. (2002) using the Workgroup Emotional Intelligence Profile (WEIP) studied the link between EQ and two measures of team performance: team process effectiveness and team goal focus on a sample of 350 Australian undergraduate students and found that low emotional intelligence teams performed at a lower level than high emotional intelligence teams. On the surface, such research offers some bold and exciting claims of the role of EI when leading. However, *caveat emptor*, as some of these studies, although in earnest, suggest a statistical sleight of hand to fashion organizational outcomes, which are often owing to personality and a host of other deciding factors as discussed in our opening paragraphs. In addition to this, Day and Carroll's (2008) comparison study of trait and ability models discovered that the EQ-i (trait) model was more open to faking than the MSCEIT (an ability model), as the participants were able to increase their EQ-i scores when motivated to do so, but could not do the same for the MSCEIT scores with the same motivation.

A review of the ability research may provide us with a more credible alternative in terms of assessing whether EI and effective leadership do in fact go hand in hand. Daus and Harris (2003) studied leadership emergence, transformational leadership, and emotional intelligence using the MEIS and found that EI predicted leadership emergence and was significantly related to the understanding branch of emotional intelligence. Cote et al. (2010) discovered similar outcomes in a study of EI and leadership emergence comparing both the ability and self-reporting (personality) approaches. In an unpublished study of 170 CEOs of architectural practices in Ireland using the managing emotions branch of the MSCEIT, Fleming (2012) found a link between leader's emotion management and their ability to commercialize innovation in their practices. In a study of South African managers, Coetzee and Schaap (2004) found that transformational leadership was related to identifying and managing emotion branches of emotional intelligence. In a recent unpublished study of 17 managers in a social work context in Malta, Kenely (2013) found that a degree of self-awareness occurs from training and education in EI which resulted in better coping strategies by leaders. She proffers that this new self-awareness allows them to learn from their own experiences and apply the learning to their leadership activities. In a study of 44 financial analysts, Lopes et al. (2004) found that those who scored higher in the MSCEIT received greater merit increases, held higher company rank, and had more leadership potential. This ability-led research has solid psychometric foundations, which we would suggest offers a basis for reality as to how EI relates to leadership within an organizational context. However, we suggest that successful leadership of contemporary human capital requires general intelligence, cognition (the ability to process information and apply knowledge rationally), self-awareness and awareness of others, along with many other skills. So, if the first are a given, how can you evolve the latter?

The Emotionally Intelligent Leader in Action

One way is through the use of the "MSCEIT Blueprint," a structured problem-solving approach to difficult emotion-based situations (see Caruso & Salovey, 2004). Although the ability model was not explicitly designed for this purpose, the model has been adapted for practical use in leadership situations. Consider the following leadership scenario where a team leader has to deliver unexpected, bad news about an important product launch to the development and marketing teams. We use the ability model to understand the underlying emotional issues behind the problems the team is facing, and then use this structured approach to develop an action plan. Table 6.5 illustrates the application of this model as a structured approach, or "blueprint," for emotion-based problem solving. In this case, a project is behind schedule. The project leader recognizes that he is anxious and angry whereas his development team is fairly complacent and satisfied. Anxiety and anger focus the leader on finding fault and blame whereas the team's complacency appears to result in feelings that all is right with the world. Importantly, the leader understands that some of his anger is due to issues unrelated to the program. The anger and anxiety is incidental to the project, or at least part of it is. Just as one can filter out noise from a signal, this leader filters out the multiple sources of his feelings and recognizes that some of the anger is justified. Rather than yelling at the team, he manages his emotions in a way that the anger energizes him and he provides an impassioned speech which grabs people's attention and makes them realize that they still have work to do.

Leaders can learn to employ this structured approach to difficult emotion-laden problems, first by applying it as a sort of after-action review. Later, as they develop confidence in their ability to use the Blueprint, they can use it to prepare for difficult interactions in a prospective or preventative manner.

Consider the CEO facing significant organizational change, perhaps a major acquisition. Some of her managers are more and some less able to cope with the stress of the changes. The "Blueprint" asks the leader to consider both her current moods and emotions and those of the top

Table 6.5   Emotional intelligence blueprint

Ability/Step	Questions	Answer
Perceive emotions	How do I feel? How does the team feel?	Anxious and angry Content
Facilitate thought	How are my feelings influencing my thinking? How are the team's feelings influencing their thinking?	The anxiety narrows my vision and my anger focuses me on assigning blame The team is oblivious—they think all is well
Understand emotions	Why do I feel this way? Why does the team feel this way?	I'm worried that the bad news will set the team back even further. And I'm angry because we could have avoided the issues if the team took them more seriously to begin with. However, some of the anxiety is also due to some problems at home and some of the anger is due to being passed over for promotion The last update was positive and the team believes that we are on target
Manage emotions	How do I manage my emotions? How do I manage the team's emotions?	I need to calm down, and I do this, in part, by acknowledging that the team is not the sole source of these emotions. I can't "lose it," but at the same time, my anger is justified I can use my anger and anxiety to motivate the team

management. Next, she asks how these feelings are impacting their thinking. The anxious managers are digging in, focused on details, worried about what can go wrong. The managers who are energized and upbeat are generating ideas for the acquisition. The CEO recognizes that she needs both types of thinking: the "blue sky" possibilities of organizational change and synergy combined with the practical, "how will this work in practice?" worry. Understanding the source of a manager's anxiety is key. For example, if one of her top people comes in worrying about one aspect of the acquisition, the emotionally intelligent CEO determines that the source of this anxiety is less due to the plan itself and more to the person's generally negative outlook on life as well as the stress he is undergoing with regard to a difficult family issue. Therefore, she checks on the executive's hypotheses, and then accordingly rejects the negative hypothesis when no supporting data are found. Finally, throughout the process the CEO manages her own emotions to focus on the plan, energizes herself before she walks out on stage to announce the acquisition, deals individually with the stress and excitement of her top staff, and spreads a message of "we can do this" throughout the organization. The four steps or branches of the ability model may be followed informally by many successful leaders, but an explicit focus on such steps can help other leaders plan for, understand, and cope, with difficult leadership challenges.

Leaders can also acquire discrete emotional skills or develop remedial strategies to compensate for deficits in emotional intelligence. A leader lacking the ability to accurately read people is sometimes coached to ask people how they are feeling. The problem with this approach is that people may not know how they feel, and if they do and there is a power distance between the leader and the person being questioned, the person may not want to reveal how they feel. Instead, a leader can ask pointed questions such as "on a scale of 0 to 100, how satisfied are you with the outcome?" An answer less than 100 percent satisfied can be followed up with "and what would bring you to 100% satisfaction?" Another critical skill for leaders to develop is to be both aware of their feelings and to accurately determine the source of their feelings. A recent study on the role of EI on making risky decisions (Yip & Cote, 2013) indicates that people low on EI are less likely to make a risky decision when feeling anxious for reasons unrelated to the decision being made than are those high on EI. However, if you tell low-EI leaders that their moods can be the result of extraneous factors, and that such moods' impact bleeds into unrelated decisions, the effect disappears. In other words, simply providing leaders with minimal information on the role of moods on decision making can enhance their decision making.

When Emotional Intelligence Goes Wrong

Is it possible to be too smart? What about too emotionally intelligent? Is there a downside to high EI in leadership.? A few studies have found that emotion regulation knowledge is negatively correlated with a measure of Machiavellianism, surely a result that allows us to breathe a sigh of relief. We can also look at the ability model of EI and posit that someone high on all four abilities would likely not use these abilities to intentionally cause pain in others. Recall that "using emotions to facilitate thought" includes emotional empathy, the ability to feel what others feel. If I feel your pain I am unlikely to intentionally cause you pain.

However, one can also imagine leaders who manipulate the emotions of others in order to further their own goals or the goals of the organizations. EI as an ability may be value-free, and so, one could utilize the ability to achieve goals which are socially objectionable (see Kilduff, Chiaburu & Menges, 2010 for a discussion of these possibilities). Such musings are interesting to consider and disconfirming evidence exists that those high on ability EI are generally lower on a measure of Machiavellianism (Cote, DeCelles, McCarthy, Van Kleef, & Hideg, 2011). However, this same study demonstrated a dark side to EI. Those who were high on

Machiavellianism and also high on emotion regulation knowledge were more socially deviant. That is, they used their emotion knowledge for the forces of evil rather than the forces of good.

It is also easy to imagine a leader high on many of the traits described in the trait-based literature on EI. A leader with very high scores on optimism may fail to see the downside of a new strategy or the possibility that something could go wrong. Such behaviors are seen in various accidents as well as in failed product launches and acquisitions. High assertiveness can lead to arrogant behavior and in combination with high self-regard may lead to narcissistic behavior.

Before we celebrate emotionally intelligent leaders and before we tout the benefits of EI training among leaders, we need to move with caution and with care, and look out for potential downsides of such abilities.

Conclusions

Although claims that emotional intelligence (EI) is twice as important as IQ, and predicts 80 percent of the variance in workplace success may be outlandish, the emergence of an alternative intelligence, that uses emotion and cognition to improve decision making should be welcomed as it offers a useful platform to enhance leader and organizational performance. It also offers a means of substantiating the importance of human emotion as a form of intelligence. It also offers contemporary leaders a simple but effective behavioral tool to manage both their people and their performance outcomes. The idea of using an inherent ability, which everyone possesses to some degree, to enhance one's leadership capability is surely a novel way to manage an organization. In Whyte's (1956) classic book the *Organization Man*, effective business people are described as logical, reasoned, and rational decision makers. However, much research since then has shown that emotion is an integral part of daily life and is inseparable from the work environment (Ashforth & Humphreys, 1995; Ashkanasy, 1996). It remains to be said that organizations should continue to hire the best people—those with the intellectual capability and technical expertise necessary to perform the job well. But for people in leadership positions, there are likely other skills which can be helpful in certain environments, those where relationships matter, and where the focus is on the long-term outlook of the organization. These other skills include emotional intelligence, especially the abilities to perceive emotions accurately, understand the causes of emotions, use emotions to facilitate thinking and decision making, and regulating emotions.

Note

Disclosure: David Caruso receives royalties from the sales of the Mayer, Salovey, Caruso Emotional Intelligence Test and the book *The Emotionally Intelligent Manager*.

References

Apelojg, B., Binder, H. D., & Schirpke, A. (2013). Emotions in school: What emotions can tell us about the effectiveness of learning and self-regulation. Conference Paper, 1st International Conference on Emotional Intelligence in the Workplace. May 29–31, Ashridge Business School, Herts, UK.

Ashforth, B. E., & Humphrey, R. H. (1995). Emotion in the workplace, A re-appraisal. *Human Relations, 48,* 97–125.

Ashkanasy, N. M. (1996). *Perceiving and managing change in the workplace.* Management Paper Series, Graduate School of Management, University of Queensland, Australia.

Avolio, B. J., Walumbwa, F. O., & Weber, T. J. (2009). Leadership: Current theories, research and future directions. *Annual Review of Psychology, 60,* 421–449.

Bolden, R., & Gosling, J. (2006). Leadership competencies: Time to change the tune? *Leadership Journal, 2*(2), 147–163.

Calvo, R. A., & D'Mello, S. K. (2010). Affect detection: An interdisciplinary review of models, methods, and their applications. *IEEE Transactions on Affective Computing, 1*(1), 18–37. doi:10.1109/TAFFC.2010.1

Calvo, R. A., Pardo, A., & Peters, D. (2013). Supporting Emotional Intelligence with Automatic Sensing of the organization's affective state. Conference Paper, 1st International Conference on Emotional Intelligence in the Workplace. May 29–31, Ashridge Business School, Herts, UK.

Caruso, D. R., & Salovey, P. (2004). *The emotionally intelligent manager.* San Francisco: Jossey-Bass.

Coetzee, C., & Shaap, P. (2004). The relationship between leadership styles and emotional intelligence. Paper presented at the 6th Annual Conference for the Society of Industrial and Organizational Psychology, Sandton, South Africa.

Cooper, R., & Sawaf, J. (1997). *Executive EQ: Emotional intelligence in leadership and organizations.* New York: Grosset/Putnam.

Côté,, S., DeCelles, K. A., McCarthy, J. M.,Van Kleef, G. A., & Hideg, I. (2011). The Jekyll and Hyde of emotional intelligence: Emotion-regulation knowledge facilitates both prosocial and interpersonally deviant behavior. *Psychological Science, 22,* 1073–1080.

Côté, S., Lopes, P. N., Salovey, P., & Miners, C. T. H. (2010). Emotional intelligence and leadership emergence in small groups. *Leadership Quarterly, 21*(3), 496–508.

Daus, C. S., & Harris, A. (2003). Emotional intelligence and transformational leadership in groups. Paper presentation of symposium, multi-level perspectives on emotions in organizations at the 18th Annual Meeting of the society for Industrial and Organizational Psychologists, Orlando, Florida.

Day, A. L., & Carroll, S. A. (2008). Faking emotional intelligence (EI) comparing response distortion on ability and trait based EI measures. *Journal of Organizational Behavior, 29,* 761–784.

Fleming, K. (2012). *Strategic leadership of architectural firms, the role of emotion management and innovation.* Doctoral Dissertation, Dublin City University, Ireland (Unpublished).

Gardner, H. (1983). *Frames of mind.* New York: Basic Books.

Gardner, L., & Stough, C. (2002). Examining the relationship between leadership and emotional intelligence in senior level managers. *Leadership and Organizational Development, 23,* 68–79.

George, J. M. (2000). Emotions and leadership: The role of emotional intelligence. *Human Relations, 53,* 1027–1055.

Goleman, D. (1995). *Emotional intelligence: Why it can matter more than IQ.* London: Bloomsbury Publishing.

Goleman, D. (1998). *Working with Emotional intelligence.* New York: Bantam.

Halsell, S., Shumate, S. R., & Blum, S. (2007). Using a model of Emotional intelligence domains to indicate transformational leaders in the hospitality industry. *Journal of Human Resources in Hospitality & Tourism, 7,* 99–113.

Herrnstein, R. J., & Murray, C. (1994). *The Bell Curve.* New York: Free Press.

Issacson, W. (2011). *Steve Jobs.* New York: Simon & Schuster.

Johnson, P. R., & Indvik, J. (1999). Organizational benefits of having emotionally intelligent managers and employees. *Journal of Workplace Learning, 11*(3), 84–88.

Jordan, P. J., Ashkanasy, N. M., Hartel, C. E. J., & Hooper, G. S. (2002). Workgroup emotional intelligence, scale development and relationship to team process effectiveness and goal focus. *Human Resource Management Review, 12*(2), 195–214.

Jung, C. (1969). *The psychology of the transference*. Princeton, NJ: Princeton University Press.

Kenely, N. (2013). Emotional intelligence and transformational leadership. Conference Paper, 1st International Conference on Emotional Intelligence in the Workplace. May 29–31, Ashridge Business School, Herts, UK.

Kilduff, M., Chiaburu, D. S., & Menges, J. I. (2010). Strategic use of emotional intelligence in organizational settings: Exploring the dark side. *Research in Organizational Behavior, 30*, 129–152.

Law, K. S, Wong, C. S., & Song, L. J. (2004). The construct and criterion validity of emotional intelligence and its potential utility for management studies. *Journal of Applied Psychology, 89*, 483–496.

Lewis, K. M. (2000). When leaders display emotion: How followers respond to negative emotional expression of male and female leaders. *Journal of Organizational Behavior, 21*, 221–234.

Lopes, P. N., Brackett, M. A., Nezlek, J., Schutz, A., Sellin, I., & Salovey, P. (2004). Emotional intelligence and social interaction. *Personality and Social Psychology Bulletin, 30*, 1018–1034.

Mandell, B., & Pherwani, S. (2003). Relationship between emotional intelligence and transformational leadership style: A gender comparison. *Journal of Business and Psychology, 17*(3), 387–404.

Mayer, J., & Salovey, P. (1990). Emotional intelligence. *Imagination, Cognition and Personality, 9,* 185–211.

Mayer, J., Salovey, P., & Caruso, D. R. (2002). *The Mayer Salovey and Caruso emotional intelligence test, version 2.0.* Multi Health Systems: Toronto, Ontario, Canada.

McGarvey, R. (1997). Final score: Get more from employees by upping your EQ. *Entrepreneur, 25*(7), 78–81.

Pisarski, A., & Brooks, C. (2013). Achieving success in the Australian mega-project environment: The role of leaders' emotional intelligence. Conference Paper, 1st International Conference on Emotional Intelligence in the Workplace. May 29–31, Ashridge Business School, Herts, UK.

Schmidt, F. L., & Hunter, J. E. (1998). The validity and utility of selection methods in personnel psychology: Practical and theoretical implications of 85 years of research findings. *Psychological Bulletin, 124,* 262–274.

Sirkwoo, J., Myeong-Gu, S., & Shapiro, D. L. (2008). Revisiting the link between leaders emotional intelligence and transformational leadership: The moderating role of emotional intensity. Academy of Management Conference proceedings.

Stodgill, R. M. (1974). *Handbook of leadership: A survey of the literature*. New York: Free Press.

Stubbs Koman, E., & Wolff, S. B. (2008). Emotional intelligence competencies in the team and team leader: A multi-level examination of the impact of emotional intelligence on team performance. *Journal of Management Development, 27*(1), 55–75.

Thor, S. (2013). Organizational leadership success: Does greater emotional intelligence lead to higher work engagement? Conference Paper, 1st International Conference on Emotional Intelligence in the Workplace. May 29–31, Ashridge Business School, Herts, UK.

Whyte, W. H. (1956). *The organization man*. New York: Simon and Schuster.

Yildirim, O. (2004). Discriminating emotional intelligence based competencies of IT employees and salespeople. *Journal of European Industrial Training, 31*(4), 274–282.

Yip, J., & Côté, S. (2012). The emotionally intelligent decision-maker: Emotion understanding ability reduces the effect of incidental anxiety on risk-taking. *Psychological Science, 24*(2013), 48–55.

Yukl, G. (2006). *Leadership in organizations* (6th ed.) New Jersey: Pearson.

CHAPTER SEVEN

Kings and Charisma, Lincoln and Leadership: An Evolutionary Perspective

GEORGE R. GOETHALS AND SCOTT T. ALLISON

Three people who dramatically and fundamentally changed American society in the mid-twentieth century were also among the most charismatic. All three were, and still are, heroes to many, in the United States and around the world. Though each one's blend of heroism and charisma was distinct from that of the other two, each one was transforming. They were all leaders, who profoundly moved and changed both individuals and groups. To be sure, they were different kinds of leaders, but all three were, as Howard Gardner (1995) defined leaders, "persons who, by word and/or personal example, markedly influence the behavior, thoughts and/or feelings of a significant number of their fellow human beings." Call them "Three Kings." One was Martin Luther King (1929–1968), a heroic leader who was central in transforming race relations in the United States. His emotionally moving speeches illustrate fundamental aspects of charisma. Another was Elvis Presley (1935–1977), "The King of rock 'n' roll," a captivating performer who transformed not only popular music but also young people's sense of how they could live and what they could be. The third is Muhammad Ali (1942–), The Champ, the self-proclaimed "King of the World," whose speed and style changed the sport of boxing and whose uncompromising stances outsider the ring changed African Americans' sense of who they could be and how they could relate to the dominant white culture.

These Three Kings illustrate many of the fundamental aspects of and close interrelationships between charisma, heroism, and transforming leadership that we will develop in this chapter. First, human beings have a need for heroes and respond to strong, charismatic leadership. They attribute exceptional qualities to those they find charismatic, and they feel a strong emotional attachment to those individuals. In attributing exceptional qualities to charismatic leaders, followers construct cognitive representations that both develop and maintain heroic images (Goethals & Allison, 2012). Furthermore, many charismatic leaders are often active participants in what we might call leadership theater, designed to give follower audiences what they wish for. John Keegan (1986) puts it well. "The theatrical impulse will be strong in the successful politician, teacher, entrepreneur, athlete and divine, and will be both expected and reinforced by the audiences to which they perform... The leader of men... can show himself to his followers only through a mask, a mask that he must make for himself, but a mask made in such form as will mark him to men of his time and place as the leader they want and need." We should add to Keegan's point the implication that followers are co-conspirators in this leadership theater. Both leaders and followers benefit from the latter's perception that the former are heroic.

Although we will use MLK, Elvis, and The Champ to make part of our argument, we concentrate on Abraham Lincoln to explore further the role of language, particularly language with religious resonance, in creating the deeply moving connections that bind leaders and followers. The chapter proceeds as follows. First, we explore theoretical perspectives on how evolution has prepared human beings for leadership and heroism. How has it predisposed us to attribute charisma and heroic qualities to some leaders, and how does it lead us to experience deep emotional reactions to those we regard as charismatic? One consequence of evolution, we might say, is that leadership happens, charisma happens, and heroism happens. Second, we consider the dynamics of charisma itself. What is it, and how and when is it experienced? Third, we consider the relationship between charisma and what James MacGregor Burns (1978, 2003) calls transforming leadership. Fourth and finally, using the example of Abraham Lincoln, we consider the role of language tinged with religious referents in creating charismatic reactions and connections.

Evolution, Leadership, Charisma, and Heroism

We start with Sigmund Freud's early essay on leadership. It is explicitly evolutionary. Freud wrote that he "took up a conjecture of Darwin's to the effect that the primitive form of human society was that of a horde ruled over despotically by a powerful male" (Freud, 1922, p. 122). These men would often "possess the typical qualities of" a group "in a particularly clearly marked and pure form" and would often "give an impression of greater force and of more freedom of libido" (p. 129). That is, they would be highly prototypical, unusually competent and very powerful. These qualities would combine with a "need for a strong chief" to "invest him with a predominance" which otherwise he might not have. And such leaders could awaken from human's "archaic heritage" the idea of "a paramount and dangerous personality" who best be followed (Freud, p. 127). They would be both loved and feared, with the fear often converted into love.

It is easy to see how such evolutionarily based dynamics could have led to people attributing to certain leaders what we now call "charisma." Max Weber (1924) argued that charisma is "a certain quality of an individual personality, by virtue of which he is set apart from ordinary men and treated as endowed with supernatural, superhuman, or at least specifically exceptional powers or qualities." The word *charisma,* of course, is from the Greek meaning "divine gift of grace" (Riggio & Riggio, 2008), and in that sense it includes a religious element. In fact, Weber noted that the qualities of charismatic individuals "are regarded as of divine origin or as exemplary." That is, charismatic leaders may seem like god-like figures. Consistent with Weber's emphasis on the divine or supernatural, Freud noted that primal horde leaders are deified in death. We respond to charismatic leaders with reverence and awe. Therefore leaders who could somehow tap into religious feeling and ideation might be seen to be especially charismatic.

Another closely related human evolutionary outcome, according to Carl Jung (1969; Jung & von Franz, 1964), is our readiness to perceive heroes and be drawn to them. Jung proposed the concept of *archetype,* the idea that due to our common evolutionary past and the experience of our ancestors in evolutionary time, we inherit a *collective unconscious* composed of unconscious or latent images, which Jung called archetypes. These latent images can be made conscious or activated when we encounter something in the world that corresponds to them. For example, there is a *God* archetype which makes people readily believe in supernatural supreme beings and to perceive divine qualities in leaders such as kings, popes, and emperors. Archetypes not only lead us to notice things, they also lead us to respond to them with strong emotions of varying kinds. For example, the emotion elicited by the God archetype may be wholly positive or may contain an element of fear, as when Herman Melville in *Moby Dick* describes Captain Ahab as a "grand, ungodly god-like man." In short, when a person experiences a person or event that seems to have supernatural properties, he or she responds with intense emotion of awe and wonder. Jung suggested that another important archetype is the *hero.* When we encounter people who resemble the unconscious, archetypical image of *hero* we both think of them as heroes and respond to them with strong positive emotions, some of which are similar to those elicited by certain god-like figures. In many cases, heroes seem charismatic, and we respond emotionally to their charismatic qualities, often, as noted above, with feelings such as reverence and awe.

Recent theory and research on leadership and evolution has developed some of these themes. Mark Van Vugt (2006) argues that leadership happens because it is evolutionarily advantageous. Reproductive success is more likely in groups that can meet challenges and solve problems, and they are more likely to do so if they can coordinate their efforts through a combination of leading and following. Groups that have too many chiefs and not enough Indians, or groups where nobody leads, fare less well than those which achieve an optimal mix of leading and following. Interestingly, that optimal mix can be achieved by some combination of evolved flexibility in individual group members, so that they can either lead or follow, depending on the situation, and "frequency-dependent selection" which produces a stable ratio of leaders to followers (Maynard-Smith, 1982). That is, optimal mixes of leaders and followers can be reached if there are some people who are leaders, some who are followers, and still others who can lead or follow depending on situational demands and group composition. Evolutionary strategies can result in all three.

More recent evolutionary theory, like Freud, also suggests that the persons who emerged as leaders in early evolutionary time were "Big Men" (Van Vugt, Johnson, Kaiser & O'Gorman, 2008), individuals who were perceived to be the most skilled, intelligent, and effective in achieving the group's goals. Humans would have evolved to make quick attributions of competence among group members, and to follow those who seemed to have it. It is far from clear that these evolutionarily based tendencies still serve us well. Van Vugt et al. suggest that evolutionarily based preferences for Big Men or other charismatic leaders may cause a mismatch between the leaders we are more or less unconsciously drawn to and the leaders who are actually most effective in the modern world. Nevertheless, the appeal of many charismatic leaders is an enduring evolutionary consequence. Malcolm Gladwell's (2005) description of Americans' attraction to the handsome, graceful, and impressive but inept Warren Harding in the presidential election of 1920 is one of many illustrations.

Thankfully, there is more to leadership selection than evolved tendencies to follow powerful individuals with "paramount and dangerous" personalities. A range of proximal factors affect the extent to which we slavishly fall under the influence of strong, charismatic leaders. First, both Freud and Van Vugt et al. point out resistances to pure despotism and dominance. "Leveling mechanisms" such as gossip and ridicule would have evolved to pave the way for "a more consensual leader-follower decision structure" (Van Vugt et al., p. 270). Weber's work is also relevant here. When Weber first discussed charisma, he argued that charismatic leaders would be most likely to emerge in times of crisis. That idea can be generalized to the notion that leadership, like heroism, is need-based and consequently different kinds of leaders will appeal in different situations, depending on salient needs (again see Allison & Goethals, this volume).

Evolutionary theory nicely accommodates this notion. While powerful, charismatic leaders may often be preferred, the precise form of leadership we are most drawn to will depend on specific situational demands. Experiments on terror management theory, for example, show that the fear of death increases the relative appeal of charismatic leaders (Solomon, Cohen, Greenberg, & Pyszczynski, 2008). That fear produces a need for reassurance that we are significant, that we are an important part of something great. Similarly, Van Vugt, and Spisak (2008) show that male leaders are preferred at times of intergroup competition but that female leaders are preferred at times of intragroup competition. The authors claim that evolution teaches us that men are better war-making leaders but women are better peace-keepers. Other research derived directly from evolutionary theory suggests that our preference for attractive leaders is greater when people are concerned about disease threats (White, Kenrick, & Neuberg, 2013). Thus the literature generally supports the idea that while evolution may frequently draw us to strong, charismatic leaders, other specific qualities such as intelligence, generosity, and fairness are also important to followers, depending on the situation.

We see then that Freud, Jung, Weber, and modern evolutionary theory in social psychology all suggest a readiness to be drawn to, to follow, and to attribute exceptional heroic qualities to certain impressive individuals. More or less explicit in their approaches is the additional idea that such individuals become at least quasi-religious figures. The term "hero-worship" suggests as much. We essentially apotheosize many heroes and charismatic leaders.

As we consider Abraham Lincoln later, it will be useful to keep in mind that Freud went further in suggesting what it is about charismatic leaders that makes them so compelling. He argued that people in groups crave leadership but that those who would be leaders must not only be powerful and charismatic, they must themselves "be held in fascination by a strong faith (in an idea) in order to awaken the group's faith." He expanded on Gustave LeBon's crowd theory and suggested that "leaders make themselves felt by means of the ideas in which they themselves are fanatical believers" and that through "the truly magical power of words" leaders acquire a "mysterious and irresistible power" which acts as "sort of domination exercised over us." This domination can be exerted "by an individual, a work or an idea." Crucially then, leaders exercise influence through their ideas and their words as well as through their personal magnetism. Both can have motivating force. In the terminology of persuasion research, leadership happens through aspects of both the communicator and the communication. Or, as Howard Gardner frames it, leaders have an impact through both the stories they relate and their embodiment of those stories, that is, through both their words and their personal example.

Three Kings and the Elements of Charisma

How do the Three Kings illustrate the concept of charisma and the elements of charismatic leadership? Martin Luther King was an unusually compelling and arousing orator. Both the "words and music" of his speeches were stirring. His voice, his pacing, and the way he stimulated his audiences to respond, and the way he responded to them in return, all made his words electrifying. His audiences were deeply moved by the charismatic qualities of his speaking style. His voice was powerful, his phrases rhythmic, thus making his speeches, in a word, beautiful. Furthermore, his speeches employed deeply resonant metaphors that touched on both religious themes and enduring American ideals and images. In his last speech in Memphis, Tennessee, in 1968, King used biblical metaphors such as "I've been to the mountain top, and I've seen the promised land." Also, he quoted the quasi-biblical anthem of Union soldiers in the Civil War, the Battle Hymn of the Republic, concluding his speech with the words "Mine eyes have seen the glory of the coming of the Lord." King used his rhetorical skills to push white America to deliver on promises of equality and "justice for all." His persona, his compelling voice, his ideas, and his passionate attachment to those ideas lent him what Freud called "some magnetic magic." He related a compelling story compellingly and he embodied it fully. Gardner added that King's story was one that was "in the air" and resonated with salient needs in the America of the 1960s.

Elvis Presley's charisma was longer on emotion and shorter on ideas than Martin Luther King's, at least on the surface. The young Elvis was extremely attractive and his sneering, gyrating, and playful performances led young women to scream in what resembled mass hysteria and young men to rock and roll. His looks, his motion, and his voice combined to make his performances electric. But was there a story that his charisma related and that he embodied? There was in fact a message, that though implicit was as profound as King's. It was that people could cut loose at least for a time, and embrace and experience their passions, and dress and sing the way they wanted to, and more generally be what they truly were. Superficially, they could have long hair and sideburns. More deeply, they could express their individuality. One element of this was noted by the photographer Alfred Wertheimer, who remarked to the effect that Elvis's performances reminded young women that they had a body below the waist, and that they could move it. A more profound element of Elvis's story was his racial crossover, the idea that a white man could move beyond conventional norms and sing songs by black artists and dress in stereotypically black clothes. Black and white audiences could enjoy the same music, whether written by or performed by blacks or whites. It may not have been Elvis's intention to relate this story, but he told it through his total embrace of black gospel and rhythm and blues and his comfort with himself in embracing it. Like King's story, Elvis's resonated with a need in the culture to break loose from outdated and stultifying mores. As Elvis' contemporary Chuck Berry expressed it: "Hail, hail rock and roll, deliver me from the days of old."

Muhammad Ali's charisma combines compelling physical and athletic artistry, wit and rhetoric that is both silly and profound, and an embodiment of religious commitment that is extraordinary. Like King, he spoke up for African Americans, but he went beyond asking white Americans to accept them. He argued that blacks should live their own lives, take their own names, marry their own women, and be exactly who they wanted to be. His humorous poems and biting repartee early in his career led him to be labeled the "Louisville Lip." He used his celebrity as a boxer and composer of clever doggerel to speak seriously about justice. By refusing to be drafted into the US Army in 1967, he showed that he was willing to sacrifice his career for his religious beliefs. To the end, he never gave up combining the serious with the ridiculous. He said of his legacy, "I guess I'd settle for being remembered only as a great boxing champion who became a preacher and a champion of his people. And I wouldn't even mind if folks forgot how pretty I was" (Remnick, 1998, p. 306). Slowly, an initially hostile white America accepted his message that black people could live as they wanted in American society. Maybe they even acknowledged that there was something to his boast, "I am the greatest."

In short, the Three Kings together illustrate fundamental aspects of charismatic and heroic leadership. All three had exceptional personas. All three made an emotional connection with their audiences. All three related and embodied compelling stories. All three enacted theatrical leadership that gave people what they wanted and needed. Finally, two of them, King and Ali, used words, delivered in riveting styles, often touching on religious precepts, to influence their fellow human beings' thoughts, feelings, and behavior.

Charisma, Heroism, and Transforming Leadership

As impressed as we are by the charisma and heroic leadership of the Three Kings, characterizing them as transforming, as we did at the outset, requires some explanation. We do in fact think of them as transforming leaders. The term "transforming leadership" was introduced and contrasted with "transactional leadership" by James MacGregor Burns in his seminal 1978 book, *Leadership*. A somewhat different distinction between transformational and transactional leadership was later detailed in research by Bernard Bass and his colleagues (e.g., Bass & Avolio, 1993). Burns preferred the initial conceptualization and developed it further in his 2003 book, *Transforming Leadership*. Transforming, or transcendent, leadership involves (1) moving followers to higher levels of motivation and morality, (2) empowering followers so much so that they might become leaders themselves, and (3) producing "radical" change that "cuts...profoundly," and that causes "a metamorphosis in form or structure, a change in the very condition or nature of a thing" (Burns, 2003, p. 24). Do the Three Kings meet this high standard? We think they do. We believe all three contributed to fundamental changes in society, especially with regard to how black and white people could both be themselves and respect each other. In the 1950s and 1960s, all three empowered people to think and move beyond the conforming and often racist pressures of America at mid-century. They all had charisma, and all used it to transform, through both their words and their example.

The Charisma of Abraham Lincoln

Perhaps the most heroic, transforming leader in American history was Abraham Lincoln. Through words and actions, he moved followers to higher levels of motivation and morality, he empowered them, and he led profound transformations in American society. Lincoln brought the country through the Civil War and thereby produced a result, the ending of slavery in the United States, which was, he said in his second Inaugural Address, more "fundamental and astounding" than either North or South had initially anticipated. Was Lincoln charismatic? We believe that not all heroes or transforming leaders are. Harry Truman comes to mind as a noncharismatic transforming leader. In Lincoln's case we have in the end, we believe—given human beings' capacity to construct charismatic images, to attribute exceptional qualities where they may not initially be obvious, and to be attached to and moved by those who seem to have those qualities—a surprisingly robust instance of charisma, deeply rooted in his words, and especially their religious resonance.

Consider first Lincoln's persona. Did it, or he, have anything like "magnetic magic" as an individual in his own time? It is useful to remember that Lincoln was a very canny politician, and certainly understood John Keegan's principles noted earlier. He was an exceptionally active participant in leadership theater, giving, as best he could, follower audiences what they needed and wished for. First, Lincoln contrived to show himself. He simply wanted to be seen. He gambled that reaction to the view would be positive, given people's tendency to view leaders through a lens of heroism. In his trilogy of Civil War narrative histories, Shelby Foote (1958, pp. 802–803) argues that Lincoln made himself unusually available to the public. As more and more people saw him, or heard from others who had, they liked what they saw or heard. Foote explains "...he received all comers, and for the most part received them with a sympathy which, by their own admission, equaled or exceeded their deserving. He shook their hands at frequent public receptions in the White House...; he attended the theater, a form of relaxation which kept him still within their view; he drove or rode, almost daily, through the spokelike streets of the hive-dense city, returning the looks and salutes of men and women and children along the way. Thousands touched him, heard him, saw him at close range, and scarcely one in all those thousands ever forgot the sight of that tall figure, made still taller by the stovepipe hat, and the homely drape of the shawl across the shoulders. Never forgotten, because it was unforgettable, the impression remained, incredible and enduring, imperishable in its singularity—and finally, dear." Similarly, in Richmond, on April 4, 1865, a formerly enslaved African American woman touched the president as he toured the largely abandoned, burning city and rejoiced "I know that I am free. I have seen father Abraham and felt him." In short, Lincoln's odd appearance and gracious manner became enduringly compelling. His persona became charismatic. That was as much as Lincoln could wish for.

Many people got a closer look through his widely distributed (often by Lincoln) photograph. Foote notes that his countenance became "the most familiar face in American history." Maybe this was not advantageous. "The Paris correspondent of *The New York Times*" said he looked like a condemned murderer of servant girls, and that "such a face is enough to ruin the best of causes." However, people's needs for a charismatic hero led many to convince themselves that his face revealed inspiring heroic qualities. Foote wrote "you saw it not so much for what it was, as for what it held. Suffering was in it; so were understanding, kindliness, and determination." A young soldier wrote after a Lincoln visit to the front: "None of us to our dying today can forget that countenance... Concentrated in that one great, strong yet tender face, the agony of the life and death struggle of the hour was revealed as we had never seen it before. With a new understanding, we knew why we were soldiers." Thus Lincoln's appearance, at a distance and close up, had an inspiring, empowering effect. It made charisma happen. A final point regarding Lincoln's appearance and persona, especially as it is described by Shelby Foote and others, is that Lincoln may have activated Jung's *wise old man* archetype. That archetypical figure is seen in fictional characters such as Obi-Wan "Ben" Kenobi from the *Star Wars* films and Dumbledore in the Harry Potter novels. Resonating with such an archetype would have heightened Lincoln's emotional impact.

Lincoln worked hardest to make an emotional connection with his words, spoken and written. Then and even more now, his impact comes through those words. They may have more impact today when read by a Sam Waterston or enacted by a Daniel Day-Lewis. Or, people reading them may imagine the weary Lincoln writing or speaking them, or call to mind Daniel Chester French's iconic sculpture in Washington, DC's Lincoln Memorial, thereby adding to their emotional and intellectual impact. Still, it is the words themselves that most move people. What is it about them that gives them such power? As with Martin Luther King, one important element is Lincoln's use of religious imagery and biblical allusion. Sometimes Lincoln uses biblical language quite directly, sometimes he simply alludes to religious themes or content. Biblical language allowed Lincoln to use rhythms and phrases that would have been familiar to large and diverse audiences. The Second Great Awakening of Christian fervor in America in the nineteenth century would have made such language highly resonant as people pondered Lincoln's meanings.

In his famous house divided speech delivered in Springfield, Illinois, upon accepting the Republican Party nomination for the US Senate in 1858, Lincoln memorably argued "A house divided against itself cannot stand. I believe this government cannot endure, permanently, half slave and half free." The house metaphor might have had impact by itself, but surely its biblical origins gave it additional power. Lincoln was speaking to an audience composed of people who would have varied widely in their education. Of course he himself had very little formal instruction. He attended "blab schools," he said, "by littles," not having much more than one full year in total of schooling. But Lincoln had read all and absorbed much of the King James edition of the Bible. His audiences would also likely be familiar with its ideas and cadences, whether they were literate or not. The house divided metaphor derived from language attributed to Jesus in Matthew 3:25: "And if a house be divided against itself, that house cannot stand." By using language from a familiar, revered text with soothing rhythms and inspirational imagery, Lincoln was more likely to move his listeners.

Similarly, Lincoln's presidential speeches and writings frequently mention or appeal to God. In doing so, he often implied that God was on his (the Union) side. At the end of his December 1862 message to Congress, a speech some of whose last words are set to music in Aaron Copland's *Lincoln Portrait,* the president concludes his appeal for Congressional support for emancipation using balanced phrasing, alliteration, and appeals to honor and eternity. And ultimately he asserts divine support for this position. "In *giving* freedom to the *slave,* we *assure* freedom to the *free*— honorable like in what we give, and what we preserve. We shall nobly save, or meanly lose, the last, best hope to earth. Other means may succeed; this could not fail. The way is plain, peaceful, generous, just—a way which, if followed, the world will forever applaud, and God must forever bless" (italics in original).

Another example comes from the Emancipation Proclamation, signed a month after Lincoln's 1862 message to Congress, on January 1, 1863. Lincoln concludes a dry, legalistic document full of "Whereas," "Now, therefore I..." and "by virtue of the power, and for the purpose aforesaid..." with appeals to important values and divine approval. The document is often criticized for its legalistic, stilted wording, and also for aspects of its substance. However, given the assertion of Constitutional prerogative in the Proclamation, that tone is appropriate. Still, Lincoln was happy to add toward the conclusion "And upon this act, sincerely believed to be an act of justice, warranted by the Constitution, upon military necessity, I invoke the considerate judgment of mankind, and the gracious favor of Almighty God."

Sometimes Lincoln's use of biblical imagery and appeals to the divine are slightly more subtle. In his First Inaugural address, a lengthy discourse on the unconstitutionality and impracticality of secession, Lincoln suggests that passions that "may have strained" and threaten to "break our bonds of affection" may be eased when "the mystic chords of memory" are touched "by the better angels of our nature." In his famous Gettysburg Address, delivered in November 1863, Lincoln's uses religious terminology without a direct appeal for God's assistance. The speech touches on themes of birth and death, nation and people, and dedication and honor. It famously begins poetically: "Four score..." That short phrase both contains a rhyme and uses a word, "score," more familiar from the Bible than anywhere else. Somewhat later Lincoln uses the words "consecrate," "hallow," and "consecrated": "But, in a larger sense, we can not dedicate—we can not consecrate—we can not hallow—this ground. The brave men, living and dead, who struggled here, have consecrated it far above our poor power to add or subtract." Toward the end, in a more explicit religious phrasing, Lincoln states that included in the "unfinished work" and "great task remaining before us" is to ensure "that this nation, under God, shall have a new birth of freedom." The speech, then, is laced with religious, quasi-religious. and biblical wording. Such wording struck a familiar chord, creating a positive association, and which added to the charismatic appeal of the speech. It helped produce a charismatic emotional reaction, or as we have framed it earlier, make charisma happen.

The text of two short speeches adorn the Lincoln Memorial in Washington, DC. The Gettysburg Address is one. The other is the Second Inaugural Address, often regarded as Lincoln's greatest speech. The first part of the latter refers to the "reasonably satisfactory and encouraging" "progress of our arms" and discusses the political fractures which brought war, even though "all dreaded it." Then Lincoln asserts that slavery was the cause of the war and notes that neither side "anticipated that the *cause* of the war might cease with, or even before, the conflict itself should cease." In the latter portions of the address, Lincoln turns to the Bible and to God, and considers the role of the divine in both starting and potentially ending the war. He includes both direct biblical quotations and allusions to biblical passages. His audience would be familiar with both. Referring to Union and Confederate sides, Lincoln said, "Both read the same Bible, and pray to the same God; and each invokes His aid against the other. It may seem strange that any men should dare to ask a just God's assistance in wringing their bread from the sweat of other men's faces; but let us judge not that we be not judged." Here Lincoln refers to both old and new testaments. "Bread from the sweat of other men's faces" touches base with Genesis 3:19 "in the sweat of thy face shalt thou eat bread," while "let us judge not that we be not judged" is Matthew 7:1. Lincoln then goes on to say "The prayers of both could not be answered; that of neither has been answered fully. The Almighty has His own purposes." This passage may call to mind Job Chapter 42, where Job speaks to God, "I know you can do all things, no purpose of yours can be thwarted ... surely I spoke of things that I do not understand ... " Here Lincoln's words reflect his immersion in the Bible though they do not quote directly. Again, to the extent that his audience has been immersed in the same text, Lincoln's words can connect with them. Later Lincoln quotes the Bible directly: "Woe unto the world because of offences! for it must needs be that offences come; but woe to that man by whom the offence cometh!" (Matthew 18:7) and "the judgments of the Lord, are true and righteous altogether" (Psalms 19:9).

Interestingly in this address Lincoln doesn't claim as much knowledge of God's will as in earlier speeches. In his December, 1862 message to Congress Lincoln talks about his way being "plain, peaceful, generous, just ... " and says that it is a way that "God must forever bless." In contrast, in the Second Inaugural, Lincoln, like Job, does not claim to understand

God's purposes. He argues that it is not illogical to think that God gave "both North and South this terrible war" but he doesn't assert that he knows God's purposes. God may or may not will "that it continue." Lincoln's uncertainty about God's will and purpose also comes into focus in the first phrases of the climatic last paragraph of the Second Inaugural: "With malice toward none; with charity for all; with firmness in the right *as God gives us to see the right*, let us strive on to finish the work we are in..." (italics added).

Regardless of the gloss Lincoln gives to his understanding of the Almighty's purpose, he adorns his views with his own sense that he is doing God's will, as best he can divine it. His characterization of himself as doing God's bidding, expressed in language either taken directly from scripture, or using scriptural forms and words, likely went far in creating a charismatic reaction in his audiences. At the time Lincoln's appearance, voice, and demeanor may have added to that reaction. Now, only the words, the photographs, and the interpretations of numerous readers and actors shape our response. For many, the response is emotional in a way that is consistent with the way Freud, Weber, and others have described the impact of charismatic leadership.

Conclusion

In considering ideas from Freud, Weber, Jung, and Burns, and the cases of our Three Kings and Abraham Lincoln, we see that elements of leadership, charisma, and heroism are closely entwined. Elsewhere we (Allison & Goethals, 2011, 2013; Goethals & Allison, 2012) have argued that all heroes are leaders. We think that many, perhaps most, heroes are also charismatic, although we pointed to Harry Truman as a heroic leader who was not charismatic. Furthermore, although many charismatic leaders and charismatic heroes are transforming, Burns and others have argued persuasively that charisma can lead to villainy as well as transforming leadership. We need look no further than Hitler or Jim Jones. Still, examples where charisma, heroism, and transforming leadership go together are legion. These elements are clearly tightly linked.

The four individuals we have discussed here illustrate the way important leaders combine the elements of charisma. Elvis Presley's music and especially his riveting performances illustrate the charismatic qualities of a magnetic physical presence. His mostly implicit message about living in ways that were not constrained by conventional standards of dress, music, and interracial interaction makes him transforming. Muhammad Ali added wit and a serious consideration of how African Americans can live freely and proudly in the United States to his physical magnetism to become a transforming, charismatic leader. Martin Luther King and Abraham Lincoln used eloquent language with religious resonance to become transforming leaders. The impact of King's words and ideas was heightened by his compelling speaking style. In Lincoln's case, there are indications that his manner and appearance made more moving the message he so eloquently expressed in his words. We hope that our consideration of these charismatic and transforming heroes will help foster a fuller understanding of the dynamics of leadership.

Note

Portions of this chapter were based on material in G. R. Goethals (2013). Charismatic reactions to individuals and ideas: Looks, language and Lincoln. *Religions, 4,* 209–215.

References

Allison, S. T., & Goethals, G. R. (2011). *Heroes: What they do and why we need them.* New York: Oxford University Press.

Bass, B. M., & Avolio, B. J. (1993). Transformational leadership: A response to critics. In M. M. Chemers & R. Ayman (Eds.), *Leadership theory and research* (Chapter 3). San Diego, CA: Academic Press.

Burns, J. M. (1978). *Leadership.* New York: Harper & Row.

Burns, J. M. (2003). *Transforming leadership.* New York: Atlantic Monthly Press.

Copland, A. (1942). *Lincoln portrait.* Orchestral work.

Foote, S. (1958). *The Civil War: A narrative, Fort Sumter to Perryville.* New York: Random House.

Freud, S. (1921). Group psychology and the analysis of the ego. In J. Strachey (Ed.), *The standard edition of the complete works of Sigmund Freud* (Vol. 28, *Beyond the pleasure principle, group psychology, and other works*). London: Hogarth Press.

Gardner, H. (2005). *Leading minds: An anatomy of leadership.* New York: Basic Books.

Goethals, G. R., & Allison, S. T. (2012). Making heroes: The construction of courage, competence, and virtue. In J. M. Olson & M. P. Zanna (Eds.), *Advances in experimental social psychology, 46,* 183–235.

Jung, C. G. (1969). *Collected Works of C.G. Jung (Vol. 9, Part 1): Archetypes and the collective unconscious.* Princeton, NJ: Princeton University Press.

Jung, C. G., & von Franz, M. L. (Eds.). (1964). *Man and his symbols.* London: Aldus Books.

Keegan, J. (1987). *The mask of command.* New York: Viking.

Lincoln, A. (1858). "House divided" speech at Springfield, Illinois. In Don E. Fehrenbacher (Ed.), *Abraham Lincoln: Speeches and writings, 1832–1858* (p. 426). New York: The Library of America, 1989.

Lincoln, A. (1862). Annual message to Congress. In Don E. Fehrenbacher (Ed.), *Abraham Lincoln: Speeches and writings, 1859–1865* (p. 415). New York: The Library of America, 1989.

Lincoln, A. (1863). Emancipation proclamation. In Don E. Fehrenbacher (Ed.), *Abraham Lincoln: Speeches and writings, 1859–1865* (p. 425). New York: The Library of America, 1989.

Lincoln, A. (1863). Address at Gettysburg. In Don E. Fehrenbacher (Ed.), *Abraham Lincoln: Speeches and writings, 1859–1865* (p. 536). New York: The Library of America, 1989.

Lincoln, A. (1865). Second Inaugural address. In Don E. Fehrenbacher (Ed.), *Abraham Lincoln: Speeches and writings, 1859–1865* (pp. 686–687). New York: The Library of America, 1989.

Maynard, S. J. (1982). *Evolution and the theory of games.* Cambridge, UK: Cambridge University Press.

Melville, H. (1851). *Moby-Dick.* Indianapolis: Bobbs-Merrill, 1964.

Remnick, D. (1998). *King of the world: Muhammad Ali and the rise of an American hero.* New York: Random House.

Riggio, R. E., & Riggio, H. R. (2008). Social psychology and charismatic leadership. In C. L. Hoyt, G. R. Goethals, & D. R. Forsyth (Eds.), *Leadership at the crossroads: Vol. 1. Leadership and Psychology* (pp. 30–44). Westport, CT: Praeger.

Solomon, S., Cohen, F., Greenberg, J., & Pyszczynski, T. (2008). Knocking on heaven's door: The social psychological dynamics of charismatic leadership. In C. L. Hoyt, G. R. Goethals, & D. R. Forsyth (Eds.), *Leadership at the crossroads: Vol. 1. Leadership and Psychology* (pp. 45–61). Westport, CT: Praeger.

Van Vugt, M. (2006). Evolutionary origins of leadership and followership. *Personality and Social Psychology Review, 10,* 354–371.

Van Vugt, M., & Spisak, B. R. (2008). Sex differences in leadership emergence in competition within and between groups. *Psychological Science, 19,* 854–858.

Van Vugt, M., Johnson, D. D. P., Kaiser, R. B., & O'Gorman, R. (2008). Evolution and the social psychology of leadership: The mismatch hypothesis. In C. L. Hoyt, G. R. Goethals, & D. R. Forsyth (Eds.), *Leadership at the crossroads: Vol. 1. Leadership and psychology* (pp. 267–282). Westport, CT: Praeger.

Weber, M. (1921). The sociology of charismatic authority. In H. H. Gerth & C. W. Mills (Eds., 1946). *From Max Weber: Essays in sociology.* New York: Oxford University Press.

White, A. E., Kenrick, D. T., & Neuberg, S. L. (2013). Beauty at the ballot box: Disease threats predict preferences for physically attractive leaders. *Psychological Science, 24,* 2429–2436.

PART II

Leadership Processes

CHAPTER EIGHT

Creating and Maintaining Trust: How and Why Some Leaders Get It Right

R O D E R I C K   M .   K R A M E R   A N D
K I M B E R L Y   D .   E L S B A C H

When asked to testify before Congress as to the lessons, if any, Americans could derive from the Iran-Contra fiasco that nearly felled the Reagan administration, then-Secretary of State George Schultz famously asserted that, when it comes to credible and effective leadership, "Trust is the coin of the realm." In some respects, Schultz's words are even more poignant and applicable to today's world, where levels of trust in both government and business leaders have dipped to dismally low levels over the past decade (Center for Public Leadership, 2010; Nye, Zelikow, and King, 1997).

It might seem all too obvious that the capacity of leaders to lead is linked, in no small measure, to the extent to which they can inculcate or garner the trust of those they hope to lead. Accordingly, both researchers and practitioners alike have argued that the ability to establish and maintain trust is vital for effective leadership (Bennis, Goleman, O'Toole, & Biederman, 2008; Brown, 1994; Covey, 2006; Whitener, Brodt, Korsgaard, & Werner, 2006). Yet, research has demonstrated just as clearly such trust is both hard won and easily lost. It is this inherent "fragility" of trust, in fact, that makes trust in leaders both coveted and problematic.

A primary aim of our chapter, accordingly, is to explicate the vital role that trust plays in the leadership process. We also examine the practical question of how such trust is built and maintained. To achieve these aims, we first provide a brief discussion of how trust, as well as the closely related construct of perceived trustworthiness, have been conceptualized by social scientists. We then examine some of the benefits that have been ascribed to trust and perceived trustworthiness, particularly as they pertain to effective leadership processes. Our chapter then elaborates on some of the foundations of trust, identifying specific processes associated with trust-building. As a concrete illustration of these issues, we describe some of the dynamics of trust within real-world organizations, including the somewhat unusual case of the Minnesota Mycological Association. Finally, we conclude with some assessments of the current state of our knowledge regarding trust and trust-building, as well as suggesting some promising directions for future research.

Conceptualizing Trust and Perceived Trustworthiness

To assert that there has been a dramatic increase of interest among social scientists in the concept of trust would be a considerable understatement. In the last two decades, the topic has been the subject of intense attention from every major social science discipline. Thus, political scientists (Hardin, 2002, 2006; Hetherington, 2005), sociologists (Cook, 2001; Sztompka, 1999), psychologists (Grant & Sumanth, 2009; Kramer & Cook, 2004; Kramer & Tyler, 1996), organizational theorists (Lane & Bachman, 1998), behavioral economists (Bohnet, 2007), and neuroscientists (Zak, 2008) have all weighed in, offering their distinctive disciplinary perspectives and emphases. Even philosophers have joined the bandwagon, elucidating the benefits and limitations of trust on normative or prescriptive grounds (Baier, 1986; Grovier, 1994; Hollis, 1998; Solomon & Flores, 2001).

In addition to developing basic theory regarding the nature of trust, social scientists have been eager also to apply these emerging ideas to a variety of real-world trust-related problems, including the enduring problem of low trust in authorities and how to remedy it (Braithwaite & Levi, 1998; Cook, Hardin, & Levi, 2005; Kramer & Lewiciki, 2010; Kramer & Pittinsky, 2012; Lane & Bachmann, 1998). Given these theoretical strides, it is hardly surprising that organizational scholars have also endeavored to apply these insights to leadership theory (Dirks, 2006; Dirks & Skarlicki, 2004; Kramer, 2011; Tyler & Deogey, 1996).

Although social scientists have afforded considerable attention to this subject, a concise and universally accepted definition of trust has remained elusive (e.g., Barber, 1983, Hardin, 2006; Uslaner, 2002). Despite differences in view and emphasis, however, most trust theorists have concurred on the basic point that trust is fundamentally a psychological state. When conceptualized as a psychological state, moreover, trust can be defined in terms of several cognitive and affective processes.

On the cognitive level, it has been widely agreed that trust entails a state of perceived vulnerability or risk. Lewis and Weigert (1985) noted, along these lines, that trust entails the "undertaking of a risky course of action on the confident expectation that all persons involved in the action will act competently and dutifully" (p. 971). Similarly, Baier (1986) characterized trust as "accepted vulnerability to another's possible but not expected ill will (or lack of good will) toward one" (p. 235). Finally,

Robinson (1996) defined trust in terms of an individual's "expectations, assumptions, or beliefs about the likelihood that another's future actions will be beneficial, favorable, or at least not detrimental to one's interests" (p. 576).

Although acknowledging the importance and centrality of these cognitive components, other researchers have argued that trust needs to be conceptualized as a more complex, multi-dimensional psychological state that includes affective and motivational components as well (Chua, Ingram, & Morris, 2008; Fine & Holyfield, 1996). To this point, Fine and Holyfield (1996) have argued that cognitive models of trust provide a necessary but not sufficient understanding of trust. Trust also embodies, they emphasize, aspects of the "world of cultural meanings, emotional responses, and social relations…one not only thinks trust, but feels trust" (p. 25).

Closely related to the issue of how we think about trust is the issue of what it takes to be perceived as trust*worthy*. In an early and influential analysis of this question, Barber (1983) posited that in order for people to believe their leaders or other authorities on whom they depend are trustworthy, they must believe those individuals are both competent and motivated to fulfill all of their perceived responsibilities and other commitments. Elsbach (2004) extended and refined this general idea by identifying three specific elements that shape people's appraisals of a leader's trustworthiness. "To possess an image of interpersonal trustworthiness," she proposes, "is to be perceived by others as displaying (now and in the future) competence, benevolence, and integrity in one's behaviors and beliefs" (p. 275). More recently, Elsbach and Currall (2012) have embellished on this formulation to include "honesty, fairness, proficiency, and compassion" (p. 217).

In elaborating on how people evaluate a leader's trustworthiness, Elsbach and Currall (2012) further argue that leaders are judged with respect to at least two major types of trust, which they characterize, respectively, as *morality-based* and *competency-based* trust. Morality-based trust is defined as the "perception that a leader can be counted on to 'do the right thing' because he or she adheres to a set of acceptable behavioral principles" (p. 217). Competence-based trust is defined in terms of the "perception that a leader can be counted on to competently do his or her job because he or she has the appropriate skills and abilities" (p. 217).

Given these characterizations, it is not hard to see why practitioners and scholars alike have assumed that trust and perceived trustworthiness are vital to an efficacious leadership process. Clearly, organizational members and external constituents will be more receptive and responsive to leaders' influence attempts and other directives if those leaders are trusted and viewed as trustworthy.

Having laid this conceptual scaffolding, we turn now to elaborating some of the benefits that have been ascribed to trust and perceived trustworthiness in leadership contexts.

Benefits of Trust and Perceived Trustworthiness

As noted earlier, the ascension of trust as a major focus of recent social science research reflects, in no small measure, steadily accumulating evidence implicating trust as a critical factor influencing a variety of desired social and organizational outcomes (Dyer & Chu, 2003, Fukuyama, 1995; Putnam, 2000; Sztompka, 1999; and Uslaner, 2002). These include the effects of trust on (1) organizational performance, (2) voluntary deference to leaders, (3) and spontaneous sociality. We consider each of these benefits in turn.

Trust and Organizational Performance

To assess the then-current state of knowledge, Dirks and Ferrin (2002) performed a valuable meta-analysis of nearly four decades of research on the positive effects of trust on leadership effectiveness and organizational performance. They found that trust in leaders had a significant relationship with respect to a variety of important outcomes, including constituents' commitment to a leader's decisions, their commitment to the organization itself, reductions in reported intentions to turnover jobs, enhanced job performance and satisfaction, and increased levels of organizational citizenship behaviors. In a similar vein, Davis, Schoorman, Mayer, and Tan (2000) found that trust in management was associated with improved sales and profits, along with reduced turnover. In yet another study, Dirks (2000) reported a relationship between players' trust in their head coach and winning in the National Basketball Association. Finally, Grant and Sumanth (2009) found that trust in leaders was associated with enhanced prosocial motivations and behaviors among employees, at least within the context of service organizations.

Voluntary Deference and Compliance

In most organizations, the leadership role is inherently hierarchical, in the sense that one or more persons, operating from positions of authority or power, exert influence over one or more others (Barber, 1983), often designated followers or subordinates (although characterized in our chapter hereafter simply as *constituents*). In less hierarchical or "flat" organizations, leaders typically assert influence over their constituents vis-à-vis their centrality, power, or decision control (Ancona, Malone, Orlikowski, & Senge, 2007). Regardless of organizational structure or design, however, leadership is exerted more successfully when constituents voluntarily accept or defer to a leader's influence.

Consistent with this general argument, one important stream of research has examined the relationship between trust in leaders and various forms of voluntary deference by constituents. In discussing the importance of this issue, Tyler and Degoey (1996) noted that if organizational leaders had to continually explain or justify their decisions, their ability to lead would be greatly diminished. Second, because of the costs and impracticality of continually monitoring constituent performance, leaders cannot detect and punish every failure to cooperate or comply, nor can they recognize and reward every cooperative or compliant act. As a result, efficient and effective organizational performance depends upon constituents' commitment to their leaders and their concomitant willingness to voluntarily comply with their directives.

In addition to situations involving voluntary compliance or deference, trust is also important when conflicts arise within organizational or social settings. To the extent that leaders are charged with resolving such conflict, trust in the leader's fairness and impartiality is vital, particularly because it influences the acceptance of dispute resolution procedures and outcomes. Indeed, research has shown that individuals are more likely to accept outcomes, even if unfavorable to themselves, when their trust in an authority's benevolent motives is high (e.g., Brockner & Sigel, 1996; Tyler & Degoey, 1996).

Additional research by Brockner and his colleagues has investigated the influence of procedural variables on attributions regarding leaders' trustworthiness. In particular, Brockner and Siegel (1996) argued and found that procedures are important because they communicate information not only about a leader's motivations and intention to behave in a trustworthy fashion, but also their ability to do so, a factor they characterize as *procedural competence*. In support of their argument, they report evidence that procedures that are perceived as structurally and interactionally fair tend to increase trust, whereas lack of perceived structural and procedural fairness tends to elicit low levels of trust in leaders.

In a follow-up study and extension of these basic findings, Brockner, Siegel, Daly, and Tyler (1997) explored some of the conditions under which trust in leaders matters more or less. They argued that, all else equal, trust matters more to constituents when the outcomes they obtain are unfavorable. In explaining why this would be true, they noted that receipt of favorable outcomes does not raise issues of leaders' trustworthiness, because the outcomes themselves constitute evidence that the leader can be trusted to make decisions and perform behaviors consistent with the constituent's well-being. As a result, issues of trust are neither salient nor critical in determining support for the leader under these favorable circumstances. When outcomes are unfavorable, in contrast, trust becomes more critical, and leaders are less likely to receive ongoing support and trust. Brockner et al. tested this prediction in three different studies and found strong support for it.

Acts of Spontaneous Sociability and
Extra-Role Behaviors

In an influential discussion of trust, Fukuyama (1995) argued that one of the important consequences of trust is the *spontaneous sociability* it engenders. When operationalized in behavioral terms, spontaneous sociability refers to the myriad forms of cooperative and altruistic behavior that individuals are willing to engage in that enhance collective well-being and further the attainment of important collective goals.

Within organizational contexts, spontaneous sociability assumes many forms. Organizational members are expected, for example, to contribute their time and attention toward the achievement of collective goals, especially those that are articulated by their leader (Olson, 1965). Additionally, they are expected to share information with other organizational members (Kramer, 2006). Finally, they are expected to exercise responsible restraint when using valuable but limited organizational resources (Tyler & Degoey, 1996) and engage in those "above-and-beyond the call of duty" extra-role behaviors that further collective goals (Tyler & Blader, 2003).

To summarize, there exists substantial evidence of the varied and consequential benefits that follow when constituents trust their leaders. This raises the question of where such trust comes from. How are these important benefits of trust initially secured and sustained? The research literatures on the foundations of trust, and in particular the dynamics of the trust-building process, provide some useful answers to these questions.

Foundations of Trust and Perceived Trustworthiness

We have presented, we hope, a convincing case for the merits of trust and perceived trustworthiness. We have yet to elaborate, however, on how these desired benefits are secured. Fortunately, theory and research on the foundations of trust between leaders and constituents, and the dynamics of the trust-building process, has shed light on this issue (Creed & Miles, 1996; Sztompka, 1999; Zucker, 1986). In general, this research has emphasized the importance of (1) psychological, (2) interpersonal or social, (3) procedural, and (4) structural factors that promote the development and ongoing stability of trust between leaders and their constituents.

Because of the size of this literature, a comprehensive review far beyond the scale and scope of the present chapter, we will organize our discussion in terms of (1) interpersonal trust-building behaviors, (2) social bases of trust, (3) a consideration of the role of rules and norms to inculcate trust, and (4) the use of image management strategies and tactics to enhance perceived trustworthiness.

Interpersonal Trust-Building Behaviors

Empirically based models of trust development have shown that individuals' perceptions of others' trustworthiness, and their concomitant willingness to engage in trusting behavior when interacting with them, are largely history-dependent, interactional processes (see Lindskold, 1978 for a review). According to such models, trust between two or more individuals increases (or decreases) as a function of their cumulative history of positive (or negative) interactions. Interaction histories give individuals, in effect, a personal "data base" that can be used in assessing another's trust-related dispositions, intentions, and competencies.

Evidence of the importance of interactional histories in judgments about trust comes from a substantial body of experimental research linking specific patterns of behavioral interaction with changes in trust. For example, a number of studies have demonstrated that reciprocity in exchange situations enhances trust, while the absence or violation of reciprocity erodes it (Lindskold, 1978; Pillisuk & Skolnick 1968). In effect, trust begets further trust and distrust begets distrust.

In noting the formative role that interaction histories play in the emergence of trust, these models draw attention to two psychological facets of trust judgments. The first is that judgments about others' trustworthiness are anchored, at least in part, on individuals' *a priori* expectations about others' behavior. Second, those expectations change in response to the extent to which subsequent experience either validates or discredits them. Boyle and Bonacich's (1970) analysis of trust development is representative of such arguments. Individuals' expectations about trustworthy behavior, they posit, tend to change "in the direction of experience and to a degree proportional to the difference between this experience and the initial expectations applied to it" (p. 130).

Drawing on this research, we suggest that leaders can initiate trust-building in two ways. First, they can demonstrate their own trustworthiness at every opportunity. Second, they can demonstrate their willingness to trust their constituents by making themselves vulnerable to those constituents' actions.

Social Foundations of Presumptive Trust

Another approach to creating trust is to exploit the psychological and social factors that lead to a sort of "presumptive trust" in others (Kramer, 2010). Human beings are exquisitely equipped social information processors, literally "hard-wired" to learn to assess others' social proclivities toward trust and trustworthiness (Zak, 2008).

One basis for such presumptive trust between leaders and their constituents, it has been shown, is information regarding their common or shared membership in a probative social or organizational category. Brewer (1981) proposed there are a number of reasons why membership in a salient category can provide a basis for presumptive trust between social actors. First, shared membership in a given category can serve as a "rule for defining the boundaries of low-risk interpersonal trust that bypasses the need for personal knowledge and the costs of negotiating reciprocity" (p. 356) when interacting with other members of that category. Further, because of the cognitive consequences of social categorization and positive ingroup bias, individuals tend to attribute favorable characteristics such as honesty, cooperativeness, and trustworthiness to other ingroup members (Brewer, 1911). As a consequence, individuals can confer a sort of *deperson-alized trust* on other ingroup members that is based simply on their awareness of their shared category membership (Kramer, Brewer, & Hanna, 1996).

The most systematic development of such ideas applied to leadership contexts remains Hogg's (2005) social identity theory of leadership. According to his theory, group members evaluate leaders on the basis of the extent to which they exemplify or embody valued group attributes. "As group membership becomes increasingly salient," he posits, "leadership perceptions, evaluations, and effectiveness become increasingly based on how group-prototypical the leader is perceived to be" (2005, p. 57). Enhanced perceived prototypicality, he further argues, results in increased influence, social attraction, and positive attributions. Hogg and his research colleagues have offered strong empirical support for this theorized relation.

In sum, on the basis of these diverse strands of theory and evidence, it seems reasonable to posit that trust in the leadership process is enhanced when an underlying basis for perceived social commonality exists between leaders and their constituents. But are there other ways leaders can rely on to create and maintain trust? The answer is yes, as we show next.

Roles as a Basis for Presumptive Trust

Role-based trust represents another important form of potential presumptive trust found within organizational settings, and one which has special relevance to the leader-constituent relation. As with category-based trust, role-based trust constitutes a form of depersonalized or de-individualized trust because it is predicated on knowledge that a leader occupies a particular role in the organization, or has specific training in a role, rather than specific knowledge about the individual's personal capabilities, dispositions, motives, and intentions.

Roles can serve as proxies for personalized knowledge about other organizational members in several ways. First, as Barber (1983) noted, strong expectations regarding technically competent role performance are typically aligned with roles in organizations, as well as expectations that role occupants will fulfill the fiduciary responsibilities and obligations associated with the roles they occupy. Thus, to the extent that people within an organization have confidence in the fact that role occupancy signals both an intent to fulfill such obligations and competence in carrying them out, individuals can adopt a sort of presumptive trust based upon knowledge of role relations, even in the absence of personalized knowledge or history of prior interaction.

Such trust develops from, and is sustained by, people's common knowledge regarding the barriers to entry into organizational roles, their presumptions, the training and socialization processes that role occupants undergo, and their perceptions of various accountability mechanisms intended to ensure role compliance. As numerous scholars (Barber, 1983; Dawes, 1994) have noted, it is not the person in the role that is trusted so much as the system of expertise that produces and maintains role-appropriate behavior of role occupants. As Dawes (1994, p. 24) suggested in this regard, "We trust engineers because we trust engineering and believe that engineers are trained to apply valid principles of engineering, moreover, we have evidence every day that these principles are valid when we observe airplanes flying." As with other bases of presumptive trust, such roles function then to reduce uncertainty regarding role occupant's trust-related intentions and capabilities. They thus lessen the perceived need for, and consequent costs of, negotiating trust when interacting with them.

Rule–Based Presumptive Trust

If trust between leaders and their constituents is predicated on constituents' positive beliefs and expectations regarding their leaders, then both explicit and tacit understandings regarding what their leaders are likely to do may be critical in creating and sustaining trust. Organizational rules, both formal and informal, capture much of the knowledge that constituents have about such behaviors (March & Olsen, 1989).

Rule-based trust is predicated not on a conscious calculation of consequences, but rather on shared understandings and beliefs regarding the system of rules regarding appropriate behaviors—for both leaders and constituents. As March and Olsen (1989, p. 27) put it, rule-based trust is sustained within an organization "not [by] an explicit contract...[but] by socialization into the structure of rules." When reciprocal confidence in both leader's and constituents' socialization into, and continued adherence to, a normative system is high, mutual trust can acquire a taken-for-granted quality. Rules bind (behavior) and therefore build trust.

One way in which rules foster trust is through their effects on individuals' self-perceptions as well as their shaping of expectations about other organizational members. As March (1994) observed in this regard, organizations function much like "stage managers" by providing "prompts that evoke particular identities in particular situations" (p. 72). Miller (1992) offers an excellent example of this kind of socially constructed and ultimately self-reinforcing dynamic. In discussing the underpinnings of cooperation at Hewlett-Packard, Miller (1992) noted that, "The reality of cooperation is suggested by the open lab stock policy, which not only allows engineers access to all equipment, but encourages them to take it home for personal use" (p. 197).

From a strictly economic perspective, this policy simply reduces monitoring and transaction costs. However, from the standpoint of a rule-based conception of trust-related interactions, its consequences are more subtle and far-reaching. As Miller (1992) observes, "The open door symbolizes and demonstrates management's trust in the cooperativeness of the employees" (p. 197). Because such acts are so manifestly predicated on trust in others, they tend to breed trust in turn.

Rule-based practices of this sort can also exert subtle influences, not only on individuals' perceptions of their own honesty and trustworthiness, but also their expectations and beliefs about other organizational members' honesty and trustworthiness. As Miller (1992) notes in this regard, by eliminating time clocks and locks on equipment room doors at Hewlett-Packard, the organization builds a "shared expectation among all the players that cooperation will most likely be reciprocated" creating "a shared 'common knowledge' in the ability of the players to reach cooperative outcomes" (p. 197). By institutionalizing trust through practices at the macro-organizational (collective) level, trust becomes internalized at the micro (individual) level.

Creating Trust by Enhancing Perceived Trustworthiness

Our trust in leaders is obviously determined, as least in part by the extent to which we perceive them as trust*worthy*. As noted earlier, to be regarded as trustworthy, it is important that leaders be perceived by constituents as possessing at least three characteristics: (1) competence, (2) benevolence, and (3) integrity. In organizational contexts, perceived competence refers to the perceived abilities and skills that allow a leader to exert power and influence effectively. Perceived benevolence refers to the leader's motivation and intentions to do good on behalf of his or her constituents. Finally, perceived integrity refers to the leader's adherence to principles, ideals, and values that constituents expect.

Recognizing its importance, researchers have investigated the conditions under which people are likely to attribute trustworthiness to individuals occupying leadership positions. In one of the earliest studies, Gabarro (1978) found that perceived integrity, benign motives, consistency, openness, discreteness, functional competence, interpersonal competence, and decision-making judgment all contributed to attributions of trustworthiness. Along similar lines, Butler (1991) found that perceived availability, competence, consistency, fairness, integrity, loyalty, openness, overall trust, promise fulfillment, and receptivity influenced subordinates' judgments of an authority's trustworthiness.

Subsequent research has refined and extended our understanding of the factors that influence trustworthiness attributions in leadership contexts. Tyler and Degoey (1996) identified several important components of trustworthiness attributions. The first of these factors they characterize as *status recognition*, which reflects the extent to which leaders recognize and validate constituents' sense of full-fledged membership in their organization. A second important factor is *trust in benevolence*, which refers to constituents' beliefs that the leaders with whom they deal are well intentioned and honest in their decisions. A third critical factor is *neutrality*, which implies perceived fairness and impartiality in a leader's decisions and adjudications.

Taking a different tact, Elsbach and Elofson (2000) investigated two characteristics of the "packaging" of decisions that they theorized would influence people's perceptions of decision makers' competence-based trustworthiness. Specifically, they explored the impact of the *understandability* of a decision, positing that the ease or difficulty of understanding communications may be construed as an indication or signal of the decision makers' intentions or motivations. In particular, they reasoned that the use of hard to understand language, such as technical language or organizational jargon, may suggest some attempt at obfuscation. Accordingly, they predicted that decisions presented in terms of easy-to-understand language would lead, all else equal, to higher evaluations of competency-based trustworthiness than decisions described in terms of harder to understand language.

A second factor they examined was the impact of the *perceived legitimacy* of the decision process, arguing that decision processes that more clearly conform with normative and legitimate processes would result in higher evaluations of decision makers' competency-based trustworthiness. Although the first hypothesis was supported, the second was not.

Another approach to understanding how people assess a leader's trustworthiness is suggested by research on effective impression management and self-presentation strategies and tactics. One self-presentation tactic, for instance, that has been shown to reliably enhance perceptions of trustworthiness is demonstrating that one possesses similar attributes as the target of one's trust. People tend, all else equal, to trust those who are similar to them along some salient and presumably diagnostic dimension (e.g., DeBruine, 2002). Consistent with this notion, Cook, Kramer, Thom, Stepanikova, Mollborn, and Cooper (2004) found that social category similarity provided an important lubricant for trust in the context of doctor-patient relationships. The bases of similarity in their study included similarity with respect to gender, age, culture, and race/ethnicity.

Additionally, judgments of physician trustworthiness were enhanced by a variety of behavioral "cues" considered diagnostic of underlying competence and motivation. These include such cues as expressions of caring and empathy, direct eye contact, and body language indicating attentiveness and approachability. Providing and explaining recommendations and prescriptions also indicated greater trust and trustworthiness. Following a parallel logic, a few studies have shown that presenting one's self as *different from* or *dissimilar to* an untrustworthy other may also improve images of one's own trustworthiness (Elsbach, 2004).

In concert, such factors show that people's judgments about trust and perceived trustworthiness are often "cue-driven," reflecting our intuition that both verbal and nonverbal behaviors can be considered diagnostic signals of underlying trust-relevant dispositions.

Trust Creation and Maintenance within the Minnesota Mycological Society: An Illustrative Case Study

From a leadership standpoint, trust-building ultimately entails effective management of the perceived risks associated with action or inaction in a given organizational context. Leaders are charged, in effect, with creating and maintaining a "climate" or culture that fosters the production of trust in their organizations (Zucker, 1986).

Doing so, however, is easier said than done. As organizational theorist and social psychologist Richard Hackman and his colleagues have noted (Hackman, 2002; Hackman & Wageman, 2005; Wageman, Nunes, Burruss, & Hackman, 2008), one of the most challenging tasks that all leaders confront is to create the "conducive conditions" for desired outcomes. From this perspective, leaders who hope to be trusted must create organizational cultures in which trust is diffuse and strong. Fine and Holyfield (1996) offer an instructive illustration of how such conditions can be created. Specifically, they examined how leaders create perceptions of mutual trust and trustworthiness among members of the Minnesota Mycological Society.

This voluntary organization is comprised of amateur mushroom aficionados and provides an unusual—and unusually rich—setting in which to study the bases of trust and perceived trustworthiness for several reasons. First, and perhaps obviously, the costs of misplaced trust in this organization can be quite severe. Should a member consume a mushroom dish that someone else in the organization has prepared and mistakenly believes is safe for consumption, the end result can be serious illness and even, in rare cases, death.

Given such palpable risks, Fine and Holyfield aptly note, trust among members is vital—and easily lost, as even a single mistake can be costly. As a consequence, both leaders and members are likely to be exceptionally vigilant when it comes to assessing and maintaining each others' trust and trustworthiness, especially when it comes to their relevant motivation- and competence-based credentials (e.g., their knowledge of mushrooms, expertise, and diligence in preparing mushroom dishes, etc.).

Second, because membership in the organization is voluntary, exit is comparatively costless. As a result, if any doubts regarding the leader's or members' trustworthiness arise, individuals can simply leave (in effect, taking their trust elsewhere). If this happens, the organization will die. Thus, the organization's very survival depends upon the leaders' ability to successfully instill and sustain perceptions of high levels of trust and perceived trustworthiness among its members. As Fine and Holyfield put it, in order to survive, the organization must function like a "cocoon to protect members from the risks of its activities" (p. 34). The reason this cocoon metaphor is appropriate, they go on to suggest, is that trust in such an organization is "interactional, interpreted, and negotiated, [and] not fully determined or calculating" (p. 35). Because eating mushrooms is potentially dangerous, the organization must provide, therefore, both the resources to experience the risks involved in the activity and the knowledge and expertise to manage that risk.

Fine and Holyfield go on to identify three important functional processes which the leader must manage if trust is to be maintained, which they termed *awarding trust, managing risk*, and *transforming trust*. One way trust is created, they observed, is to award trust to other members even when full or adequate confidence in them (in terms of personal knowledge about the other and sufficient opportunity to vet their expertise) may be lacking. For example, considerable social pressure is exerted on newcomers to the organization, who are often also novices to the art of mushroom preparation and consumption, to eat dishes at banquets prepared by other members. As Fine and Holyfield put it, there is an insistence on members' trust. Thus, even if individuals remain privately anxious, their public behavior connotes high levels of trust—they eat and with enthusiasm (at least its display!). Collectively, these displays constitute a potent form of "social proof" to members that their individual acts of trust are sensible.

This shared, consensual insistence on trust is adaptive, of course, only if collective trustworthiness is actually in place within the organization (i.e., the members preparing and offering dishes really know what they are doing!). Accordingly, a second crucial element related to the management of trust within this organization occurs through practices and arrangements that ensure competence and due diligence.

How is this result achieved? One way to create competence and instill the discipline of due diligence is through the meticulous socialization of newcomers to the organization. For example, newcomers are encouraged to collaborate with more experienced individuals who know what is safe to eat and how to prepare it properly. Newcomers are motivated to participate in these socialization processes with appropriate levels of commitment because it helps them not only manage the risks of mushroom eating, but also, and not trivially, secure a place in the social order of the group. Newcomers want to learn, but they also want to achieve the status of accepted members in good standing. In turn, more seasoned organizational members teach newcomers out of a sense of obligation, having themselves benefited from instruction from those who came before them. This repaying of their own instruction constitutes an interesting temporal (trans-generational) variant of depersonalized trust and reciprocity. Experienced members also accept the responsibility of exercising vigilance over newcomers—watching what they do and with what level of motivation and care and conscientiousness.

Over time, Fine and Holyfield then go on to argue, new members acquire knowledge about the organization, and in so doing the nature of their trust is transformed. Early on, the organization is simply a "validator" of trust for the new member—they sense the organization is functioning well and has survived the test of time. Thus, it becomes in time an "arena in which trusting relations are enacted and organizational interaction serves as its own reward" (p. 29). As with trust in engineers and other professionals who have been thoroughly educated into a role and set of expertise associated with that role, this form of trust is not simply trust in the expertise of specific individuals, but more importantly, trust in a system that reliably produces expertise. To the extent all of these activities are shared by members, we should point out, leadership in this organization is to some degree shared or *distributed* (cf., Ancona, Malone, Orlikowski, & Senge, 2007).

There are other examples we could invoke of organizational leaders who explicitly proclaim the importance of trust in their organizations—and who "walk their talk"—by designing organizational cultures that foster it. For example, Ed Catmull, creative leader of the animation studio Pixar, has emphasized the importance of creating a trusting culture where everyone feels psychologically safe. The Pixar approach to trust-building and maintenance, he goes on to elaborate, is to "construct an environment that nurtures trusting and respectful relationships and unleashes everyone's creativity. If we get that right, the result is a vibrant community where talented people are loyal to one another and their collective work...I know what I'm describing is the antithesis of the free-agency practices that prevail in the movie industry, but that's the point: I believe that community matters" (p. 67).

Along similar lines, John Mackey, the founder and co-CEO of Whole Foods, counts both trust and trustworthiness as among the core values of his organization, noting that "trust in an essential human attribute and virtue. Trusting others and being trustworthy oneself are central to what it means to be fully human" (quoted in Mackey & Sisodia, 2013, p. 220). Accordingly, he has striven to diligently demonstrate his own trust in his employees and to create opportunities for them to demonstrate their trustworthiness in return. Mackey achieves this partly through his generous and shrewd delegation of discretion, authority, and accountability for decisions that affect the reliability and consistency of his organization's performance.

Conclusions, Enduring Questions, and Promising Directions for Future Research

In this chapter, we have hopefully demonstrated the considerable progress that has been made with respect to understanding the importance of trust between leaders and their constituents, as well as some of the foundations for that trust. Specifically, we have identified some of the psychological, social, and organizational factors that contribute to trust creation and maintenance. We have also elaborated on some of the benefits of such trust.

Despite the impressive strides in our understanding of these issues, some important lacunae or gaps persist in our knowledge. One area where our knowledge remains incomplete pertains to our understanding of the *structural* underpinnings of trust in leader-constituent relations. By structural underpinnings, we mean the features of organizational design that influence how leaders and their constituents interact, including how often and on what basis. Future research should explore these structural considerations, including how to *design* more effective and collaborative governance processes (Braithwaite & Levi, 1998). We also need to develop a better understanding of the structural factors that foster greater transparency and higher levels of perceived accountability (Bennis, Goleman, O'Toole, & Biederman, 2008). Already, preliminary inroads in this direction have been made (see, e.g., Braithwaite & Levi, 1998; Gillespie, Hurley, Dietz, & Bachman, 2012; Lorsch, Berlowitz, & Zelleke, 2005), but clearly more research is needed.

There also remains a dearth of well-developed theory and evidence pertaining to the effects of gender on trust in leaders. Most revealing in this regard is the fact that, in their comprehensive and impressive assessment of the gender and leadership literature, Eagly and Carli (2007) remain largely silent regarding the role trust plays in the process of leader development and success. This gap in our knowledge is particularly important because of accumulating evidence that women leaders are not only becoming more prevalent in leadership ranks, but also exert effective and sometimes even superior influence. Moreover, when gender is thrown into the causal mix, the relationships may be subtle and complex. For example, although her research did not examine these issues in a leadership context per se, Bohnet (2007) reported some provocative differences with respect to how men and women think about and respond to trust dilemmas, at least in the context of simple laboratory-based trust games. Similarly, Cook et al. (2004) found in their study of trust in doctor-patient relations, that the gender of the physician was often perceived by patients and sometimes physicians themselves as an important factor affecting trust levels, especially for female patients and female physicians. Such results clearly suggest gender may be an important factor affecting the level of trust and perceived trustworthiness between leaders and their constituents.

Another important area where our knowledge remains incomplete concerns cross-cultural differences in how leaders build trust. We do not know, for example, whether there are subtle cross-cultural variations in the verbal and nonverbal behaviors that are effective at conveying impressions of underlying trustworthiness. Similarly, we don't know whether the self-presentational strategies identified as effective in studies largely involving Western leaders and their constituents translate into equal efficacy in other countries.

We also don't know much about the specifics of trust-building in leadership contexts that involve cross-cultural interactions or collaborations. One promising direction for approaching this question is research on cultural intelligence. One of the most prominent researchers in this area, Christopher Earley (2002) has defined this construct in terms of "a person's capability to adapt effectiveness to new cultural contexts" (p. 274). Earley and Ang (2003) review an impressive body of evidence demonstrating that *cultural intelligence* is useful in helping individuals work effectively in a variety of cross-cultural contexts. It would be interesting to know specifically, however, whether leaders high in cultural intelligence might be more adept at understanding how to build trust across cultural divides.

Such trust-building skills may be especially vital for leadership success in our increasingly global and, in some respects, fractured and polarized world. Despite its *prima facie* importance, our lack of current knowledge regarding this relation is suggested by several observations. First, the extensive and impressive single-spaced, 890-page *Handbook of Cultural Psychology* (Kitayama & Cohen, 2007) contains not a single reference in its subject index to leadership. Moreover, it contains only a small handful of sentences pertaining to trust scattered over a scant five-pages. Similarly, Gelfand, & Brett's (2004) outstanding *Handbook of Negotiation and Culture* contains no references to leadership in its subject index, and only two brief references to trust. Pittinsky (2009) has recently argued the need for models of intergroup leadership to address problem of trust and distrust that cross cultural divides. These are, of course only a few of the promising directions that future inquiries might address.

Acknowledgments

We are grateful for the numerous and insightful comments provided by Al Goethals, Scott Allison, and David Messick to an earlier version of this chapter.

References

Ancona, D., Malone, T. W., Orlikowski, W. J., & Senge, P. M. (2007). In praise of the incomplete leader. *Harvard Business Review, 85*, 92–100.

Baier, A. (1986). Trust and antitrust. *Ethics, 96*, 231–260.

Barber, B. (1983). *The logic and limits of trust.* New Brunswick, NJ: Rutgers University Press.

Bennis, W., Goleman, D., O'Toole, J., & Biederman, P. (2008). *Transparency: How leaders create a culture of candor.* San Francisco, CA: Jossey-Bass.

Bohnet, I. (2007). Why women and men trust others. In B. S. Frey and A. Stutzer (Eds.), *Economics and psychology: A promising new cross-disciplinary field* (pp. 89–110). Cambridge, MA: MIT Press.

Boyle, R., & Bonacich, P. (1970). The development of trust and mistrust in mixed-motive games. *Sociometry, 33*, 123–179.

Braithwaite, V., & Levi, M. (1998). *Trust and governance.* New York: Russell Sage Foundation.

Brewer, M. B. (1981). Ethnocentrism and its role in interpersonal trust. In M. B. Brewer and B. E. Collins (Eds.), *Scientific inquiry and the social sciences* (pp. 345–359). San Francisco, CA: Jossey-Bass.

Brockner, J., & Siegel, P. A. (1996). Understanding the interaction between procedural distributive justice: The role of trust. In R. M. Kramer and T. Tyler (Eds.), *Trust in organizations* (pp. 390–413). Thousand Oaks, CA: Sage.

Brockner, J., Siegel, P. A., Daly, J. P., & Tyler, T. (1997). When trust matters: The moderating effects of outcome favorability. *Administrative Science Quarterly, 43*, 558–583.

Butler, J. (1991). Toward understanding and measuring conditions of trust: Evolution of a conditions of trust inventory. *Journal of Management, 17*, 643–663.

Catmull, E. (2008). How Pixar fosters collective creativity. *Harvard Business Review, 86*, 65–72.

Center for Public Leadership (2010). *National leadership index 2010: A national study of confidence in leadership.* Cambridge, MA: Harvard Kennedy School.

Chua, R., Ingram, P., & Morris M. W. (2008). From the head and the heart: Locating cognition-based and affect-based trust in manager's professional networks. *Academy of Management Journal, 51*, 436–452.

Cook, K. S. (2001). *Trust in society.* New York: Russell Sage Foundation.

Cook, K. S., Hardin, R., & Levi, M. (2005). *Cooperation without trust.* New York: Russell Sage Foundation.

Cook, K., Kramer, R. M., Thom, D. H., Stepanikova, Mollborn, S. B., & Cooper, R. M. (2004). Trust and distrust in physician-patient relationships: Antecedents and consequences. In R. M. Kramer and K. S. Cook (Eds.), *Trust in Organizations: Dilemmas and Approaches* (pp. 65–98) (Russell Sage Foundation Trust Series, Volume VII) New York: Russell Sage Foundation.

Covey, S. M. R. (2006). *The speed of trust: The one thing that changes everything.* New York. Free Press.

Creed, W. D., & Miles, R. E. (1996). *Trust in organizations: A conceptual framework.* In R. M. Kramer and T. R. Tyler (Eds.), *Trust in organizations* (pp. 16–38). Thousand Oaks, CA: Sage.

Davis, J., Schoorman, F. D., Mayer, R. C., & Tan, H. (2000). The trusted general manager and business unit performance: Empirical evidence of a competitive advantage. *Strategic Management Journal, 21*, 543–576.

Dawes, R. M. (1994). *House of cards.* New York: Free Press.

DeBruine, L. (2002). Facial resemblance enhances trust. *Proceedings of the Royal Society of London, 269*, 1307–1312.

Dirks, K. T. (2000). Trust in leadership and team performance: Evidence from NCAA basketball. *Journal of Applied Psychology, 85*, 1004–1012.

Dirks, K. T. (2006). Three fundamental questions regarding trust in leaders. In R. Bachmann & A. Zaheer (Eds.), *Handbook of trust research* (pp. 15–28). Northhampton, MA: Edward Elgar.

Dirks, K. T., & Ferrin, D. L. (2002). Trust in leadership: Meta-analytic findings and implications for organizational research. *Journal of Applied Psychology, 87*, 611–628.

Dirks, K. T., & Skarlicki, D. P. (2004). Trust in leaders: Existing research and emerging issues. In R. M. Kramer and K. S. Cook (Eds.), *Trust and distrust in organizations: Dilemmas and approaches* (pp. 21–40). New York: Russell Sage Foundation.

Dyer, J. H., & Chu, W. (2003). The role of trustworthiness in reducing transaction costs and improving performance: Empirical evidence from the United States, Japan, and Korea. *Organization Science, 14*, 121–142.

Eagly, A. H., & Carli, L. L. (2007). *Through the labyrinth: The truth about how women become leaders.* Boston, MA: Harvard Business School Press.

Earley, C. (2002). Redefining interactions across cultures and organizations: Moving forward with cultural intelligence. In B. M. Staw & R. M. Kramer (Eds.), *Research in organizational behavior* (Vol. 24, pp. 272–299.) New York: Elsevier.

Earley, C., & Ang, S. (2003). *Cultural intelligence.* Stanford, CA: Stanford Business Books.

Elsbach, K. D. (2004). Managing images of trustworthiness in organizations. In R. M. Kramer & K. S. Cook (Eds.), *Trust and distrust in organizations* (pp. 275–292). New York: Russell Sage Foundation.

Elsbach, K. D., & Currall, S. C. (2012). Understanding threats to leader trustworthiness: Why it's better to be called "incompetent" than "immoral." In R. M. Kramer & T. L. Pittinsky (Eds.), *Restoring trust in organizations* (pp. 217–240). New York: Oxford University Press.

Elsbach, K. D., & Elofson, G. (2000). How the packaging of decision explanations affect perceptions of trustworthiness. *Academy of Management Journal, 43*, 80–89.

Fine, G., & Holyfield, L. (1996). Secrecy, trust and dangerous leisure: Generating group cohesion in voluntary organizations. *Social Psychology Quarterly, 59*, 22–38.

Fukuyama, F. (1995). *Trust: The social virtues and the creation of prosperity.* New York: Free Press.

Gabarro, J. J. (1978). The development of trust and expectations. In A. G. Athos & J. J. Gabarro (Eds.), *Interpersonal behavior: Communication and understanding in relationships* (pp. 290–303). Englewood Cliffs, NJ: Prentice Hall.

Gelfand, M. J., & Brett, J. M. (2004). *The Handbook of negotiation and culture.* Stanford, CA: Stanford University Press.

Gillespie, N., Hurley, R., Dietz, G., & Bachman, R. (2012). Restoring institutional trust after the global financial crisis: A systemic approach. In R. M. Kramer & T. L. Pittinsky (Eds.), *Restoring trust in organizations* (pp. 185–216). New York: Oxford University Press.

Grant, A. M., & Sumanth, J. J. (2009). Mission possible? The performance of prosocially motivated employees depends on manager trustworthiness. *Journal of Applied Psychology, 94*, 927–944.

Grovier, T. (1994). An epistemology of trust. *International Journal of Moral and Social Studies, 8*, 155–174.

Hackman, J. R. (2002). *Leading teams: Setting the stage for great performances.* Boston, MA: Harvard Business School Press.

Hackman, J. R., & Wageman, R. (2005). When and how team leaders matter. In B. M Staw & R. M. Kramer (Eds.), *Research in organizational behavior* (Vol. 26, pp. 37–75). New York: Elsevier.

Hardin, R. (2002). *Trust and trustworthiness.* New York: Russell Sage Foundation.

Hardin, R. (2004). *Distrust.* New York: Russell Sage Foundation.

Hardin, R. (2006). *Trust.* Cambridge, UK: Polity Press.

Hetherington, J. J. (2005). *Why trust matters: Declining political trust and the demise of American liberalism.* Princeton, NJ: Princeton University Press.

Hogg, M. (2005). Social identity and leadership. In D. M. Messick & R. M. Kramer (Eds.), *The psychology of leadership* (pp. 53–80). Thousand Oaks, CA: Sage.

Hollis, M. (1998). *Trust within reason.* Cambridge, UK: Cambridge University Press.

Kitayama, S., & Cohen, D. (2007). *Handbook of cultural psychology.* New York: Guilford.

Kramer, R. M. (1996). Divergent realities and convergent disappointments in the hierarchic relation: The intuitive auditor at work. In R. M. Kramer & T. R. Tyler (Eds.), *Trust in organizations: Frontiers of theory and research* (pp. 216–245). Thousand Oaks, CA: Sage Publications.

Kramer, R. M. (2006). Social identity and social capital: The collective self at work. *International Public Management Journal, 9*, 25–45.

Kramer, R. M. (2011). Trust and distrust in the leadership process: A review and assessment of theory and evidence. In A. Bryman, D. Collinson, K. Grint, B. Jackson, & M. Uhl-Bien (Eds.), *Sage handbook of leadership* (pp. 136–150). Thousand Oaks, CA: Sage Publications.

Kramer, R. M., Brewer, M. B., & Hanna, B. J. (1996). Collective trust and collective action: The decision to trust as a social decision. In R. M. Kramer and T. R. Tyler (Eds.), *Trust in organizations* (pp. 357–389). Thousand Oaks, CA: Sage Publications.

Kramer, R. M., & Cook, K. S. (2004). *Trust and distrust in organizations.* New York: Russell Sage Foundation.

Kramer, R. M., & Lewicki, R. J. (2010). Repairing and enhancing trust: Approaches to reducing organizational trust deficits. In J. P. Walsh & A. P. Brief (Eds.), *Academy of management annals* (Vol. 4, pp. 245–278). New York: Academy of Management and Routledge (Taylor and Francis Group).

Kramer, R. M., & Pittinsky, T. (2012). *Restoring trust in organizations and leaders: Enduring problems, emerging perspectives.* Oxford, England: Oxford University Press.

Lane, C., & Bachamn, R. (1998). *Trust within and between organizations.* New York: Oxford University Press.

Lewicki, R. J., & Bunker, B. B. (1995). Trust in relationships: A model of trust development and decline. In B. B. Bunker & J. Z. Rubin (Eds.), *Conflict, cooperation and justice.* San Francisco: Jossey-Bass.

Lewis, J. D., & Weigert, A. (1985). Trust as a social reality. *Social Forces, 63*, 967–85.

Lindskold, S. (1978). Trust development, the GRIT proposal, and the effects of conciliatory acts on conflict and cooperation. *Psychological Bulletin, 85*, 772–793.

Lorsch, J. W., Berlowitz, L., & Zelleke, A. (2005). *Restoring trust in American business.* Cambridge, MA: MIT Press.

Mackey, J., & Sisodia, R. (2013). *Conscious capitalism: Liberating the heroic spirit of business.* Boston, MA: Harvard Business Review Press.

March, J. G. (1994). *A primer on decision making.* New York: Free Press.

March, J. G., & Olsen, J. P. (1989). *Democratic governance.* New York: Free Press.

Miller, G. J. (1992). *Managerial dilemmas.* New York: Cambridge University Press.

Nye, J. (2008). *The powers to lead.* New York: Oxford University Press.

Nye, J. S., Zelikow, P. D., & King, D. C. (1997). *Why people don't trust government.* Boston, MA: Harvard University Press.

Olson, M. (1965). *The logic of collective action.* New Haven, CT: Yale University Press.

Pillisuk, M., & Skolnick, P. (1968). Inducing trust: A test of the Osgood proposal. *Journal of Personality and Social Psychology, 8,* 121–133.

Pittinsky, T. (2009). *Crossing the divide: Intergroup relations and leadership.* Boston, MA: Harvard Business School Press.

Putnam, R. D. (2000). *Bowling alone: The collapse and revival of American community.* New York: Simon and Schuster.

Robinson, S. L. (1996). Trust and breach of the psychological contract. *Administrative Science Quarterly, 41,* 574–99.

Solomon, R. C., & Flores, F. (2001). *Building trust in business, politics, relationships, and life.* New York: Oxford University Press.

Sztompka, P. (1999). *Trust: A sociological theory.* Cambridge, UK: Cambridge University Press.

Tyler, T. R., & Blader, S. L. (2003). The group-engagement model: Procedural justice, social identity, and cooperative behavior. *Personality and Social Psychology Review, 7,* 349–361.

Tyler, T. R., & Degoey, P. (1996). Trust in organizational authorities: The influence of motive attributions on willingness to accept decisions. In R. M. Kramer & T. R. Tyler (Eds.), *Trust in organizations: Frontiers of theory and research* (pp. 331–356). Thousand Oaks, CA: Sage.

Uslaner, E. M. (2002). *The moral foundations of trust.* Cambridge, UK: Cambridge University Press.

Wageman, R., Nunes, E. A., Burruss, J. A., & Hackman, J. R. (2008). *Senior leadership teams: What it takes to make them great.* Bostson, MA: Harvard Business School Press.

Whitener, E. M., Brodt, S. E., Korsgaard, M. A., & Werner, J. M. (2006). Managers as initiators of trust: An exchange relationship for understanding managerial trustworthy behavior. In R. M. Kramer (Ed.), *Organizational trust: A reader* (pp. 140–169). New York: Oxford University Press.

Zak, P. J. (2008). The neurobiology of trust. *Scientific American Mind,* June issue, pp. 88–95.

Zucker, L. G. (1986). Production of trust: Institutional sources of economic structure. *Research in Organizational Behavior, 8,* 53–111.

CHAPTER NINE

Leaders and Their Life Stories: Obama, Bush, and Narratives of Redemption

Dan P. McAdams

In *Leading Minds: An Anatomy of Leadership*, Howard Gardner (1995) wrote: "Leaders achieve their effectiveness chiefly through the stories they relate" (p. 9). Leaders express stories in the way they live their own lives, and they aim to evoke stories in the lives of those they lead. "The artful creation and articulation of stories constitutes a fundamental part of the leadership vocation," Gardner claimed. Further, "it is *stories of identity*—narratives that help individuals think about and feel who they are, where they come from, and where they are headed—that constitute the single most powerful weapon in the leader's literary arsenal" (Gardner, 1995, p. 43).

Gardner's (1995) assertion is the starting point for my own psychological explorations of the lives and the leadership styles of two American presidents: Barack Obama and George W. Bush (McAdams, 2011, 2013a, 2013b). Despite the dramatic differences between these two leaders, both personified stories of personal and national *redemption*—quintessentially American life stories of the sort that many Americans, for better and for worse, seem to hold dear. In this chapter, I will frame my case studies of Obama and Bush within a growing empirical literature in personality, developmental, social, cognitive, and cultural psychology on the role of life stories in the formation and expression of human identity (Habermas & Bluck, 2000; Hammack, 2008; McAdams, 1996, 2013c; McAdams & McLean, 2013; McLean, Pasupathi, & Pals, 2007; Singer, 2004). In the spirit of Gardner (1995), moreover, I will consider how this literature might further inform the social-scientific study of political leadership. If a political leader's life story exists as a powerful resource for leadership itself, as Gardner (1995) maintained, then social scientists are sure to ask questions like these: How do the personal stories of political leaders relate to the public policy positions they take? What kinds of stories are effective in promoting a leader's agenda? And to what extent do leaders project their own life stories onto those whom they lead?

Leadership and Narrative

Storytelling is a powerful and versatile form of human communication (Bruner, 1990). Therefore, it should not be surprising to learn that leaders tell stories with great frequency and for many different purposes. In daily interactions, for example, leaders may use narratives to explain or illustrate a policy initiative, to persuade others to adopt their point of view, or to burnish a desired image as a forceful, competent, or compassionate authority. In a broader sense, leaders may work to craft the narrative of the organizations they lead. Boal and Schultz (2007) write: "Through dialogue and storytelling, strategic leaders shape the evolution of agent interactions and construct the shared meanings that provide the rationale by which the past, the present, and the future of the organization coalesce" (p. 411). If organizations themselves can be said to affirm and exemplify certain stories about their own identity and mission (Gabriel, 2000), then the leaders of organizations may often function as influential tellers of those tales.

Leaders may tell many different kinds of stories, but among the most powerful in their repertoire of narratives are those that draw directly upon personal, autobiographical experience. Through casual anecdotes, formal interviews, memoires and books, and other venues, leaders may project a life story that illuminates their values and life goals and that accounts for how they came to be the persons they are. Life storytelling is an especially common rhetorical strategy among charismatic leaders (Frese, Beimel, & Schoenborn, 2003), but its usage is widespread in many other leadership contexts as well.

Followers may evaluate the life story projected by a political leader in order to gauge how much they like, admire, and trust the leader (Weischer, Weibler, & Petersen, 2013). Life stories speak to a leader's *authenticity*, or the extent to which his or her actions, words, and identity correspond with each other. As Shamir and Eilam (2005) put it, "Leaders are authentic to the extent that they act and justify their actions on the basis of the meaning system provided by their life stories" (p. 396). In order to assess authenticity, their constituencies may evaluate the believability and coherence of a leader's life story, may search the story for an explanation of the leader's origins, and may look for what Pittinsky and Tyson (2004) call *authenticity markers*, or experiences in the leader's life that legitimate his or her status as an authentic group member, a leader who is "one of us" or "like me" and thereby worthy of my support.

In order to convey some degree of authenticity and verisimilitude, a leader's life story needs to provide a credible account of personal *development*. Shamir and Eilam (2005) suggest that such developmental accounts often articulate one or more of four classic themes. First, the story may identify early-emerging traits in a leader's life, to suggest that he or she was *born to lead*. Second, the story may describe a *learning process* whereby the protagonist gained lessons about leadership from mistakes made in life and from the influences of positive and negative mentors. In a third form, the story may illustrate how the leader *found a larger cause or ideological platform* with which to line up his or her personal aspirations. Finally, stories of leadership development often depict in vivid terms the *obstacles and adversities* that the protagonist needed to overcome in order to emerge as a leader.

Stories about overcoming adversity carry strong meaning in certain cultural contexts. They may, for example, suggest a *redemptive* understanding of human nature and a *progressive* vision for society. In that the protagonist endures tribulations to emerge strengthened in the end, the story asserts that people in general may be delivered from suffering to an enhanced status or state, and, correspondingly, that society itself may evolve from the negative realities of contemporary social life to a better world promised for the future. As Bennis (2003) writes, "authentic leaders create their own legends and become the authors of their own lives in the sense of creating new and improved versions of themselves" (p. 334). At the same time, their transformational personal visions may become templates for the kind of societal change they seek to bring about (Parameshwar, 2006). In the life stories of certain political and religious leaders, personal suffering is, moreover, the crucible within which truth and mission are forged. Winner of the Nobel Peace Prize for her fight against cultural discrimination in Central America, Rigoberta Menchu (1986) wrote of how her call to leadership originated in the suffering she experienced in her own life and witnessed in the lives of others:

> Through all my experiences, through everything I'd seen, through so much pain and suffering, I learned what the role of a Christian on this earth is... The work of revolutionary Christians is above all to condemn and denounce the injustices committed against the people... that is my cause. As I've already said, it wasn't born out of something good, it was born out of wretchedness and bitterness. (Menchu, 1986, pp. 246–247)

Many scholars have offered conjectures regarding the role of early suffering and adversity in the lives and life stories of leaders. Simonton (1994) observed that early trauma—such as parental loss, physical disability, and poverty—was especially prevalent in the biographies of leaders and those who have made outstanding creative contributions in the arts and sciences. In a study of 120 biographies of prominent leaders in the twentieth century, Ligon, Hunter, and Mumford (2008) found that those who were judged to be especially effective experienced more events in their lives wherein negative circumstances were transformed into positive outcomes. In addition, effective leadership was associated with empathy for others' suffering and with showing more kindness and compassion for other people, as well as experiencing more kindness and compassion as expressed by others. Whether the biographies written about leaders relate what has really happened in their lives or the subjective narratives that leaders and their followers have formed about the leader's life remains, in many instances, an open question. What seems clear, though, is that certain kinds of life stories enjoy favor over other kinds, when it comes to evaluating leaders (Weischer et al., 2013). How leaders, their followers, and their biographers tell the life story, therefore, matters greatly in determining a leader's identity in the here-and-now and his or her legacy for the future.

Narrative Identity

You don't have to be a leader to have a life story. Over the past three decades, social scientists and other scholars have articulated a rich assortment of conceptual variations on the general thesis that human beings create identity through life storytelling (e.g., Eakin, 1999; Freeman, 1993; McAdams, 1985, 1996; Shotter & Gergen, 1989). Within personality and developmental psychology, researchers have focused on the concept of *narrative identity*, which may be defined as an internalized and evolving story of the self that explains how the person came to be and where his or her life may be heading (McAdams & McLean, 2013). Combining one's personal reconstruction of the past with imagined scenarios for the future, narrative identity functions to provide one's life with a sense of meaning, purpose, and continuity. It is a person's own tale of becoming the person that he or she is, more of a *personal myth* than an objective accounting of the past. In constructing narrative identity, then, people become autobiographers of the self. Even if they never keep a diary or publish a memoir, many people *author their own lives* in the sense of creating and refining their identities through life narrative. And they frequently share those stories with others.

The cognitive tools for the construction of narrative identity begin to become available to aspiring authors in the adolescent years (Habermas & Bluck, 2000). Teenagers exhibit *autobiographical reasoning* when they draw upon specific episodes in their lives to formulate assertions about the self. For example, a young woman may explain why she wants to be a lawyer by recalling childhood experiences in which she enjoyed debating with other people, which led to her enjoying classes in high school in which she argued about politics and the law. She constructs a causal chain of events that explain, for herself and for others, how she came to be and where her life may be going. Or a young man may conclude that he is the kind of person who "stands up for the oppressed" after noting numerous events in his life in which he sided with the underdog. In the case of the lawyer-to-be, her autobiographical reasoning expresses what Habermas and Bluck (2000) term *causal coherence*, in that she is able to string personal events together to explain what she believes to be a causal sequence in her life. The young man exhibits *thematic coherence* in his life story, by deriving a superordinate theme that underlies different concrete events. Research suggests that as they move through adolescence and into their 20s, young people create life narrative accounts that exhibit increasing levels of causal and thematic coherence, as well as illustrating other markers of life-narrative facility like identifying clear beginnings and endings and incorporating foreshadowing, retrospective reflection, and vivid illustrations of personal growth and development (Habermas & de Silveira, 2008; McAdams et al., 2006; McLean & Breen, 2009).

As adolescents become more proficient in using the tools of autobiographical reasoning, they typically encounter many experiences with peers, parents, and teachers that encourage them to begin thinking more seriously about who they are and what kind of an adult they will someday be. Ever since Erik Erikson (1950) wrote about the identity challenges of youth, social scientists have identified the late teens and 20s as the prime developmental period for constructing a coherent sense of self and finding a self-affirming niche in society (Arnett, 2000; Kroger & Marcia, 2011; McAdams, 1985). From adolescence through the emerging adulthood years, young people construct narrative identity through a process of experiencing events, narrating those experiences to others, monitoring the reactions of others to those narrations, editing the narrations in response to the reactions, experiencing new events, narrating those new events in light of past narrations, and on and on. Over developmental time, then, selves create stories, which in turn create new selves, all in the context of significant interpersonal relationships and group affiliations (McLean et al., 2007). Narrative identity emerges gradually, through daily conversations and social interactions, through introspection, through decisions young people make regarding work and love, and through normative and serendipitous passages in life, as when a student meets with a vocational counselor to discuss "What do I want to do with my life?" or a young couple sit down to write their marriage vows.

Gender, ethnicity, race, and social class strongly shape the process of formulating a life story. Women tell different kinds of stories than men tell, based both on different experiences and different cultural expectations regarding the kinds of narratives women and men are supposed to tell (Franz & Stewart, 1994). Culture provides a menu of images, metaphors, and plots for the construction of narrative identity (Hammack, 2008; McAdams, 2013a). Adolescents and emerging adults sample from the menu in constructing individual life stories, aiming to find narrative forms that capture their own personal experiences, allow for their own limitations and constraints, and convey their aspirations for the future. They appropriate models for living that prevail in the cultures wherein their lives have their constituent meanings. In this sense, the authoring of a narrative identity is rarely experienced as an act of full authorial freedom, but rather as a cobbling together of life narrative that works within a particular sociohistorical context, given prevailing opportunities and constraints.

Generativity and the Redemptive Self

People continue to work on their life stories as they move into and through the midlife years. The work may be fast and furious during periods of personal upheaval, as with divorce or significant occupational changes, but it may involve no more than minor editing and tweaking of the life story during times of relative quiescence. As parents, teachers, and mentors, adults may tell stories about their lives to younger people, sometimes simply to entertain and at other times to provide moral instruction, cautionary tales, and the like (Bluck, 2003). As Erikson (1950) argued, adults become increasingly preoccupied with the psychosocial issue of *generativity* as they move into their midlife years. Generativity is an adult's concern for and commitment to promoting the well-being of future generations, as evidenced in parenting, mentoring, leadership, and engaging in a wide range of behaviors aimed at leaving a positive legacy of the self for future generations (McAdams & de St. Aubin, 1992). Research has demonstrated wide individual differences in the strength and salience of generativity among midlife adults, with high scores on measures of generativity showing positive associations with psychological well-being, effective parenting, positive social networks, religious and civic engagement, volunteering, and leadership (e.g., Hart, McAdams, Hirsch, & Bauer, 2001; McAdams, 2013d; Zacher, Rosing, Henning, & Frese, 2011). Self-storytelling may serve the function of generativity for many adults, especially those with strong generative inclinations. Through telling stories about their own lives, generative adults may try to help young people solve their own problems and meet their developmental needs.

What kinds of life stories do especially generative adults tell? In a series of empirical reports and case studies, McAdams and colleagues have shown that American adults scoring high on standardized measures of generativity tend to narrate their lives as tales of *redemption* (McAdams, 2013a; McAdams, Diamond, de St. Aubin, & Mansfield, 1997; McAdams et al., 2001). Compared to their less generative counterparts, highly generative American adults describe more scenes in their lives in which negative events were redeemed by positive outcomes. In some instances, the positive outcome follows directly from the negative event, as when the protagonist of the story is fired from a job but then meets his future wife the next day. In other instances, the narrator looks back upon the negative event as ultimately teaching a positive lesson or insight, fostering personal development, or leading to some manner of life enhancement many years down the road. For example, the narrator may conclude that his parents' divorce ultimately taught him important and life-enhancing lessons about love and commitment.

The theme of redemption lies at the center of a constellation of related themes that frequently characterize the life stories told by highly generative American adults (McAdams, 2013a). These stories often begin with the protagonist's receiving a unique blessing or advantage early in life, as if to suggest that he or she has been chosen for a positive destiny. Moreover, the young protagonist may be strongly affected by witnessing the suffering or misfortune of other people. Thus, highly generative adults are significantly more likely than those low in generativity to narrate early scenes in which they (1) experienced an early advantage compared to others and (2) witnessed suffering, oppression, injustice, and the like. The implicit message in these kinds of stories is this: *I am blessed, but others suffer.* Or, *I am the gifted protagonist who journeys forth into a dangerous world.* Typically, the protagonist commits the self steadfastly to a clear personal ideology that supports a generative mission in life, be that ideology religious, political, or ethical. Across the temporal landscape of the narrative, the protagonist repeatedly encounters negative events in the form of defeats, setbacks, losses, and the like. But negative events are often redeemed by positive outcomes. Looking to the future, the protagonist expresses hope and optimism that his or her efforts to make the world a better place will ultimately pay off. Taken together, then, the five themes of (1) enjoying an early advantage, (2) sensitivity to the suffering of others, (3) moral steadfastness, (4) redemption sequences, and (5) hope in prosocial goals for the future comprise an ideal narrative prototype for highly generative American adults, what McAdams (2013a) calls *the redemptive self.* Thematic patterns that bear striking resemblance to the redemptive self have been observed in the life stories of moral exemplars (Colby & Damon, 1992) and adults who have been recognized for lifetime achievements in promoting the social good (Walker & Frimer, 2007).

From adolescence onwards, life stories function as psychological resources for people, helping them solve various life problems and justify important life decisions (McAdams & McLean, 2013). As such, the redemptive self appears to be well designed for supporting a generative life at midlife. Working to promote the well-being of future generations—be it through raising children or engaging in political activism—is rarely easy. But if an adult's life story celebrates the power of redemption, he or she may be better equipped, psychologically speaking, to endure the hardships that typically come with generative efforts, confident that difficulties today will lead to positive results in the future. Moreover, if a midlife adult's life story suggests that he or she was blessed or advantaged early on in life, and sensitized early on to the suffering of others, that same adult may work hard to *give back* to society, in gratitude for the early advantage. The adult may come to believe that he or she has been chosen by God, fate, good luck, good genes, or some other mechanism to make a positive mark on society, to fulfill a generative destiny. The thematic dynamic here is reminiscent of what Parameshwar (2006) and other scholars in the leadership literature have described as the development of higher purpose through experiences of suffering. Leadership itself, especially in political and religious contexts, may invoke feelings of generativity, so it should not be surprising to learn that highly generative adults and certain types of leaders may construct similar kinds of stories about their lives.

Finally, it is important to note that the themes articulated in the redemptive self carry substantial cultural meaning. McAdams (2013a) has argued that the redemptive self is a characteristically *American* brand of narrative identity, reflecting themes that have been historically cherished and contested in American cultural life. As reflected in Hollywood movies, American political discourse, folk conceptions in American history and heritage, and many other cultural expressions, Americans love redemptive narratives, even as they realize how limited and unrealistic these stories can sometimes be. Among the favorites in the canonical American anthology of redemptive tales are stories of (1) atonement, (2) upward social mobility, (3) liberation, and (4) recovery.

Going back to the Massachusetts Bay Puritans and forward to the born-again tales of Christian evangelicals, stories of *atonement* trace the redemptive move—sometimes sudden, sometimes gradual—from sin to salvation. Canonized as the American Dream, stories of *upward mobility* found their earliest expression in Benjamin Franklin's iconic autobiography (1771). They have been reworked ever since in Horatio Alger stories (the late nineteenth century), immigrant narratives of aspiration, and countless other tales about how America is the land of boundless opportunity. Contemporary stories of personal *liberation* have their deepest cultural roots in the nineteenth-century narratives of escaped African American slaves, an extraordinarily powerful and elastic line of discourse that may be traced forward to movements for civil rights, women's liberation, and (most recently) the rights and dignity of gays, lesbians, and other oppressed groups. Finally, stories of *recovery* describe how protagonists have lost some kind of valued quality—health, wholeness, innocence, purity—and now seek to get it back. As expressed in 12-step programs, tales of psychotherapy, recidivism, and a host of other popular forms, recovery narratives chart the redemptive move from sickness, addiction, crime, or abuse to the restoration of the good inner self (Dunlop & Tracy, 2013; Maruna, 2001). Once upon a time, I was good and pure. And then the bad things happened. Now, I am seeking to recover the goodness that was lost.

A Redemptive Tale of Liberation: Barack Obama

In his early 30s, Barack Obama sat down to write his own life story. Published in 1995, *Dreams from My Father* provides a vivid account of Obama's childhood in Hawaii and Indonesia, his college years in California and New York, his work as a community organizer in Chicago, and a trip he took, in his 20s, to Kenya in order to spend time with his deceased father's extended family. His parents divorced shortly after his birth. Raised by his White mother, Ann Dunham, and her parents, the young Barry Obama met his father only once, when Barack Sr. returned to Hawaii for a short visit in 1971 (Barry was 10 years old). At one level, *Dreams* is about how the son came to terms with his dreams and fantasies about his absent father and how he searched to discover who his father really was. It is also about the protago-nist's struggle to figure out how to be a Black American man. Because very few African Americans attended the Punahou School in Honolulu, Barry Obama earnestly studied up on African American culture—he learned how to be Black—by watching television shows about African American life, listening to African American music, and reading magazines and books featuring such African American icons as Ralph Ellison, Langston Hughes, and Malcolm X. Born to a White mother and Black father, he struggled to reconcile the racial polarities that he experienced in high school:

> I learned to slip back and forth between my black and white worlds, understanding that each possessed its own language and customs and structures of meaning, convinced that with a bit of translation on my part the two worlds would eventually cohere. Still, the feeling that something wasn't quite right stayed with me, a warning that sounded whenever a white girl mentioned in the middle of a conversation how much she liked Stevie Wonder; or when a woman in the super-market asked me if I played basketball; or when the school principal told me I was cool. I did like Stevie Wonder, I did love basketball, and I tried my best to be cool at all times. So why did such comments set me on edge? (Obama, 1995, p. 82)

At Occidental College, Obama took classes in politics, history, and litera-ture mainly, and he made friends with the more politically active Black students on campus. After his sophomore year, he transferred to Columbia University, desiring a more urban and diverse social environment. In his early 20s, Obama went through an especially intense period of identity search. As he described it years later, "questions of identity, questions of purpose, ques-tions of, not just race, but also the international nature of my upbringing" all came to a head at Columbia (Remnick, 2011, p. 114). Obama "did a lot of reading and a lot of thinking and a lot of walking through Central Park," and "somehow I emerge[d] on the other side of that ready to take a chance in what is a pretty unlikely venture: moving to Chicago and becoming an organizer. So I would say that's a moment when I gain[ed] a seriousness of purpose that I had lacked before" (Remnick, 2011, p. 114).

At age 24, Obama moved to Chicago to take a position as a community organizer under the direction of Jerry Kellman. A White Jewish activ-ist from New York, Kellman headed a coalition of churches and com-munity groups in an area of abandoned steel mills, dilapidated housing, high crime rates, and bad schools. Kellman needed a Black organizer for the largely African American citizenry on the far south side of Chicago. By dint of complexion and vocation, Barack Obama fit the part. Obama worked in various capacities with neighborhood groups, churches, the police, and politicians in Chicago. He organized neighborhood cleanups and crime-watch programs, sponsored career days for area youth, and worked to secure agreements from city alderman to improve sanitation service. The assignments were grueling, and Obama experienced more failures than successes in the early months. Despite the setbacks, however, he felt irresistibly drawn to community organizing for what he described as its "promise of redemption" (Obama, 1995, p. 135).

In his biography of Obama, David Remnick (2011) characterizes *Dreams* as a "narrative of ascent." In a narrative of ascent, the protagonist "begins in a state of incarceration or severe deprivation. He breaks those bonds so that he may go out, discover himself, and make his imprint on the world" (Remnick, 2011, p. 231). To give *Dreams* this kind of narrative feel, Obama (1995) opens the book with a dark and foreboding sequence. Age 21 and living in New York, he first learns of the death of an old man, whose body is found on the third floor landing of his apartment building. Next, he receives a phone call from his sister, telling him that their father is dead. Known as "the Old Man" back in Africa, Barack Sr. died drunk behind the wheel of his wrecked automobile. The narrator remarks: "At the time of his death, my father remained a mystery to me, both more and less than a man" (Obama, 1995, p. 5). Obama then circles back to tell the story of his more-or-less happy childhood in sunny Hawaii. But the early scenes leave a dark cloud to remind the reader that this is fundamentally a redemptive narrative, tracking the move from suffering to enhancement. In Obama's case, the suffering is less his own than it is the collective experience of African American men and women. Even though he never experienced slavery itself, nor even the kind of Jim Crow discrimination that many American Blacks endured in the twentieth century, the protagonist of *Dreams* eventually comes to identify with his African American forerunners. When a friend visited Obama at Harvard Law School, the friend noticed that he was reading Taylor Branch's *Parting of the Waters*, a celebrated history of the civil rights movement. "What do you think of Branch's book?" the friend asked. Obama nodded at the book and then said with absolute confidence and not a trace of irony, "Yes, it's *my* story" (Remnick, 2011, p. 13).

In the narrative identity that Barack Obama began to construct for his life in his 20s, community organizing became part of a broader political vocation that he associated with the grand narrative of African American—and more generally *American*—liberation and progress. His own story becomes part of the long arc of history that bends toward justice, as Obama described it, quoting Martin Luther King, Jr., running from the Emancipation Proclamation to King himself, and encompassing women's suffrage, civil rights, and the expansion of freedom and equality. Moreover, the search to discover the story—the soul-searching quest to examine one's life closely in order to find one's generative calling in life—is part-and-parcel of the story itself. The narrator of *Dreams* sees himself as a relentless explorer and questioner of the self who finally comes to understand that he is the culmination of a redemptive narrative of American liberation. The protagonist may not have directly battled oppression in his own life, but because others before him did, he is able to carry forth the banner of liberation, justice, and equality. As much as his personal gifts of oratory and his boundless ambition, Obama's personal story of redemption through liberation is a key to his political success. The story of self-exploration and the resultant psychological and political identification with a long arc of justice continues to inspire millions of Americans, especially those drawn to liberal political causes (McAdams et al., 2008; McAdams, Hanek, & Dadabo, 2013). It is a redemptive story that, to quote the iconic lines from Jesse Jackson, "keeps hope alive."

Obama's personal story supports a progressive policy agenda in American politics. It also suggests a particular style of leadership itself, one that emphasizes reasoned analyses, conciliation, and compromise while adhering to underlying principles of social justice, egalitarianism, and progress through government intervention. Obama's story tells us that, over the long haul, progress will be achieved through dialogue, as polarized factions eventually find common ground and potentially reasonable people eventually learn to pursue common goals. As the biracial protagonist travels back and forth between groups in search of a common ground for identity in high school, so too does the middle-aged protagonist, now occupant of the White House, endeavor to split the differences between various factions in Congress and the American electorate, in search of a policy consensus.

While praiseworthy in principle, Obama's conciliatory and doggedly hopeful approach to leadership may frustrate those allies, like liberal activists, who want a more muscular strategy, and it may be viewed as weakness by the opposition. The president of the United States is not a mere community organizer, after all. Moreover, his emphasis on reasoned analysis and rational deliberation suggests to some critics that he might have done better to stay at the University of Chicago Law School, where he once taught constitutional law. President Obama achieved the one notable victory of passing health care reform in 2010, but as I write this (November of 2013), he has yet to find a way, after five years, of developing coalitions between Democrats and Republicans on the most important issues facing the United States, such as the budget and foreign affairs. Despite the fact that he and his story both proclaim the power of conciliation, common ground, and human reason, his detractors view him to be extraordinarily polarizing. So far, the disconnect between his story and his legacy as president is striking, and serves as a deep source of disappointment to the millions of supporters whose personal and political identifications resonate with a redemptive American narrative of liberation. As a rejoinder, however, I suspect that Barack Obama might quote Martin Luther, King, Jr. The arc of history is long...

Redemption through Recovery and Atonement:
George W. Bush

If Barack Obama needed to find the father who had abandoned him, George W. Bush needed to lose the father he had known all his life.

By the time George W. Bush enrolled in Yale University in 1964, his father—George Herbert Walker Bush—was already a millionaire businessman and a rising star in the Republican Party. A decorated fighter pilot in World War II, a varsity athlete, and top student during his own time at Yale, a fabulously successful oil tycoon in Texas, and an all-around nice guy with hundreds of close friends and a matchless family pedigree, the father was an impossible act to follow—and yet the son sought to follow it. Like his father, George W. Bush attended the elite Andover Academy for high school and was inducted into the secret Skull & Bones Society at Yale, but his grades were always mediocre and he excelled at fraternity beer pong rather than varsity baseball. Like his father, he flew fighter jets during wartime (the Vietnam War), but over the sunny skies of Texas as a member of the Texas Air National Guard, rather than in actual battle. In a coincidence that typically only happens in Victorian novels, he proposed marriage to a coed from Smith College at the age of 20, which was the age at which George Bush Sr. proposed marriage to Barbara Pierce, who happened to be a student at Smith College in her day. George Sr. and Barbara eventually became president and first lady, 1989–1993; the son's engagement to Cathy Wolfram broke off during his senior year. And like his father, George W. Bush tried to make his fortune in the oil industry, but in the son's case every hole his companies ever drilled, during his 20s and 30s, came up dry. In terms of narrative identity, George W. Bush spent the bulk of his emerging adulthood years fashioning a story for his life that followed, chapter and verse, the heroic narrative of his father. The authorial effort failed miserably; the first draft of the son's narrative identity never went to press.

There were at least two reasons that George W. Bush was never able to create the kind of story for his life that his father constructed, even though he, like his brothers (Jeb, Marvin, and Neal), idolized his father. First, the son was nothing like the father, in terms of temperament, intellect, and life experiences. Achievement-oriented and goal-focused from an early age onward, the father grew up fast in wartime and felt strong urgency to launch an adult life of hard work and serious responsibility at the war's end. By contrast, the son spent his 20s and early 30s in what he described as a "nomadic period," lacking purpose and direction. The second reason, related to the first, is that George W. Bush abused alcohol from college onwards, for over two decades. The Delta Kappa Epsilon (DKE) fraternity parties at Yale were like the movie *Animal House*, and George W. Bush regularly played the role made famous by John Belushi. As one fraternity brother recalled those times, "we drank heavily at DKE. It was absolutely off the wall—appalling. I cannot for the life of me figure out how we made it through" (Andersen, 2002, p. 64). Throughout his 20s and 30s, George W. Bush drank so heavily that friends and family members worried that he was becoming an alcoholic. Even as he held down various jobs, started a family, and taught Sunday school at the local Methodist church, Bush continued to live a life that was dominated by what he called "the 4 Bs": "beer, bourbon, and B & B" (Andersen, 2002, p. 106). On more than one occasion, his wife threatened to leave him. "Its me or Jim Beam!" she is reported to have told him. For a long time, it was not clear what choice he would make.

In his 30s, George W. Bush began to turn his life around. Importantly, the effort involved (1) making decisive changes in behavior and commitments and (2) creating a new story about who he was and who he might become. As described in many biographical sources and his two autobiographies (Bush, 1999, 2010), George W. Bush began to construe his life as a story of redemption through atonement and recovery. It would become a story about atoning for his sins and recovering the innocence, goodness, and sobriety of an earlier time (McAdams, 2011). Whereas Obama's story affirmed self-exploration and the grand American narrative of social progress, Bush affirmed an equally powerful narrative of self-regulation and the restoration of a golden age. Whereas the cultural and political sources for Obama's story may be traced to nineteenth-century slave narratives and the powerful rhetoric of personal emancipation, Bush's personal story, which is also deeply political, recalls the New England Puritans, Christian revivals, and a powerful strand of conservative sentiment in American history that celebrates American exceptionalism and longs for a renewal of American greatness. As different as these two stories are, both are deeply redemptive and quintessentially American.

In Bush's case, the narrative is marked by three life turning points. First, marrying Laura Welch at age 31 helped to settle his wanderlust and reinforce a new image of himself as a responsible adult who is capable of commitment. Bush (1999) characterized his marriage to Laura as "the best decision I ever made" (p. 79). Second, Bush experienced a profound religious conversion in his late 30s, partly as a result of private consultations with an itinerant preacher named Arthur Blessitt. In the spring of 1984, Blessitt and Bush prayed together in a Holiday Inn coffee shop in Midland, Texas, where Bush followed the evangelical practice of accepting Jesus as his lord and savior. In doing so, he incorporated into his narrative identity a set of culturally mediated metaphors and concepts for the life course—ideas regarding sin and salvation, the story of the prodigal son, the sense of being chosen by God, the role of epiphany in self-development—that have colored the life narratives of American evangelicals for nearly 200 years, going back to the Christian tent revivals of the early nineteenth century (McAdams, 2013a). Third, on the morning after his fortieth birthday celebration, still suffering from a killer hangover, Bush went for his customary run, and upon returning pledged to Laura that he would never drink again. If the public record is to be believed (and there is no reason to doubt it), he never did. He gave it all up, cold turkey. In the redemptive story Bush regularly tells, he traces his subsequent success in business (as part-owner of the Texas Rangers baseball team) and in politics to his swearing off alcohol. And he mainly credits Laura and Jesus for his dramatic self-regulatory accomplishment. Along with the father he so wanted to be, they are the main heroes in George W. Bush's narrative identity, the powerful and virtuous agents who helped to redeem the story's protagonist.

As a story of recovery, Bush's narrative identity puts into a meaningful sequence more than the protagonist's triumph over alcohol addiction. It also accounts for and celebrates his recovery of the lost innocence and freedom of his youth, growing up in Midland, Texas (McAdams, 2011). In Bush's personal mythology, Midland symbolizes a psychological and social Eden. It represents the values of self-reliance, social responsibility, and freedom—political freedom in the sense that men and women are free to pursue happiness and the best that life and liberty have to offer, and psychological freedom from the forces that hold people back in the pursuit of happiness, like alcohol. "When you step outside in Midland, Texas," Bush (1999, p. 56) wrote, "your horizons suddenly expand. The sky is huge." "Appropriately, 'the sky is the limit' was the slogan in Midland when I arrived [returned] in the mid-1970s, and it captured the sense of unlimited possibilities that you could almost feel and taste in the air." Recalling childhood, Bush (1999) painted Midland in sentimental and romantic hues as the paradigmatic American small town where children are safe, adults are self-reliant and responsible, and everybody looks out for everybody else:

> Midland was a small town, with small-town values. We learned to respect our elders, to do what they said, and to be good neighbors. We went to church. Families spent time together, outside, the grown-ups talking with neighbors while the kids played ball or with marbles and yo-yos. Our homework and school work were important. The town's leading citizens worked hard to attract the best teachers to our schools. No one locked their doors, because you could trust your friends and neighbors. It was a happy childhood. I was surrounded by love and friends and sports. (Bush, 1999, p. 18)

Bush's personal story of atonement and recovery functioned as a psychological resource to sustain his midlife commitments to work, family, and government service. He believed that God had chosen him for a special destiny in life not so much because he was born into a famous American family but because of his struggles with alcohol and faith. A sinner now saved, he was freed up to pursue his own manifest destiny, which he believed would take him all the way to the White House, which of course it did. Moreover, his personal story inspired millions of Americans who often struggle with the same impediments to personal freedom that tormented Bush in his nomadic period—alcohol, drugs, and other addictions that keep men and women from working hard and being safe, that is, those forces that keep men and women from enjoying the fruits of Midland. In the beginning was Midland, and Midland was good. Midland represents universal values, God-given, inalienable goods that people the world over should enjoy.

In its longing to return to the golden age of Midland, the redemptive story that George W. Bush constructed in midlife affirms, on a political level, many of the values and favored images of American conservatism (Sullivan, 2006). At its heart, conservatism seeks to *conserve* cherished elements from an imagined past. Among American conservatives today, the most cherished values they hope to conserve include liberty, self-reliance, and personal responsibility. Anything that is perceived to stand in the way of these values—like government regulation, higher taxes, threats to traditional authority, or alcohol addiction—is held in great suspicion. The greatest threat to life in Midland is tyranny, of the sort displayed by *dictators such as Iraq's Saddam Hussein*. In the same way that God (and his own focused determination) had helped Bush to overcome the tyranny of alcohol and restore freedom and goodness to his own life, so too might President Bush, with the blessing of God and history, overcome the greatest enemy to liberty in the Middle East, Saddam Hussein.

In *George W. Bush and the Redemptive Dream* (McAdams, 2011), I argue that among the many reasons that President Bush launched a pre-emptive invasion of Iraq in March of 2003 was his sincere belief that Iraqi citizens deserved to live in Midland, too. Bush (consciously and unconsciously) aimed to achieve many ends with the Iraq invasion—finding and destroying weapons of mass destruction, stabilizing the Middle East and protecting Israel, opening up business opportunities for American oil interests, avenging threats to his own father, George Bush Sr., delivered by Hussein years before, and protecting the homeland in the wake of 9/11. In the mix, however, one cannot dismiss his inclination to project his own story onto world affairs, a psychological move that proved to bring disastrous consequences. By delivering the Iraqi people from their evil dictator, Bush could restore what he imagined to be the primal state of freedom and goodness. It is a weird coincidence, no doubt, that Baghdad sits near the imagined site of the mythical Garden of Eden, where the Tigris and Euphrates Rivers flowed. Both energized and *trapped* by his own life story (he could, unfortunately, see the world no other way), Bush felt compelled to bring freedom to Iraq.

In George W. Bush's redemptive story for America, he was chosen to lead the struggle against evil tyranny, so as to restore God's gift of security and freedom, both for America and for Iraq. It is with respect to this redemptive story, he believed, that he and his presidency would ultimately be judged. "What matters [most] is the emergence of a free society where people realize their lives are better off," he told the journalist Bob Woodward (2004, p. 424). "And where they work through their traumas so they can seize the moment...It is *the story of the 21st century*."

President Bush's response to Woodward captures perfectly the basic narrative arc of his own redemptive life story. People need to "work through their traumas so they can seize the moment," just as George W. Bush himself worked through his own difficulties in life, before he seized the moment by finding Jesus and giving up alcohol forever. The result of the

redemptive move is the "emergence of a free society where people realize their lives are better off." What matters is the restoration of Midland,
with its God-given values of security, freedom, and self-determination. It
is, Bush believed, "*the* story of the 21st century." Instead, it turned out to
be *his* story projected onto *our* time.

Conclusion

Like most adults living in modern societies, men and women who become
leaders in business, religion, politics, and other arenas construct stories to
make sense of their own lives. These internalized and evolving narratives
of the self explain to the self and others how the person came to be the
person that he or she is becoming. By reconstructing the remembered
past and connecting it to an imagined future, the life story—or narrative identity—provides a person's life with a sense of unity, meaning, and
purpose. Adults derive psychological sustenance from their own narrative
identities. Moreover, leaders may draw upon their life stories to enhance
their status and promote their agenda among those whom they have been
chosen to lead. Self-storytelling is a powerful tool for leadership itself. In
some contexts, especially those linked to religion or politics, followers
may look to the leader's life story for authenticity and inspiration.

Presidents Barack Obama and George W. Bush personified and articulated personal life stories that have inspired millions of Americans in the
first two decades of the twenty-first century. If they had not done so, they
would have never been elected president. Of course, Obama and Bush
appeal to dramatically contrasting constituencies. There indeed may be no
individual American alive at the moment who finds *both* of their stories to
be inspiring! Yet both stories draw from a wellspring of characteristically
American imagery and rhetoric about the power of human redemption.
Although he suffered relatively little by way of discrimination and oppression as a boy and young man, Barack Obama came to identify his life with
the progressive American narrative of expanding civil rights, traced back
to African American slave narratives from the nineteenth century and forward to the discourse of equal rights for women, people of color, gays and
lesbians, and other groups who have historically been marginalized, dis-
enfranchised, and even enslaved. George W. Bush drew upon an equally
compelling tradition of myth and rhetoric centered on Christian atonement and the recovery of American goodness, a line that can be traced
back at least as far as the stories of the Massachusetts Bay Puritans and
forward to the rhetoric of American entrepreneurship, self-help, and self-
reliance. Not surprisingly, Obama's story appeals, in style and substance,
to a generally liberal political sensibility in contemporary American politics, whereas Bush's narrative appeals to many conservatives.

In articulating redemptive stories for their own lives, Obama and Bush
are creating narrative identities that bear resemblance to the stories that

many highly generative American adults construct to make sense of their remembered past and imagined future. Whether they affirm liberation or recovery, equal rights or individual responsibility, redemptive life narratives help to sustain hope and confidence as generative adults work hard to provide for their families and contribute in positive ways to their communities. For many people, redemptive stories can promote psychological health and resilience, as many empirical studies have shown. For leaders, these same kinds of stories can animate their leadership agendas and inspire their followers.

At the same time, personal stories of redemption may bring with them unintended negative consequences for the leaders who construct these stories. It is surely too soon to pass historical judgment, but it seems plausible to assert that President Bush's powerful personal narrative of redemption through recovery may have worked, along with other factors, to motivate an ill-conceived invasion of another nation. His commitment to his own redemptive story about restoring the goodness and freedom that was Midland may have colored his understanding and severely narrowed his range of policy options in the months following 9/11. In the case of President Obama, his steady commitment to a progressive narrative of expanding rights and personal liberation, along with his dogged belief in the power of reason and compromise, may contribute to a leadership style that some have criticized as overly restrained, aloof, and diffident. One might provisionally suggest that both presidents may have invested too much faith into their respective redemptive narratives—leading one to strike out rashly in order to restore a desired end, and the other to wait patiently for a desired end that he implacably believes will surely come to be, in the very long run.

Note

Preparation of this chapter was supported by a grant from the Foley Family Foundation to establish the Foley Center for the Study of Lives at Northwestern University. Send correspondence to Dan P. McAdams, Psychology Department, 2120 Campus Drive, Evanston, IL 60208.

References

Andersen, C. (2002). *George and Laura: Portrait of an American marriage.* New York: William Morrow.

Arnett, J. J. (2000). Emerging adulthood: A theory of development from the late teens through the twenties. *American Psychologist, 55,* 469–480.

Bennis, W. G. (2003). The crucibles of authentic leadership. In J. Antonakis, A. T. Gianciolo, & R. J. Sternberg (Eds.), *The nature of leadership* (pp. 331–342). Thousand Oaks, CA: Sage.

Bluck, S. (2003). Autobiographical memory: Exploring its functions in everyday life. *Memory, 11,* 113–123.

Boal, K. B., & Schultz, P. L. (2007). Storytelling, time and evolution: The role of strategic leadership in complex adaptive systems. *The Leadership Quarterly, 18,* 411–428.

Bruner, J. (1990). *Acts of meaning.* Cambridge, MA: Harvard University Press.

Bush, G. W. (1999). *A charge to keep.* New York: Harper.

Bush, G. W. (2010). *Decision points.* New York: Random House.

Colby, A., & Damon, W. (1992). *Some do care: Contemporary lives of moral commitment.* New York: Free Press.

Dunlop, W. L., & Tracy, J. L. (2013). Sobering stories: Narratives of self-redemption predict behavioral change and improved health among recovering alcoholics. *Journal of Personality and Social Psychology, 104,* 576–590.

Eakin, P. J. (1999). *How our lives become stories: Making selves.* Ithaca, NY: Cornell University Press.

Erikson, E. H. (1950). *Childhood and society.* New York: Norton.

Franz, C., & Stewart, A. J. (Eds.). (1994). *Women creating lives: Identity, resilience, resistance.* Boulder, CO: Westview Press.

Freeman, M. (1993). *Rewriting the self: History, memory, narrative.* New York: Routledge.

Frese, M., Beimel, S., & Schoenborn, S. (2003). Action training for charismatic leadership: Two evaluations of studies of a commercial training module on inspirational communication of a vision. *Personnel Psychology, 56,* 671–698.

Gabriel, Y. (2000). *Storytelling in organizations: Facts, fictions, and fantasies.* New York: Oxford University Press.

Gardner, H. (1995). *Leading minds: An anatomy of leadership.* New York: Basic Books.

Habermas, T., & Bluck, S. (2000). Getting a life: The emergence of the life story in adolescence. *Psychological Bulletin, 126,* 748–769.

Habermas, T., & de Silveira, C. (2008). The development of global coherence in life narrative across adolescence: Temporal, causal, and thematic aspects. *Developmental Psychology, 44,* 707–721.

Hammack, P. L. (2008). Narrative and the cultural psychology of identity. *Personality and Social Psychology Review, 12,* 222–247.

Hart, H., McAdams, D. P., Hirsch, B. J., & Bauer, J. J. (2001). Generativity and social involvements among African Americans and white adults. *Journal of Research in Personality, 35,* 208–230.

Kroger, J., & Marcia, J. E. (2011). The identity statuses: Origins, meanings, and interpretations. In S. J. Schwartz, K. Luyckx, & V. L. Vignoles (Eds.), *Handbook of identity theory and research* (pp. 31–53). New York: Springer.

Ligon, G. S., Hunter, S. T., & Mumford, M. D. (2008). Development of outstanding leadership: A life narrative approach. *The Leadership Quarterly, 19,* 312–334.

Maruna, S. (2001). *Making good: How ex-convicts reform and rebuild their lives.* Washington, DC: American Psychological Association Press.

McAdams, D. P. (1985). *Power, intimacy, and the life story: Personological inquiries into identity.* Homewood, IL: Dorsey Press.

McAdams, D. P. (1996). Personality, modernity, and the storied self: A contemporary framework for studying persons. *Psychological Inquiry, 7,* 295–321.

McAdams, D. P. (2011). *George W. Bush and the redemptive dream: A psychological portrait.* New York: Oxford University Press.

McAdams, D. P. (2013a). *The redemptive self: Stories Americans live by* (revised and expanded edition). New York: Oxford University Press.

McAdams, D. P. (2013b). Life authorship: A psychological challenge for emerging adulthood, as illustrated in two notable case studies. *Emerging Adulthood, 1,* 151–158.

McAdams, D. P. (2013c). The psychological self as actor, agent, and author. *Perspectives on Psychological Science, 8,* 272–295.

McAdams, D. P. (2013d). The positive psychology of adult generativity: Caring for the next generation and constructing a redemptive life. In J. Sinnott (Ed.), *Positive psychology: Advances in understanding adult motivation* (pp. 191–205). New York: Springer.

McAdams, D. P., Albaugh, M., Farber, E., Daniels, J., Logan, R. L., & Olson, B. (2008). Family metaphors and moral intuitions: How conservatives and liberals narrate their lives. *Journal of Personality and Social Psychology, 95,* 978–990.

McAdams, D. P., Bauer, J. J., Sakaeda, A. M., Anyidoho, N. A., Machado, M. A., Magrino, K.,..., & Pals, J. L. (2006). Continuity and change in the life story: A longitudinal study of autobiographical memories in emerging adulthood. *Journal of Personality, 74,* 1371–1400.

McAdams, D. P., & de St. Aubin, E. (1992). A theory of generativity and its assessment through self-report, behavioral acts, and narrative themes in autobiography. *Journal of Personality and Social Psychology, 62,* 1003–1015.

McAdams, D. P., & McLean, K. C. (2013). Narrative identity. *Current Directions in Psychological Science, 22,* 233–238.

McAdams, D. P., Hanek, K. J., & Dadabo, J. (2013). Themes of self-regulation and self-exploration in the life stories of American conservatives and liberals. *Political Psychology, 34,* 201–219.

McAdams, D. P., Diamond, A., de St. Aubin, E., & Mansfield, E. D. (1997). Stories of commitment: The psychosocial construction of generative lives. *Journal of Personality and Social Psychology, 72,* 678–694.

McAdams, D. P., Reynolds, J., Lewis, M., Patten, A., & Bowman, P. J. (2001). When bad things turn good and good things turn bad: Sequences of redemption and contamination in life narrative, and their relation to psychosocial adaptation in midlife adults and in students. *Personality and Social Psychology Bulletin, 27,* 472–483.

McLean, K. C., & Breen, A. V. (2009). Process and content of narrative identity development in adolescence: Gender and well-being. *Developmental Psychology, 45,* 702–710.

McLean, K. C., Pasupathi, M., & Pals, J. L. (2007). Selves creating stories creating selves. *Personality and Social Psychology Review, 11,* 265–278.

Menchu, R. (1986). *Rigoberta Menchu: An Indian woman in Guatemala.* London: Versu and NLB.

Obama, B. (1995). *Dreams from my father.* New York: Three Rivers Press.

Parameshwar, S. (2006). Inventing higher purpose through suffering: The transformation of the transformational leader. *The Leadership Quarterly, 17,* 454–474.

Pittinsky, T. L., & Tyson, C. J. (2004). *Leader authenticity markers: Findings from a study of African American political leaders.* Paper presented at the Gallup—University of Nebraska Leadership Institute Summit, Omaha, NE.

Remnick, D. (2011). *The bridge: The life and rise of Barack Obama.* New York: Vintage.

Shamir, B., & Eilam, G. (2005). "What's your story?" A life-stories approach to authentic leadership development. *The Leadership Quarterly, 16,* 395–417.

Shotter, J., & Gergen, K. (Eds.) (1989). *Texts of identity.* London: Sage.

Simonton, D. K. (1994). *Greatness: Who makes history and why.* New York: Guilford Press.

Singer, J. A. (2004). Narrative identity and meaning-making across the adult lifespan: An introduction. *Journal of Personality, 72,* 437–459.

Sullivan, A. (2006). *The conservative soul: Fundamentalism, freedom, and the future of the right.* New York: Harper.

Walker, L. J., & Frimer, J. A. (2007). Moral personality of brave and caring exemplars. *Journal of Personality and Social Psychology, 93,* 845–860.

Weischer, A. E., Weibler, J., & Petersen, M. (2013). "To thine own self be true": The effects of enactment and life storytelling on perceived leader authenticity. *The Leadership Quarterly, 24,* 477–495.

Woodward, B. (2004). *Plan of attack.* New York: Simon & Schuster.

Zacher, H., Rosing, K., Henning, T., & Frese, M. (2011). Establishing the next generation at work: Leader generativity as a moderator of the relationship between leader age, leader-member exchange, and leadership success. *Psychology and Aging, 26,* 241–252.

CHAPTER TEN

"Now He Belongs to the Ages": The Heroic Leadership Dynamic and Deep Narratives of Greatness

SCOTT T. ALLISON AND GEORGE R. GOETHALS

We have only to follow the thread of the hero-path. And where we had thought to find an abomination, we shall find a god; where we had thought to slay another, we shall slay ourselves; where we had thought to travel outward, we shall come to the center of our own existence; and where we had thought to be alone, we shall be with all the world.
—Joseph Campbell (1949), *The Hero with a Thousand Faces*

When legendary South African president Nelson Mandela passed away on December 5, 2013, the world responded with an outpouring of heartache for the loss mixed with reverence for his heroic leadership. Foremost among the tributes to Mandela was a statement made by US president Barack Obama, who observed that Mandela "no longer belongs to us. He belongs to the ages" (Parnes, 2013). Obama surely was aware that his words mirrored those made a century and a half earlier by Secretary of War Edwin Stanton upon the death of President Abraham Lincoln. Of Lincoln, Stanton is said to have uttered, "Now he belongs to the ages," although some claim that Stanton actually said, "Now he belongs to the angels" (Gopnik, 2007). Whether ages or angels, Stanton's meaning was as clear as that of Obama. When extraordinary, transformative leaders perish, we construct rhetoric to ensure that their life legacies transcend the small time period in which they lived. Our language forges great leadership in eternity.

The human tendency to bestow a timeless quality to heroic leadership is the culmination of a pervasive narrative about human greatness that people have been driven to construct since the advent of language. In this chapter, we argue that these narratives fulfill important psychological needs for both individuals and collectives. Narratives that detail the lives of legendary heroes provide ageless wisdom and inspiration that allow humans to survive and even thrive. We begin our analysis by tracing the evolutionary source of the human need to construct heroic tales.

Narratives of Greatness

Most scholars of human evolution agree that Thomas Hobbes (1651, 1988) was only slightly exaggerating when he described the quality of life for early humans as "solitary, poor, nasty, brutish, and short" (Robertshaw & Rubalcaba, 2005; Stearns & Koella, 2008). For our hominid ancestors, an early death was the norm, either from disease or from danger. Human tribes were wracked by hunger, sickness, injury, and fatigue. Evidence indicates that at the end of each day, tribe members huddled around fires for warmth, safety, and security (Balter, 1995; McCrone, 2000; Wuethrich, 1998). While fire satisfied many of the physical needs of early humans, tribe members gathered around fire for a social activity that fulfilled equally important psychological needs. This activity was storytelling.

Good stories were a salve for tribe members' psychological wounds. In addition to nursing physical ailments, early humans no doubt experienced as much fear and emotional distress as modern humans, and perhaps more (Solomon, Greenberg, Schimel, Arndt, & Pyszczynski, 2014). Our early ancestors gathered around the fire each night for stories that would bring them some understanding of their misery, some sense of meaning to buoy their spirits. The earliest known human stories that healed and inspired the ancients were stirring accounts of the exploits of heroes and heroic leaders (Kerenyi, 1978). These ancient hero stories from around the globe included the tales of Hesiod, Su Wu, Vishnu, Gilgamesh, Etana, Sundiata, Beowulf, Samson, Thor, Leonidas, Guan Yu, among others (Durant, 2002; Hamilton, 1999).

After examining thousands of mythic tales of heroes from around the globe and across different periods of human history, comparative mythologist Joseph Campbell (1949) found that all ancient hero tales follow a clear and predictable pattern. This universality prompted him to refer to the classic hero narrative as a *monomyth*, a single hero story to which all humans resonate. The monomythic hero story begins with an ordinary person, usually a male, who is called to leave his safe, familiar world and must enter a special world fraught with danger. At the outset of the journey, the hero is missing some important quality, usually self-confidence, humility, or a sense of his true purpose in life. The hero journey is always a journey toward vast personal discovery and transformation. Receiving assistance from enchanted and unlikely sources, the hero shows remarkable cunning, courage, and resourcefulness to triumph. Once successful, the hero returns to his original familiar world to bestow a boon to the entire community.

As early humans soaked in these hero stories, they became transformed in profound ways. Hero narratives allayed their fear, nourished their hopes, and underscored important values of strength and resilience. Life now had greater purpose and meaning. We believe that contemporary humans are no different from their ancient counterparts in deriving essential psychological benefits from narratives about heroes and heroic leaders. Lifespans are longer and general health is better today than millennia ago, but there seems little doubt that people today still seek out powerful hero narratives as a tonic for their anxieties and fears.

In this chapter, we introduce the term *Heroic Leadership Dynamic* (HLD) to describe the ways in which heroes and hero stories nourish the human mind and spirit. The HLD illuminates the myriad psychological processes implicated in our drive to create heroes in our minds, in our storytelling, in our behavior, and in virtually every crevice of every human culture. Central to the HLD is the idea that hero stories fulfill important cognitive and emotional needs, such as our need for wisdom, meaning, hope, inspiration, and growth. The HLD includes the term *dynamic*, along with its multiple meanings, intentionally. In its noun form, dynamic refers to an interactive system or process that unfolds over time. Used as an adjective, dynamic describes a system or process that is energizing and always in motion, a system that drives us toward rising heroes or away from fallen ones. We frame the dynamic as *heroic leadership* rather than as simply heroism because we argue that although not all leaders are heroes, all heroes are leaders (Allison & Goethals, 2011, 2013; Goethals & Allison, 2012). The HLD describes how our most basic human needs can account for our thirst for heroic leaders, and how these needs explain why we are drawn to heroic leaders, how we benefit from them, why we stick with flawed ones, and why we repudiate heroes only after they have outlived their psychological usefulness.

Psychological Benefits of Stories

Over the past two decades, a growing number of scholars have begun to recognize the significance of narrative storytelling for both individuals and collectives (Bennis, 1996; Boje, 1995; Cajete, Eder, & Holyan, 2010; Gardner, 1996; Jameson, 2001; McAdams, 1997; Sternberg, 2011). Stories crystallize abstract concepts and imbue them with contextual meaning (Boje, 1995). Gardner (1995) and Sternberg (2011) point to numerous examples of effective leaders using stories to win the minds and hearts of followers. Stories are not just tools of social influence directed toward others; they also can precipitate self-change. McAdams (1997; this volume) has argued that personal self-narratives play a prominent role in determining our life trajectories and the maintenance of our subjective well-being. Stories are vivid, emotionally laden capsule summaries of wisdom for which the human mind was designed (Haidt, 2012; Wyer,

1995). Price (1978) has gone so far as to claim that "a need to tell and hear stories is essential to the species Homo sapiens—second in necessity apparently after nourishment and before love and shelter" (p. 3).

A core principle of the HLD is that hero stories fulfill two principal human functions: an *epistemic* function and an *energizing* function. The epistemic function refers to the knowledge and wisdom that hero stories impart to us. The energizing function refers to the ways that hero stories inspire us and promote personal growth. We examine these two functions below.

The Epistemic Function of Hero Stories

Stories of heroic action impart wisdom by providing mental models, or scripts, for how one could, or should, lead one's life. Ronald Reagan and Winston Churchill are striking examples. Both felt destined for greatness, and were immensely informed by heroic accounts they read as young boys, stimulating them to aspire to ascend to comparable leadership positions (Hayward, 2006). At the same time, tales of heroic leadership provide a way for those who are disposed to be followers to relate to such leaders through their admiration or awe.

Heroic narratives also teach us how we should behave in crisis situations (Allison & Goethals, 2011; Goethals & Allison, 2012). Consider the wisdom imparted by the heroic actions of Wesley Autrey, a construction worker living in Harlem. In 2007, Autrey received international acclaim when he rescued a complete stranger from an oncoming New York subway train. Autrey was with his two daughters, age four and six, when he witnessed the victim of an epileptic seizure fall on the subway tracks just as a train was approaching. Realizing he had no time to move the man from the tracks, Autrey lay down on top of him in-between the rails as the train passed over them both. Only one-half inch separated Autrey from severe injury or death. Soon after performing this heroic act, Autrey received hundreds of letters from people thanking him for showing them how to live their lives and how to respond in emergency situations (Kolker, 2007). In short, Autrey provided a script for heroic action to millions of New York citizens hungry for such a script. Heroes such as Autrey are role models who perform behaviors that affirm our most cherished world views (Kinsella, Ritchie, & Igou, 2014; Solomon et al., 2014).

Hero stories are far more than simple scripts prescribing prosocial action. Richard Rohr (2011) argues that effective hero stories feature an abundance of *transrational* phenomena, which he defines as experiences that resist or defy rational analysis. Transrational phenomena contained in hero stories reveal truths and life patterns that our limited minds have trouble understanding using our best logic or rational thought. Examples of transrational experiences that routinely appear in hero stories include *suffering, sacrifice, meaning, love, paradox, mystery, God,* and *eternity.* The ultimate transrational phenomenon may be the eternal battle between good and evil, a theme that pervades all of human literature and is a universal characteristic of the human condition. Transrational phenomena beg to be understood but cannot be fully known using conventional tools of human reason. Hero stories help unlock the secrets of the transrational.

How do hero stories help us understand transrational experience? We believe that heroic narratives and their meaningful symbols serve as metaphors for easing our understanding of complex, mysterious phenomena. Over the past two decades, scholars have accumulated an abundance of evidence supporting the idea that metaphors facilitate learning (Lakoff, 2003). According to Leary (1994), "All knowledge is ultimately rooted in metaphorical modes of perception and thought" (p. 2). William James himself claimed that the use of metaphor was characteristic of all human understanding. Heroic narratives may bring transrational phenemona to life by providing, in James's words, "similar instances" which operate as "pegs and pigeonholes—as our categories of understanding" (James, 1878/1983, p. 12). We believe that hero stories promote wisdom in at least three ways: Hero stories (a) reveal deep truths, (b) illuminate paradox, and (c) develop emotional intelligence.

Hero Stories Reveal Deep Truths. According to Joseph Campbell (1949), hero stories reveal life's deepest psychological truths. Truths are considered deep when their insights about human nature and motivation are not only profound and fundamental but also hidden and nonobvious. Campbell believed that most readers of mythic hero stories are oblivious to deep truths, their meaning, and their wisdom. Deep truths contained in hero myths are difficult to discern and appreciate because they are disguised within symbols and metaphors. As a result, readers of mythology underestimate the psychological value of the narratives, prompting Campbell to observe that "mythology is psychology misread as biography, history, and cosmology" (p. 219).

One way that hero narratives reveal deep truths is by sending us into *deep time*, meaning that the truths contained in stories enjoy a timelessness that connects us with the past, the present, and the future. Rohr (2011) notes that deep time is evident when stories contain phrases such as, "Once upon a time," "A long time ago in a galaxy far, far away," and "they lived happily ever after." As noted earlier, Barack Obama forged Nelson Mandela in deep time by proclaiming that Mandela "belongs to the ages." By sending heroic leaders into deep time, hero stories reinforce timeless values and ageless truths about human existence.

Hero stories also reveal *deep roles* in our human social fabric. Moxnes (2012) has argued that the deepest roles are archetypal family roles such as mother, child, maiden, and wise old man or grandparent. Family role archetypes abound in classic hero tales and myths, where there are a wealth of kings and queens, parents, stepparents, princesses, children, and stepchildren. Moxnes's research shows that even if hero stories do not explicitly feature deep role family characters, we will project these archetypal roles onto the characters. Moreover, in a process much like Freud's transference, we tend to project these deep family roles onto others in our social environments (Moxnes, 2007). Moxnes's conclusion is that the family unit is an ancient device, still useful today, for understanding our social world.

Hero Stories Illuminate Paradox. Another epistemic function of hero stories is their ability to shed light on meaningful life paradoxes. We believe that most people have trouble unpacking the value of paradoxical truths unless the contradictions contained within the paradoxes are illustrated inside a good story. Hero stories are saturated with paradoxical truths, such as those mentioned by Joseph Campbell in one of his best-known quotes that opens this chapter. Let's unpack each of the paradoxes in that quote:

★ *Where we had thought to find an abomination, we shall find a god.* Carl Jung is known for his apocryphal edict, "what you resist persists," which cautions us to question our avoidance of the people and issues we fear most in life. Campbell (1949) notes that every human being encounters painful challenges in life and that they are an integral part of our own individual hero journeys. "Where you stumble," wrote Campbell, "there lies your treasure" (p. 75). Hero stories teach us that only by confronting our dragons can we sow the seeds of our redemption.

★ *Where we had thought to slay another, we shall slay ourselves.* When heroes face their greatest fears, they are entering the dragon's lair, and only when they defeat the dragon is their personal transformation complete. According to Campbell (1949), every human life encounters metaphorical dragons during the hero's journey. When we slay our dragons, we are slaying our false selves or former selves, thereby allowing our true heroic selves to emerge.

★ *Where we had thought to travel outward, we shall come to the center of our own existence.* In the opening act of every hero story, the hero leaves her safe, familiar world and enters a dangerous, unfamiliar world. Going on a pilgrimage of some type is a necessary component of the classic hero journey. Hero stories teach us that we have to leave home to find ourselves.

★ *Where we had thought to be alone, we shall be with all the world.* The hero's journey is far from over once the dragon has been slain. Campbell (1949) observes that the now-transformed hero in myth and legend must return to his original familiar world and transform it in significant ways. The hero, once alone on his journey, becomes united and in communion with the world.

Hero Stories Develop Emotional Intelligence. Emotional intelligence refers to the ability to identify, understand, use, and manage emotions (Caruso, Fleming, & Spector, this volume; Mayer, Salovey, Caruso, & Sitarenios, 2001; Salovey & Mayer, 1989). Psychoanalyst Bruno Bettelheim believed that children's fairy tales are useful in helping people, especially children, understand emotional experience (Bettelheim, 1976). The heroes of these fairly tales are usually subjected to dark, foreboding experiences, such as encounters with witches, evil spells, abandonment, neglect, abuse, and death. Listeners to these tales vicariously experience these dark stimuli, allowing them to develop strategies for resolving their fears and distress. Bettelheim believed that even the most distressing fairy tales, such as those by the Brothers Grimm, add clarity to confusing emotions and give people a greater sense of life's meaning and purpose. The darkness of fairy tales allows children to grow emotionally, thus developing their emotional intelligence and preparing them for the challenges of adulthood.

The Energizing Function of Hero Stories

Hero stories energize and inspire us. The recent work of Jonathan Haidt and his colleagues suggests that heroes and heroic action may evoke a unique emotional response which Haidt calls *elevation* (Algoe & Haidt, 2009; Haidt, 2003). Haidt borrowed the term elevation from Thomas Jefferson, who used the phrase "moral elevation" to describe the euphoric feeling one gets when reading great literature. According to Haidt, when people experience elevation, they feel a mix of awe, reverence, and admiration for a morally beautiful act. Haidt describes elevation as the opposite of disgust. His research team has demonstrated that exposure to stories about morally exemplary action triggers elevation (Algoe & Haidt, 2009). Participants in elevation studies describe the emotion as similar to calmness, warmth, and love. Importantly, elevation also includes a desire to become a better person.

Consistent with research on elevation, Kinsella et al. (2014) propose that heroes serve important life-enhancing functions. Heroes who "behave in ways that benefit others, sometimes at great personal risk, are likely to increase positive feelings towards the hero and others, reminding people of the good in the world" (p. 7). Heroes take risks that inspire us. Franco, Blau, and Zimbardo (2011) argue that this risk-taking component differentiates heroism from altruism, with heroes taking risks and making self-sacrificing decisions in ways that altruists do not. In fact, Zimbardo (2011) calls altruism "heroism-light." Franco et al. argue that the risk-taking aspect of heroism is what makes heroism especially desirable and emotionally moving. We propose that hero stories energize us in three ways: by healing our psychic wounds, by inspiring us to action, and by promoting personal growth. We examine these ideas next.

Hero Stories Heal Psychic Wounds. Hero stories serve a healing function in several ways. First, storytelling is a community-building activity. For early humans, just the act of gathering around communal fires to hear stories established social connections with others. This sense of family, group, or community was, and remains, central to human emotional well-being (Aberson, Healy, & Romero, 2000; Brewer, 1979, 1999; Leary & Baumeister, 2000). The content of hero stories also promotes a strong sense of social identity. If the hero is an effective one, he or she performs actions that exemplify and affirm the community's most cherished values. The validation of a shared world view, told vividly in storytelling, serves important healing and self-esteem-building functions (Leary & Baumeister, 2000; Solomon et al., 2014).

Group storytelling is not unlike group therapy in that it involves bringing people together to share stories about how to overcome traumatic, anxiety-provoking situations. We believe that hero stories provide many of the benefits of group therapy as identified by Yalom and Leszcz (2005). These benefits include the instillation of hope; the relief of knowing that others share one's emotional experiences; the sharing of information; the development of socialization skills; the acquisition of modeling behavior; the fostering of self-awareness; the building of group cohesiveness; the relief of stress; and the development of a sense of existential meaning about life. The anxiety-buffering role of heroic action is consistent with the tenets of terror management theory (Solomon et al., 2014). Moreover, many 12-step recovery groups, such as Alcoholics Anonymous, also promote healing through the open sharing of members' stories. Some clinical psychologists even use hero stories in their practice to help their clients develop the heroic traits of strength, resilience, and courage (Garloch, 2013).

Hero Stories Inspire Us. The classic mythic hero is often an underdog or "everyman" who is summoned on a journey fraught with extraordinary challenges. Our research on underdogs shows that we identify with them, root for them, and judge them to be highly inspiring when they triumph (Allison & Goethals, 2008; Kim, Allison, Eylon, Goethals, Markus, & McGuire, 2008; see also Vandello, Goldschmeid, & Richards, 2007). Kinsella et al. (2014) present data suggesting that the inspiring quality of heroes is what sets heroes apart from altruists, helpers, and leaders. Allison and Goethals (2011) asked participants to generate traits describing heroes and, using factor and cluster-analytic statistical procedures, found eight general categories of traits. Called *The Great Eight*, these trait categories consist of *smart, strong, charismatic, reliable, resilient, selfless, caring,* and *inspiring*. When asked which of the great eight are the most important descriptors of heroes, a different group of participants reported that the traits of *inspiring* and *selfless* are the most important (Allison & Goethals, 2011).

Charisma's presence in the great eight underscores the idea that heroes are inspiring. As we note elsewhere in this volume, people are highly inspired by charismatic individuals, viewing them with reverence and awe (Goethals & Allison, this volume). Charismatic leaders are perceived to possess god-like characteristics, an idea conveyed by Weber (1924) who wrote that charismatic individuals are "treated as endowed with supernatural, superhuman, or at least specifically exceptional powers or qualities." Perhaps we should not be surprised by these deific attributions, as divine intervention on behalf of the hero is a central element of Campbell's (1949) hero monomyth. The hero in classic mythology is often summoned by a higher power to a great journey, and the catalytic agent of this journey is some type of deficit or wounding suffered by the hero. This wounding, divine in origin, emerges in countless stories of ugly ducklings, Cinderellas, and other underdogs who through magic or the help of a deity turn their wounds into triumph. Heroes use their wounds to transform themselves and to redeem the world, much like the crucifixion and resurrection of Jesus in the New Testament. Unlocking the divine secret of our wounds is the surest path to heroism. With divine involvement so fundamental to hero stories, we should not be surprised that the trait of charisma—the "divine gift of grace" (Riggio & Riggio, 2008)—is so readily attributed to heroes.

We endow our most charismatic and transformative leaders with god-like immortality, as seen in Obama's description of Mandela as belonging "to the ages." Assigning immortality to heroes can assume many tangible and emotionally significant forms. We erect permanent monuments and shrines to honor heroes. Stamps, coins, and paper currency bear their likeness. Roads and buildings are named after heroes. Epic stories and poems are composed. Statues, cities, and children bear the names of our departed heroes. Martin Luther King, Jr., has almost 800 streets in America named after him. We tend to place heroes who die young on an especially high pedestal, and apparently there can never be enough physical reminders of these heroes in the form of memorabilia, films, plays, parks, and museums. The fact that there continue to be Elvis Presley sightings is a powerful reminder that we cannot seem to let go of some of our most treasured and iconic heroes (Simpson, 2013).

Hero Stories Promote Personal Growth. According to Stern (1966), "the evolution of human growth is an evolution from an absolute need to be loved towards a full readiness to give love." This developmental trend is consistent with Erich Fromm's (1956) classic view of love for others as first requiring self-respect and self-love. It also nicely summarizes the transformation that a mythic hero undergoes during the hero journey. Joseph Campbell (1949) believed that the hero journey paralleled human developmental stages. All young adults, according to Campbell, are driven out of their safe, familiar worlds and into the fearful real world, and "the big question is whether you are going to be able to say a hearty yes to your adventure" (p. 43). Eric Erikson's (1975) stages of development suggest a hero trajectory during the human lifespan, with young adults driven to establish competencies and carve out an *identity* for themselves. Older adults reach a stage of *generativity*, which Erikson defines as people's desire to create things that will outlast them and to give back to the society that has given them so much. Hero stories remind us that we are all developmentally equipped to pursue a lifelong hero-like journey.

Campbell's (1949) stages of the hero's journey culminate with the gift, boon, or elixir that the hero bestows upon the society from which he originated. Both Campbell and Erikson believed that personal transformation is the key to reaching the generativity stage of development and, finally, the apex of *integrity*. In all good hero stories, the key to achieving transformation is the discovery of an important missing inner quality that has heretofore hindered personal growth. Good heroic leaders use the power of transformation not only to change themselves for the better, but also to transform the world. Campbell (1988) describes the power of mythic transformation in this way: "If you realize what the real problem is—losing yourself, giving yourself to some higher end, or to another—you realize that this itself is the ultimate trial. When we quit thinking primarily about ourselves and our own self-preservation, we undergo a truly heroic transformation of consciousness. And what all the myths have to deal with is transformations of consciousness of one kind or another" (p. 112).

This type of gift-giving is apparent in 12-step recovery groups, which require members to undergo 11 steps of self-discovery followed by a 12th and final step requiring them to "carry the message" to others in need. The co-founder of Alcoholics Anonymous, Bill Wilson, maintained that the key to the recovered alcoholic's continued personal growth, and even his sobriety, is to carry the message of AA to other alcoholics (Smith & Wilson, 2013). Moreover, all 12-step programs underscore the importance of sponsorship. Healing and sobriety are not likely to be maintained unless one is willing and able to sponsor newcomers, a process that involves shepherding them through the 12 steps.

The journey of personal growth within the context of the hero narrative is consistent with Lawrence Kohlberg's theory of moral development. According to Kohlberg (1969), children possess a preconventional, or Level I, sense of morality. At this level children are concerned with rewards for good behavior and punishments for bad. By the teenage years, children display Level II or conventional morality. At this stage teens consider what other people will think of them and what society and the law require. For example, people might mention a sense of honor as compelling them to steal food or medicine to save a loved one, or not wanting to be dishonest or criminal as reasons for not stealing. Finally, starting in late adolescence or early adulthood, some people begin reasoning at Level III, using postconventional morality. Here people become more concerned about following mutually agreed upon moral principles and their own ethical values. Their thinking revolves around abstract principles such as justice and equality. They might decide that stealing food to save someone is the right thing to do, even though it violates the law. With postconventional morality comes considerations of morality that transcend rules and take into account the greatest good for the greatest number of people.

There are two crucial points about Level III postconventional morality. First, it very much involves taking other people's perspectives into account and thinking about the common good as well as one's own interests. Second, not many people, even as mature adults, get to this level of thinking. Campbell and Erikson both acknowledge that not everyone completes the hero journey or achieves the goals of generativity or integrity. But we do encounter heroic leaders who illustrate this kind of moral growth. Princess Diana was jarred out of a conventional life dominated by conventional morality when she discovered Prince Charles's infidelities and encountered disdain from the tabloid press, and even some of the royal family. She decided to concentrate on being a good mother to her two sons, and working on causes that she independently believed to be important, whether they were conventional choices or not. Diana made commitments that reflect an emphasis on important moral principles, such as equality and the value of human life (Allison & Goethals, 2011).

Level III postconventional moral reasoning is also vividly seen in President John F. Kennedy's 1963 speech in which he rallied the nation behind his civil rights legislation. First, Kennedy appealed directly to the country's conscience and morality. He explicitly asked "every American" to "stop and examine his conscience" and stated "We face, therefore, a moral crisis as a country and a people." Invoking the theme of deep time, he argued that "it is as old as the Scriptures." Second, he invoked principles of equality and justice, and values as fundamental as the golden rule. He reminded the nation that "it was founded on the principle that all men are created equal" and declared that "every American ought to have the right to be treated as he would wish to be treated." He appealed to "a sense of human decency" and asked "who among us would be content with the counsels of patience and delay" in the face of injustice. Not every listener was prepared to think at this level, but as a leader Kennedy tried to raise the nation's level of moral reasoning (Allison & Goethals, 2011).

Temporal and Dynamic Components of the HLD

Earlier we noted that the dynamic component of the HLD refers to manner in which the psychology of heroism unfolds over time. The HLD and its temporal component can be viewed as a story itself. At the beginning sits our craving for heroes, borne out of a longing for an understanding of the vicissitudes of life. We've shown how hero stories fulfill our epistemic and energizing needs, and a key aspect of the HLD is the myriad ways in which heroes satisfy our ever-changing drives and motives. As people age, their needs shift in accordance with developmental trends. When young children are asked to name their heroes, they typically list people who show great competencies, especially athletic prowess (Goethals & Allison, 2012). Superman, for example, is idolized by young children for his ability to leap tall buildings and overpower locomotives, but in later stages of childhood Superman's role as a crime-fighter is listed as the main reason for his heroism. As people develop more sophisticated notions of morality, their heroes evolve accordingly. Goethals and Allison (2012) have used the term *transitional heroes* to describe heroes that correspond to particular stages of development. These transitional heroes are placeholders that fulfill our need for heroes until better ones come along that meet different or higher-level needs.

The Johnny Carson Effect

In 1983, the legendary *Tonight Show* host Johnny Carson was embroiled in a contentious divorce from his third wife Joanna. The divorce turned out to be a costly one for Carson, both emotionally and financially. One night, during his *Tonight Show* opening monologue, Carson couldn't resist making light of his difficult divorce. "I remember being a kid, age 7 or 8," he said. "Babe Ruth was my hero. Then when I first got into show business, Jack Benny was my hero. Now my hero is Henry VIII" (Carson, 2003). With this joke, Carson illustrates the need-based origin of heroism as well as the dynamic nature of heroic leadership. Our psychological needs dictate our choice of heroes, and as these needs inevitably shift over time, so do our preferences for heroes and heroic leaders. Johnny Carson's quip has inspired us to call our tendency to choose heroes that match our current needs the *Johnny Carson Effect*.

The Johnny Carson effect suggests that changes in our needs bring about changes in our choice of heroes. To provide evidence for this effect, we recently asked 85 people between the ages of 18 and 80 to think of a time in their lives when they faced a significant life challenge. We then asked our participants to list the people whom they considered to be their heroes during this period. The results showed a striking relationship between our respondents' needs and their choice of heroes. When they reported having a severe health problem, they chose heroes at that time who had overcome their specific malady. For example, a participant who overcame testicular cancer reported that his hero was Lance Armstrong, who is famous for triumphing over this form of cancer. Another participant overcame a severe depression and reported that her uncle, who also suffered from and overcame depression, was her hero.

We also asked a different group of participants to think back to a time when they had a hero whom they no longer consider to be a hero. These participants revealed that their former heroes helped them cope with difficult circumstances unique to that time in their lives. For example, many of our college student participants reported that the Power Rangers were once their heroes because the Rangers exuded skill and confidence when our participants lacked those qualities. Another middle-aged participant revealed that the famed soccer player Pelé was once his hero because, as captain of his soccer team, he felt pressure to excel at his sport. Our choice of heroes is dynamic, reflecting inevitable changes in our needs and life circumstances.

Hero Retention and Repudiation

Social psychologists have long been interested in what attracts us to people, and one of the most robust findings in the attraction literature is the observation that human beings are drawn to successful, competent others (Berscheid & Reis, 1998). In a classic study, Cialdini, Borden, Thorne, Walker, Freeman, and Sloan (1976) demonstrated a phenomenon that they called *basking in reflected glory*, or BIRGing. People associate themselves with successful others to such an extent that another's success can become one's own success. We suspect that BIRGing can help explain how one's identity can become psychologically attached to another's accomplishment and heroism. Cialdini et al. noted that these associations can shift as the fortunes of the target of our associations shift. This idea is consistent with the HLD in suggesting that our attachments to heroes come and go, but the HLD extends this idea by suggesting that these shifts reflect the ever-changing nature of our needs. We also suspect that people resist changing their heroes when such change threatens deeply held self-identities. How might this work?

To the extent that people's identities are enmeshed with another's heroism, we may see people remain staunchly loyal to the hero, even when the hero has fallen in the eyes of most others. The case of Lance Armstrong offers a powerful example. For years, Armstrong denied allegations of doping and even showed a vicious streak toward anyone who dared to make these allegations. Armstrong's supporters were people who, for many years, believed his denials and were inspired by Armstrong's ability to overcome cancer and win seven Tour de France titles. When Armstrong finally admitted using performance-enhancing drugs, he lost most of his admirers but, curiously, he retained a small but fervent fan base that continued to place him on a heroic pedestal. These followers could not or would not be deterred by Armstrong's confession of doping. They downplayed the significance of the doping ("everyone in cycling cheats"); they accused the cycling governing body of corruption ("they were out to get him"); they focused on Armstrong's heroic battle with cancer ("he beat the disease"); or they pointed to his charitable work ("the Livestrong Foundation raises millions"). Armstrong's supporters had shown such a personal investment in Armstrong's heroism and bore identities that were so deeply connected to his legendary status that they could not repudiate a fallen hero (Levy, 2012).

According to the HLD, the stories we tell about our heroes, even our fallen ones, are designed to impart wisdom and inspiration. We contend that stories about the rise of heroes, and even the fall of heroes, fulfill an important epistemic function by showing us paths to success as well as paths to ruin. In our earlier work on heroes, we discuss two types of heroes who can suffer a reversal of fortune—*tragic heroes* and *transposed heroes* (Goethals & Allison, 2012). Both of these hero types offer a cautionary tale of the fragility of human success. The wisdom we glean from such stories satisfies invaluable needs and inspires us to perform exemplary action in life. The ways in which people benefit from both rising and falling heroes are an integral part of the HLD.

Final Thoughts

Our human craving for heroes, our need for the psychological benefits that heroes offer, and our desires over time either to retain our heroes or to repudiate them, all comprise the constellation of phenomena that we call the *Heroic Leadership Dynamic*. In this chapter we've identified a number of key psychological processes that are implicated by the HLD. These processes include the mental construction of scripts and schemas about heroic behavior; the processing of transrational phenomena in hero stories that defy rational analysis; the analysis of deep truths and paradoxes inherent in hero stories; the development of emotional intelligence, the healing power of group storytelling; the inspiring nature of charismatic leaders and triumphant underdogs; various mechanisms underlying personal growth and developmental health; and the psychology of associating with, and disassociating from, heroes and heroic leaders over time. A central driving mechanism underlying the HLD is the every-changing state of human needs. The Johnny Carson effect describes what we call need-based heroism—the human tendency to choose heroes based on one's current set of needs, motives, and drives.

We began this chapter by acknowledging the human tendency to cement our greatest leaders in deep time. We recently submitted the phrase "one for the ages" to a Google search and obtained hundreds of hits, all of which directed us to remarkable people and unforgettable accomplishments that are forever etched in time. In addition to Abraham Lincoln and Nelson Mandela, our "one for the ages" search yielded references to actress Betty White's career, Arnold Schwarzenegger's role in *The Terminator*, Jack Nicklaus's victory at the 1986 Master's Tournament, Michael Jackson's musicianship, Pat Tillman's ultimate sacrifice, Mark McGwire's home run record, and 100 slain NYPD officers honored by New York's mayor (Campanile, 2005). Because heroic leadership is so valuable to society, and also because it is so rare, human beings take steps—usually in the form of storytelling—to ensure that these heroic leaders never leave our collective memories. Our hope is that this chapter offers some initial insights and observations about the psychology of the human effort to immortalize our most exemplary leaders.

Note

This research was supported by a John Templeton Foundation Grant (#35279) awarded to Scott Allison.

References

Aberson, C. L., Healy, M. R., & Romero, V. L. (2000). Ingroup bias and self-esteem: A meta-analysis. *Personality and Social Psychology Review, 4*, 157–173.

Algoe, S. B., & Haidt, J. (2009). Witnessing excellence in action: The "other-praising" emotions of elevation, gratitude, and admiration. *Journal of Positive Psychology, 4,* 105–127.

Allison, S. T., & Goethals, G. R. (2008). Deifying the dead and downtrodden: Sympathetic figures as inspirational leaders. In C.L. Hoyt, G. R. Goethals, & D. R. Forsyth (Eds.), *Leadership at the crossroads: Psychology and leadership*. Westport, CT: Praeger.

Allison, S. T., & Goethals, G. R. (2011). *Heroes: What they do and why we need them.* New York: Oxford University Press.

Allison, S. T., & Goethals, G. R. (2013). *Heroic leadership: An influence taxonomy of 100 exceptional individuals.* New York: Routledge.

Balter, M. (1995). Did homo erectus tame fire first? *Science, 268,* 1570.

Bennis, W. (1996). The leader as storyteller. *Harvard Business Review, 74*(1), 154–161.

Berscheid, E., & Reis, H. T. (1998). Attraction and close relationships. *The handbook of social psychology, 4th edition,* 193–281.

Bettelheim, B. (1976). *The uses of enchantment: The meaning and importance of fairy tales.* New York: Knopf.

Boje, D. M. (1995). Stories of the storytelling organization: A postmodern analysis of Disney as Tamara-land. *Academy of Management Journal, 38,* 997–1035.

Brewer, M. B. (1979). Ingroup bias in the minimal intergroup situation: A cognitive-motivational analysis. *Psychological Bulletin, 86,* 307–324.

Brewer, M. B. (1999). The psychology of prejudice: Ingroup love or outgroup hate? *Journal of Social Issues, 55*(3), 429–444.

Cajete, G., Eder, D., & Holyan, R. (2010). *Life Lessons through storytelling: Children's exploration of ethics.* Bloomington: Indiana University Press.

Campanile, C. (2005). Police salute is one for the ages. *New York Post,* Retrieved on December 8, 2013 from http://nypost.com/2005/11/16/police-salute-is-one-for-the-ages/

Campbell, J. (1949). *The hero with a thousand faces.* New York: New World Library.

Campbell, J. (1988). *The power of myth, with Bill Moyers.* New York: Doubleday.

Carson, J. (Host, Executive Producer). (2003). *The Ultimate Carson Collection Vol. 3* [DVD]. USA: Carson Productions.

Caruso, D. R., Fleming, K., & Spector, E. D. (2015). Emotional intelligence and leadership. In G. R. Goethals, S. T. Allison, R. Kramer, & D. Messick (Eds.), *Conceptions of leadership: Enduring ideas and emerging insights.* New York: Palgrave Macmillan.

Cialdini, R. B., Borden, R. J., Thorne, A., Walker, M. R., Freeman, S., & Sloan, L. R. (1976). Basking in reflected glory: Three (football) field studies. *Journal of Personality and Social Psychology, 34,* 366–375.

Durant, W. (2002). *Heroes of history: A brief history of civilization from ancient times to the dawn of the modern age.* New York: Simon and Schuster.

Erikson, E. H. (1975). *Life history and the historical moment.* New York: Norton.

Franco, Z. E., Blau, K., & Zimbardo, P. G. (2011). Heroism: A conceptual analysis and differentiation between heroic action and altruism. *Review of General Psychology.* doi: 10.1037/a0022672

Fromm, E. (1956). *The art of loving.* New York: Harper & Row.

Gardner, H. E. (1995). *Leading minds: An anatomy of leadership.* New York: Basic Books.

Garloch, K. (2013). *Charlotte psychologists use movie and comic book superheroes to help clients find strength and resiliency.* Retrieved on November 29, 2013, from http://www.charlotteobserver.com/2013/09/02/4276377/charlotte-psychologists-use-movie.html#.UpksHY1RYT7

Goethals, G. R., & Allison, S. T. (2012). Making heroes: The construction of courage, competence and virtue. *Advances in Experimental Social Psychology, 46,* 183–235.

Goethals, G. R., & Allison, S. T. (2015). Kings and charisma, Lincoln and leadership: An evolutionary perspective. In G. R. Goethals, S. T. Allison, R. Kramer, & D. Messick (Eds.), *Conceptions of leadership: Enduring ideas and emerging insights.* New York: Palgrave Macmillan.

Gopnik, A. (2007). Angels and ages. *The New Yorker.* May 28.

Haidt, J. (2003). Elevation and the positive psychology of morality. In C. L. M. Keyes & J. Haidt (Eds.), *Flourishing: Positive psychology and the life well-lived* (pp. 275–289). Washington, DC: American Psychological Association.

Haidt, J. (2012). *The righteous mind: Why good people are divided by politics and religion.* New York: Pantheon.

Hamilton, E. (1999). *Mythology: Timeless tales of gods and heroes.* New York: Grand Central Publishing.

Hayward, S. F. (2006). *Greatness: Reagan, Churchill, and the making of extraordinary leaders.* New York: Three Rivers Press.

Hobbes, T. (1651, 1988). *Leviathan.* London: Penguin Books.

James, W. (1983). Brute and human intellect. In *Essays in psychology* (pp. 1–37). Cambridge, MA: Harvard University Press. (Original published in 1878.)

Jameson, D. A. (2001). Narrative discourse and management action. *Journal of Business Communication, 38*, 476–511.

Kerenyi, K. (1959—Reissue edition 1978). *The heroes of the Greeks*. Thames & Hudson.

Kim, J., Allison, S. T., Eylon, D., Goethals, G., Markus, M., McGuire, H., & Hindle, S. (2008). Rooting for (and then abandoning) the underdog. *Journal of Applied Social Psychology, 38*, 2550–2573.

Kinsella, E. L., Ritchie, T. D., & Igou, E. R. (2014). *On lay-conceptions of heroes: Their psychological and social functions*. Unpublished manuscript, University of Limerick.

Kohlberg, L. (1969). Stage and sequence: The cognitive-developmental approach to socialization. In D. A. Goslin (Ed.), *Handbook of socialization: Theory and research*. Boston: Houghton Mifflin.

Kolker, R. (2007). This is the part where the superhero discovers he is mortal. Retrieved on December 1, 2013, from http://nymag.com/news/features/30636/

Lakoff, G., & Johnson, M. (2003). *Metaphors we live by*. Chicago: University of Chicago Press.

Leary, D. E. (1994). *Metaphors in the history of psychology*. Cambridge: Cambridge University Press.

Leary, M. R. (2005). Sociometer theory and the pursuit of relational value: Getting to the root of self-esteem, *European Review of Social Psychology, 16*, 75–111.

Leary, M. R., & Baumeister, R. F. (2000). The nature and function of self-esteem: Sociometer theory. In M. Zanna (Ed.), *Advances in experimental social psychology* (Vol. 32, pp. 1–62). San Diego, CA: Academic Press.

Levy, D. (2012). Lance Armstrong's true believers refuse to believe the new truth about him. Retrieved on December 5, 2013, from http://bleacherreport.com/articles/1375671-lance-armstrongs-true-believers-refuse-to-believe-the-new-truth-about-him-them.

Mayer, J. D., Salovey, P., Caruso, D. L., & Sitarenios, G. (2001). Emotional intelligence as a standard intelligence. *Emotion, 1*, 232–242.

McAdams, D. P. (1997). *The stories we live by: Personal myths and the making of the self*. New York: Guilford Press.

McAdams, D. P. (2015). Leaders and their life stories: Obama, Bush, and narratives of redemption. In G. R. Goethals, S. T. Allison, R. Kramer, & D. Messick (Eds.), *Conceptions of leadership: Enduring ideas and emerging insights*. New York: Palgrave Macmillan.

McCrone, J. (2000). Fired up. *New Scientist, 166*, 30.

Moxnes, P. (2007). Deep-roles—a model of implicit roles in groups: First facts. Paper presented at invited symposium Small group research in Scandinavia (Convenor: Prof. Stefan Jern), *10th European Congress of Psychology*, Prague, Czech Republic.

Moxnes, P. (2012). Deep roles: Are they real? A model of positive and negative interpersonal fantasies. *International Journal of Psychology, 47*, Special Issue: SI Supplement: 1 Pages: 724–725.

Parnes, A. (2013). Obama: Mandela "belongs to the ages." Retrieved on December 6, 2013, from http://thehill.com/blogs/blog-briefing-room/news/192267-obama-mandela-belongs-to-the-ages

Price, R. (1978). *A Palpable God*. New York: Atheneum, p. 3.

Robertshaw, P., & Rubalcaba, J. (2005). *The early human world*. New York: Oxford University Press.

Rohr, R. (2011). *Falling upward*. New York: Jossey-Bass.

Salovey, P., & Mayer, J. D. (1989). Emotional intelligence. *Imagination, cognition, and personality, 9*(3), 185–211.

Simpson, T. R. (2013). *Could Elvis Presley be alive?* Retrieved on December 1, 2013, from http://memphis.about.com/od/memphismusic/f/Could-Elvis-Presley-Be-Alive.htm.

Smith, B., & Wilson, B. (2013). *The big book of alcoholics anonymous*. New York: Createspace.

Solomon, S., Greenberg, J., Schimel, J., Arndt, J., & Pyszczynski, T. (2014). *Human awareness of mortality and the evolution of culture*. Unpublished manuscript.

Stearns S. C., & Koella J. K. (2008). *Evolution in health and disease* (2nd ed.). Oxford [Oxfordshire]: Oxford University Press.

Stern, K. (1966). *Institute of man symposium on neurosis and personal growth*, Duquesne University, Pittsburgh, PA, November 18.

Sternberg, R. J. (2011). Leadership and education: Leadership stories. In M. Harvey & R. Riggio (Eds.), *Leadership studies: The dialogue of disciplines*. New York: Edward Elgar.

Vandello, J. A., Goldschmied, N. P., & Richards, D. A. R. (2007). The appeal of the underdog. *Personality and Social Psychology Bulletin, 33*, 1603–1616.

Wilber, K. (2007). *The integral vision*. New York: Shambhala.

Wuethrich, B. (1998). Geological analysis damps ancient Chinese fires. *Science, 281*, 165.

Wyer, R. S. (1995). *Knowledge and memory: The real story*. New York: Erlbaum.

Yalom, I., & Leszcz, M. (2005). *Theory and practice of group psychotherapy*. New York: Basic Books.

Zimbardo, P. (2011). *What makes a hero?* Retrieved on December 1, 2013, from http://greatergood.berkeley.edu/article/item/what_makes_a_hero

CHAPTER ELEVEN

How Do Leaders Lead? Through Social Influence

DONELSON R. FORSYTH

From 1933 to 1944, US president Franklin D. Roosevelt used a series of radio broadcasts—his famous "fireside chats"—to persuade Americans to remain calm through a continuing series of financial, domestic, and military crises. In the early 1980s IBM hired Bill Gates to write an operating system for that company's computers, but Gates convinced IBM to allow him to market the system through his own start-up company, which he named Microsoft. In 2013 Secretary of State John Kerry threatened Syria's leaders, warning them the United States would launch a military strike against that country unless they curtailed their weapons program. In 1978 Jim Jones, the leader of a religious sect known as the Peoples Temple, ordered his followers to commit suicide, and nearly all complied with his deadly demand.

Leaders must have many skills. They must be able to organize complex tasks so that the efforts of each person are integrated in a collective enterprise. They must be able to identify the social and interpersonal needs of the group, and take steps to make certain their followers are relatively satisfied. They must envision future outcomes and events and put in place procedures that will facilitate the attainment of their organization's mission. But, among these myriad responsibilities, the one most crucial to the leader's success is the capacity to influence others. As Bass (2008, p. 19) explained, leadership is the "successful influence by the leader that results in the attainment of goals by the influenced followers." Yukl (2013, p. 7) considered leadership to be the "process of influencing others," as did Northouse (2013, p. 5): Leadership is "a process whereby an individual influences a group." Leaders are, as Gardner (1995, p. 6) concluded, "individuals who significantly influence the thoughts, behaviors, and/or feelings of others." Neustadt (1990, p. 150) describes successful US presidents as individuals who are skilled in wielding "personal influence of an effective sort on the behavior of men" and women, and US president Harry S. Truman put it this way: A leader is a person who "has the ability to get other people to do what they don't want to do, and like it" (Truman, 1958, p. 139).

This chapter considers leadership to be a social influence process that derives from multifarious sources, manifests itself in a variety of forms, and generates outcomes both extraordinary and commonplace. However, it cuts through some of influence's complexities by distinguishing between two oft-contrasted forms of influence: the direct and the indirect (Falbo, 1977; Kipnis, 1984). Military leaders, as legitimate authorities in the services, can and do issue orders to subordinates who are duty-bound to follow those orders. Politicians speak directly to their constituents, explaining their policies and asking for support. Team leaders identify the subtasks that must be completed by the group as it pursues its goals, and then assign different members of the team to each subtask. But other leaders influence their followers in more subtle and less perceptible ways. They rarely issue any orders or directives, but instead put in place organizational procedures and structures that constrain their followers' actions in ways that often go unnoticed. Their persuasive messages convince listeners not by presenting rational arguments and information, but by appealing to their emotions and unconscious motivations. And some lead by setting an example that they hope others might follow. For every leader who orders, demands, and requires is a leader who persuades, cajoles, and maneuvers.

This chapter applies this basic assumption—that leaders influence others in ways that range from the direct to the indirect—to the analysis of influence in two stages. The chapter first reviews the historical antecedents of the scientific study of influence. Early investigators, intrigued by the sometimes surprisingly substantial impact of one person on many others, examined such topics as propaganda, persuasion, contagion, social climates, and suggestion. These investigations documented the many ways in which leaders influence others, but highlighted one of the paradoxes of influence: indirect forms of influence are often veiled within the situation yet they are just as powerful as direct ones. The second section of the chapter further explores this paradox by examining three topics that have attracted the enduring interest of social psychologists: persuasion, compliance, and obedience. Each of these forms follows its own path to influence; persuasion, for example, relies more on communication of information, compliance on extracting acquiescence, and obedience on acceptance of authority. But this chapter highlights their commonality: all three draw on both direct and indirect social influence processes to achieve results.

Investigating Influence: Historical Foundations

Philosophers and political theorists down through the ages have concluded that leadership is a form of influence. Homer's great leader Odysseus not only relied on his status as a warlord and king to take command over his crew, but he also made use of guile and cunning to overcome adversity during their long journey home. Shakespeare's plays are filled with vivid descriptions of the way leaders use coalitions and strategic initiatives to influence others. Centuries ago political savant Niccolò Machiavelli explained when leaders should use indirect (the fox) rather than direct (the lion) influence styles. The social psychological analysis of leadership, however, is scarcely a century old, for it originated in the field's earliest empirical explorations of suggestibility, propaganda, and contagion.

Crowds and Contagion

The scientific study of social influence began near the end of the nineteenth century when a number of scholars in a variety of fields simultaneously expressed a shared fascination with crowds, mobs, and masses. Le Bon (1895/1960), for example, undertook one of the first systematic analyses of the forces acting within crowds. He noted that, in many cases, the mob's influence can be traced to its leader—a charismatic individual who exhorts a large mass of followers to act in ways that run counter to accepted practice—"as soon as a certain number of living beings are gathered together, whether they be animals or men, they place themselves instinctively under the authority of a chief" (p. 117). Leaders of such groups, he believed, influence the masses through affirmation—they make claims without any supporting proof or evidence—and repetition—they repeat their message over and over again. But even though Le Bon concluded "the multitude is always ready to listen to the strong-willed man, who knows how to impose himself upon it" (pp. 118–119), he also recognized a second unifying process operating within large groups: contagion. Unlike a leader's direct exhortation of the crowd, contagion is a more subtle, localized process, for it generates uniformity in members' actions and outlooks as emotions, ideas, and information are passed from one member to the next. The result: "the heterogeneous is swamped by the homogenous" (Le Bon, 1895/1960, p. 29).

Le Bon's speculations stimulated the development of more rigorous analyses of influence, particularly in psychology (e.g., Freud, 1913, 1922) and sociology (e.g., Weber, 1921/1946). Freud (1922), in his characteristic search for the hidden motivators of human behavior, described the psychologically binding relationship between the leader and followers who identify with the leader and so develop strong libidinal ties to one another. Weber (1921/1946), in contrast, identified three distinct, but potentially overlapping, pure types of influence: traditional, legal-rational, and charismatic. Traditional leaders, such as priests, monarchs, or patriarchs, can influence others because their followers recognize and accept their legitimate right to exercise authority. Legal-rational leaders derive their influence from the impersonal rules of social order that define rights and responsibilities. But charismatic leaders, in contrast, inspire and motivate others more directly: "Every charismatic authority...preaches, creates, or demands new obligations—most typically, by virtue of revelation, oracle, inspiration, or of his own will" (Weber, 1921/1946, p. 243).

Attitudes and Opinions

Whereas Le Bon and other crowd theorists studied how leaders influence people who are massed together, other early researchers explored the leader's influence on widely dispersed followers. Studies of rumor transmission, propaganda, and mass persuasion all suggested individuals, in seeking information about their world, are significantly influenced by the opinions of other people, but particularly leaders (Lasswell, 1927). Studies of propaganda, for example, examined the way leaders in business, government, politics, and education systematically influenced others' attitudes and opinions, often by using methods that appealed more to emotion and bias rather than rationality and critical analysis. As Biddle (1931, p. 283) explained, many types of influence "create emotional disturbance in the coerced, resentments, overcompensations, or desires for revolt. Propaganda is different in that it controls without occasioning antagonistic emotions. Each individual behaves as though his response were his own decision. Many individuals may be coerced to behave alike, each apparently guided by his or her own independent judgment." Leaders, he concluded, sometimes make clear their intent to persuade, but more frequently their ultimate intent is kept hidden as they exploit emotions, related attitudes, and slogans.

In the 1940s and 1950s, Hovland and his colleagues (Hovland, Janis, & Kelly, 1953; Hovland, Lumsdaine, & Sheffield, 1949) conducted their groundbreaking experimental studies of persuasion and propaganda to understand how leaders could influence the nation's opinions during wartime. Their learning model was based on the three elements of any persuasive encounter: the source of the persuasive message, the nature of the message, and the characteristics of the receiver. Their work confirmed what previous studies only suggested: that persuasive communications are influential when they capture listeners' attention, offer convincing arguments, and leave a lasting impression. But they also discovered that persuasion does not depend only on these overt and more obvious aspects of the source, message, and receiver, but also on relatively subtle aspects of the persuasion setting. They discovered, for example, that listeners were sensitive to cues that helped them estimate the source's credibility. Listeners were also more accepting of a message from a communicator who was similar to them in some minor, even trivial, way. Moreover, some carefully crafted messages that provided listeners with the information they needed about an issue proved to be remarkably ineffective because they triggered fear and denial. They concluded the most effective, persuasive messages were ones that sought to change people's attitudes using a combination of both direct and indirect methods.

Normative Social Influence

Le Bon (1895/1960) suggested a relatively quotidian process—social influence—was responsible for the sometimes extraordinary behavior of crowds, but it remained for Sherif (1936) and Newcomb (1943) to verify this process empirically. Sherif studied this subtle form of social influence by asking individuals seated in a darkened room to publicly report their estimates about the distance a dot of light appeared to move (the autokinetic effect). Sherif found that, in this ambiguous situation, people gradually aligned their judgments until a consensus spontaneously emerged. His procedures provided a paradigm for subsequent studies of social influence, such as Asch's (1955) investigations of conformity.

Newcomb's (1943) field study of attitude change among the students at Bennington College yielded corroborating evidence of the ubiquity of social influence. Newcomb noted that many students at Bennington changed their political attitudes during the time they were students at the college becoming more liberal in their political outlook. This change, Newcomb concluded, was not brought about by some direct campaign to influence the students. Instead, it resulted from what became known as normative social influence—the tailoring of one's thoughts, emotions, and actions to match those displayed by others. The Bennington community at that time was a relatively liberal one, and many of the new students unwittingly accepted this outlook as their own. The more liberal attitudes created by the group remained a part of the beliefs of many of the graduates some 25 years later (Newcomb, Koenig, Flacks, & Warwick, 1967). Newcomb's work stimulated subsequent studies of two closely related social influence processes: reference groups (Hyman, 1942) and social comparison (Festinger, 1950, 1954).

Autocratic and Democratic Leaders

At about the same time that Hovland and his colleagues were studying persuasion and attitude change Lewin, Lippitt, and White (1939) were investigating the differential impact of three forms of leadership on group productivity and morale. They studied boys working in small groups on hobby projects. A young man was appointed the leader of each group, and this leader was trained to adopt one of three different styles of leadership. The autocratic leader was highly directive; he gave the boys orders, criticized them, and remained aloof from the group. The democratic leader, in contrast, adopted a more indirect, participatory leadership style; he explained long-term goals and the steps to be taken to reach the goals and rarely gave the groups orders. The laissez-faire leader's style was the most restrained of all; he provided information on demand but did not offer advice, criticism, or guidance spontaneously.

All three types of leadership generated changes in group behavior. A leader who influenced others directly—by issuing orders and monitoring the group's actions—created a leader-centered, work-focused atmosphere. His groups worked more diligently than groups with a laissez faire leader, although in some cases this productivity declined when he was not physically present to monitor their actions. Some of the autocratically led

groups also resisted their leader, but others accepted his authority without question. Overall, however, followers were more involved with their
groups and more satisfied when their leader's influence style was democratic rather than autocratic and, in some respects, more indirect rather
than direct.

Direct and Indirect Influence in Persuasion, Compliance, and Obedience

How did Roosevelt garner support for his relief, recovery, and reform
efforts? How did Bill Gates convince computer manufacturers to install
his software rather than his competitors' on their machines? How did
Secretary of State John Kerry gain international support for sanctions
against Syria for human rights violations? How did Jim Jones convince his
followers to take their own lives? How do leaders influence others?

The earliest studies of leadership conducted by pioneering psychologists and sociologists provided partial answers to these questions. Le
Bon (1895/1960) and Weber (1921/1946) described leaders who guided
their constituents' thoughts, actions, and emotions through spoken
and written communications. Work inspired by Hovland and the Yale
Communications researchers indicated that the leader, as the source of
the message, determines the magnitude of the message's impact on recipi-
ents (Hovland et al., 1953). Sherif (1936) and Newcomb (1943) confirmed
people's willing acceptance of others' responses as a normative guidelines,
and Lewin and his colleagues (1939) changed the actions and emotions of
task-focused groups simply by changing the leadership style of the leader.

Subsequent researchers, building on these foundational investigations,
examined three types of influence: *persuasion*, *compliance*, and *obedience*.
Roosevelt speaking to Americans during the Great Depression and Gates
explaining to IBM's executives why they should use his operating system
are examples of persuasion: the use of facts, arguments, and information
in a deliberate attempt to influence other's attitudes, beliefs, or outlooks.
Compliance, like persuasion, can result in a change in thoughts, feelings, and action, but in most cases compliance is behaviorally focused:
it seeks first and foremost acquiescence rather than private acceptance.
Obedience, in contrast, results when leaders draw on their power and
authority to change others. The devotee who drinks the poisoned punch
and the accountant who follows the boss's order to doctor the failing company's ledger are obeying a leader whose influence they cannot resist.

The analysis will not only detail how leaders persuade, seek compliance,
and extract obedience, but also consider the two sides of each of these
forms of influence: the direct and the indirect. Leaders can, for example,
persuade their followers in one of two ways: (1) through a direct, central
route that involves communicating reasons and arguments and (2) by a
more indirect, peripheral route that exploits the listener's emotions and

motivations. Similarly, although compliance and obedience are generally considered to be direct, obvious means of influence, in many cases followers comply and obey not only because they are the targets of direct forces, but also because compliance and obedience are taken-for-granted requirements in the situation where they find themselves. As we will see, these basic social response forms—persuasion, compliance, and obedience—are sustained by both direct and indirect social influence processes.

Two Sides to Persuasion

Studies of persuasion and propaganda, in explaining when a listener will be influenced by a persuasive message, assumed that people learn new ways of thinking by listening to a message's content, processing and understanding its meaning, and then evaluating the strength of its arguments. But, in many cases, people change their attitudes but do not remember or understand the content of a message. In some cases, leaders persuade people not by presenting cogent messages, but by appeals to followers' emotions, biases, and unconscious motivations.

Several theoretical models account for these two kinds of persuasion. Petty and Cacioppo's (1984) Elaboration Likelihood Model (ELM), for example, distinguishes between the central route and the peripheral route to persuasion. Central route processing requires cognitive elaboration of the message. If this elaboration generates favorable thoughts then people are persuaded, but if the message stimulates negative thoughts then the original attitude may become even stronger. If people lack the motivation or ability to examine the message closely, then peripheral cues in the situation—vivid images, emotionally charged phrasings, slogans, and so on—influence their attitudes. Chaiken and Eagly's heuristic-systematic model (HSM) similarly suggests that systematic processing requires careful analysis of the message but that heuristic processing relies on rules-of-thumb that are accurate enough for most purposes (Chaiken, Liberman, & Eagly, 1989).

Both routes lead to persuasion, but they do so through very different mechanisms. The leader who takes a central route to persuasion assumes that followers will consider the quality of the arguments, search their memories for information on the subject, and revise their attitudes if these processes generate pro-attitudinal cognitions. A message that leads to negative responses, however, may produce a boomerang effect: the listener may become strongly opposed to the advocated position. And a message that generates neutral thoughts or a mix of positive or negative thoughts may prompt the listener to rely more on such peripheral route cues as voice tone, warmth, attractiveness of the speaker, and so on. Thus, what matters most during central processing is the listener's cognitive response to the message. People who can list all the claims made by a leader may still resist his or her message, but followers who respond with many positive thoughts about the speaker, the message, or the situation will likely do what the leader suggests even if they cannot remember the substance of the leader's message (Mackie & Asuncion, 1990).

When should a leader use a central route rather than a peripheral route? The ELM offers two answers. First, the likelihood of cognitive elaboration decreases when followers are not motivated to process information systematically. Younger workers, for example, may not be persuaded by a leader who stresses retirement benefits, whereas this issue may substantially influence older workers' attitudes. Second, if followers lack the cognitive resources and abilities needed for elaboration, then the leader may find more persuasive success by shifting to the peripheral route. When people are distracted, have a prior opinion, or just cannot make any sense out of the message they are less likely to think carefully about the information. In such cases they instead shift to a heuristic mode of thought that sacrifices precision but improves processing efficiency. Followers who trust their leader do not try to pick apart the arguments in a persuasive message, but just assume that their leader knows what he or she is talking about. Past experience with leaders has taught them that, in general, "leaders can be trusted," "my leader cares about me," and "my leader is effective," so they rely on these rules-of-thumb to reach a conclusion or decision.

Dual-process models of persuasion predict that when followers rely on heuristics rather than systematic processing they will respond differently to the same persuasive appeal. Axsom, Yates, and Chaiken (1987) tested this assumption by asking college students to listen to a tape-recorded debate in which one speaker argued that probation programs are more effective than imprisonment methods. The researchers, to prompt some people to use heuristic rather than systematic processing, manipulated the listeners' involvement in the issue. They created high involvement by stressing the importance of the debate and its relevance for their community, and low involvement by telling listeners to just "sit back and relax" since this study was just a preliminary analysis of the idea. They also varied the strength of the arguments in the message and audience's reaction to the message. Subjects could hear, in the background of the tape-recording, the apparent response of the original audience. In some cases the audience responded with great enthusiasm—bursts of clapping and cheers of approval—but in others the audience rarely clapped and even heckled the speaker.

A dual-process model argues that these two factors—the quality of the arguments and the audience's reaction to the speech—should have very different effects on the listeners who are processing information systematically rather than heuristically. Systematic thinkers should agree more with a speaker who presents strong rather than weak arguments, but they should not be influenced by the audience's responses. Heuristic thinkers, in contrast, should respond more favorably when the audience responds positively. After all, the consensus heuristic argues that "if other people think a message is correct, then it probably is correct" (Axsom et al., 1987, p. 31). The results provided considerable support for the heuristic model. People who were involved in the issue (and presumably were processing information systematically) were more persuaded by a speech with strong arguments rather than weak ones. They weren't influenced to any great extent by the audience's response to the speech. People who were not involved in the issue (and presumably were processing information heuristically), in contrast, were more likely to agree with a strong speaker whose ideas were well received by the audience. These heuristic thinkers were not completely oblivious to the quality of the arguments—they did not agree with a low-quality argument even if the audience liked it—but they nonetheless let the audience's approbation guide their conclusions when the speech was sound.

Leaders need not choose, however, between direct and indirect approaches in their persuasive messages, for astute communicators structure their presentations so they appeal to both engaged and less-engaged followers. Olson and Haynes (2008), for example, examined the persuasive methods used by former US vice president Al Gore in his climate change film *An Inconvenient Truth*. This documentary seeks to convince viewers of the need to support environmental reforms and makes ample use of facts and information to support its case. Gore presents findings from climate science research in both numeric and graphic form and offers a detailed account of the effect of greenhouse gases on temperatures. However, Gore does not use only strong, compelling arguments in his message. He also guides the viewer's emotional reactions by presenting dramatic images of glacier meltdown and a catastrophic prediction of the impact of rising seawater on large population centers. He continually reaffirms his credibility by frequently referring to his close association with leading climate scientists and his long-term personal commitment to environmental issues. He capitalizes on audience cues to increase the acceptance of his message, for much of his presentation was filmed with a live audience that responds very enthusiastically to his message. This skillful combination of direct and indirect persuasive tactics means that both engaged and unengaged viewers will find his arguments compelling and so may, in consequence, change their minds and agree with the position he advocates.

Two Sides to Compliance

The executive who constructs a fact-filled report about a new corporate initiative, the politician who appeals to his constituents' commitment to their political party, and the propagandist who convinces others to take up a cause by delivering emotionally arousing speeches are influencing through persuasion. In other cases, however, leaders are more interested in changing their follower's behaviors rather than their minds. The police officer requires others to obey the law; the safety compliance specialist puts into place regulations to reduce risk in the workplace; the team leader requires every member of the team to attend the daily briefing sessions. Compliance, unlike attitude change, requires acquiesce that is in some cases relatively transitory and may or may not be driven by individuals' privately held beliefs.

Compliance is in many cases achieved by the direct imposition of the leader's will on followers. Leaders can and do issue orders, promulgate and enforce regulations, and punish noncompliance. Compliance tactics also include more indirect, even stealthy, means of influencing others. These indirect forms of influence, Pratkanis (2007) suggests, work by creating a favorable cognitive response in listeners, so that their thoughts when they consider the proposed course of action are positive ones, and any negative thoughts that might warn them against following the suggestion are disrupted. Taxonomies of compliance-inducing tactics have generated substantial lists of the many and varied ways leaders influence their followers, including complaining, building coalitions, exchanging favors, making demands, manipulating moods, persisting, enacting fait accompli, manipulations, supplications, evasion, lying, and so on (Cialdini & Griskevicius, 2010; Yukl, 2013). These tactics can be arrayed on a continuum from direct to indirect, as suggested here, but other dimensions of difference are also important to consider. Raven and his colleagues (Pierro, Kruglanski, & Raven, 2012), for example, distinguish between hard and soft tactics, as does Nye (2004). The harder tactics limit the "freedom an influence recipient is allowed in choosing whether or not to comply with a request or a demand" (Pierro, Kruglanski, & Raven, 2012, p. 41). Bullying, enforcing, or invoking standards, punishing, and delivering contingency-based rewards are examples of hard tactics. Soft tactics, in contrast, exploit the relationship between the influencer and the target to extract compliance. When individuals use such methods as collaboration, socializing, friendships, personal rewards, and ingratiation, they influence more indirectly and interpersonally. Hard tactics are often described as harsh, forcing, or direct, but they are not necessarily more powerful than soft ones; threatening people with exclusion from a group or public embarrassment may lead to substantially greater change than the threat of some material deprivation or corporal punishment (Fiske & Berdahl, 2007).

Soft compliance methods are not just noncoercive, but subtle and indirect rather than forceful or threatening. When researchers led students to believe that they had administered painful electric shocks to other students, the students felt guilty for what they had done and so were more likely to comply with a request to donate their time to a worthy cause (Carlsmith & Gross, 1969). Leaders who phrase their request in an unusual way pique their follower's interest in the request, thereby short-circuiting the default "I refuse" response (Santos, Leve, & Pratkanis, 1994). Norms of fairness and reciprocity, too, can be exploited by leaders to increase compliance, for individuals who receive something from another person—a gift, a favor, a reward, or even a smile—tend to feel obligated to give something back in return, even if the item that was received was unsolicited and not even desired. Across a number of studies, researchers have confirmed that people are more likely to comply with another person's request—to help with a task, to make a monetary donation to a charitable cause, to serve as a volunteer—if the person making the request previously did something that provided a benefit to the target of the request (e.g., Boster, Rodriguez, Cruz, & Marshall, 1995). Individuals who are negotiating a deal are more likely to offer a concession if the other party in the negotiation has previously offered one (e.g., Burger, 1986) and followers are more cooperative if the leader has acted in a cooperative, rather than coercive manner, in previous interactions (Komorita, Parks, & Hulbert, 1992).

Not every leader uses the full range of tactics. Those who are more concerned with being accepted and liked by their followers use more indirect and rational tactics than direct and nonrational strategies, but those who enjoy manipulating others instead use indirect and nonrational as opposed to direct and rational ones. Men use more of the tactics than women do, and they are the ones who are most likely to rely on the more direct strategies (Instone, Major, & Bunker, 1983). In general, people who use more rational methods of influence, such as reasoning, compromise, expertise, bargaining, or persuasion to influence others are better liked than those who use less rational influence tactics, such as deceit, evasion, or threats (Falbo, 1977; Yukl, 2013).

Leaders also use different tactics depending on their level of authority and their degree of power relative to their followers. A leader, for example, will more likely use such direct tactics as demands, threats, or promises when dealing with a subordinate, but indirect ones when trying to influence a superior. Also, when the target of the influence resists, people shift to more direct tactics (see Kipnis, 1984). However, some direct tactics are also harsh tactics, and so generate a range of negative emotions (e.g., hostility, depression, fear, and anger), whereas indirect tactics are often softer tactics, and so elicit compromise and cooperation (Fiske & Berdahl, 2007). Hence, although coercive leaders may be successful initially, influence becomes more difficult over time as their followers' anger and resistance to pressure grow. Followers will, however, tolerate the use of coercive methods when the group is successful, the leader is trusted, and the use of such tactics is justified by the group's norms (Forsyth, 2013).

Two Sides to Obedience

In many everyday situations leaders nudge rather than push; they suggest rather than pressure. But in other cases their influence can be extraordinarily strong. Rather than subtly shaping opinions and choices, leaders can compel obedience even when their followers resist that influence. Lewin, Lippitt, and White (1939), by finding that most of the young boys submitted to the autocratic leader's requirements, hinted at the power leaders could wield, but it was Milgram's (1963) behavioral study of obedience that fully confirmed it. This study, which is one of the most widely known studies in the social sciences, tested the limits of a leader's authority by creating a situation in which a legitimate authority ordered subordinates to do something they would usually not do—in this case, significantly harm another person who was innocent of any wrongdoing. Through a series of subterfuges and manipulations, Milgram arranged for unwitting participants to take the role of the teacher in a simulated learning situation. As the teacher, subjects were told to deliver shocks of increasing intensity to another participant—the learner—each time the learner made a mistake on a simple task. The learner was, however, actually part of the research team, deliberately made mistakes to test the teacher's willingness to obey, and did not actually receive any shocks.

The situation was a realistic one for participants, and served as a laboratory analog to real-world settings where leaders give orders to subordinates. Milgram expected few would follow the authority's orders, and that most would refuse when the shocks reached dangerous levels, yet 65 percent of the participants he tested were fully obedient. Even when he altered aspects of the situation to make the learner's suffering more salient, and limited the apparent credibility of the experimenter, participants still exhibited surprisingly high levels of obedience. Replications of Milgram's study using different procedures and participants have generally confirmed his initial findings (Burger, 2009) and studies of obedience in natural settings suggest that the levels of obedience that Milgram documented in his laboratory matches levels found in medical, military, organizational, and educational settings (Fiske, Harris, & Cuddy, 2004).

So extraordinary a human capacity—to compel others to do one's bidding even though they wish to resist—seems to require an extraordinary explanation. Freud (1922), for example, believed obedience resulted from an unconscious identification with the father figure and a psychological merging with the primal horde. Milgram (1963, 1974) posited a transformational psychological condition, which he labeled the agentic state, where normal cognitive functioning gives way to a mindless subservience to another. Yet obedience, like persuasion and compliance, is sustained by both direct and indirect processes. Followers' obedience springs, in part, not only from coercion and fear, but also from a cooperative orientation that recognizes that following maximizes both the follower's and the group's well-being. Milgram's experimenter commanded participants to continue and many participants obeyed—but only because the experimenter forced them to do so. Others, however, continued because they trusted the experimenter, respected his authority, and wanted to help the researchers achieve what they thought were scientifically laudable goals. In Milgram's experiment, as in many leadership situations, a variety of social forces—some direct and some more indirect—combined to create a situation where obedience was probable and disobedience improbable.

Blass (2000) examined this possibility by asking a group of unbiased observers to review a 12-minute videotape of Milgram's procedures before ranking possible reasons for why the participant obeyed. Blass drew the reasons for obedience from French and Raven's (1959) seminal analysis of the five bases of power: reward power, coercive power, legitimate power, referent power, and expert power. Two of the bases of power in the French and Raven model—reward and coercive power—can be considered direct forms of influence. Leaders with reward power extract obedience from followers because they control the distribution of rewards given or offered, including tangible resources but also intangible, personal types of rewards. Leader with coercive power have the capacity to threaten and punish those who do not comply with his or her requests or demands. Tangible threats and punishments include noxious physical events, such as abuse, fines, low grades, and firings, whereas intangible, social threats and punishments include disapproval, insults, and expressions of contempt. When the experimenter in the Milgram's experiment (1974) told the participants "The experiment requires that you continue" and "You have no other choice, you must go on," he was relying on coercive power.

Did Blass's (2000) observers think the experimenter in the Milgram's experiment used direct methods to influence the participants? Yes, but they emphasized his coercive power more than his reward power in their analyses. These observers also suggested, however, that much of the experimenter's capacity to influence participants derived from the more indirect sources of power identified by French and Raven: legitimate power, expert power, and referent power.

Unlike reward and coercive power, legitimate power stems from the influencer's recognized right to require and demand the performance of certain behaviors. The employer has a legitimate right to require a certain level of productivity because of the contractual relationship between employer and employee. Similarly, the teacher can insist that students refrain from using cell phones in class if both the students and the teacher recognize that this demand is among the teacher's prerogatives. Legitimate power arises from an internalized sense of duty, loyalty, obedience, or normative obligation rather than a desire to gain rewards or avoid punishments. Many subjects in the Milgram's study felt that when they agreed to participate in the study they had entered into an oral contract that obliged them to obey. In consequence, the experimenter had a legitimate right to control their actions and the learner had no right to quit the study. Unlike reward or coercive power, which diminishes when the authority loses control over the resources, authorities who achieve their position through methods that the group considers fair or proper generally find that their decisions are accepted, without resistance, by others in the group (Tyler, 2005).

The remaining two bases of power identified by French and Raven (1959), referent and expert power, can also generate obedience but do so in nonobvious ways. Leaders who are well-liked or admired possess referent power, for others look to them to define their beliefs and behavior. Bosses who enjoy the unswerving loyalty of their employees may be able to increase productivity simply by looking at a worker. Teachers who are high in referent power—the friendly teacher who all the students like and the tough but well-respected teacher—may be able to maintain discipline in their classes with little apparent effort because the students obey every request. The participants in Milgram's study respected the experimenter because he worked at a major university and was conducting scientific research. He was not particularly likable, however, so this source of referent power was likely relatively weak (Blass, 2000).

When followers believe that their leader is an expert—perhaps because of his or her special training, experience, or aptitude—then that leader enjoys expert power. An employee may refuse to follow the suggestion of a younger supervisor, but comply with the same request made by someone who is older and thought to be more experienced. Similarly, students may be reluctant to disagree with a teacher who seems to be an expert in his or her field. Milgram's experiment, because it involved electricity, placed many subjects at a disadvantage in terms of expertise, since few understood the effect of high voltage on humans. Because they considered the experimenter to be an expert, they believed him when he said "Although the shocks may be painful, there is no permanent tissue damage" (Milgram, 1974, p. 21).

Conclusion

Leadership is one of the great mysteries of social life. Most people, in most situations, proclaim their independence and individuality, yet they often sacrifice their autonomy and accept a leader's influence. But even though the word *follower* suggests to some a person who is weak or insecure, accepting a leader's influence is an adaptive process that helps people deal with situations that vary from the cooperative and collaborative to those rife with conflict, tension, and animosity. As an evolutionary account of leadership suggests, people accept influence from others because such behavioral responses are adaptive (Keltner, Van Kleef, Chen, & Kraus, 2008). When people join forces to achieve an outcome, individuals must step forward and guide the group toward it goals and others must accept that guidance. Followers struggle, in some cases, against their leader's influence, particularly when that influence takes the form of heavy-handed, exceptionless mandates, orders, and decrees. But, rare is the leader who relies only on direct forms of influence to keep followers persuaded, compliant, and obedient. Most mix the direct with the indirect, and as a result leaders' influence is often so subtle that it is scarcely noticed by their followers. So long as leaders are motivated by collective goals and not seeking their own selfish ends, then their followers will benefit when they accept their leaders' guidance (Tiedens, Unzueta, & Young, 2007). Homo sapiens thrive through the skilled use of, and judicious response to, social influence.

References

Asch, S. E. (1955). Opinions and social pressures. *Scientific American, 193,* 31–35.
Axsom, D., Yates, S., & Chaiken, S. (1987). Audience response as a heuristic cue in persuasion. *Journal of Personality and Social Psychology, 53,* 30–40.

Bass, B. M., with R. Bass. (2008). *The Bass handbook of leadership: Theory, research, and managerial applications* (4th ed.). New York: Free Press.

Biddle, W. W. (1931). A psychological definition of propaganda. *The Journal of Abnormal and Social Psychology, 26*(3), 283–295.

Blass, T. (2000). The Milgram paradigm after 35 years: Some things we now know about obedience to authority. In T. Blass (Ed.), *Obedience to authority: Current perspectives on the Milgram paradigm* (pp. 35–59). Mahwah, NJ: Erlbaum.

Boster, F. J., Rodríguez, J. I., Cruz, M. G., & Marshall, L. (1995). The relative effectiveness of a direct request message and a pregiving message on friends and strangers. *Communication Research, 22*(4), 475–484.

Burger, J. M. (1986). Increasing compliance by improving the deal: The that's-not-all technique. *Journal of Personality and Social Psychology, 51*(2), 277–283.

Burger, J. M. (2009). Replicating Milgram: Would people still obey today? *American Psychologist, 64*(1), 1–11.

Carlsmith, J. M., & Gross, A. E. (1969). Some effects of guilt on compliance. *Journal of Personality and Social Psychology, 11*(3), 232–239

Chaiken, S., Liberman, A., & Eagly, A. H. (1989). Heuristic and systematic information processing within and beyond the persuasion context. In J. S. Uleman & J. A. Bargh (Eds.), *Unintended thought* (pp. 212–252). New York: Guilford Press.

Cialdini, R. B., & Griskevicius, V. (2010). Social influence. In R. F. Baumeister & E. J. Finkel (Eds.), *Advanced social psychology: The state of the science* (pp. 385–417). New York: Oxford University Press.

Falbo, T. (1977). The multidimensional scaling of power strategies. *Journal of Personality and Social Psychology, 35,* 537–548.

Festinger, L. (1950). Informal social communication. *Psychological Review, 57,* 271–282.

Festinger, L. (1954). A theory of social comparison processes. *Human Relations, 7,* 117–140.

Fiske, S. T., & Berdahl, J. (2007). Social power. In A. W. Kruglanski & E. T. Higgins (Eds.), *Social psychology: Handbook of basic principles* (2nd ed., pp. 678–692). New York: Guilford.

Fiske, S. T., Harris, L. T., & Cuddy, A. J. C. (2004). Why ordinary people torture enemy prisoners. *Science, 306,* 1482–1483.

Forsyth, D. R. (2013). Social influence and group behavior. In I. B. Weiner (Ed. in-chief), H. Tennen & J. Suls (Vol. Eds.). *Handbook of psychology* (Vol. 5, pp. 305–328). New York: Wiley.

French, J. R. P., Jr., & Raven, B. (1959). The bases of social power. In D. Cartwright (Ed.), *Studies in social power.* Ann Arbor, MI: Institute for Social Research.

Freud, S. (1913). *Totem and taboo: Some points of agreement between the mental lives of savages and neurotics.* New York: Norton.

Freud, S. (1922). *Group psychology and the analysis of the ego* (J. Strachey, trans.). London: Hogarth Press and the Institute of Psycho-analysis.

Gardner, H. (1995). *Leading minds: An anatomy of leadership.* New York: Basic Books.

Hovland, C. I., Janis, I. L., & Kelley, H. H. (1953). *Communication and persuasion; psychological studies of opinion change.* New Haven, CT: Yale University Press.

Hovland, C. I., Lumsdaine, A. A., & Sheffield, F. D. (1949). *Experiments on mass communication* (Studies in social psychology in World War II, Vol. 3.). Princeton, NJ: Princeton University Press.

Instone, D., Major, B., & Bunker, B. B. (1983). Gender, self-confidence, and social influence strategies: An organizational simulation. *Journal of Personality and Social Psychology, 44,* 322–333.

Keltner, D., Van Kleef, G. A., Chen, S., & Kraus, M. W. (2008). A reciprocal influence model of social power: Emerging principles and lines of inquiry. *Advances in Experimental Social Psychology, 40,* 151–192.

Kipnis, D. (1984). The use of power in organizations and in interpersonal settings. *Applied Social Psychology Annual, 5,* 179–210.

Komorita, S. S., Parks, C. D., & Hulbert, L. G. (1992). Reciprocity and the induction of cooperation in social dilemmas. *Journal of Personality and Social Psychology, 62,* 607–617.

Lasswell, H. D. (1927). *Propaganda technique in the World War.* Oxford, England: Knopf.

Le Bon, G. (1960). *The crowd: A study of the popular mind [La psychologie des foules].* New York: Viking Press (original work published in 1895).

Lewin, K., Lippitt, R., & White, R. (1939). Patterns of aggressive behavior in experimentally created "social climates." *Journal of Social Psychology, 10,* 271–299.

Mackie, D. M., & Asuncion, A. G. (1990). On-line and memory-based modification of attitudes: Determinants of message recall-attitude change correspondence. *Journal of Personality and Social Psychology, 59*(1), 5–16.

Milgram, S. (1963). Behavioral study of obedience. *Journal of Abnormal and Social Psychology, 67,* 371–378.

Milgram, S. (1974). *Obedience to authority.* New York: Harper & Row.

Neustadt, R. E. (1990). *Presidential power and the modern presidents.* New York: Free Press.

Newcomb, T. M. (1943). *Personality and social change.* New York: Dryden.

Newcomb, T. M., Koenig, K., Flacks, R., & Warwick, D. (1967). *Persistence and change: Bennington College and its students after 25 years.* New York: Wiley.

Northouse, P. G. (2013). *Leadership: Theory and practice* (6th ed.). Thousand Oaks, CA: Sage.

Nye, J. S., Jr. (2004). *Soft power: The means to success in world politics.* Cambridge, MA: Perseus Books.

Olson, J. M., & Haynes, G. A. (2008). Persuasion and leadership. In C. L. Hoyt, G. R. Goethals, & D. R. Forsyth (Eds.), *Leadership at the crossroads: Leadership and Psychology* (Vol. 1, pp. 199–212). Westport, CN: Praeger.

Petty, R. E., & Cacioppo, J. T. (1984). The effects of involvement on responses to argument quantity and quality: Central and peripheral routes to persuasion. *Journal of Personality and Social Psychology, 46*(1), 69–81.

Pierro, A., Kruglanski, A. W., & Raven, B. H. (2012). Motivational underpinnings of social influence in work settings: Bases of social power and the need for cognitive closure. *European Journal of Social Psychology, 42*(1), 41–52.

Pratkanis, A. R. (2007). An invitation to social influence research. In A. R. Pratkanis (Ed.), *The science of social influence: Advances and future progress* (pp. 1–15). New York: Psychology Press.

Santos, M. D., Leve, C., & Pratkanis, A. R. (1994). Hey buddy, can you spare seventeen cents? Mindful persuasion and the pique technique. *Journal of Applied Social Psychology, 24*(9), 755–764.

Sherif, M. (1936). *The psychology of social norms.* New York: Harper & Row.

Tiedens, L. Z., Unzueta, M. M., & Young, M. J. (2007). An unconscious desire for hierarchy? The motivated perception of dominance complementarity in task partners. *Journal of Personality and Social Psychology, 93*(3), 402–414.

Truman, H. S. (1958). *Memoirs.* New York: Doubleday.

Tyler, T. R. (2005). Introduction: Legitimating ideologies. *Social Justice Research, 18,* 211–215.

Weber, M. (1946). The sociology of charismatic authority. In H. H. Gert & C. W. Mills (Trans. & Eds.), *From Max Weber: Essay in Sociology* (pp. 245–252). New York: Oxford University Press (original work published in 1921).

Yukl, G. A. (2013). *Leadership in organizations* (8th ed.). Boston: Pearson.

CHAPTER TWELVE

Leader-Follower Relations and the Dynamics of Inclusion and Idiosyncrasy Credit

EDWIN P. HOLLANDER

Leadership is not a solo activity, but involves an interdependent relationship with followers. It is variously affected by how followers perceive and respond to a leader, and their being able to exert an upward influence, instead of being shut down by dominance or other constraints of social control.

Though there is no leadership without followers, followers usually are given far less attention. However, an effective leader is interested in such followers' qualities as needs, perceptions, and identities because these play an essential role in the leadership process, and how leaders are seen and accepted. Political scientist Garry Wills (1994) asserted that from the outset "followers judge leaders" (p. 210) and "much of leadership is the projection of an image that will appeal to followers" (p. 274). In politics especially, such images are likely to be self-serving, even deceptive, as in an epigram attributed to Mark Twain, "If you get a reputation as an early riser, you can sleep 'til Noon."

Voters electing a candidate "legitimate" that leader's role as an official to be "followed," to some acceptable degree. There is the expectation that he or she will perform duties consistent with public needs. Another expectation, often revised by reality, is that in office a leader will produce policies promoted to be elected. Also, even if appointed, leaders benefit by acceptance. As John Gardner (1987, p. 6) said, "Executives can be given subordinates, but a following must be earned." Leaders can gain what Katz and Kahn (1978) called an "influence increment" beyond their authority, by personal standing, considered here as "credit" earned from followers.

Follower Acceptance of and Effects on Leaders

Findings about such follower perceptions are revealed in the *Globe Research Program* (House, Hanges, Javidan, Dorfman, & Gupta, 2004), an international study of leadership across world societies. Its goal was to learn what is considered effective leadership, regarding criteria of psychological welfare and international competitiveness. Among its conclusions from responses of 17,000 workers in 900 organizations in 62 societies around the world was that, "Leaders who are accepted by their followers are more effective than leaders who are not. An effective leader will, over time, be increasingly accepted because a leader's demonstration of competence improves follower's attitudes toward the leader, resulting in increased acceptance" (p. 580).

These findings are consistent with a history of scholars urging recognition how followers evaluate and respond to their leaders. Fillmore Sanford (1950) was an early proponent of this point that followers are crucial to any leadership event, and deserve more attention. In a prescient view, Sanford said, "There is some justification for...arguing that research directed at the follower will eventually yield a handsome payoff. Not only is it the follower who accepts or rejects leadership, but it is the follower who perceives both the leader and the situation" (p. 4). Indeed, we have now seen the actuality of the losing faction of an electorate refusing to accept and follow the election's winner as a leader, which is one form of what is called "nullification."

Expanding on Sanford's insights, a chapter of mine on the importance of followers granting this "leader legitimacy" was subtitled "relational features of leadership." It further stated that "follower responses to a leader can and do moderate the strength of a leader's influence, the style of a leader's behavior, and the performance of the group, through processes of perception, attribution, and judgment. Both influence and power require legitimacy, which is still determined or affected by followers and their response to leaders" (Hollander, 1993, p. 29; also in 2009, p. 140).

Lord and Dinh (2014, p. 159) seek to separate perception from effectiveness of leadership. In that pursuit, their first principle of four they propose is that, "Leadership is a socially constructed, enacted process that involves bidirectional influence among multiple individuals." However, Harms and Spain (2014, p. 188) emphasize that "the leader's actions are seasoned by the follower's perceptual biases," which are part of the social construction. It can be, in system terms, these feed back to the motivational question of choosing to follow and stay with a particular leader. "Why follow?" has complex answers (Kelley, 1992; Maccoby, 2008, p. 210). Though a great deal rests on perceived leader legitimacy, how the leader behaves toward them, and succeeds or fails in reaching mutual goals and fulfilling their needs matter. James MacGregor Burns (1978) wrote, "Only the followers themselves can ultimately define their own true needs...[given] a choice" (p. 36). Concretely, Warren Bennis (1999, p. 19) put it in these terms: "Whether in a corporation...or an entire nation, constituents seek four things: meaning or direction, trust in and from the leader, a sense of hope and optimism, and results."

Mary Parker Follett was a forward-looking, independent thinker about leadership in organizations. She stressed the important role of followers in her concept of "power with," in the early 1930s (Follett, 1949; Graham, 1995). In her view, the dynamic between the leader and the follower rather than the ability of the leader to dominate his or her followers was critical to team success. Chester Barnard (1938) was an executive who wrote a book about that role. In his *Acceptance Theory of Authority*, Barnard contended that in organizations, followers make a judgment about a leader's order by whether they understood it; believed it was not inconsistent with organizational or personal goals; had the ability to comply with it; saw more rewards than costs in so doing; and wanted to remain in the organization or group.

Social Exchange

Leadership usually involves a "social exchange," in which the leader gives something and gets something (Homans, 1958, 1961). This does not mean a literal return of the same thing received. In any leadership setting, there are expectancies about fulfilling the leader role. David Messick (2005) wrote, "A leader, in contrast to an individual, is expected to have the best interest of the group or organization in mind and to operate so as to promote this interest. The equilibrium or exchange between leaders and followers comes about in my view as the result of the natural social psychological processes that are involved when groups of people organize themselves to solve common problems" (p. 92). Messick added that followers follow because they may get such benefits from leaders as vision and direction, protection and security, achievement and effectiveness, inclusion and belongingness, and pride and self-respect. In turn, leaders may receive such benefits from followers as focus and self-direction, gratitude and loyalty, commitment and effort, cooperation and sacrifice, respect and obedience.

As a result of this exchange relationship, Messick (2005) asserted, "Leaders can make their followers feel respected as individuals, and trusted as group members who can cause a team or organization to succeed or fail. In other words, good leaders make the followers feel important as individuals...not [by] deception [but by] empowerment at an individual level" (p. 86).

Inclusive Leadership through Participation by Followers

Underlying the mutually beneficial relationship of exchanging benefits is the followers' acknowledgment of the leader's legitimacy as leader, and responsiveness by both to each other. For instance, a key question is whether a leader is capable of learning from followers. Peter Vaill (1996) said it was essential to good leadership. Two-way influence is a basis for "Inclusive Leadership" (IL) (Hollander, 2009), which seeks to "do things with people rather than to people" (p. 4). Dennis Tourish (2013) points to inclusion as necessary in "normal" business organizations, instead of Transformational Leadership (TF), he says, promoting "group dynamics found in cults" (p. 39). An alternative, favorable account of TF leadership is presented in Bass and Riggio (2006).

Listening is respectful in improving the leader-follower relationship and in optimizing team performance in groups and organizations. Bill Gates, a founder and former head of Microsoft, was described by an early coworker as "trying to get the right answer...not his answer...always great about saying 'What do you think?'" (Maffei, 2011). Gates earned respect, and credit, by opening up discussion and then probing intently, seeking a conclusion with coworkers. Newer leadership practices encourage decision making through good teamwork (e.g., Day, Gronn, & Salas, 2004) as a departure from traditional top-down power-wielding. Performing well at an organization's peak depends on the CEO's capacity as team leader (Schwartz, 2007). J. W. Marriott, Jr. (2013), former CEO of his family-named hotel chain, also reported using that basic "What do you think?" question with his staff, which was asked of him as a new officer by President Dwight Eisenhower. Other examples are leaders who encouraged inputs from followers, as revealed in interviews with CEOs, such as reply from the head of Continental Airlines, who listened to workers because, "I quickly realized that I knew a lot less about a lot of areas than the people who worked for me" (Kellner, 2009). But at failed Lehman Brothers Bank, CEO Dick Fuld discouraged staff comments and questions (Sorkin, 2009).

Increasing participation also has been justified on grounds of the higher-order value of involvement, democratic process, and increased effectiveness (Hollander & Offermann, 1990). Followers can team with leaders to improve the quality and success of the decision and its implementation (Howard, 1997), exemplified by European "workers' councils." Such participation was called an "ethical imperative" by Sashkin (1984). Optimally, organizational leaders ought to take account of follower needs and expectations (Lord & Maher, 1990, 1991). These follower expectations about leader qualities do affect whom they accept as right for the role, and how they respond to that leader (Lord, DeVader, & Alliger, 1986).

Essentials of Idiosyncrasy Credit (IC)

Issues of follower acceptance of a leader, based on perceptions and expectations about him or her, are essential to the "Idiosyncrasy Credit" concept of leader-follower relations (Hollander, 1958, 1964, 1978, 2004a). The IC model provides a means of grasping this set of elements by conceiving of followers giving credit to a leader, when seen as "one of us" and performing well. These credits exist in others' perceptions, and, as shown in the next sections, can account for leader emergence and added latitude of leader action, beyond legitimacy of authority. Credits are a way of spurring "upward influence" (Hollander, 2004b) by followers indicating that their views matter. A succinct definition of idiosyncrasy credits has been given as, "The accumulation of positive impressions of an individual acquired through achievements or past behavior, which are associated with greater ability to deviate from expectations without sanctions" (Phillips, Rothbard, & Dumas, 2009, p. 722).

The idea of credit accorded by followers also drew on concepts of attraction from "Sociometry," pioneered by Jacob Moreno (1934, 1960), which was basic to my early studies of peer nominations in leadership and followership (e.g., Hollander, 1954; Hollander & Webb, 1955; both in Hollander, 1964). Earning credit was derived from a view of leader qualities as interpersonal links to others that can affect their shared activities, a distinct departure from the traditional way of seeing these qualities as fixed. What is different in this approach was that it presented a process by which followers accord or withdraw support for a leader, via credit. Here the leader is not the only focus of attention; instead it is the relationship that is emphasized, as a two-way "inclusive" process. Mutual actions or inactions then help determine the success of the enterprise and the well-being of its members. The emphasis is studying leadership and followership together in an interdependent system (Hollander, 1992, 2007, 2009), as in Follett's (1949) "power with" idea.

The applicability of the IC concept is seen in everyday speech, where "giving or taking credit" and "being discredited" are understood as expressing approval or disapproval. For example, Michael Porter (1985) observed that, "Managers are reluctant to spend time and resources on interrelationship projects if they are uncertain to receive credit for them" (p. 389).

Leader Emergence through Credit

The IC model of leadership deals with a dynamic process of interpersonal evaluation. Individuals earn standing in the eyes of present or eventual followers and then have latitude for actions, including innovations associated with the leader role, which would be unacceptable for those without such status. With more credits than others, an individual may emerge as a leader. An initial purpose of the IC model was to account for how leaders emerge in an open system that is not limited by external institutional control from above or internal agreement, such as a rotating leadership. In this "input" stage, credits are earned by perceptions that other members have about one's contributions to the group's task, called "perceived competence," and loyalty to the group by adhering to its norms, called "perceived conformity." Both are inputs to credits in the eyes of relevant others, and they form "accorded status" associated with leader emergence.

Later, it was clear that the "conformity" term was easily mistaken for "slavish" conformity, when, in fact, it was meant only to signify what Brown (1936) called "member character," as a needed leader quality of identity with and loyalty or fidelity to the group. On the basis of the credit an individual has earned, he or she can do and say things in the "output" stage with more acceptance and less criticism than others with relatively less credit. In short, the IC model indicates how credits accrue and have operational significance in permitting innovations that would be perceived to be deviations, if introduced by another person with less credit.

Seniority also can contribute to gaining credits, but without a constant input that is linear, given that it is likely to reach a plateau. A person may also benefit from having "derivative credit"—a favorable reputation from another group or in society, such as high socioeconomic and/or celebrity status, and expertise. Credits are most often gained among followers by the display of competence and loyalty to group and institutional norms. These credits can then be drawn on for greater acceptance of a leader's initiatives, but also may be lost for failing to take expected needed actions in time. Overall, favorably perceived behavior provides credits to use for later influence and, importantly, independence from usual group pressure.

Credit Earned and Spent

The input and output stages of credit essentially mean that, "You earn them, and then get to spend them." However, spending is not just done in any way one likes because the expectations of others about suitable role behavior are involved. Furthermore, subsequent work with the IC model and related publications by this author (Hollander, 1958, 1960, 1961, 1964, 1978, 1992a,b, 1993, 2004a,b, 2007, 2009) and others (e.g., Estrada, Brown, & Lee, 1995; Winkler, 2008; Stone & Cooper, 2009; Shapiro et al., 2011) indicates that, in addition to the potential for gaining a leader role, credits make possible being distinctive, to break away and become more independent. The topic of overcoming impediments to independence is addressed in Hollander (1975; 2009, ch.18).

The IC model was not intended to propose how things ought to be in a normative way. Rather, it was to be descriptive of how things seem to operate in relatively noncoercive, open systems, where power is not absolute but depends on the conditions and interactions of the persons there. Despite this disclaimer, some have the impression that the model at least implies keeping a low profile early in interactions within a group and thereby earning credits by conformity. That was neither intended nor accurate because a person's perceived competence also matters. If he or she speaks up and contributes something that is productive, that person earns credits, and, thereby, may emerge as a leader.

Illustrative Research on the IC Model

The IC model postulates that "early signs of competence and conformity will permit later nonconformity to be better tolerated" (Hollander, 1958,

p. 120). When at Carnegie Tech (now Carnegie Mellon University), this prediction was supported in an experiment with groups of male engineering students who were to arrive at joint decisions (Hollander, 1960). Then, when at Washington University, it was also confirmed with male and female college students responding to how status level they had assigned to others affected their perceptions of those others' deviant actions (Hollander, 1961). Ridgeway (1981) found that early nonconformity could be a basis for influence, concluding this disconfirmed the IC model. Sheer volume of interaction though may earn credits by first speaking out and gaining high visibility on a matter of concern to the group. However, members' early reactions may then give way to a reversal, if shown later to be unsupported. This was the finding of an experiment revealing that initially quantity of participation was related to ratings of leadership ability. Later, judgments of quality became the basis for these ratings (Sorrentino & Boutillier, 1975). Relatedly, a longitudinal study showed how credits were being acquired by members of work groups (Estrada, Brown, & Lee, 1995).

A recognized limitation of laboratory research on leadership is that the groups studied have no past or future, unless these are induced. In an experiment precisely on this point, a group discussion task centered around urban problems was used (Lewis, Langan, & Hollander, 1972). Half the participants were told that they would have future interaction—that is, their group would have an extended life—and the other half were not. Crosscutting this treatment, the attractiveness of the decision alternatives in the problems varied, based on pretests. When participants believed that there would be future interaction and the alternatives were of relatively equal attractiveness, there was the greatest conformity to the group's majority judgments. By contrast, the greatest nonconformity occurred with a lack of anticipated future interaction, and unequal attractiveness of alternatives. This finding shows the possibility of creating an engaging reality to test hypotheses about group processes, and to see the greater pressure to conform to majority judgments in long-term groups. As already noted here, more effort is needed in such groups to justify one's different views.

Earlier, Alvarez (1968) found that credit loss, using his term "esteem," was significantly less for a leader's nonconformity when the organization was successful rather than failing. The IC model also postulates that unused credits can be lost by a leader who fails to live up to follower expectations for action. The loss may be higher by overpromising, and then seeming not to act in the face of need. Not least, the leader's self-serving and other negatively viewed behaviors can also drain credits, as can perceptions of weak motivation, incompetence, and avoiding responsibility for failure. But taking responsibility can have an initially favorable effect, as was found when President Kennedy did so soon after the loss at the 1961 Bay of Pigs invasion of Cuba.

In sum, experimental and other research has examined and in varying degrees supported the IC process (Stone & Cooper, 2009; Winkler,

2008), and indicated refinements of it. The sequence revealing changing evaluations was studied in the first two IC experiments (Hollander, 1960, 1961, 1964, chs. 17 and 18). An experiment by Hollander, Fallon, and Edwards (1977) on the effects of success and failure on leader standing and change in groups, and those reported in Hollander and Julian (1970, 1978), showed the relevance of perceived competence in the IC model. Competence is recognized generally as a major variable in interpersonal evaluation. That is certainly so in seeing a leader as successful or not, though it can be highly affected by bias and other situational factors. Among these are institutional structure and culture, as well as changed circumstances over which one had no control, yet may still be evaluated and responsible. Fair or not, a leader's competence is judged by perceived results, also attributed to how achieved, revealing that leader motives and "style" matter in attributions made by followers.

The IC model anticipated this later "attributional approach," conceptually and empirically. It was furthered in the work of Calder (1977), Pfeffer (1977), and Lord, DeVader, and Alliger (1986) related it to Implicit Leadership Theory (ILT), referring to follower expectations about leader qualities. IC also resonates with the Leader Member Exchange (LMX) of George Graen and his colleagues (e.g., Graen & Uhl-Bien, 1995), and justice concerns of George Homans (1958, 1961, 1962).

Leader Legitimacy and Follower Needs

Legitimacy is essentially the leader's basis for being considered a leader. It has a pivotal part in this relationship because it affects how followers perceive and respond to a leader. Among its manifestations, legitimacy implicates such qualities as credibility, trust, loyalty, and the leader's ability to be effective in exercising power and influence. At the outset, it brings credits from a leader's validation dealing with how a leader attained that status. However, Read (1974) noted that it goes on to involve a complex interaction of attitudes toward the leader and source of authority, with a leader's behavior adding to continuing legitimacy (p. 203).

Followers respond differently to a leader's source of legitimacy, so that elections and appointments create different psychological climates or conditions among leaders and followers (Hollander & Julian, 1970, 1978). Election is an obvious form of emergence, and is closest to the concept of followers having a sense of responsibility for an investment in according credit to the leader. Using an urban-problems task about a city called *Colossus*, an experiment on source of authority studied the effects on appointed or elected leaders of disagreements with their followers. Cast within the IC model, the purpose was to determine the leader's willingness to deviate from group decisions about the rankings of programs to alleviate typical urban problems (Hollander, Julian, & Sorrentino, 1969; included in Hollander & Julian, 1970). A "strong" or "not strong" support treatment was introduced cutting across the conditions of leader election or appointment. Elected leaders who had been *told they had strong group support were significantly more likely to make total reversals of their group's decision*, which was the dependent measure. Their mean number of reversals on the critical trials was significantly greater than those for leaders in the other conditions. In addition, *elected leaders with strong support showed lower conciliation in their responses to group judgments, based on a content analysis of their messages to the group. Evidently, elected leaders in this condition felt freer to expend credits by challenging group judgments, in line with the IC model's prediction.*

A subsequent series of experiments in our laboratory pursued this line of research on source of authority. The same Colossus task was used to reach group judgments on ranking solutions to urban problems. In general, elected leaders had more influence on these group judgments than did appointed ones. Furthermore, the influence of elected but not appointed leaders increased after the first failure feedback, and decreased after success feedback. This effect was interpreted via Hamblin's (1958) concept that a "crisis," in this case created through an apparent failure, produced the effect of "rallying around" the elected leader, at least initially. In the success condition, with no crisis, group members acted out of a greater security in their own judgments, and the leader did not gain that benefit. When the groups were studied for still another phase, however, the elected leader in the failure condition showed a distinct loss of status, with credits depleted and followers willing to depose the leader. Other research (e.g., Tyler & Caine, 1981; Sorrentino & Field, 1986) broadly supported these effects of reciprocal leader-follower influence found in our research.

Further experiments were done on responses to and by elected and appointed leaders in task groups. In one by Ben-Yoav, Hollander, and Carnevale (1983), we found followers rated elected leaders more responsive to their needs, more interested in the group task, and more competent than appointed leaders. In another experiment, by Elgie, Hollander, and Rice (1988), we studied the responses in a problem-solving task of elected or appointed leaders to positive or negative feedback from followers who were high or low in their task activity. Elected leaders were found to be more positive in their judgments of followers in the negative feedback condition, but similar to appointed leaders in the positive condition.

One explanation for why followers make a higher demand on the elected leader comes from the social-exchange view presented here earlier. Jacobs (1970) said the group gives the leader a "reward" in advance, by electing him or her, and then has a claim for "paying back" by producing favorable outcomes. Its counterpart is exemplified in the disappointment among political supporters when expectations for policies and other actions are not met once a candidate holds office. Overpromising loses credits. Elected leaders not performing up to expectation are found more vulnerable to criticism than appointed leaders, particularly if seen by supporters to be capable of doing better. As stated before, to be effective, even appointed organizational leaders need a "following" from going beyond just exercising legitimacy of authority.

"Idiosyncrasy" as "Exceptionalism": Distinctiveness Positive and Negative

The term "idiosyncrasy" was chosen to indicate that a leader could behave differently from others, at least in areas such as innovation. However, the term was open to misunderstandings, as long ago became apparent. In his book *Leadership Ethics*, Terry Price (2008) helped clarify this issue by referring to "leader exceptionalism." Building on the IC model's approach to leader-follower relations, his philosophically based analysis explained that leader initiatives are likely to be seen by followers as acceptable rule-breaking. Using the study of ethics and moral theories, he said that leaders have special latitude to behave in different ways.

On a related theme, Debra Shapiro and her colleagues (2011) studied IC effects on follower responses to exceptionally bad leader behaviors. They referred to these as "transgressions," including immoral and illegal action, abusiveness, procedural inconsistencies, and capriciousness. Their respondents (N = 162) were full-time employees enrolled in a university business administration master's program, who completed a survey rating leaders by the Graen and Uhl-Bien's (1995) LMX measure. Those perceived to be able and inspirationally motivating, who displayed such transgressions, were "less punitively evaluated." Consistent with the IC model, these findings confirmed that, "the greater latitude typically given when evaluating leaders with more positive attributes occurs even when leaders behave in transgressing, not merely idiosyncratic, ways" (p. 419). It is probable that trangressors often understand implicitly the credit concept and flagrantly abuse their status, expecting to get by through gaming the system. Many examples come to mind of such abusers, private ones observed in the work setting, and public ones in current events.

A key issue in Shapiro et al.'s research, regarding the IC model, is how followers relate to such abusers. The results show they are not so punitively judged if valued by followers. An analysis of this kind of relationship is in Jean Lipman-Blumen's (2005) *Toxic Leaders*. Another, earlier contribution on "toxic followers," is by Lynn Offermann (2004). Price's concept and the IC model are "relational" in stressing follower attention to leader behavior, often disregarded but of interest now (e.g., Chaleff, 2003; Uhl-Bien, 2006; Kellerman, 2008; Riggio, Chaleff, & Lipman-Blumen, 2008). Attention to "upward influence" and "inclusion" (Hollander, 2004, 2009) also show followers active in the leadership process, with more to come here.

The IC model is dynamic, postulating an "open system" of relatively free status mobility, where "power over" is not a major constraint. Differential needs of constituent groups mean that there are varying "credit balances," as, for example, in a politician's multiple constituencies. Credits are depleted if not restored by further inputs. A leader's failure to take appropriate action can rapidly deplete credits, by not spending them to fulfill expectations that a manifest need will be met. This phenomenon, which is variously called "sitting on your credits" or "being a dead hand on the wheel," is damaging to a leader's credibility and can undermine trust in authority, as chief executives continue to find. The point is, "use it, or lose it," as in the old saying. An instance of this in politics is seen in not using one's popularity to move with a program (Verba, 1961). This idea of "political capital" is similar to IC, but less dynamic in omitting such variables as perceived competence.

Also basic to the IC model is a positive emotion. As the "entrance gate" to earn credit, a leader must elicit positive emotion from others. Credit is neither earned, nor good qualities seen, if the others' emotion is negative, as when a leader is disliked. Whatever President Barack Obama's appeal for many of his followers, his detractors have shown little willingness to have him receive any credit, or even for many to accept him as a constitutional president. This denial by them has revealed a way to try to "discredit" a leader, by delegitimating him (Hollander, 2013a, 2014), a form of nullification. They said he was not a citizen born in this country, even after he produced his long-form birth certificate from Hawaii, which they had demanded.

Journalist Dexter Filkins (2013) also highlighted the detractors' negativity toward Obama and any of his policies. Indeed, they even switch their positions on policies they had advocated, such as demanding he aid the Libyan opposition to the dictator Quaddafi, which he ordered and was done. The next day, Filkins said, these Obama critics began complaining, "What have you just done?" (p. 49). An earlier flagrant instance was bringing a lawsuit to the Supreme Court against Obama's affordable health care law (ACA), as unconstitutional with its "individual mandate," though it was already in the Massachusetts Law passed under Republican Governor Mitt Romney, and was proposed originally by the conservative Heritage Foundation.

Some detractors, including major media figures, continue to insist Obama is a Muslim, thus separating him "as not one of us." He has asserted he is and has been a Christian, and never otherwise. He wrote about how he came to his religious faith many years ago in his autobiography (Obama, 1995). In 2012 polls during primaries in the South, over a third of Republicans said he was a Muslim. Former Speaker Newt Gingrich, seeking their presidential nomination votes, repeatedly promoted Dinesh D'Souza's slur that Obama had a "Kenyan, anti-colonial worldview" (Stein, 2010).

Realistically, the IC model cannot operate in these and other restrictive conditions, and will not always apply. A major lack is that the basic condition is not fulfilled of an "open system," unconstrained by authority pressures, such as those found in top-down organizations. As Graen

(2013) points out, administrative roles are distinct from leadership and can override individual choices in relations, thus limiting the operation of credit (pp. 170–171). In an example of mine, a supervisor turning down a request because it would violate company policy ought not to lose credit. Understandably, if this supervisor were somehow to get around the policy, this would please the requester. However, whatever credit gained from this could be lost by a sense of favoritism others feel, with a reverse effect, plus probable problems from superiors.

The IC model's essential thrust is innovative leadership and the latitude that followers allow a leader to make changes, beyond legitimacy of authority. The model describes a process in which the effects of leader authority are not fixed, but, instead, are determined significantly by the support of followers. Failing to recognize that element may explain why my French colleagues, Serge Moscovici and Claude Faucheux (1972), incorrectly asserted that "if Lenin had followed this scheme described by Hollander, he would first have had to become Czar of Russia before transforming it into a socialist country" (pp. 175–176). Given that the Czar is a hereditary monarch, this seemed a very strange example for these sophisticated colleagues to have chosen. Lenin was an emergent leader, supported by his immediate circle of followers. That is often the case for dictators initially, as leaders of a movement advance and extend control over a party, society, and nation. Dov Seidman (2011) called "personal charisma" that which brings trust in the leader derived from moral authority, versus "charisma from position," that is, formalized authority, similar to Graen's (2013) distinction noted above regarding administration versus leadership.

Heroes are a subset of leaders who stand out as having demonstrated achievements in challenging circumstances. Also, as Allison and Goethals contend, not all leaders are heroes, but those who are can be role models with a compelling "story." They often are able to draw a following, according them an abundance of credit, though not consistently, nor necessarily used in a constructive way.

IC Implications for Action

The IC model indicates how earned credits permit a leader to emerge and take actions that would be perceived to be deviations if someone with less credit introduced them. Credits can also increase a person's status in a group, without that person necessarily being seen as or becoming a leader, by providing more independence and influence. As noted, seniority also can contribute to gaining credits, although less so than other factors, and this influence eventually reaches a plateau. Also as noted, a person may gain "derivative credit," drawn from external status and actions, as seen with public figures and other celebrities.

Most often, however, a newcomer in a group wishing to bring about change needs desired qualifications to have derivative credit, and/or must display competence to gain credit. In the latter case, even when maximizing on the competence factor, someone may not earn credit as readily if perceived to be different, such as a woman in an otherwise male group, as Wahrman and Pugh (1974) found. This occurs in situations described as having "tokenism," with only one "different" member. His or her burden may be reduced by adding more such members. Newcomers usually are expected to "learn the ropes," by observation, and instruction, too. For example, a manager, after his first departmental meeting, was told by his director, "In our meetings, we don't speak up to disagree." Not least, new leaders, whether appointed or elected, still need to earn credits by building a following. New college and university presidents were found by Estelle Bensimon (1993) to need to establish credit with their faculties, and maintain it, before embarking on major changes. To sum up, this research was said to indicate that,

> the idiosyncracy credit (IC) model (Hollander, 1958)...is of particular relevance to the understanding of leader influence in academic organizations....The IC model...explains why new presidents initially may find it beneficial to [get] to know their institution's history, culture, and key players before proclaiming changes....[This] study...suggests that first-time presidents, not wanting to appear indecisive, may overlook the potential benefits of "getting to know" and "becoming known" by the institution. (Bensimon, Neuman, & Birnbaum, 1989, p. 39; see Hollander, 2013c)

IC, Charismatic, and Transforming Leadership

Charisma refers to a leader's appeal that creates positive attachment, accompanied by emotional arousal, seen in devotion and enthusiasm (see Goethals & Allison, this volume). However, charisma is not a quality a leader possesses, as much as an attribute invested by followers, which can be accorded or withdrawn by them. Its major proponent, Max Weber (1947), said charisma depends on perceptions by followers "who can withdraw it,...if the leader is long unsuccessful " (p. 360). Therefore, though the term comes from the Greek word for "divine gift," it can be viewed more aptly as followers giving a leader an abundance of credit.

Weber said further that a charismatic leader had an emotional appeal and great hold over followers, especially in a time of crisis when there are strong needs for direction. Weber contrasted this mode of leadership with the traditional kind, handed down from parent to child, as in a monarchy, and the legal, constitutional kind, determined by a democratic voting process. He also said charisma provides "personal authority" that evokes awe in followers, which is less likely with other leaders. On the contrary, Robert House (1977) explained charisma as a leader motivating followers on the path to a goal (House, 1962), and rejected some unique emotional attribute. In IC terms, it can be seen as a higher level of exceptionalism, like a guru, who is accorded a super-leader status.

Burns (1978; 2003) critiqued charisma as "so overburdened as to collapse under close analysis" (1978, p. 243; see also Yukl, 1999). In this vein, John Corry (1993), who was a *New York Times* reporter then, covered the acknowledged appeal of John Lindsay, Republican mayor of New York in the 1960s. If anything, Lindsay raised excessively high expectations so that "there was no way he could meet them." Charisma," said Corry, "is the most attractive but least substantive of political qualities and is useless as a guide to predicting what a candidate will do after he is elected. By the end of Lindsay's first term as Mayor, New York was having second thoughts" (1993, p. 111). Though his charisma seemed gone, Lindsay had enough credit to win on the Liberal Party line as an "independent," expressing contrition for what he said "had gone wrong," beating Republican and Democratic opponents.

Peter Drucker (1988) affirmed the major point that charisma should not be confused with performance. "Doing, not dash," he said, is what counts, and "avoid their [charismatic leaders'] belief in their own infallibility." Charisma's basis in emotional arousal and identification has limited permanence and carries such other negative features as narcissism (Howell & Avolio, 1992; Howell & Shamir, 2005).

A link can be seen between IC and Burns's concept of "transforming leadership" (TF) and "transactional leadership" (TA) because TF leaders, wishing to bring about change, *provide benefits to followers that earn credit from them*. Hollander and Julian (1969) had long since pointed out that the two benefits a leader can provide regarding change are "defining a situation" and "giving direction to activity." Accordingly, Burns's concept of a TF leader bringing people together for higher purposes by leaders interested in more than garnering votes (Burns 1984, p. 103) rests on a transactional/exchange process that Burns (2007) calls a gradient.

Indeed, Stone and Cooper (2011) considered the career of Nelson Mandela to exemplify this TA credit pattern, with his eventual emergence as a TF leader who became president of South Africa. They said his case therefore illustrates the link between the TA and TF leadership concepts.

Though charisma and TF are often linked in the literature, charisma may also be seen in TA leadership. Charisma is imputed to TF leaders, for example, in Bernard Bass's (1985) first presentation of TF, and House and Shamir's (1993) work. However, it can also be part of TA, and for similar reasons. The research by Ehrlich, Meindl, and Viellieu (1990) suggested that "more transactionally-oriented activities by a leader may also contribute to a leader's charismatic appeal" (p. 242). Critiquing the emphasis on the leader, in the "romance of leadership," Meindl and Ehrlich (1987) also asserted that, "Conceptually, the basis for either form of leadership is relational and perceptual exchange developed between a leader and his or her subordinates" (p. 96). As its basis, charisma is attributed to a leader by followers, and, therefore, they are likely to withdraw it, which was the essence of the earlier quote here from Max Weber.

In a new book on the "dark side" of TF leadership, Dennis Tourish (2013), as noted here at the outset, asserts, "[T]he dominant models within the rubric of transformational leadership are fundamentally flawed . . . they promote, unintentionally or otherwise, group dynamics often found in cults. . . . More inclusive and participatory models of the leadership process are required" (p. 39).

Consequences of "Good" and "Bad" Leadership on Leader–Follower Relationships

The followers' view is instructive in understanding leader behavior and its effects, as a counterpart to their according credits to leaders. Our own research program, summarized in Hollander (2006), used the "critical incidents technique" (Flanagan, 1952), a mode of event analysis. We drew our total sample of 293 respondents, about half male and half female, primarily from organizationally based master's degree students enrolled in evening university courses on organizational behavior or leadership. Two-thirds held professional and/or administrative positions, and the great majority (four-fifths) were employed full time.

We asked these respondents to write a description of an incident that had occurred between them and a superior in which either good leadership (the set given one half of the respondents) or bad leadership (given the other half) was displayed. To protect anonymity, no names or other identifying information was requested. Other follow-up questions then asked were what they found rewarding or not from what that superior did or said as leader, what their own response was, and what effect this event had on the relationship with this superior. Respondents also rated the leader on seven leader characteristics (e.g., involvement and directiveness), as representative of major qualities of leader reported in the literature. In addition, respondents evaluated the leader in the incident on semantic differential scales (e.g., capable-incapable and helpful-unhelpful).

Content analyses of the first open-ended question indicated that, in good leadership, leaders were seen to be supportive, have good communication skills in providing clarity and/or being good listeners, be action/results oriented, delegate to and/or empower subordinates, and be fair. In bad leadership, leaders were reported to be unsupportive, show a lack of communication skills; to be uninvolving, unfair, angry or harsh, autocratic; and at times to be poor managers of resources.

The major findings of this research showed that relational qualities were emphasized in reports and evaluations distinguishing good from bad leadership. Most notably, these included providing personal and professional support, communicating clearly as well as listening, taking needed action, and delegating. We found that the experience of good leadership was associated most with such intangible rewards as "provided a clear message which helped me interact more effectively" and support "backed up his staff." Conversely, bad leadership elicited accounts of poor communication and such unrewarding behaviors as unfairness, "rules do not go for everyone," and harshness, "constantly sought to demean me." Other examples on the negative, dysfunctional side included instances of character flaws, in self-seeking at others' expense, lying, misjudgment, vacillation, and illegal conduct, which could drop a leader's standing with followers, as a loss of credit. Corruption, in addition to incompetence, was found to be an important detriment by Barbara Kellerman (2004).

Particularly significant findings in the long run were the consequences of the good or bad leadership behavior on the relationship and follower subsequent actions. Respondents in the good condition reported that the incident developed/strengthened their relationship with the leader and increased their respect for him or her. In the bad condition, respondents often mentioned a loss of respect, passivity/withholding, discouragement, alienation, and weakening of that relationship, ending in departure from the unit or organization. An implication of a leader losing credit may also be the movement of followers, or needing to remain, but discontented.

Perceived attainments of leaders often result from team effort, said Robert Reich (1987), and so, "We need to honor our teams more, our aggressive leaders and maverick geniuses less" (p. 78). Especially vital, though, are leaders who deserve credit for showing the ability to engage followers toward successful outcomes. Counter to the usual view of "leader-centrism," many everyday tasks of leadership are accomplished as acts of support, not alone by one person, or only by those in authority. Help from followers by open communication, with influence flowing both ways, can optimize needed functions. Moreover, as followers perceive a leader to be responsive, fair, competent, and accountable, their trust in and loyalty to that leader grows and is more likely to be sustained.

Summing Up

Basic to leadership is how followers perceive and respond to a leader in a two-way interdependent relationship. Recognizing the influence of followers from how they perceive the attributes, actions, and motives of a leader has been of major importance. It has to some extent moved attention away from the dominant theme of a leader's effects on followers to a more balanced view. Studying the leader-follower relationship is now seen as essential to understanding leadership phenomena. As Robert Lord (2008) put it, "Followers play many critical roles in making organizations successful, both individually and as members of larger collective structures" (p. 256).

The Idiosyncrasy Credit (IC) Model highlighted here conveys some of the dynamics of how leadership and followership relate to bring about action and change in teams, organizations, and nations. The process involved can be understood as credit that followers may accord or withhold from their leaders, when seen as "one of us" and performing well, which then provides latitude for action that is undergirded by a bond of trust and loyalty. Charisma can be understood as representing a leader's abundance of credits received from eliciting positive emotions in others. This dynamic process begins with the leader's perceived legitimacy by followers, as in election and appointment. Leadership then carries on through two-way influence and interpersonal evaluation, with followers responding to the leader in terms of their needs and expectations, including performance and equity issues.

Followers are usually the leader's most attentive strategic audience, so their support is vital to leader-follower cooperative arrangements. They also are a resource for a leader who listens for a range of information and ideas, regarding ends as well as means (Hollander, 1985, p. 526).

The principles of Inclusive Leadership (IL), which draws upon active followership, emphasize giving respect, recognition, responsiveness, and responsibility both ways. IL takes seriously involving followers in the tasks of leadership to optimize the benefits of increasing the flow of ideas and creating a climate for implementing change. In the political sphere, IL affirms the "consent of the governed," and being responsible for informing constituents, and remaining accountable to them. Fundamentally, good leadership depends on and is enriched by good followership.

Note

Portions of this chapter are drawn from the author's chapter 8 in M. Rumsey (Ed.), *The Oxford handbook of leadership* (Hollander, 2013b), with permission of Oxford University Press.

References

Allison, S. T., & Goethals, G. R. (2013). *Heroic leadership: An influence taxonomy of 100 exceptional individuals*. New York: Routledge.

Alvarez, R. (1968). Informal reactions to deviance in simulated work organizations: A laboratory experiment. *American Sociological Review, 33*, 895–912.

Barnard, C. I. (1938). *The functions of the executive*. Cambridge, MA: Harvard University Press.

Bass, B. M. (1985). *Leadership and performance beyond expectations*. New York: Free Press.

Bass, B. M., & Riggio, R. E. (2006). *Transformational leadership* (2nd ed.). Mahwah, NJ: Erlbaum.

Bennis, W. G. (1999). The leadership advantage. *Leader to leader, 12*(Spring), 18–23.

Bensimon, E. M. (1993). New presidents' initial actions: Transactional and transformational leadership. *Journal for Higher Education Management, 8*(2), 5–17.

Bensimon, E. M., Neuman, A., & Birnbaum, R. (1989). *Making sense of administrative leadership*. ASHE-ERIC Report No. 1, Washington, DC: George Washington University.

Ben-Yoav, O., Hollander, E. P., & Carnevale, P. J. D. (1983). Leader legitimacy, leader-follower interaction, and followers' ratings of the leader. *Journal of Social Psychology, 121*, 111–115.

Brown, J. F. (1936). *Psychology and the social order*. New York: McGraw-Hill.

Burns, J. M. (1978). *Leadership*. New York: Harper & Row.

Burns, J. M. (1984). *The power to lead: The crisis of the American presidency*. New York: Simon & Schuster.

Burns, J. M. (2007). Foreword. In R. A. Couto (Ed.), *Reflections on leadership* (pp. v–viii). Lanham, MD: University Press of America.

Calder, B. J. (1977). An attribution theory of leadership. In B. M. Staw & G. R. Salancik (Eds.), *New directions in organizational behavior* (pp. 179–204). Chicago: St. Clair Press.

Chaleff, I. (2003). *The courageous follower* (2nd ed.). San Francisco: Berrett-Koehler.

Corry, J. (1993). *My Times.* New York: Putnam. [Note: Times is capped. It's the newspaper.]

Day, D. V., Gronn, P., & Salas, E. (2004). Leadership capacity in teams. *The Leadership Quarterly, 15*(6), 857–880.

Drucker, P. F. (1988, January 6). Leadership: More doing than dash. *Wall Street Journal*, p. 14.

Ehrlich, S. B., Meindl, J. R., & Viellieu, B. (1990). The charismatic appeal of a transformational leader: An empirical case study of a small, high-technology contractor. *Leadership Quarterly, 14*, 229–248.

Elgie, D. M., Hollander, E. P., & Rice, R. W. (1988). Appointed and elected leader responses to favorableness of feedback and level of task activity from followers. *Journal of Applied Social Psychology, 16*, 1361–1370.

Estrada, M., Brown, J., & Lee, F. (1995). Who gets the credit? Perceptions of Idiosyncracy Credit in work groups. *Small Group Research, 26*(1), 56–76.

Filkins, D. (2013, May 13). The thin red line. *The New Yorker*, p. 41.

Flanagan, J. C. (1954). The critical incident technique. *Psychological Bulletin, 51*, 327–358.

Follett, M. (1949). The essentials of leadership. In L. Urwick (Ed.), *Freedom and coordination* (pp. 47–60). London: Management Publication Trust.

Gardner, J. W. (1987). Leaders and followers. *Liberal Education, 73*(2), 6–8.

Gleason, J. M., Seaman, F. J., & Hollander, E. P. (1978). Emergent leadership processes as a function of task structure and Machiavellianism. *Social Behavior and Personality, 6*, 33–36.

Goethals, G. R, & Allison, S. T. (2014). Charisma (in this volume).

Graham, P. (1995). *Mary Parker Follett: Prophet of management.* Boston: Harvard Business School Press.

Graen, G. B. (2013). Overview of future research directions for team leadership. In M. G. Rumsey (Ed.), *Oxford handbook of leadership* (pp. 167–183). New York: Oxford University Press.

Graen, G. B., & Uhl-Bien, M. (1995). Relationship-based approach to leadership: Development of leader-member exchange (LMX) theory of leadership over 25 years—Applying a multi-level multi-domain perspective. *Leadership Quarterly, 6*, 219–247.

Hamblin, R. L. (1958). Leadership and crises. *Sociometry, 21*, 322–335.

Harms, P. D., & Spain, S. M. (2014). Follower perceptions deserve a closer look. *Industrial and organizational psychology: Perspectives on science and practice, 7*(2), 187–191.

Hollander, E. P. (1954). Authoritarianism and leadership choice in a military setting. *Journal of Abnormal and Social Psychology, 49*, 365–370.

Hollander, E. P. (1958). Conformity, status, and idiosyncrasy credit. *Psychological Review, 65*, 117–127.

Hollander, E. P. (1960). Competence and conformity in the acceptance of influence. *Journal of Abnormal & Social Psychology, 61*, 361–365.

Hollander, E. P. (1961). Some effects of perceived status on responses to innovative behavior. *Journal of Abnormal and Social Psychology, 63*, 247–250.

Hollander, E. P. (1964). *Leaders, groups, and influence.* New York: Oxford University Press.

Hollander, E. P. (1975). Independence, conformity and civil liberties: Some implications from social psychological research. *Journal of Social Issues, 31*(2), 55–67.

Hollander, E. P. (1978). *Leadership dynamics: A practical guide to effective relationships.* New York: Free Press/Macmillan.

Hollander, E. P. (1985). Leadership and power. In G. Lindzey & E. Aronson (Eds.), *The handbook of social psychology* (3rd ed.), pp. 485–537. New York: Random House.

Hollander, E. P. (1992a). The essential interdependence of leadership and followership. *Current Directions in Psychological Science, 1*, 71–75.

Hollander, E. P. (1992b). Leadership, followership, self, and others. *Leadership Quarterly, 3* (1), 43–54.

Hollander, E. P. (1993). Legitimacy, power, and influence: A perspective on relational features of leadership. In M. Chemers & R. Ayman (Eds.), *Leadership theory and research: Perspectives and directions* (pp. 29–47), San Diego, CA: Academic Press.

Hollander, E. P. (2004). Idiosyncrasy credit; Upward influence. Two essays In G. R. Goethals, G. J. Sorenson, & J. M. Burns (Eds.), *Encyclopedia of leadership* (pp. 696–701; 1606–1610). Thousand Oaks, CA: Sage.

Hollander, E. P. (2006). Influence processes in leadership-followership: Inclusion and the idiosyncrasy credit model. In D. Hantula (Ed.), *Advances in social and organizational psychology* (pp. 293–314). Mahwah, NJ: Erlbaum.

Hollander, E. P. (2007). Relating leadership to active followership. In R. A. Couto (Ed.), *Reflections on leadership* (pp. 57–66). Lanham, MD: University Press of America.

Hollander, E. P. (2009). *Inclusive leadership: The essential leader-follower relationship.* New York: Routledge.

Hollander, E. P. (2013a). American presidential leadership: Leader credit, follower inclusion, and Obama's turn. In R. Riggio & M. Bligh (Eds.), *When far is near and near is far: Exploring "distance" in leader-follower relationships* (pp. 274–312). New York: Routledge.

Hollander, E. P. (2013b). Inclusive leadership and idiosyncrasy credit in leader-follower relations. In M. G. Rumsey (Ed.), *Oxford handbook of leadership* (pp. 122–143). New York: Oxford University Press.

Hollander, E. P. (2013c). Leadership in higher education. In M. G. Rumsey (Ed.), *Oxford handbook of leadership* (pp. 311–326). New York: Oxford University Press.

Hollander, E. P. (2014). Barack Obama and inclusive leadership in engaging followership. In D. Sharma & U. Gielen (Eds.), *The Global Obama: Crossroads of Leadership in the 21st Century* (pp. 59–80). New York: Routledge.

Hollander, E. P. (2015). Further ethical challenges in the leader-follower relationship. In J. Ciulla (Ed.), *Ethics, the heart of leadership* (3rd ed.). Westport, CT: Praeger.

Hollander, E. P., & Julian, J. W. (1969). Contemporary trends in the analysis of leadership processes. *Psychological Bulletin, 71,* 387–397.

Hollander, E. P., & Julian, J. W. (1970). Studies in leader legitimacy, influence, and innovation. In L. Berkowitz (Ed.), *Advances in experimental social psychology* (Vol. 5, pp. 33–69). New York: Academic Press.

Hollander, E. P., & Julian, J. W. (1978). A further look at leader legitimacy, influence, and innovation. In L. Berkowitz (Ed.), *Group processes* (pp. 153–165). New York: Academic Press.

Hollander, E. P., & Offermann, L. (1990). Power and leadership in organizations: Relationships in transition. *American Psychologist, 45,* 179–189.

Hollander, E. P., & Webb, W. B. (1955). Leadership, followership, and friendship: An analysis of peer nominations. *Journal of Abnormal and Social Psychology, 50,* 163–167.

Hollander, E. P., Julian, J. W., & Sorrentino, R. M. (1969). *The leader's sense of constructive deviation.* ONR Technical Report No. 12, Buffalo: State University of New York Psychology Department. Reported in Hollander & Julian (1970).

Hollander, E. P., Fallon, B. J., & Edwards, M. T. (1977). Some aspects of influence and acceptability for appointed and elected group leaders. *Journal of Psychology, 95,* 289–296.

Homans, G. C. (1958). Social behavior as exchange. *American Journal of Sociology. 63,* 597–606.

Homans, G. C. (1961). *Social behavior: Its elementary forms* (rev. ed. 1974). New York: Harcourt, Brace & World.

Homans G. C. (1962). *Sentiments and activities.* New York: Free Press.

House, R. J. (1971). A path-goal theory of leader effectiveness. *Administrative Science Quarterly, 16,* 321–338.

House, R. J. (1977). A 1976 theory of charismatic leadership. In J. G. Hunt & L. L. Larson (Eds.), *Leadership: The cutting edge.* (pp. 189–207). Carbondale: Southern Illinois University Press.

House, R. J., Hanges, P., Javidan, M., Dorfman, P., & Gupta, V. (2004). *Culture, leadership, and organizations: The GLOBE study of 62 societies.* Thousand Oakes, CA: Sage.

House, R. J., & Shamir, B. (1993). Toward the integration of transformational, charismatic and visionary theories. In M. M. Chemers and R. Ayman (Eds.), *Leadership theory and research: Perspectives and directions* (pp. 81–107). San Diego: Academic Press.

Howard, A. (1997). The empowering leader: Unrealized opportunities. In E. P. Hollander & L. R. Offermann. (Eds.), *The balance of leadership and followership* (pp. 31–44). A Kellogg Leadership Study Project (KLSP) Report. Burns Academy of Leadership, University of Maryland, College Park.

Howell, J. M., & Avolio, B. J. (1992). The ethics of charismatic leadership: Submission or liberation? *Academy of Management Executive, 6*(2), 43–54.

Howell, J. M., & Shamir, B. (2005). The role of followers in the charismatic leadership process: Relationships and their consequences. *Academy of Management Review, 30*(1), 96–112.

Jacobs, T. O. (1970). *Leadership and exchange in formal organizations* (p. 80). Alexandria, VA: Human Resources Research Organization.

Katz, D., & Kahn, R. L. (1978). *The social psychology of organizations* (2nd ed.). New York: Wiley.

Kellerman, B. (2004). *Bad leadership.* Boston: Harvard Business School Press.

Kellerman, B. (2008). *Followership: How followers are creating change.* Boston: Harvard Business School Press.

Kelley, R. E. (1992). *The power of followership.* Garden City, NY: Doubleday.

Kellner, L. W. (2009, September 27). Corner office. Bad news or good, tell me now. *New York Times,* Sunday Business, p. 2.

Lewis, S. A., Langan, C. J., & Hollander, E. P. (1972). Expectation of future interaction and the choice of less desirable alternatives in conformity. *Sociometry, 35,* 440–447.

Lipman-Blumen, J. (2005). *The allure of toxic leaders.* New York: Oxford University Press.

Lord, R. G. (2008). Followers' cognitive and affective structures and leadership processes. In R. E. Riggio, I. Chaleff, and J. Lipman-Blumen (Eds.), *The art of followership* (pp. 255–266). San Francisco: Jossey-Bass.

Lord, R. G., & Maher, K. J. (1990). Leadership perceptions and leadership performance: Two distinct but interdependent processes. In J. Carroll (Ed.), *Advances in applied social psychology: Business settings* (Vol. 4, pp. 129–154). Hillsdale, NJ: Erlbaum.

Lord, R. G., & Maher, K. J. (1991). *Leadership and information processing.* Cambridge, MA: Unwin Hyman.

Lord, R. G., DeVader, C. L., & Alliger, G. M. (1986). A meta-analysis of the relation between personality traits and leadership perceptions: An application of validity generalization procedures. *Journal of Applied Psychology, 71,* 402–409.

Lord, R. G., & Dinh, J. E. (2014). What have we learned that is critical in understanding leadership perceptions and leader-performance relations? *Industrial and organizational psychology: Perspectives on science and practice, 7*(2), 158–177.

Maccoby, M. (2008). What kind of leader do people want to follow? In R. E. Riggio, I. Chaleff, & J. Lipman-Blumen (Eds.), *The art of followership.* San Francisco: Jossey-Bass, 209–217.

Maffei, G. B. (2011, January 9). Quoted in A. Bryant. Corner office. *New York Times,* p. B2.

Marriott, J. W., Jr. (2013, May 26). Corner office. What Eisenhower taught me about decision-making. *New York Times,* p. B2.

Meindl, J. R., & Ehrlich, S. B. (1987). The romance of leadership and the evaluation of organizational performance. *Academy of Management Journal, 30,* 90–109.

Messick, D. M (2005). On the psychological exchange between leader and followers. In D. M. Messick & R. M. Kramer (Eds.), *The psychology of leadership: New perspectives and research* (pp. 83–98). Mahwah, NJ: Erlbaum.

Moreno, J. L. (1934). *Who shall survive?* New York: Beacon House.

Moreno, J. L. (Ed.) (1960). *The sociometry reader.* Glencoe, IL: Free Press.

Moscovici, S., & Faucheux, C. (1972). Social influence, conforming bias, and the study of active minorities. In L. Berkowitz (Ed.), *Advances in experimental social* (Vol. 6, pp. 149–202). New York: Academic Press.

Obama, B. (1995). *Dreams from my father: A story of race and inheritance.* New York: Times Books.

Offermann, L. R. (2004). When followers become toxic. *Harvard Business Review, 87*(1), 55–60.

Pfeffer, J. (1977). The ambiguity of leadership. In M. W. McCall, Jr. & M. M. Lombardo (Eds.), *Leadership: Where else can we go?* (pp. 13–36). Durham, NC: Duke University Press.

Phillips, K. W., Rothbard, N. P., & Dumas, T. L. (2009). To disclose or not to disclose? Status distance and self-disclosure in diverse environments. *Academy of Management Review, 34,* 710–732.

Porter, M. E. (1985). *Competitive advantage.* New York: Free Press.

Price, T. (2008). *Leadership ethics.* New York: Cambridge University Press.

Read, P. B. (1974). Source of authority and the legitimation of leadership in small groups. *Sociometry, 37,* 189–204.

Reich, R. B. (1987). Entrepreneurship reconsidered: The team as hero. *Harvard Business Review, 65*(3), 77–83.

Ridgeway, C. L. (1981). Nonconformity, competence, and influence in groups: A test of two theories. *American Sociological Review, 46,* 333–347.

Riggio, R. E, Chaleff, I., & Lipman-Blumen, J. (Eds.) (2008). *The art of followership.* San Francisco: Jossey-Bass.

Sanford, F. (1950). *Authoritarianism and leadership.* Philadelphia: Institute for Research in Human Relations.

Sashkin, M. (1984). Participative management is an ethical imperative. *Organizational Dynamics, 12,* 4–22.

Schwartz, N. D. (2007, November 10). C.E.O evolution phase 3: After empire builders and repair experts, the team captain. *New York Times,* p. C1.

Seidman, D. (2011). *How.* Hoboken, NJ: Wiley.

Shapiro, D. L., Boss, A. D., Salas, S., Tangirala, S., & Von Glinow, M. A. (2011). When are transgressing *leaders* punitively judged? An empirical test. *Journal of Applied Psychology, 46*(2), 412–422.

Sorkin, A. R. (2009). *Too big to fail.* New York: Viking.

Sorrentino, R. M., & Boutillier, R. G. (1975). The effect of quantity and quality of verbal interaction on ratings of leadership ability. *Journal of Experimental Social Psychology,* 11, 403–411.

Sorrentino, R. M., & Field, N. (1986). Emergent leadership over time: The functional value of positive motivation. *Journal of Personality and Social Psychology, 50,* 1091–1099.

Stein, S. (2012). Gingrich slammed for saying Obama may hold "Kenyan, anti-colonial" worldview. *Huffpost,* September 12, p. 1.

Stone, T. & Cooper, W. (2009). Emerging credit. *Leadership Quarterly, 20,* 785–798.

Tourish, D. (2013). *The dark side of transformational leadership: A critical perspective.* London: Routledge.

Tyler, T. R., & Caine, A. (1981). The influence of outcomes and procedures on satisfaction with formal leaders. *Journal of Personality and Social Psychology, 41,* 642–655.

Uhl-Bien, M. (2006). Relational leadership theory: Exploring the social processes of leadership and organizing. *Leadership Quarterly, 17,* 654–676.

Vaill, P. B. (1996). *Learning as a way of being.* San Francisco: Jossey-Bass.

Vaill, P. B. (1982). The purposing of high-performing systems. *Organizational Dynamics, 11*(2), 23–39.

Verba, S. (1961). *Small groups and political behavior: A study of leadership.* Princeton, NJ: Princeton University Press.

Wahrman, R., & Pugh, M. (1974). Sex, nonconformity and influence. *Sociometry, 37,* 137–147.

Wallace, J. L. (1996). An examination of comparable behavioral and motivational features of transactional and transformational leadership as regards effectiveness and follower satisfaction. Unpublished doctoral dissertation, Baruch College and the Graduate Center, City University of New York.

Weber, M. (1947). *The theory of social and economic organization.* T. Parsons & A. M. Henderson (Ed. and Trans.) New York: Oxford University Press. Wills, G. (1994) *Certain trumpets: The nature of leadership.* New York: Simon & Schuster.

Yukl, G. (1999). An evaluation of conceptual weakness in transformational and charismatic leadership theories. *Leadership Quarterly, 10*(2), 285–305.

CHAPTER THIRTEEN

Power and Influence at the Top: Effective and Ineffective Forms of Leader Behavior

RODERICK M. KRAMER

Social psychologists have long recognized the intimate and reciprocal relationship that exists between the power leaders possess and their capacity to exert influence over others (French & Raven, 1959; McClelland, 1975). The effective use of social influence, it has been argued, helps aspiring leaders obtain and consolidate power (McClelland and Burnham, 1976; Pfeffer, 2010). Power, in turn, enhances their ability to retain their positional advantage and exert effective influence once they become leaders (Neustadt, 1990; Pfeffer, 1992).

Given these important theorized linkages between power and influence, it is hardly surprising that social scientists have afforded considerable attention to the study of how leaders acquire power and influence, as well as how, in turn, they use that power and influence when trying to achieve their desired goals. Richard Neustadt (1990), one of the most distinguished scholars to study power, even went so far as to characterize power in terms of "personal influence of an effective sort" (p. ix). Subsequent studies have only reinforced and deepened our understanding of this fundamental and important relationship (see, e.g., Kellerman, 1994). These studies document, in particular, the relationship between the effective use of power and influence by perceptive and politically skilled leaders and the attainment of often difficult personal, institutional, and organizational goals (Caro, 2002; Gergen, 2000).

After decades of sustained inquiry, the extant literature on this topic has grown substantially, and a comprehensive overview far beyond the scope of the present chapter. Accordingly, the primary and more modest goals of this chapter are, first, to provide a brief historical review of some of the major early social psychological research on leader power and influence. Second, I examine some more recent theoretical developments and empirical contributions. In particular, I explore some of the forms of effective and ineffective leader influence behaviors that social psychologists have examined when studying the leadership process. In so doing, I draw on some of my own case studies on effective (Kramer, 2006) and ineffective (Kramer, 2003) uses of leader power and influence. In concert, these studies suggest that leaders at times display considerable "political genius" (cf., Caro, 1975, 1982, 2002; Kearns-Goodwin, 2006) in the pursuit of their aspirations and aims, followed by stints of surprising and even startingly perplexing folly.

To illustrate this general theme of leader "genius and folly" when using power and influence, I draw primarily on several examples from the US presidency. Not surprisingly, given the importance of the office, the study of power and influence within the Oval Office has been the subject of considerable scholarly interest. On the one hand, one would hardly be surprised to discover that US presidents have proven quite adept at thinking about and using their power and influence. After all, in the long road to that office they are the victors of countless political contests and skirmishes. Their political mettle has been measured and proven—again and again. On the other hand, history provides no shortage of examples of striking political miscalculation and flagrantly ineffectual behaviors by presidents—often when they are seemingly at the top of their game. Thus, these leaders provide particularly rich and provocative fodder for the study of the complexities and sometimes perplexing variability in the effective and ineffective use of power and influence by experienced and presumably politically savvy leaders.

A Brief History and Review of Research on
Leader Power and Influence

Historically, the concept of power has been readily invoked to explain how leaders achieve a host of important organizational processes and outcomes, including how their power is exercised (Galinsky, Gruenfeld, & Magee, 2003; Keltner, Gruenfeld, & Anderson, 2003), how organizational resources are allocated (Pfeffer, 1992), how important decisions are made (Neustadt, 1990), and how conflicts are resolved (Boulding, 1966, 1989).

The concept of power has been routinely employed, moreover, not only to explain why leaders are able to make desired or intended things happen, but also why they sometimes fail in their efforts. Given this impressive spectrum of demonstrated consequences, Bertrand Russell's (1938) cogent observation that power is a "fundamental concept" in the social sciences remains as true today as it was when he first uttered it, and never more true as when applied to the voluminous literature on leadership.

Conceptualizing Leader Power and Influence

When it comes to conceptualizing power, most theorists have adopted some variant of physical metaphor, suggesting that the concept of power entails "the intuitive notion of *struggle*, with outcomes determined by the relative strength of *contending forces*" (March, 1994, p. 140, emphases added). Along similar lines, Blau (1964) proposed that actors possess power when they can "*induce* others to accede to wishes by rewarding them for doing so" (p. 115, emphasis added). More recent definitions (e.g., Wong, 1979) continue this conceptual tradition, characterizing power as the "capacity of some persons to *produce intended* and *foreseen effects* on others" (p. 2, emphases added). In such accounts, power is treated almost as a vector force that influences the movement of bodies through a space.

Along parallel lines, conceptualizations of social influence reflect physical images of push and pull. Influence has been characterized, for example, as a process entailing the successful induction of change in other people's attitudes, beliefs, perceptions, feelings, values, and behaviors by means of one's own behavioral tactics (Pratkanis, 2007). Thus defined, the use of effective influence tactics has been the subject of considerable prior theory and research (Cialdini, 1988; Kramer & Neale, 1998; Levine, 2003; Pratkanis & Aronson, 1992, 2001; Zimbardo, Ebbesen, & Maslach, 1977).

Effective versus Ineffective Influence Behaviors

Within the context of previous leadership studies, considerable attention has focused on the effective use of power and influence. In elaborating on the nature of this process, some important and enduring distinctions have been drawn by previous scholars. The first of these is the distinction between *transactional* and *transformational* leadership processes. In an early and insightful discussion of this distinction, Bass (1984) noted that transactional leadership processes focus primarily on the provision of contingent rewards and punishments as means of influencing constituents' attitudes, feelings, and behaviors. Transformational leadership, in contrast, entails the use of individualized attention and consideration, intellectual challenge and stimulation, and charismatic modes of influence (such as inspiring rhetoric and imagery).

One of the more important distinctions to have gained traction in recent years—among academics and practitioners alike—concerns the "hard" versus "soft" nature of power that leaders deploy during the influence process. In his influential work on this topic, Nye (2008) notes that hard power entails use of the proverbial sticks at a leader's disposal to induce compliance and conformity with directives or requests. Soft power, in contrast, favors the appeal and allure of organizational carrots. If the former is coercive, Nye notes, the latter is seductive. Neither form of power, he goes on add, is inherently superior or dominant, noting that the comparative efficacy of hard versus soft forms of power is contingent on the specific context within which the leader is operating. Accordingly, Nye argues, leaders' "contextual intelligence" (i.e., their deft and contingent assessment of which influence approach is needed in a given situation) plays a vital role in determining the ultimate effectiveness of their influence attempts.

In an impressive series of original empirical studies, as well as theoretical integrations, Hackman and his associates (Hackman, 2002; Hackman & Wageman, 2005; Wageman, Nunes, Burruss, & Hackman, 2008) have done much in recent years to advance and deepen our understanding of the core influence processes that contribute to effective leadership. According to their framework, effective leader influence consists of creating and maintaining a set of conditions that are conducive to effective organizational performance. Specifically, the five conditions that leaders can influence include (1) contributing to the *composition* and development of a well-functioning group, (2) providing a *compelling direction* for the group's work, (3) providing an *enabling structure* that facilitates rather than impedes coordination and collaboration, (4) providing and maintaining a *supportive organizational context*, and (5) providing ample *expert coaching* when needed.

Because the literature on effective influence is so well established and substantial, with abundant overviews and compilations available elsewhere (Kenrick, Goldstein, & Braver, 2012; Kramer & Neale, 1998; Pratkanis, 2007), I now turn our attention to a comparatively neglected, but no less important, topic—namely, the self-defeating or counterproductive use of power and influence by leaders.

It is important to note at the outset that self-defeating influence behavior by leaders—behavior that proves counterproductive or self-destructive— represents a rather provocative and only poorly understood behavioral phenomenon. Indeed, it seems almost paradoxical or, at the very least, ironic, that leaders can shoot themselves in the proverbial foot with such alacrity. After all, if self-preservation and the pursuit of self-interest are among the hallmarks of rational behavior," then self-defeating influence behaviors must be counted as among the most peculiar and vexing demonstrations of leader irrationality (Baumeister & Scher, 1988, p. 3).

Self-defeating influence behavior by experienced and successful leaders is particularly puzzling because, on prima facie grounds, one might argue such behavior should be rather rare. After all, when political novices use influence processes ineptly, it is easy to discount their mistakes as reflecting simply lack of sophistication or requisite experience. Their mistakes can be attributed, for example, to naive misperceptions or miscalculations that undermine their influence attempts. When experienced and politically savvy leaders make such mistakes, however, there is often a more perplexing and paradoxical quality to their actions. Because they are seasoned and proven power players and influence purveyors, we might expect, powerful and well-established leaders should be fairly discriminating when it comes to sizing up influence situations and equally adept at finding the "right" (i.e., most effective) influence strategies to use in that situation.

As myriad social, corporate, and political scandals over the past decade have amply documented, however, even the savviest and most experienced leaders are capable of shooting themselves in the proverbial foot

(Kramer, 2003a). Indeed, when we examine the recurrent and persistent self-defeating behavior of political virtuosos such as Presidents William Clinton and Richard Nixon, or someone with a proven track record of savvy prosecution and media manipulation, such as Eliot Spitzer—to invoke just three recent examples—who has not asked, "What were they thinking? How could they have been so stupid?" What accounts for the stunning ability of such leaders to snatch such absolute and total defeat from the jaws of victory?

In trying to make sense of this phenomena, there is fortunately a small literature nestled at the intersection of social and clinical psychology (Berglas & Baumeister, 1993). Baumeister and Scher (1988) provided one of the first comprehensive literature reviews of this literature, defining self-defeating behavior as "any deliberate or intentional behavior that has clear, definitely or probably negative effects on the self or on the self's projects" (p. 3). They go on to posit that the behavior "must be intentional, although harm to self did not have to be the intended or primary goal of the action" (p. 3).

Much of the initial research in this area focused on what social psychologists call "motivated" forms of self-defeating behavior. Baumeister and Scher characterized these as *deliberate* or *primary self-destructive behaviors.* An assumption behind this early emphasis was that decision makers' willingness to engage in, and persist with, obviously self-destructive behaviors suggests they must have some sort of psychological investment or stake in the negative outcomes or failure those behaviors were producing (see, e.g., Berglas & Baumeister, 1993, 1996).

As Baumeister and Scher (1988) themselves noted in their careful assessment of such research, however, the evidence that people deliberately engage in behavior that harms the self in a foreseeable and desired way is actually quite thin. Consequently, they concluded, the range of normal adult self-defeating behaviors they examined simply "does not conform to the pattern of deliberate self-destruction" (p. 7). A more fruitful approach, therefore, seemed to pursue psychological and social processes that might impel even normal, ordinary decision makers to unintentionally engage in, and persist with, self-defeating modes of judgment and action. Thus, the second category of self-defeating behavior Baumeister and Scher addressed involves situations where decision makers do not desire, intend, or foresee the harmful or self-destructive consequences of their acts. This category includes situations where a decision maker "seeks some positive goal, but uses a technique or strategy that impairs the chances of success.... The focus is neither on normal behaviors that occasionally turn out badly, nor on isolated accidents or mishaps. Rather, it is on *systematic behavior patterns that... lead reliably to self-harmful outcomes*" (Baumeister & Scher, 1988, p. 12, emphases added). It is this category of self-defeating leader behavior with which this chapter is particularly concerned.

Because this topic has received so little systematic attention from social psychologists, I next identify some of the specific forms that self-defeating influence behaviors take. I then examine some of the possible determinants and dynamics of such behavior. This will hopefully help give a flavor of the sorts of causal factors that might drive such behavior. I follow this discussion with a consideration of some of the psychological and social dynamics that contribute to the persistence of self-defeating influence behaviors. I close the chapter by discussing briefly some of the implications of the framework for our understanding of self-defeating power and influence behavior by leaders.

Forms of Self-Defeating Leader Power and
Influence Behaviors

In their review of the literature, Baumeister and Scher (1988) identified several general forms of self-defeating behavior, any one of which, I will argue, can adversely affect leaders' influence behaviors. The first is *irrational persistence* or *perseveration*. As Baumeister and Scher (1988) have aptly noted, "Although persistence is often regarded as a virtue, misguided persistence can waste time and resources, and therefore defeat one's chance of success at superordinate goals" (p. 12). One classic example of such counterproductive perseverance in the leadership realm was Lyndon Johnson's persistence in simultaneously pursuing his political objectives of successful prosecution of the Vietnam war (he did not want to be the first president to lose a major war) and the attainment of his Great Society goals, especially in the realm of civil rights and education (he was determined to "out-Roosevelt Roosevelt" when it came to domestic achievements). Johnson's unwillingness to make the necessary, even if difficult, trade-offs between "guns and butter" ultimately compromised the successful pursuit of both programs. Equally importantly, it defeated his often-stated goal of being remembered as one of the greatest and most beloved US presidents (Dallek, 2003; Kearns-Goodwin, 1976).

A second category of self-defeating behavior identified by Baumeister and Scher (1988) that might adversely affect a leader's effectiveness as an influence agent is *choking under pressure*. Individuals are said to "choke under pressure" when they select an influence strategy that they are unable to carry out successfully in a situation where performing it well is vitally important. Many journalists and political commentators have noted the almost uncanny ability of Dan Quayle to choke under pressure when confronted with difficult or embarrassing questions—his speech slows and his gaze freezes giving the impression of a "deer caught in the high beams of an onrushing pick-up truck."

Counterproductive bargaining strategies constitute another important category of self-defeating behaviors and one directly related to ineffective influence in leadership contexts. Leaders use bargaining as a route of influence when dealing with the diverse preferences of their opponents. Used effectively, bargaining behavior allows leaders and those they deal with to achieve integrative or "win–win" (joint gain) outcomes (Kramer, Newton, & Pommerenke, 1993). Bargaining behavior becomes counterproductive, in contrast, when leaders' strategic choices lead to suboptimal agreements or even stalemates. This can occur when leaders' influence attempts are based on misperceptions of either the bargaining situation and/or the nature of their opponent. For example, leaders can misperceive the payoff structure or bargaining range in a situation. A classic example is the tendency to perceive the situation as more "zero sum" than it really is, resulting in an inability to find integrative or "win–win" solutions (Thompson, 1988). Alternatively, bargainers can underestimate the cooperativeness or trustworthiness of their opponents, resulting in adoption of overly harsh influence strategies that produce reactance and retaliation from their opponents or resistance from their constituents (Bendor, Kramer, & Stout, 1991). Finally, they can underestimate the resources or resilience of an adversary. Nixon famously repeatedly underestimated both the resources and durability of his political foes during the escalation Watergate crisis that ultimately felled his administration.

Another interesting category of self-defeating behavior discussed by Baumeister and Scher (1988) consists of *ineffective ingratiation* strategies. Such behaviors entail misjudgment as to how the target of an influence attempt will interpret or respond to one's behavior. As a consequence, "the person overestimates the likelihood of a positive response to flattery or doing a favor" (p. 15). For example, an influence agent might attempt to use ingratiation to curry favor, only to discover that the target of his or her influence attempt devalues the effort, attributing not positive but negative qualities to the agent. A famous instance in the leadership realm occurred when President Richard Nixon decided to surprise some protestors, encamped in Washington to oppose the Vietnam War, in the middle of the night. Nixon wandered among the group of protestors, trying to engage them in friendly banter about surfing and football. Rather than winning them over, however, he only caused them to feel more estranged from his leadership and policies. They had come to Washington not to talk sports, but to end the war and save lives.

Another provocative form of self-defeating behavior can arise when group members—finding their group under external threat—take steps to protect and maintain a shared sense of the group's positive social identity (Turner, Pratkanis, Probasco, & Leve, 1992). In so doing, group members may find themselves able to collectively justify actions that individually they might hesitate to endorse. The extreme, illegal behaviors of numerous members of Richard Nixon's inner circle proved enormously costly to his presidency and to themselves in retrospect. Yet, at the time they felt justified in doing everything necessary to defend what they perceived as an unjustly beleaguered presidency (Dean, 1972; Raven, 1974).

As such examples make clear, when applied to the realm of leaders behavior, a leader's influence behaviors can be self-defeating or counterproductive in several different ways. First, influence behaviors that are intended to advance a chosen goal can unintentionally backfire, under-mining achievement of that goal. Relatedly, leaders may try to employ a variety of impression management attempts that can fail to produce their intended effects (Elsbach & Kramer, 2003; Ginzel, Kramer, & Sutton, 1993; Sutton & Kramer, 1986). Third, influence behaviors aimed at reduc-ing or resolving identified problems can make them worse rather than better. For example, conflict resolution attempts can lead to escalation of conflict rather than reduction of conflict (Pruitt & Rubin, 1986). Finally, influence attempts intended to generate constructive change can instead produce reactance, hardening resistance to a chosen course of action rather than softening it (Kramer, Pradhah-Shah, & Woerner, 1995).

Some Determinants of Self-Defeating Leader Influence Behaviors

A large body of social cognitive (Gilovich, 1991) and decision making (Dawes, 2001) research has illustrated how various forms of misperception and judgmental bias can contribute to the misconstrual and misevaluation of social situations. Some illustrative examples can help provide a flavor of the kinds of variables that recent research has examined.

The Shadow of the Past: How History Sometimes Hurts

When leaders are trying to decide which influence strategy or tactic to use when endeavoring to influence another party, they are likely to search for past situations and experiences for guidance. In other words, they may try to compare their current situation with prior examples that might be informative or salient. Thus, they are likely to search for previous exam-ples of effective influence that might be successfully applied once again. Conversely, in order to avoid repeating the mistakes of the past, they are likely to look for mistakes they and other leaders have made.

In their systematic examination of the role such historical analogies have played in leader judgment and decision making, Neustadt and May (1986) argued along such lines that contemporary leaders often compare their current situation with situations faced by earlier leaders in similar-seeming circumstances. For example, when President Kennedy was try-ing to decide how much toughness and resolve to display to the Soviets in dealing with the Berlin crisis, he compared the situation he faced with Khruschev to British decisions with respect to Hitler's increasingly bold gestures in Europe. (The British analogy, it should be noted, may have been especially salient to President Kennedy because he had written at length himself about the dangers of complacency and inaction in his best-selling book, *Why England Slept*).

Although analogies can be informative in terms of providing useful points of comparison and raising important caveats, they can also mislead a leader by providing false assurance or fueling unrealistic optimism. An archival study of President Lyndon Johnson's decisions about how much toughness to display toward Ho Chi Mingh in dealing with the escalating conflict in Vietnam revealed more than a dozen specific references made by the president to analogies between his situation and situations faced by previous presidents, including allusions to Abraham Lincoln, Franklin Roosevelt, Harry Truman, Dwight Eisenhower, and President Kennedy (Kramer, 1995, 1998). For example, when not only his critics but even his advisors and friends suggested Lyndon Johnson might be perceived as a greater president if he were to bring an end to what had become an enormously unpopular conflict, Johnson retorted, "Everything I know about history proves this absolutely wrong. It was our lack of strength and our failure to show stamina, our hesitancy and vacillation...that caused all our problems before World War I, World War II, and Korea.... You see, I deeply believe we are quarantining aggressors over there...just like FDR [did] with Hitler, just like Wilson [did] with the Kaiser. You've simply got to see this thing in historical perspective" (cited in Kearns-Goodwin, 1976, p. 313). As he said on another occasion, "I read all about Lincoln and his problems, yet Lincoln persevered and history rewarded him for his perseverance" (Kearns-Goodwin, 1976, p. 314). (Interestingly, in pondering his own more recent political difficulties, Secretary of Defense Rumsfeld sought reassurance in the past as well, "I've been reading a book about the Civil War and Ulysses Grant—and I'm not going to compare the two, don't get me wrong, and don't anybody rush off and say he doesn't get the difference between Iraq and the Civil War...[but] the fact of the matter is, the casualties were high, the same kinds of concerns that we're expressing here were expressed then...[the people then] were despairing, they were hopeful, they were concerned, they were combative...the carnage was horrendous, *and it was worth it*" (Bumiller, 2004, p. A12, emphasis added).

Self-Enhancing Cognitive Illusions in Influence Situations

When leaders select a given influence strategy, it is reasonable to assume that they believe the use of that strategy will, more likely than not, move them closer to achieving their aims. The definition of self-defeating influence presented earlier, in fact, presupposes that leaders' behaviors are intendedly adaptive, and emphasizes the unintended and unforeseen consequences of one's influence behaviors. This raises the question, "What psychological factors might inadvertently affect leader's judgments regarding the efficacy or probability of success of a given influence strategy?" Certainly near the top of our list should be those various well-documented cognitive illusions that influence individuals' risk assessment and risk-taking behavior. Many studies have shown, for example, that decision makers maintain a variety of positive illusions about themselves and their behaviors. These cognitive illusions include overly positive self-evaluations, unrealistic optimism, exaggerated perceptions of control, and illusions of personal invulnerability (Taylor & Brown, 1988). In an experimental investigation of the role positive illusions played in negotiation situations, Newton, Pommerenke, and I showed that negotiators in a good mood tended to overestimate how well they had done in extracting value from the other party (Kramer, Newton, & Pommerenke, 1993).

Social Contextual Factors That Contribute to
Self-Defeating Influence Behaviors

Although the primary focus of this analysis is on social cognitive factors that contribute to leaders' self-defeating influence behaviors, it is important to note that there are many social contextual and organizational factors that can contribute to such behaviors. For example, role embeddedness can constrain leaders' strategic choices. Leaders are expected, after all, to enact the role they have assumed. Such perceived role requirements can make it difficult for leaders to change their behavior, even when that behavior is recognized as counterproductive (Kahn, Wolfe, Quinn, Snoek, & Rosenthal, 1964). Leaders' interpretations of what their role requires, for example, can force them to draw a distinction between what they would like to do personally (e.g., end a costly conflict) versus what they believe fulfilling the obligations of role dictates (e.g., a US president can never afford to show weakness or vacillation). Lyndon Johnson repeatedly voiced a strong antipathy toward the war in Vietnam and a deep personal anguish over the loss of American lives in that conflict. Yet, in the role of president, he felt he had a moral obligation to fulfill US treaty commitments around the globe. Perceived role-constraints of this sort can be reinforced also by historical, institutional imperatives that dictate compliance with past traditions and requirements.

The structure and organization of advice that surround a leader can also influence the options he or she perceives as available. The key role presidential advisors play in helping presidents select their influence strategies is amply documented (Barrett, 1993; Berman, 1982; George, 1980). To the extent advisors help broaden the panoply of considerations to which leaders attend and provide richer data for decision, such advisors can play a critical role in improving the quality of the decision-making process. However, to the extent leaders engage in homosocial reproduction when selecting advisors—selecting those who think and act like them—the range and quality of inputs can be sharply curtailed (Janis, 1983, 1989; Kramer, 1998). Advisors often shave their views to placate or please leaders. A nice illustration of this tendency emerges in one of the early Nixon tapes. When Richard Nixon was discussing the likely reaction of the public to the Watergate break-in, he predicted, "My view is…that in terms of the reaction of people…I think the country doesn't give much of a shit about it other than the ones we've already bugged…most people around the country think that this is routine, that everybody's trying to bug everybody else.... Look, breaking and entering and so forth, without accomplishing it, is not a hell of a lot of crime" (reported in Kutler, 1997, pp. 54–55). Nixon's aides were more than willing to aid and abet such misperception. In a meeting with aide Charles Colson, Nixon speculated, "They [the public] don't give a shit about repression and bugging and all the rest." To which Colson replied helpfully, "I think they expect it. As I've said to you, they think political parties do this all the time." "They do, they certainly do," chimes in Nixon. Colson embellishes, "They think that companies do this. You know, there have been marvelous stories written about industrial espionage." Nixon adds eagerly, "Sure, sure, sure. Well, they do." Colson then adds, "How Henry J. Ford sends agents into General Motors to get the designs. People just sort of expect this." Nixon quickly agrees, "Governments do it. We all know that" (reported in Kutler, 1997, p. 59).

Implications and Conclusions

From the standpoint of assessing where we stand with respect to the state of our current knowledge regarding power, influence, and leader influence processes, several points might be made. First, the present analysis suggests leaders have a variety of effective influence tools at their ready disposal when trying to do their work. At the same time, as we have seen, there are many points of vulnerability that leaders confront when attempting to make sense of influence opportunities and dangers they confront. First, it is clear that leaders' can seriously misjudge influence situations, based on their erroneous assumptions, misperceptions, and misinterpretations. These misjudgments, in turn, can adversely affect their strategic choices regarding which influence behaviors to use in addressing the situation. For example, leaders' strategic choices can backfire badly when they opt to use a conciliatory or "soft" influence tactic when the target of their influence attempt happens to disparage weakness and timidity. When President Kennedy first encountered Premier Nikita Khruschev in Vienna early in his presidency, he felt a reasonable dialogue about political realities would help establish common ground between them and lay the foundations for the beginning of a constructive working relationship. Accordingly, he tried to engage Khruschev in an intellectual debate regarding the respective political philosophies of their countries and their merits. By all accounts, that strategic intent backfired badly when Khruschev dismissively began to lecture Kennedy on the historical roots and justification for Marxism and, in the end, concluded that Kennedy was a young, inexperienced, tentative and unsteady leader—one who would back down if push ever came to shove (Reeves, 1933; Dallek, 2003).

Second, even if predicated on a prudent and circumspect assessment of a given situation, leaders' influence behaviors can be poorly executed or implemented. Thus, leaders can intend to employ an influence tactic with a constructive aim in mind, only to see it backfire or fail. Based upon his decades of experience influencing Washington politicians, Lyndon Johnson believed that the most effective way to influence Ho Chi Mingh was to treat the conflict in Vietnam as essentially a political bargaining problem, the solution to which required simply identifying the right mixture of "carrots and sticks" that would bring Mingh to the bargaining table. Accordingly, he offered to build dams and provide other forms of aid, on the same model of the Tennessee Valley Authority—an approach that was brilliantly executed on the domestic front, but a disaster internationally. Johnson completely misread Ho's own construal of the situation and his resolve never to negotiate or compromise Vietnam's future sovereignty, independence, or nationality with its enemies.

Third, in any influence situation, considerable room exists for the misconstrual of the efficacy of an influence attempt. Leaders can draw erroneous inferences regarding the efficacy of their actions in many ways including believing they were effective even when they were not. And even if efficacious, leaders can be mistaken about the reasons for their effectiveness. They may, for example, attribute their success to their social perceptiveness or political skill when, in fact, non-self-relevant causes played a major, determining role. Most famously, perhaps, British Prime Minister Neville Chamberlain returned from his personal meeting with Adolf Hitler having concluded that a genuine rapport and constructive relationship between the two leaders had been established.

In concluding, I should note that one of the primary aims of this chapter was to document the central importance that power and influence processes play in understanding leadership behavior. In order to successfully implement their visions and transact business, leaders must be adept at using both their formal, positional power and interpersonal persuasive power to get things done. Second, but no less important, the chapter attempted to focus attention on exploring a more neglected, but important and recurrent, aspect of leaders' behavior, namely, their use of self-defeating or counterproductive influence strategies and tactics. At times, today, it sometimes seems as if the misuse of power and influence is more prevalent today than its proper and effective use, as we watch our leaders fumble and stumble in front of the media and when trying to carrying out their mandates.

As the examples provided throughout this chapter also hopefully make clear, the costs of misguided or ineffective influence attempts by leaders can be substantial. In that spirit, this chapter has laid some theoretical grounds and conceptual foundations for further thinking on the origins and dynamics of self-defeating forms of influence. The framework presented here hopefully helps us understand how and why it sometimes happens that even politically savvy, experienced, and otherwise intelligent leaders might embark on, and persevere in, self-destructive and costly courses of action.

Given the enormously serious consequences that arise when powerful leaders escalate their commitment to costly, counterproductive influence behaviors in pursuing their objectives, it is imperative that we develop a better understanding of the forms, dynamics, and remedies for such behaviors. At the moment of greatest tension during the Cuban Missile Crisis, Chairman Khrushchev sent President Kennedy a message in which he appropriately raised his concern about the possibility they were racing toward a point of no return, "The harder you and I pull, the tighter this knot [of war] will become. And a time may come when this knot is tied so tight that the person who tied it is no longer capable of untying it." A more thorough understanding of the causes and dynamics of self-defeating power dynamics and influence behaviors may help leaders avoid such knots in the future and, even if encountering them, can untie them and thereby avoid catastrophic errors.

Author's Acknowledgments

The author gratefully acknowledges the support of the William R. Kimball family and a research fellowship from the Stanford University Graduate School of Business. Preliminary versions of this paper were presented at the Academy of Management Annual Meetings, Harvard Business School, Harvard Law School's Negotiation Roundtable, Harvard Kennedy School, London Business School, Ohio State University, and University of Michigan. I am grateful for comments from participants at those annual meetings and colloquia. I also thank Al Goethals, Scott Allison, and Dave Messick for their numerous constructive comments and thoughtful insights.

References

Axelrod, R. (1997). *The complexity of cooperation: Agent-based models of competition and collaboration.* Princeton, NJ: Princeton University Press.

Barrett, D. M. (1993). *Uncertain warriors: Lyndon Johnson and his Vietnam advisors.* Kansas University Press.

Baumeister, R. F., & Scher, S. J. (1988). Self-defeating behavior patterns among normal individuals: Review and analysis of common self-destructive tendencies. *Psychological Bulletin, 104,* 3–22.

Bendor, J., Kramer, R. M., & Stout, S. (1991). When in doubt: Cooperation in the noisy prisoner's dilemma. *Journal of Conflict Resolution, 35,* 691–719.

Berglas, S., & Baumeister, R. F. (1993). *Your own worst enemy: Understanding the paradox of self-defeating behavior.* New York: Basic Books.

Berman, L. (1982). *Planning a tragedy: The Americanization of the war in Vietnam.* New York: Norton.

Blau, P. M. (1964). *Exchange and power in social life.* New York: Wiley and Sons.

Boulding, K. B. (1966). *Conflict and defense.* New York: Harper & Row, 1966.

Boulding, K. B. (1989). *Three faces of power.* Thousand Oaks, CA: Sage.

Brockner, J., & Rubin, J. (1985). *Entrapment in escalating conflicts.* New York: Springer-Verlag.

Bumiller, E. (2004, May 12). Stolid Rumsfeld soldiers on, but weighs ability to serve. *New York Times,* A12.

Burns, J. M. (1978). *Leadership.* New York: Harper & Row.

Campbell, D. T., & Fiske, D. W. (1959). Convergent and discriminant validation by the multitrait-multimethod matrix. *Psychological Bulletin, 56,* 81–105.

Caro, R. (1975). *The power broker: Robert Moses and the fall of New York.* New York, Vintage.

Caro, R. A. (1982). *The path to power: The years of Lyndon Johnson.* New York: Vintage Books.

Caro, R. (2002). *Master of the Senate: The years of Lyndon Johnson.* New York: Alfred Knopf.

Caro, R. (2013). *The passage of power: The years of Lyndon Johnson.* New York: Vintage Press.

Cialdini, R. B. (1988). *Science and practice* (2nd ed.). Glenview, IL: Scott, Foresman.

Dallek, R. (2003). *An unfinished life: John F. Kennedy, 1917–1963.* New York: Little, Brown.

Dawes, R. M. (1988). *Rational choice in an uncertain world.* New York: Wiley.

Dawes, R. M. (2001). *Everyday irrationality: How pseudo-scientists, lunatics, and the rest of us systematically fail to think rationally.* Boulder, CO: Westview.

Dean, J. (1972). *Blind ambition.* New York: Scribners.

Elsbach, K. D., & Kramer, R. M. (1996). Members' responses to organizational identity threats: Encountering and countering the Business Week rankings. *Administrative Science Quarterly, 41,* 442–476.

Elsbach, K. D., & Kramer, R. M. (2003). Assessing creativity in Hollywood pitch meetings: A dual process model of creativity judgment. *Academy of Management Journal, 46,* 3, 283–301.

Emerson, R. M. (1962). Power-dependence relations. *American Sociological Review, 27,* 31–40.

French, J. R. P., Jr., & Raven, B. (1959). The bases of social power. In D. Cartwright (Ed.), *Studies in social power* (pp. 150–167). Ann Arbor, MI: University of Michigan.

Galinsky, A., Gruenfeld, D. H., & Magee, J. (2003). From power to action. *Journal of Personality and Social Psychology, 85,* 453–466.

Gardner, H. (1995). *Leading minds: An anatomy of leadership.* New York: Basic Books.

George, A. (1980). *Presidential decisionmaking in foreign policy: The effective use of information and advice.* Boulder, CO: Westview.

Gergen, D. (2000). *Eyewitness to power: The essence of leadership from Nixon to Clinton.* New York: Simon & Schuster.

Gilovich, T. (1991). *How we know what isn't so: The fallibility of human reason in everyday life.* New York: Free Press.

Ginzel, L. E., Kramer, R. M., & Sutton, R. I. (1993). Organizational impression management as a reciprocal influence process: The neglected role of the organizational audience. In L. L. Cummings and B. M. Staw (Eds.), *Research in organizational behavior, 15,* 227–266. Greenwich, CT: JAI Press.

Greenhalgh, L., & Kramer, R. M. (1986). Strategic choice in conflicts: The importance of relationships. In R. L. Kahn & M. N. Zald (Eds.), *Organizations and nation-states: New perspectives on conflict and cooperation* (pp. 181–220). San Francisco: Jossey-Bass.

Herring, G. C. (1993). The reluctant warrior: Lyndon Johnson as Commander in Chief. In D. L. Anderson (Ed.), *Shadow on the white house: Presidents and the Vietnam War, 1945–1975* (pp. 87–112). Kansas: University of Kansas Press.

Hitlin, S. (2003). Values as the core of personal identity: Drawing links between two theories of the self. *Social Psychology Quarterly, 66,* 118–137.

Hoffman, J. (1995). *Theodore H. White and journalism as illusion.* Columbia, MI: University of Missouri Press.

Janis, I. L. (1983). *Groupthink* (2nd ed.). Boston: Houghton Mifflin.

Janis, I. L. (1989). *Crucial decisions.* New York: Free Press.

Jervis, R. (1976). *Perception and misperception in international politics.* Princeton, NJ: Princeton University Press.

Jones, E. E., & Berglas, S. (1999). Control of the attributions about the self through self-handicapping strategies: The appeal of alcohol and the role of underachievement. In R. Baumeister (Ed.), *The self in social psychology* (pp. 430–435). New York: Psychology Press.

Kahn, R. L., & Kramer, R. M. (1986). Untying the knot: De-escalatory processes in international conflict. In R. L. Kahn & M. N. Zald (Eds.), *Organizations and nation-states: New perspectives on conflict and cooperation* (pp. 139–180). San Francisco: Jossey-Bass.

Kahn, R. L., Wolfe, D. M., Quinn, R. P., Snoek, J. D., & Rosenthal, R. A. (1964). *Organizational stress: Studies in role conflict and ambiguity.* New York: Wiley.

Kearns-Goodwin, D. (1976). *Lyndon Johnson and the American dream.* New York: New American Library.

Kearns-Goodwin, D. (2006). *Team of rivals: The political genius of Abraham Lincoln*. New York: Simon and Schuster.

Kellerman, B. (1994). *The political presidency: Practice of leadership from Kennedy through Reagan*. Oxford, England: Oxford University Press.

Keltner, D., Gruenfeld, D. H., & Anderson, C. (2003). Power, approach, and inhibition. *Psychological Review, 110*, 265–284.

Kenrick, D. T., Goldstein, N. J., & Braver, S. L. (2012). *Six degrees of social influence*. New York: Oxford University Press.

Kramer, R. M. (1995). In dubious battle: Heightened accountability, dysphoric cognition, and self-defeating bargaining behavior. In R. M. Kramer & D. M. Messick (Eds.), *Negotiation as a social process* (pp. 95–120.) Thousand Oaks, CA: Sage.

Kramer, R. M. (1998). Revisiting the Bay of Pigs and Vietnam decisions 25 years later: How well has the groupthink hypothesis stood the test of time? *Organizational Behavior and Human Decision Processes, 73*, 236–271.

Kramer, R. M. (2003a). The harder they fall. *Harvard Business Review, 81*, 58–68.

Kramer, R. M. (2003b). The imperatives of identity: The role of identity in leader judgment and decision making. In D. van Knippenberg & M. A. Hogg (Eds.), *Leadership and power: Identity processes in groups and organizations* (pp. 184–196). London: Sage Publications.

Kramer, R. M. (2004). Perceptions of conspiracy. In D. M. Messick & R. M. Kramer (Eds.), *The psychology of leadership*. Mahwah, NJ: Earlbaum.

Kramer, R. M. (2006). The great intimidators. *Harvard Business Review, 84*, 88–97.

Kramer, R. M., & Carnevale, P. G. (2001). Trust and distrust in intergroup negotiations. In R. Brown & S. Gaertner (Eds.), *Blackwell Handbook in Social Psychology, Volume 4: Intergroup processes* (pp. 431–450). Malden, MA: Blackwell Publishers.

Kramer, R. M., & Hanna, B. A. (1998). Under the influence. In R. M. Kramer & M. A. Neale (Eds.), *Power and influence in organizations* (pp. 145–180). Thousand Oaks, CA: Sage.

Kramer, R. M., & Neale, M. A. (1998). *Power and influence in organizations*. Thousand Oaks, CA: Sage.

Kramer, R., Newton, E., & Pommerenke, P. (1993). Self-enhancement biases and negotiator judgment: Effects of self-esteem and mood. *Organizational Behavior and Human Decision Processes, 56*, 110–133.

Kramer, R., Pommerenke, P., & Newton, E. (1993). The social context of negotiation: Effects of social identity and accountability on negotiator judgment and decision making. *Journal of Conflict Resolution, 37*, 633–654.

Kramer, R. M., Pradhan-Shah, P., & Woerner, S. L. (1995). Why ultimatums fail: Social identity and moralistic aggression in coercive bargaining. In R. M. Kramer & D. M. Messick (Eds.), *Negotiation as a social process* (pp. 285–308). Thousand Oaks, CA: Sage.

Kutler, S. I. (1997). *Abuse of power: The new Nixon tapes*. New York: Free Press.

Levine, R. (2003). *The power of persuasion: How we're bought and sold*. New York: John Wiley.

Lord, C. G., Ross, L., & Lepper, M. R. (1979). Biased assimilation and attitude polarization: The effects of prior theories on subsequent considered evidence. *Journal of Personality and Social Psychology, 55*, 396–409.

March, J. G. (1994). *A primer on decision making: How decisions happen*. New York: Free Press.

McClelland, D. C. (1975). *Power: The inner experience*. New York: Irvington.

McClelland, D. C., & Burnham, D. H. (1976). Power is the great motivator. *Harvard Business Review, 54*, 100–110.

Pfeffer, J. (1992). *Managing with power: Politics and influence in organizations*. Boston, MA: Harvard Business School Press.

Neustadt, R. E. (1990). *Presidential power and the modern presidents: The politics of leadership from Roosevelt to Reagan*. New York: Free Press.

Neustadt, R. E., & May, E. R. (1986). *Thinking in time: The uses of history for decision makers*. New York: Free Press.

Nye, J. (2004). *Soft power*. New York: Oxford University Press.

Pfeffer, J. (1981). Management as symbolic action. In L. L. Cummings & B. M. Staw (Eds.), *Research in organizational behavior* (3, pp. 1–52). Greenwich, CT: JAI Press.

Pfeffer, J. (1992). *Managing with power*. Cambridge, MA: Harvard Business School Press.

Pfeffer, J. (2010). *Power: Why some people have it and others don't*. New York: HarperBusiness.

Plous, S. (1985). Perceptual illusions and military realities: The nuclear arms race. *Journal of Conflict Resolution, 29*, 363–389.

Pratkanis, A. R. (2007). *The science of social influence: Advances and future progress*. New York: Psychology Press.

Pratkanis, A., & Aronson, E. (1992). *The age of propaganda: The everyday use and abuse of persuasion*. New York: W. B. Freeman.

Pratkanis, A., & Aronson, E. (2001). *The age of propaganda* (2nd ed.). New York: W. H. Freeman & Co.

Pruitt, D. G., & Rubin, J. Z. (1986). *Social conflict: Escalation, stalemate, and settlement*. New York: Random House.

Raven, B. (1974). The Nixon group. *Journal of Social Issues, 30*, 297–320.

Reeves, R. (1993). *President Kennedy: Profile of power*. New York: Simon & Schuster.

Reeves, R. (2001). *President Nixon: Alone in the White House*. New York: Simon & Schuster.

Russell, B. (1938). *Power: A new social analysis*. London: Allen & Unwin.

Sutton & Kramer, R. M. (1990). Transforming failure into success: Spin control in the Iceland Arms Control Talks. In R. L. Kahn & M. Zald (Eds.), *Organizations and nation-states* (pp. 221–248). San Francisco: Jossey-Bass.

Swann, W. B. (1987). Identity negotiation: Where two roads meet. *Journal of Personality and Social Psychology, 53*, 1038–1051.

Swann, W. B. (1996). *Self-traps: The elusive quest for higher self-esteem*. San Francisco, CA: Freeman.

Swann, W. B., Pelham, B. W., & Roberts, D. C. (1987). Causal chunking: Memory and inference in ongoing interaction. *Journal of Personality and Social Psychology, 53*, 858–865.

Thompson, L. (1998). *The mind and heart of the negotiator*. Upper Saddle River, NJ: Prentice Hall.

Turner, M. E., Pratkanis, A. R., Probasco, P., & Leve, C. (1992). Threat, cohesion, and group effectiveness: Testing a social identity maintenance perspective on groupthink. *Journal of Personality and Social Psychology, 63*, 781–796.

Webb, E. J., Campbell, D. T., Schwartz, R. D., & Sechrest, L. (1966). *Unobtrusive measures: Nonreactive research in the social sciences*. New York: Rand McNally.

Weick, K. E. (1993). Sensemaking in organizations: Small structures with large consequences. In J. K. Murnighan (Ed.), *Social psychology in organizations: Advances in theory and practice* (pp. 10–37). Englewood Cliffs, NJ: Prentice-Hall.

Wrong, D. H. (1979). *Power: Its forms, bases, and uses*. Oxford: Basil Blackwell.

Zimbardo, P. G., Ebbesen, E. B., & Maslach, C. (1977). *Influencing attitudes and changing behavior*. Reading, MA: Addison-Wesley.

CONTRIBUTORS

Scott T. Allison is professor of psychology at the University of Richmond where he has published nearly 100 articles on positive social behavior, leadership, and heroism. His books include *Heroes, Heroic Leadership, Reel Heroes,* and *Conceptions of Leadership.* His work has been featured in media outlets such as *National Public Radio, USA Today, The New York Times,* the *Los Angeles Times, Slate Magazine, MSNBC, CBS, Psychology Today,* and *The Christian Science Monitor.* He has received the University of Richmond's *Distinguished Educator Award* and the Virginia Council of Higher Education's *Outstanding Faculty Award.*

Max H. Bazerman is the codirector of the Behavioral Insights Group, the codirector of the Center for Public Leadership at the Harvard Kennedy School of Government, and the Jesse Isidor Straus Professor at the Harvard Business School. His awards include a 2006 honorary doctorate from the University of London (London Business School), the Lifetime Achievement Award from the Aspen Institute, and the Distinguished Educator Award from the Academy of Management. His research focuses on ethics, decision making, negotiation, leadership, and the connection of these topics to policy.

David R. Caruso is a psychologist who conducts leadership development on emotional intelligence, is a research affiliate at the Yale Center for Emotional Intelligence, and has a part-time role as the special assistant to the dean of Yale College for organization development.

Kimberly D. Elsbach is professor of management and Stephen G. Newberry Chair in Leadership at the Graduate School of Management, University of California, Davis and International Research Fellow at the Center for Corporate Reputation, Oxford University. She is also the cofounder and organizer of the Davis Conference on Qualitative Research. Her research focuses on perception—specifically how people perceive each other and their organizations. She is currently studying how crying at work affects perceptions of professional women and why fans identify with NASCAR. Her book *Organizational Perception Management* was recently published by Lawrence-Erlbaum as part of its Organization and Management Series.

Kerrie Fleming is the head of the leadership department at Ashridge Business School, director of the leadership research center, and a practicing member of faculty specializing in leadership development with a particular expertise in leader emotional intelligence (EI) and its practical application for individuals and organizations.

Donelson R. Forsyth, a social and personality psychologist, holds the Colonel Leo K. and Gaylee Thorsness Endowed Chair in Ethical Leadership at the Jepson School of Leadership Studies at the University of Richmond. A fellow of the American Psychological Association, he researches and writes about leadership, ethics, groups, and related topics.

George R. Goethals holds the E. Claiborne Robins Distinguished Professorship in Leadership Studies at the University of Richmond. Previously at Williams College he served as chair of the Department of Psychology, founding chair of the Program in Leadership Studies, and provost. With Georgia Sorenson and James MacGregor Burns, he edited the *Encyclopedia of Leadership* (2004). With Gary McDowell he edited *Lincoln's Legacy of Leadership* (2009). With Scott T. Allison he coauthored *Heroes: What They Do & Why We Need Them* (2011) and *Heroic Leadership: An Influence Taxonomy of 100 Exceptional Individuals*. His recent scholarship explores presidential leadership and race relations.

Edwin P. Hollander has been CUNY Distinguished Professor of Psychology at Baruch College and the Graduate Center since 1989. Now emeritus, his latest book, *Inclusive Leadership* (2009), capped six decades studying leadership beginning when he was a naval aviation psychologist at Pensacola, where his research included his social psychology dissertation at Columbia, PhD awarded 1952, after a BS in psychology from Case Western Reserve in 1948. Starting in 1954 at Carnegie Mellon, he taught at Washington (St. Louis), and American Universities, then at SUNY Buffalo, founding and directing the Doctoral Program in Social/Organizational Psychology, then serving as provost of social sciences. His visiting appointments include Istanbul University (Fulbright), London's Tavistock Institute, Harvard, Oxford, Wisconsin, and Paris Institute of American Studies.

Crystal L. Hoyt completed her doctorate in social psychology at UC Santa Barbara and is currently an associate professor of leadership studies and psychology at the University of Richmond. Her research focuses on both the experiences and the perceptions of identity threatened individuals. She examines the role of beliefs, such as self-efficacy, implicit theories, and political ideologies, in the experiences and the perceptions of women and minorities in leadership or STEM fields, or the overweight.

Roderick M. Kramer is the William R. Kimball Professor of Organizational Behavior at the Stanford Business School. He received his PhD in social psychology from the University of California, Los Angeles in 1985. He is the author or coauthor of more than 100 scholarly articles and essays. His work has appeared in leading academic journals, such as the *Journal of Personality and Social Psychology*, *Administrative Science Quarterly*, and the *Academy of Management Journal*, and has been published in popular journals, such as the *Harvard Business Review*. He is the author or coauthor of numerous books, including *Negotiation in Social Contexts, The Psychology of the Social Self, Trust in Organizations, Power and Influence in Organizations, Psychology of Leadership, Trust and Distrust in Organizations* and, most recently, *Restoring Trust in Organizations and Leaders*.

Jean Lipman–Blumen is the Thornton F. Bradshaw Professor of Public Policy and Professor of Organizational Behavior at Claremont Graduate University's Peter F. Drucker and Masatoshi Ito Graduate School of Management. She has published extensively on leadership, crisis management, public policy, organizational behavior, and gender issues. Her book, *The Connective Edge*, was nominated for a Pulitzer Prize. In 2010, she received the International Leadership Association's Lifetime Achievement Award. She holds bachelor's and master's degrees from Wellesley College, a doctorate from Harvard Graduate School of Arts and Sciences, and did post-doctoral work at Carnegie Mellon University and Stanford University.

Dan P. McAdams is the Henry Wade Rogers Professor of Psychology at Northwestern University. A personality and developmental psychologist, his research focuses on conceptions of self and identity in the lives and the life stories of midlife adults, with an emphasis on themes of power, love, redemption, and generativity. He is the author of more than 200 scientific articles and chapters and 7 books, including most recently, *George W. Bush and the Redemptive Dream: A Psychological Portrait*.

David M. Messick received his BA in psychology from the University of Delaware, and his MA and PhD in psychology from the University of North Carolina, Chapel Hill. He served on the faculty of the University of California, Santa Barbara, from 1964 through 1991, when he accepted the Morris and Alice Kaplan Chair of Ethics and Decision in Management at the Kellogg School of Management at Northwestern University. He retired in 2007. His research focus has been on social and ethical aspects of decision making and information processing, and most recently, leadership in large and small organizations, from corporations to basketball teams. He served as editor-in-chief of the *Journal of Experimental Social Psychology*, and was the recipient of two Fulbright fellowships to support research in the Netherlands, and a national Academy of Science East/West Fellowship to pursue research in Budapest, Hungary.

Dean Keith Simonton is Distinguished Professor of Psychology at the University of California, Davis. His more than 470 publications—including 13 books—concern genius, creativity, and leadership. He most recently edited *The Wiley Handbook of Genius* (2014). Honors include the William James Book Award, the Sir Francis Galton Award for Outstanding

Contributions to the Study of Creativity, the Rudolf Arnheim Award for Outstanding Contributions to Psychology and the Arts, the George A. Miller Outstanding Article Award, the Theoretical Innovation Prize in Personality and Social Psychology, the E. Paul Torrance Award for Creativity, and three Mensa Awards for Excellence in Research.

Ethan D. Spector was a senior majoring in economics at Wesleyan University and is now an analyst at Cornerstone Consulting.

INDEX

Printed and bound by CPI Group (UK) Ltd, Croydon, CR0 4YY